Understanding Public Opinion

Understanding Public Opinion

Edited by

Barbara Norrander
University of Arizona

Clyde Wilcox
Georgetown University

A Division of Congressional Quarterly
Washington, D.C.

Understanding public opinion / edited by Barbara Norrander and Clyde
  Wilcox.
       p.   cm.
     Includes bibliographical references and index.
     ISBN 1-56802-153-4 (cloth : alk. paper). -- ISBN 1-56802-156-9
(pbk. : alk. paper)
     1. Public opinion--United States.   2. United States--Politics and
  government--1993-   3. Political psychology.   I. Norrander, Barbara,
  1954-   . II. Wilcox, Clyde, 1953-   .
HN90.P8U53   1996
303.3'8--dc20   96-23904

To our mothers

Lorraine Norrander and Sarah Louis Wilcox

Contents

List of Tables and Figures

TABLES

FIGURES

Contributors

Alan I. Abramowitz is the Alben W. Barkley Professor of Political Science at Emory University. He has published numerous articles on elections and voting behavior in political science journals. His most recent book is *Senate Elections,* coauthored with Jeffrey Segal.

Kristi Andersen is professor of political science in the Maxwell School of Citizenship and Public Affairs, Syracuse University. Her research concentrates on political parties and women and politics. She is the author of *The Creation of a Democratic Majority, 1928–1923* and *After Suffrage: Women in Partisan and Electoral Politics Before the New Deal.*

Barbara Bardes is the dean of Raymond Walters College, a campus of the University of Cincinnati. Her research areas include public opinion and foreign policy, Congress and foreign policy, and women and politics. Among her publications are *American Government and Politics Today,* coauthored with Steffen W. Schmidt and Mack C. Shelley II, and *Declarations of Independence: Women and Political Power in Nineteenth-Century American Fiction,* written with Suzanne Gossett.

M. Margaret Conway is professor of political science at the University of Florida. She has written extensively on political participation, political socialization, and electoral behavior. She is the author of *Political Participation in the United States* and coauthor, with David W. Ahern and Gertrude A. Steuernagel, of *Women and Public Policy: A Revolution in Progress.*

Elizabeth Adell Cook is the coauthor of *Between Two Absolutes: Public Opinion and the Politics of Abortion,* and coeditor of *The Year of the Woman: Myths and Realities.* She has written extensively on abortion politics and feminism.

Robert S. Erikson is the Dr. Kenneth L. Lay Professor of Political Science at the University of Houston. He is coauthor of *Statehouse Democracy,* with Gerald C. Wright and John P. McIver, and *American Public Opinion,* with Norman R. Luttbeg and Kent L. Tedin. A former editor of the *American Journal of Political Science,* he frequently writes on public opinion and elections.

Doris A. Graber is professor of political science at the University of Illinois at Chicago and a faculty associate in the Department of Communications. She is the author of many articles and books dealing with political communications. Her most recent books include *Mass Media and American Politics, Processing the News: How People Tame the Information Tide,* and *Virtual Political Reality: Learning About Politics in the Audio-Visual Age.* Professor Graber is editor-in-chief of *Political Communications.*

John R. Hibbing is professor of political science at the University of Nebraska, Lincoln. His articles on legislatures and voting behavior have been published in numerous journals, including the *American Political Science Review,* the *Journal of Politics,* and the *British Journal of Political Science.* He is the author of *Choosing to Leave* and *Congressional Careers.* Professor Hibbing also has served as coeditor of the *American Politics Quarterly* and *Legislative Studies Quarterly.*

John E. Hughes is an assistant professor in the Political Science Department at Monmouth University in New Jersey. His general research interests include political participation and vote choice. His most recent work has been on the roles and effects of technology in political processes.

William G. Jacoby is an associate professor in the Department of Government and International Studies at the University of South Carolina. Professor Jacoby wrote *Data Theory and Dimensional Analysis* and has published articles in such journals as the *American Journal of Political Science* and the *Journal of Politics.* He is conducting research on statistical graphics and on ideological thinking within the American electorate.

Ted G. Jelen is professor of political science at Benedictine University in Lisle, Illinois. His research focuses on religion and politics, the politics of abortion, feminism, and democratic theory. His recent books include *The Political Mobilization of Religious Beliefs* and *The Political World of the Clergy.*

Kathleen Knight is associate professor of political science at the University of Houston. Her articles on ideology in the American electorate have appeared in the *Journal of Politics, American Politics Quarterly,* and other journals.

Thomas Marshall is professor of political science at the University of Texas at Arlington. His latest book is *Public Opinion and the Supreme Court.* His other research focuses on public opinion, campaigns, and elections.

Barbara Norrander is associate professor of political science at the University of Arizona. She is the author of *Super Tuesday: Regional Politics and Presidential Primaries*. Her research on presidential nominations and party identification appears in the *American Journal of Political Science, Journal of Politics*, and *Political Research Quarterly*.

Lyn Ragsdale is professor of political science at the University of Arizona. The author of *Presidential Politics* and *Vital Statistics on the Presidency*, she writes frequently on the presidency and on legislative elections. Professor Ragsdale is coeditor of *Political Research Quarterly*.

Lee Sigelman is professor and chair of the Department of Political Science at George Washington University and former director of the political science program at the National Science Foundation. He has written widely in the fields of political attitudes and behavior and has a special interest in race politics. With Susan Welch, he is the author of *Black Americans' View of Racial Inequality: The Dream Deferred*.

Elizabeth Theiss-Morse is associate professor of political science at the University of Nebraska, Lincoln. She has published research on citizenship, political tolerance, and methodology. Professor Theiss-Morse is coauthor of *Congress as Public Enemy: Public Attitudes Toward American Political Institutions*, with John Hibbing, and *With Malice Toward Some: How People Make Civil Liberties Judgments*, with George E. Marcus, John L. Sullivan, and Sandra L. Wood.

Steven A. Tuch is associate professor of sociology at George Washington University. His research focuses on issues and problems related to race relations, social stratification, and mobility. He has written extensively on the racial attitudes of blacks and whites and on the measurement and tracking of shifts in these attitudes.

Clyde Wilcox is professor of government at Georgetown University. He has written extensively on religion and politics, gender politics, and campaign finance. His most recent coauthored books include *Serious Money: Fundraising and Contributing in Presidential Nomination Campaigns* and *Second Coming: The Christian Right in Virginia Republican Politics*.

Preface

Having taught courses in public opinion and political behavior for many years, we have been increasingly frustrated by the difficulty of introducing students to real political science research. Most journal articles on public opinion contain statistical analyses that are far too complex for undergraduates, and often for beginning graduate students. Textbooks generally summarize the results of research but fail to show students anything about the process by which the results were obtained. Clearly, a need existed for a book that would expose students to both the substance of public opinion and a bit of the process of that research.

We designed this collection of essays to meet that need. We developed a broad outline of the main topics covered in courses in public opinion and political behavior and then selected specific topics in these areas on which there has been ongoing, interesting research. We approached scholars who had conducted some of that research and asked them to contribute an original research essay to this collection. Each author was asked to meet three requirements: first, the chapter should be both comprehensible and interesting to upper-division undergraduates yet rich enough to sustain the attention of graduate students; second, the chapter should pose an interesting question or questions about American public opinion and use appropriate data to find answers; third, the chapter should shed light on public opinion at the turn of the century.

The book that emerged has met our goals, and we have each of the contributors to thank for this. Teachers of courses in public opinion and political behavior at both the undergraduate and graduate levels will find this text helpful as they present topics and approaches in the field. With these essays they can show how scholars approach a question, what their research looks like, and how their conclusions are derived. In addition to students enrolled in political science courses, those studying journalism, sociology, and communications will find much of interest in this book.

Understanding Public Opinion is organized into five parts. The first considers some key factors that influence individuals' opinions—gender, race, religion, and the media. The second part explores how opinion is organized through ideology and partisanship. The content of public opinion in relation to specific issues is the subject of the third part, with individual chapters on abortion, foreign policy, and economic policy. Public opinion's roles in elections and political participation are examined in the fourth part. The final part addresses the relationship of public opinion to the three branches of American government.

Many of the authors relied on familiar national surveys such as the American National Election Studies and the General Social Survey. Both data sources are made available to the academic community through the Inter-University Consortium for Political and Social Research. Others have conducted their own surveys and focus groups.

We thank the people who helped us through the process of putting this book together. Ray Harris read each article and gave us suggestions on editing. We also received helpful comments from Stephen Craig and an anonymous reviewer. At CQ Press, Brenda Carter was closely involved throughout the project. She helped us develop our outline, read the chapters, made helpful suggestions, and helped coordinate the project. Nola Healy Lynch was our copy editor, and Kerry Kern shepherded the book through the various stages of production.

1 The Diverse Paths to Understanding Public Opinion

Clyde Wilcox

If you are reading this sentence in the daytime or early evening, it is likely that somewhere in the United States small groups of citizens are sitting around tables sharing their political opinions with focus group moderators. If you are reading this at night, it is likely that various kinds of political polls are being conducted—polls commissioned by candidates to assess their popularity and understand how they might win the election, polls commissioned by newspapers or television stations to gauge public sentiments on some topic in the news, and polls conducted for interest groups to help them understand how to attract and keep members or how to frame a particular political issue to their best advantage. It is also likely that some academic survey is in the field, and it is possible that a scholar is conducting a long, in-depth interview with a citizen or an activist.

In many cases, the data gathered from these studies will be made available to the academic community—to scholars and students who want to understand the causes and consequences of public opinion. In fact, as you are reading this sentence, it is likely that several political scientists, sociologists, psychologists, and students are performing statistical analysis on surveys and polls that others have previously collected. There are now more academics, journalists, and political professionals engaged in the study of public opinion than at any time in history.

Approaches to Public Opinion

Scholars, journalists, and pollsters do not all agree on how we should study public opinion. Professional associations such as the American Association for Public Opinion Research allow professional pollsters, journalists, and academics to meet and share their views, and such organizations publish journals to help them air their differences and improve their techniques. Perhaps more important, those who study public opinion do not agree on what questions are interesting, what theories and approaches are best, what methods are the most appropriate, or even on the nature of public opinion. The increase of academic, journalistic, and political interest in public opinion has led to a flowering of diversity in the field.

Consider, for example, the sharp decline in the popularity of President George Bush during 1991 and 1992. In March 1991, in the afterglow of the U.S. victory in the Persian Gulf War, fully 90 percent of Americans told pollsters that they approved of Bush's handling of the presidency—the highest approval rating registered since Gallup began assessing presidential approval in 1938. As public attention shifted to the stagnant domestic economy, however, Bush's popularity dropped precipitously, and in 1992 his approval rating hit a low of 29 percent—one of the lowest ever.

When those who study public opinion investigate the drop in Bush's approval, they ask different kinds of questions. Some focus primarily on citizens' emotional reactions to the Gulf War and to Bush's seeming indifference to the economic recession. Others are interested instead in the cognitive dimension of presidential approval. These researchers investigate whether people believed that Bush could have personally prevented the recession or ameliorated its harsh effects on the lives of many citizens, and how individuals with complex or relatively simple sets of beliefs processed news accounts of the Gulf War and the recession. Still others are interested in the behavioral consequences of approval—the impact of declining job approval ratings on primary and general election voting.

Some study aggregate opinion—the percentage of Americans who approved of Bush's presidency—and seek to correlate that approval with media coverage, economic conditions, and other events. Others look at individual opinion and seek to determine whether men and women, blacks and whites, veterans and nonveterans, Democrats and Republicans responded differently to the Gulf War and the economic downturn.

The data for these studies come from many sources. Some researchers have studied Bush's popularity with a series of polls that tracked opinion over time. Others conducted focus groups where a small number of citizens shared and debated their views of the Bush presidency. Some used electronic devices such as pulsemeters (dials that register approval or disapproval) to allow respondents to react immediately to elements of Bush's speeches or campaign commercials. Some scholars conducted in-depth interviews with small numbers of citizens to determine just how they thought of Bush.

Public opinion is therefore a field characterized by diversity: diversity of concepts and theories, diversity of questions, and diversity of methods. In this book we have sought to capture some of this diversity while adopting a common focus on the changing sources, content, and implications of public opinion in the past decade.

The first part of the book investigates many of the important sources of public opinion—sex, race, religion, and media—and the second part discusses the broad political dispositions, including ideology and partisanship, that help structure political attitudes and cognition. The third part explores the content of opinion on social issues, foreign policy issues, and economic issues. The fourth part investigates how attitudes influence political behavior, and the final part examines public opinion about and in relation to American political institutions.

Diversity of Conceptions and Theories

In political science, the central concept of most public opinion research remains the attitude. There are countless definitions of attitudes in circulation, each emphasizing different characteristics. In 1935, Gordon Allport reviewed many different definitions, then suggested that an attitude is "a mental or neural state of readiness, organized through experience, exerting a directive or dynamic influence upon the individual's response to all objects and situations with which it is related" (p. 810). Some forty years later, Martin Fishbein and Icek Ajzen suggested that a consensus had been reached that an attitude is "a learned predisposition to respond in a consistently favorable or unfavorable manner with regard to a given object" (1975, 6). Although the two definitions differ in defining attitudes as mental states or response tendencies, they both emphasize consistent responses to objects. Moreover, Allport (1935) stated that attitudes are learned. Thus theorists agree that attitudes are learned and involve consistent responses to objects and situations.

Attitudes have three main components: a cognitive element that links the object to information, an affective element that links the object to an evaluation or emotional reaction, and a conative element that may link the object to actual behavior. Consider, for example, one hypothetical attitude toward President Bill Clinton's decision in late 1995 to commit U.S. troops to Bosnia. A cognitive element of an attitude toward the troop commitment might be "the Bosnian conflict is likely to escalate, trapping U.S. troops in the midst of an age-old struggle." An affective element would be "I fear that many U.S. troops will die in Bosnia." A conative element would be "I will write my senator urging her to oppose the troop deployment."

Of course, not all attitudes are so consistent in their elements. A citizen's attitude on Bosnia might include the cognitive element that the genocide in Bosnia must be stopped no matter the cost, the affective element of fear that the U.S. casualty count would be high, and no conative element at all (that is, no intention to take action). Such conflicting attitude elements have been frequently explored in attitude research, but no consensus has emerged on precisely how these three attitude elements affect one another.

Perhaps more important, there is no consensus on just how attitudes relate to other concepts, such as values, beliefs, opinions, habits, and identifications (that is, aspects of personal identity). Most political scientists would consider values to be a more general concept, linking many related attitudes (for instance, equality values involve attitudes on gender, race, sexual preference, and disability), and that beliefs and opinions are specific cognitive elements of attitudes (for instance, opinions on equal pay for equal work). Yet the meaning of these terms and the relations between them remain imprecise, primarily because these are words from our ordinary language and therefore carry many meanings. The chapters of this book contain various combinations of these terms, and their usages are typical of the way public opinion scholars use these terms today.

There is no single attitude theory, but rather many different theories (Fishbein and Ajzen 1975). Some theories focus on how attitudes are learned, others on how various attitudes relate to one another, still others on how attitudes influence behavior. Probably the most frequently used attitude theory in political science has been cognitive dissonance theory. Leon Festinger theorized that inconsistent attitudes or beliefs should cause some psychological discomfort and thus "motivate the person to try to reduce the dissonance and achieve consonance" (1957, 3). Much as dissonant chords in music evoke in the listener a "need for resolution into a consonant interval" (Piston 1978, 6), so inconsistent beliefs should evoke in the citizen a desire to eliminate the dissonance.

This formulation of cognitive dissonance suggests that people should be aware when their beliefs appear contradictory and that they should seek to resolve the problem. Yet research has shown that Americans often hold inconsistent beliefs. Doris Graber (1984) reported that many respondents in her experimental study of information processing did not perceive that the attitudes they were expressing were inconsistent. Jennifer Hochschild (1981) found that the men and women she interviewed at length about their attitudes toward equality held conflicting, ambivalent feelings stemming from their commitment to opposing values. Many were well aware of the contradictions among their values and beliefs, and some were bitter about their inability to resolve these inconsistencies. John Zaller summarizes the results of a great deal of scholarly research when he writes that "most people are relatively uncritical of the ideas they internalize . . . they fill up their minds with large stores of only partially consistent ideas, arguments, and considerations" (1992, 119).

If attitudes remain the central concept in public opinion research, in recent years the schema concept has gained popularity with some researchers. Borrowed from psychological research on memory structures, schemata (the plural form of *schema*) are often defined as "cognitive structures that represent organized knowledge about a given concept or type of stimulus" (Fiske and Taylor 1984, 140). A schema contains an abstract form of information about an object, as well as elements about the attributes of the object and elements that relate these attributes to each other. A schema about a politician, for example, might include a few general characteristics—that politicians often are not entirely honest, that they value reelection more highly than other goals, that they are willing to help constituents if that helps them win reelection. Some schemata may be more complex than others; for example, they may involve distinguishing among various types of politicians, including Republicans or Democrats, conservatives or liberals, honest or dishonest, and male or female.

A schema differs from an attitude in several important ways. First, in schema theory an active individual receives information, processes that information, chooses perhaps to retain some of it, and chooses perhaps to alter the schema based on the information. In contrast, attitudes are generally posited to be learned through relatively passive means—reinforcement of responses, imitation of parents, or pairings of an image with a specific reinforcement. Sec-

ond, schemata are entirely cognitive structures—they do not directly involve affect or cona-
tion, although some researchers have attempted to investigate the role of affect in shaping
schemata and of schemata in shaping affect. Finally, the schema concept has most often been
used by scholars interested in how individuals attend to and process political information
(for example, Graber 1984). The cognitive information-processing theories used by these
researchers have often used the computer as underlying metaphor: for example, one line of
research seeks to determine whether information is stored "on line" or whether it is used to
alter the cognition "in storage."

Although the schema concept has been used by many scholars in the 1980s and 1990s, it
has yet to become the dominant concept in the field.[1] Indeed, in recent years scholars
appear to have shifted back slightly toward the language of attitudes. Most of the essays in
this volume use the language of attitude theory.

Diversity of Questions

Analysts who study public opinion seek to answer many kinds of questions, as the following chapters demonstrate. First, scholars ask where attitudes and opinions come from.
Studies that ask that question use attitudes themselves as dependent variables, then try to
explain who holds specific attitudes by referencing other characteristics. Some studies investigate the connection between attitudes of parents and those of children, and then track the
connection as children and parents move through the life cycle (Jennings and Niemi 1981).
Scholars who study political socialization focus on how children acquire their opinions from
their parents, peers, schools, and the media, and what factors foster greater learning.

Another way to investigate the sources of opinion is to see just how attitudes differ
among demographic groups. The differences in men's and women's attitudes, generally
called the "gender gap," have been the source of a great deal of research (Shapiro and Maja-
han 1986; Conover 1988; Cook and Wilcox 1991). Studies have not only investigated the differences in the attitudes of men and women, but have also explored differences in how men
and women reason about politics (Gilligan 1982). Most political scientists assume that gender differences arise out of different life circumstances, even between men and women
from similar backgrounds. From birth, parents, friends, and strangers respond differently
to boys and girls, and children quickly learn the roles they are expected to play. Some scholars, however, have argued that there may be essential differences between men and women
that lead them to different positions on some kinds of issues (Ruddick 1980).

For more than thirty years, scholars have examined closely the impact of race on public
opinion. Racial differences in political attitudes and behavior are often large, and scholars have
devoted considerable attention to explaining these differences. The enormous gulf between
black and white opinion on the O. J. Simpson verdict in 1995 showed that on many issues blacks
and whites bring different histories, cultural assumptions, and reasoning to bear.

Similarly, scholars, especially in the past decade, have paid increasing attention to the many ways that religion molds political attitudes. Some people attend churches where the pastor preaches politics from the pulpit, distributes campaign materials in the church, and even endorses candidates. Others frequently watch televangelists who stake out very conservative positions on social and other issues. Some reach their political positions through their doctrine—and try to reconcile politics with the teachings of the Bible or of their church. Others interact frequently with the members of their church and take cues from the most politically astute congregants (see Leege and Kellstedt 1993 for an extended discussion). In this book, we include chapters on the impact of several demographic characteristics on political attitudes: sex and gender by Kristi Andersen (Chapter 2), race by Steven Tuch and Lee Sigelman (Chapter 3), and religion by Ted Jelen (Chapter 4).

Finally, some scholars who seek the sources of opinion focus on the role of the media in molding public thinking. Most Americans learn about politics directly from television and newspapers and indirectly by talking to others who have learned from those sources. There is some controversy on precisely how much influence the media have on public thinking, but there is a general consensus that they can increase the salience of issues in the public mind and "prime" citizens to focus on certain aspects of public problems (Zaller 1992). Yet not all citizens are equally influenced by mass media—some resist media news accounts, while others have too little background to fully process news stories (Graber 1984). In Chapter 5 of this book, Doris Graber considers how new media such as the World Wide Web might influence public levels of information, political opinion, and democracy.

A second set of questions frequently asked by scholars concerns the organization of public opinion. Although attitude theorists in the 1950s had focused on the cognitive pressures that people might feel to make their opinions internally consistent, Phillip Converse reported in 1964 that there was little evidence of attitude consistency in the general public. Converse argued that as they adopted positions people might be constrained in two ways. First, they might reason deductively from an ideological position—for example, a libertarian should be constrained against adopting a position in favor of sodomy laws, since they inhibit personal liberty. Second, they might adopt packages of ideas that have been assembled by elites or social groups—for example, fundamentalist Christians might oppose abortion and gay rights because their church teaches that these activities are sinful. Yet Converse found that the attitudes of most Americans were not constrained in these ways, and that Americans in general understood little of the ideological language used in campaigns.

Converse's findings sparked a raging debate about the sophistication of the American electorate that continues today. Often this debate hinged on the interpretation of similar empirical results, with one camp arguing that the coffee mug was half full, the other that it was half empty. A number of scholars now argue that we can most profitably think of this question by segmenting the public into those who are relatively sophisticated in their understanding of politics and those who are less sophisticated. In Chapter 6, Kathleen Knight and Robert Erikson separate out those they term ideologically sophisticated from those who do not understand ideological terms. The more sophisticated citizens can use ideology, partisanship, and feelings toward social groups to help structure their beliefs.

For example, Republicans in Congress are considering a bill that would impose a flat tax on income over a certain threshold, abolishing most deductions and eliminating the taxes on capital gains. How might citizens determine their position on that kind of issue? For many Americans, the tax code is simply too complex to even try to understand; some are cynical enough to believe that any change in the code will hurt the average American and so they pay no attention to the details. Others will rely on certain cognitive cues to help them sort out the issue. Liberals may object that a flat tax gives big tax breaks to rich Americans and that the proposed law would end up taxing wages but not profits from stocks and bonds. Republicans might support the proposal because it comes from their party's leadership. African Americans might oppose it because blacks in general would be hurt more than helped, and civil rights leaders would certainly send cues to their constituents that this is a policy to oppose. In this book, Knight and Erikson examine the impact of ideology in structuring attitudes (Chapter 6) and Barbara Norrander focuses on the role of partisanship (Chapter 7).

Another type of research asks about the content of public opinion. Some scholars have focused on the substance of opinion in a particular domain (Mueller 1994; Cook, Jelen, and Wilcox 1992), while others have examined the changes over time in the direction of opinion in a particular area. In this book we include chapters that focus on attitudes toward social issues (abortion) by Elizabeth Adell Cook (Chapter 8), foreign policy issues by Barbara Bardes (Chapter 9), and economic issues by William Jacoby (Chapter 10)—all issues stressed by candidates and parties in recent elections. Events can raise the salience of these issues, as the Supreme Court's decision in *Webster v. Reproductive Health Services* (1989) did for abortion, the Gulf War did for foreign policy, and the recession of 1991 did for the economy. In the campaigns leading up to the 1996 presidential election, the abortion issue remained alive with the Republican candidates, most of whom took a prolife pledge. And the presence of U.S. troops in Bosnia brought foreign policy forward once more.

The most common area of investigation is the impact of opinions on electoral participation and vote choice. Scholars study the impact of political attitudes on vote choice and seek to determine the relative importance of attitudes toward parties, candidates, and issues. Other studies examine the impact of an issue such as abortion on vote choice (Abramowitz 1995; Cook, Jelen, and Wilcox 1995). In this book, John Hughes and Margaret Conway (Chapter 11) investigate the role of opinions in influencing decisions on whether to vote, and Alan Abramowitz (Chapter 12) explores the impact on vote choice of people's attitudes on moral issues.

Scholars are also often interested in the intersection between public opinion and government institutions. Several issues in this area interest political scientists, including the sources of support of the president and Congress, the uses of public opinion by congressional leaders and the president, and the congruence between aggregate public preferences and the policies produced by governmental institutions. In this book, we include a chapter by Lyn Ragsdale (Chapter 13) that investigates the sources of presidential popularity and discusses the source of a long-term decline in Americans' evaluations of their presidents. A chapter by John Hibbing and Elizabeth Theiss-Morse (Chapter 14) explores the sources of public dissatisfaction with Congress, and one by Tom Marshall (Chapter 15) examines the congruence between Supreme Court decisions and public opinion. Finally, some scholars study public opinion as an independent variable—that is, they seek to determine the impact of opinion on behavior and public policy. Some study how high presidential approval improves the president's position in bargaining with Congress over legislation, others how Congress responds to constituency pressures. Some studies focus on the congruence between opinion and policy at the state or national level (Norrander and Wilcox 1994).

Diversity of Methods

With this diversity of conceptualizations, theories, and research questions, it should come as no surprise that there is a diversity of research methods as well. There is variety both in the kinds of data collected to answer these questions and in the statistical techniques used to manipulate those data.

By far the most common sources of public opinion data are polls and surveys. These two terms are often used interchangeably, although some scholars use *polls* to describe data gathered for candidates, newspapers, or political groups and *surveys* to describe longer interviews designed to test social science theories. In any event, a poll or survey consists of interviews of a sample of individuals who represent a larger population, and is designed to measure their preferences, opinions, attitudes, values, or behavior.

Methodologies

Types of Polls and Surveys

There are many kinds of polls. Academic surveys consist of long interviews designed to gather information to explain attitudes or behavior, often after the fact. For example, every two years the Survey Research Center at the University of Michigan conducts an American National Election Study, which includes a postelection interview with a sample of American citizens. These data are used by scholars to answer questions such as who voted and what kinds of voters supported each candidate. Scholars may write books or articles based on these surveys, sometimes many years after the election.

To help scholars answer their questions, academic surveys include many questions designed to measure concepts that can help explain attitudes and behavior. For example, the American National Election Studies (ANES) include a long battery of items on religion to help measure denomination, doctrine, practice, experience, and identity. Scholars have found that each of these aspects of religion is relevant in explaining political thinking and behavior (Kellstedt and Leege 1993). Over time the ANES board has experimented with questions to better measure feminism, group consciousness, feelings toward parties, and other concepts that have become important in theories of political thinking and behavior. Similarly, the General Social Survey (GSS) included a large set of special religion questions in 1989. The ANES and GSS are used in several of the chapters in this book.

Media polls, in contrast, generally seek more to report opinion than to explain it. Although leading national newspapers such as the *Washington Post* and the *New York Times* do feature detailed postelection analyses, a majority of the polls they conduct are used to describe opinion—who is ahead in the presidential race, whether the public thinks that the United States should send troops to Bosnia, whether Congress should adopt a flat tax, or how people view term limits for members of Congress. Media polls usually do not include many questions that would help explain opinions—they may have a single religion question, for example, if any.

Strategic polls seek to help consultants achieve a goal—electing a candidate, enacting a policy, enabling a political group to grow, helping a company market its products more effectively. Strategic polls therefore may not seek to determine precisely why some individuals strongly oppose or favor a candidate, but they do focus extensively on how to convince uncommitted voters to support their candidate. Frequently candidates' polls test potential arguments for or against a candidate and evaluate voters' assessments of the candidates' characteristics. Strategic polls are generally coordinated with a client's advertising campaigns to help determine whether particular ads are moving public opinion in the desired direction.

Finally, advocacy polls are surveys done to present a distorted picture of public opinion. Scholars and survey research experts know that subtle changes in the wording of questions can produce shifts in public opinion, and not-so-subtle changes can produce large shifts. For example, consider the following two possible survey questions:

1. Millionaire Steve Forbes has proposed a flat income tax that would result in rich Americans paying the same tax rate as those who work for wages. Do you support Forbes's plan?
2. Some Americans favor a flat tax, which would eliminate most deductions and tax all citizens at the same rate. Others support a progressive tax, in which those with higher incomes pay a higher rate. Which do you support?

The first question is obviously biased, for it provides cues that the person proposing the plan is himself rich and would benefit from the policy, and it contrasts rich Americans with those who work for wages. The second question provides two positions with no bias in favor of either and allows the respondent to choose. A few polling firms are willing to write questions to provide misleading results, but their reputation quickly suffers and few then take their results seriously.

In early 1996, Republican officials admitted that polls conducted by Frank Luntz and used by GOP leaders to document support for the Contract with America were quite similar to advocacy polls. Luntz's questions did not directly measure support for the Republican contract, but instead tested various arguments that might be used to increase support. For example, the survey asked respondents whether "we should stop excessive legal claims, frivolous lawsuits, and overzealous lawyers," and counted those who agreed as supporting the Republican plan for tort reform. Such obviously biasing words as *excessive, frivolous,* and *overzealous* created artificially high levels of agreement with the question, making it worthless as a measure of genuine political support. Republican officials distanced themselves from the poll and privately complained that they had not been aware of the precise wording of his questions.

Types of Interviews

Those who conduct surveys can gather responses in three ways. First, they can send the interviewer into the respondent's home to ask questions in person. This technique has the advantage of allowing the interviewer to carry cue cards and visual materials. In addition, in-person interviews are generally of the highest quality because the interviewer and the respondent both work harder at the survey. But in-person interviews are expensive, for they involve increased training costs and salaries as well as extensive travel costs. Moreover, in-person interviews must be scheduled in advance, and it often takes several weeks to complete a survey that uses this technique. Some academic surveys continue to be conducted in person, because academics value the quality of the data and generally do not worry about speed. However, many researchers cannot afford the high costs of this method.

Phone surveys have the advantage of speed. A large company can interview several hundred respondents in an evening, providing a quick estimate of public opinion. For this reason, political campaigns rely heavily on phone polls, often performing a small number of interviews every night to track opinion change. Phone surveys present their own problems, however. Most important is the difficulty in reaching a truly random sample of citizens: not everyone has a phone, young people are often out in the evenings and difficult to reach by phone, busy professionals use answering machines to screen their calls and do not pick up when interviewers call, and couples with young children are not available to answer political questions while their babies are crying.

Finally, mail surveys have the advantage of low cost—for the price of two first-class stamps (the second is for the return envelope) you can send a survey to a respondent. Mail surveys are frequently used to obtain information from political elites such as campaign contributors and party activists (Brown, Powell, and Wilcox 1995; Rozell and Wilcox 1996). Yet mail surveys also have problems. Many Americans routinely throw away surveys instead of answering them, and typically half or more of those sampled never respond to a mail survey despite repeated mailings. Mail surveys are of course slow. Finally, there is no way to know whether the addressee actually filled out the survey—a spouse, child, nanny, or friend might have done so instead.

Although each of these techniques has its limitations, polling experts have developed ways of minimizing the problems and increasing the reliability of the data. Today there are more surveys and polls conducted than ever before. Political scientists have available a wealth of information on public opinion and behavior. The vast majority of public opinion studies in political science use survey data to test their hypotheses, and the chapters in this book rely heavily on survey research as well.

Non-Survey Techniques

Although surveys are by far the most important source of data for scholars who study public opinion, there are many other techniques for measuring public opinion. Professional pollsters now conduct about as many focus groups as surveys for corporate and political clients. For a focus group a small number of individuals generally sit around a table, and a moderator directs the discussion. Because this small number of participants is not representative of the large American public, political scientists have until recently only seldomly used focus groups. But focus groups have the advantage of allowing citizens to talk about politics in their own words, and to make and respond to arguments. At its best, focus group research allows scholars to see just how individuals express and defend their opinions and how they process opposing arguments (Conover, Crewe, and Searling 1991; Hibbing and Theiss-Morse 1995; Jelen and Wilcox 1995; Meyers in press). In this book, John Hibbing and Elizabeth Theiss-Morse (Chapter 14) combine focus groups and survey data to explore attitudes toward Congress.

Professional pollsters use other techniques that are less frequently used by academics, including electronic devices that allow individuals to register a continuous range of positive or negative evaluations at all times during political speeches or commercials. These pulsemeters enable public opinion specialists to determine who reacts positively to precisely what parts of a speech or advertisement. Some polling firms have equipment that enables them to determine precisely what portion of an advertisement the subjects are watching when they respond, enabling the advertising firm to fine-tune the message.

Political scientists also occasionally use techniques, such as experiments or participant observation, that are not used by professional pollsters. Experiments allow more precise control of conditions, enabling researchers to pinpoint the exact source of a response. Participant observation can allow scholars to observe the effects of social interaction in settings that may not be otherwise accessible, especially in small groups.

Finally, both scholars and public opinion professionals often rely on in-depth interviews to inform them of how individuals think about politics. These interviews may last for several hours, and help us better understand the worldview of particular groups of Americans. In one such study, Jennifer Hochschild interviewed a number of citizens with varying incomes and education about equality and justice (Hochschild 1981). In another, Kristin Luker interviewed activists in prolife and prochoice groups and compared their world views (Luker 1984). Both studies show the rich insights that can be gained from this technique. Public opinion professionals often use structured in-depth interviews to develop maps of values and opinions.

Statistical Manipulation of Data

When social scientists examine survey data, they use statistics as tools to better understand the content, sources, and consequences of attitudes. The appendix to this book is a primer in which we describe some of the statistics used in this book in greater detail. This chapter will provide a brief overview of the kinds of statistics used and why we use them.

Some statistics are simple and descriptive: they might report the percentage of Americans who believes that abortion should never be allowed, or who rate Clinton's job performance as excellent. Other simple descriptive statistics report a central tendency of public opinion. The *mean* is the arithmetic average of a variable: for example, we might say that the average rating of Clinton on a 1–10 scale is 5.5. The *median* is the middle score in a distribution, and this is often used when there are some extreme scores on a variable. For example, a very small number of Americans have very high incomes, so it is common to report median incomes rather than means.[2] The *mode* is the most frequent score, and is often used in a general way to describe opinion. On most issues, opinion is unimodal, with the largest number of Americans in the moderate position. On a few issues, however, opinion may be bimodal, with roughly equal numbers of conservatives and liberals.

Although many of the chapters in this book report some of these simple descriptive statistics, social scientists are usually interested in understanding the relationship between two or more variables. For example, we might want to know just how closely related two seemingly similar opinions are—for example, support for gay rights and support for abortion rights. We usually measure the strength of that association with some kind of correlation coefficient. If most Americans who support gay rights also support abortion rights, and if most of those who oppose gay rights oppose legal abortion, then there will be a strong positive correlation. If most Americans who support gay rights oppose abortion rights (a very unlikely result), then there will be a strong negative correlation, because high scores on one variable are associated with low scores on another. If there is no relationship between these two attitudes—if knowing someone's position on gay rights would tell us nothing about their position on legal abortion, then the correlation will be very close to 0. We can examine the correlations between several different opinions, and if they are all high we can build a scale to measure a more general attitude. For example, if there are high correlations between opinions on abortion, gay rights, school prayer, and the role of women in society, then we can build a scale to measure attitudes on these social and moral issues.

Usually we are interested in the relationships between more than one independent variable and a dependent variable that we think may be influenced by them. Consider, for example, the relationship between race and support for legal abortion. Most surveys in the 1980s reported that blacks were less likely to support legal abortion than whites. Yet we might suspect that it is not race that is the source of this difference but rather other characteristics that are associated with race. We know that blacks in America for various reasons are less likely to complete college than whites, and we also know that blacks attend church more often and hold more conservative religious views. Both education and religion are associated with attitudes toward legal abortion. So we might ask whether blacks are less supportive of legal abortion *because* of their differences from whites in education and religion, or whether there are racial differences beyond those caused by these other factors.

To answer this question we *control* for education and religion, and examine the relationship between race and attitudes toward legal abortion. What we seek to do in this process is compare blacks and whites who are similar with regard to education and religion. For example, we compare whites and blacks with high school educations who attend church weekly, and we also compare separately whites and blacks with college degrees who attend church only occasionally. To make these comparisons physically would be quite cumbersome, for there are many possible combinations of religion and education upon which to compare. Moreover, we might suspect that other differences between blacks and whites might also affect this relationship—blacks are on average younger than whites, they are more likely to live in the South, more likely to live in urban areas, and so on. Thus the possible combinations of factors on which to compare is very large.

We can statistically hold constant a number of variables simultaneously, using techniques such as multiple regression, logistic regression, and probit. Many of the chapters in this book use these techniques to assess the independent impact of one variable on the dependent variable once all others are held constant. For example, we might include a variety of variables in an attempt to explain abortion attitudes: religion, region, race, age, sex, education, income, attitudes on women's roles, attitudes on the sanctity of life, attitudes on sexual morality, partisanship, and ideology. When we estimate these relationships using regression, we learn that blacks are actually more supportive of legal abortion than whites if all of these other factors are held constant. In other words, blacks are more liberal on abortion than whites who occupy similar social locations and have similar attitudes. A closer look reveals that black women are far more liberal than white women on abortion, and that black men are slightly more conservative than white men (Cook, Jelen, and Wilcox 1992).

This example illustrates the way in which statistical research can answer one question and raise others. If we look only at the simple percentage of blacks and whites who favor legal abortion, we learn that blacks are less supportive than whites. Yet we can entirely explain that difference by racial differences in region, religion, education, and attitudes. Once we have estimated a complete statistical model, a new question emerges: Why are black women more liberal than white women who have similar demographic characteristics and attitudes, while black men are slightly more conservative than comparable white men?

The process of answering one question while raising another may sound a bit like Sisyphus rolling the stone up the mountain—there are always new questions to be answered and so the work of a public opinion scholar is never done. Yet for those who study public thinking, this process can be fun. Herbert Kritzer writes that if we could always answer our questions quickly and thoroughly, our task would be boring, but that instead it is fun because "data occasionally tell us things we did not know; they often confuse and confound us . . ." (1996, 26). James Stimson writes that the pleasures of analysis are "what sensible people experience when they read or watch detective thrillers" (1984, 76).

Although public opinion specialists try to apply scientific methods to their analysis, their work also involves creativity and can be thought of as part art and part science. Often the best scholars use statistical techniques in creative ways to understand an issue. For example, in Chapter 11, Margaret Conway and John Hughes use statistical techniques to transform 1992 voters into 1964 voters. They first estimate the probability that each person in 1992 will vote based on the person's education, age, and attitudes, and then substitute the average education, age, and attitudes of 1964 voters for the actual values in 1992. This all seems quite complicated, but it is an act of imagination: if voters today had the same levels of education and trust in the system as they did in 1964, what would turnout be like? This simulation enables researchers to determine just how much of the decline in turnout since 1964 is attributable to changing attitudes, and how changing levels of education have helped cushion the effects of growing cynicism and distrust.

C. Wright Mills (1959) described a "sociological imagination" as the ability to connect broad trends in society, politics, and technology with individual biographies. There are many forms of imagination in public opinion scholarship, and the joy of public opinion research is the opportunity to investigate interesting questions, solve puzzles, and use that imagination. For most scholars, a puzzling result is like a mosquito bite—it has to be scratched, investigated, and thought about. Some of the anomalies we are left with can be explained with better theory, some can be resolved with better data, and some resist explanation for a time.

The chapters in this book show the variety that characterizes the study of public opinion, the creativity of the investigation, and the joy of the enterprise.

Notes

1. For different views on the utility of the schema concept, see Hastie (1986); Kuklinski, Luskin, and Bolland (1991); and Wilcox and Williams (1990).

2. Means are distorted by extreme cases, while medians are less distorted. To see how, imagine that we surveyed five Americans and asked their income. Four had identical incomes of $35,000, the fifth had an income of $35,000,000. The median, or middle score, is $35,000. The mean, or average score, is $7,028,000.

Part 1   The Sources of Public Opinion

When Steve Forbes first began to attract attention in the 1996 contest for the Republican nomination for president, he used the occasion to promote his favorite idea—a flat 17 percent tax on all wage income, with no taxes on profits from the sale of stock or property. Forbes's flat tax provoked strong opposition from some Americans and aroused enthusiastic support from others. Many Republican voters were forced to confront the issue for the first time, and they felt that they had to take a position on the flat tax proposal.

When Patrick Buchanan won the New Hampshire primary, he used the occasion to warn moderate Republicans that they could not afford to abandon the party's commitment to making abortion illegal. Abortion was an established issue in American politics, and Buchanan's candidacy probably did not force Republican voters to evaluate their stand on this issue. Most Republicans, and indeed most Americans, held firm positions on the issue that were unlikely to change as a result of an election campaign.

Where do political opinions and attitudes come from? How do Americans come to hold long-standing positions such as those on abortion, or to formulate views on new issues like the flat tax? The earliest research in political science focused on how children learn their attitudes from their parents. There were ample reasons to believe that children would share their parents' political opinions—most children and parents lived in the same communities, were members of the same social class and race, and attended the same churches. Yet M. Kent Jennings and Richard Niemi (1974) found that only on issues that we now label easy and that have a moral or lifestyle component is there even a moderate correlation between parent's and children's attitudes.

More recently, researchers have focused on how social group membership, identity, and mobilization can affect attitudes. Social movements have transformed American politics in important ways. Civil rights, feminist, gay and lesbian, and Christian Right groups work hard to mold a consensus on policy issues among group members and sympathizers. Even those who are not members of social movement organizations may have their attitudes molded by common experiences based on their social characteristics: black college students see security guards touch their guns when they enter jewelry stores, women find their views are ignored in corporate headquarters, and conservative Christians live in a secular world that promotes values different from their own (and which they believe pokes fun at them because of their religious commitment).

In this part of the book, we begin with a chapter by Kristi Andersen on gender differences in public opinion. Andersen discusses not only actual opinion differences between men and women, but also the importance of a broader understanding of how gender shapes politics. Next, Steven Tuch and Lee Sigelman investigate how race and class influence attitudes toward government programs to help the disadvantaged. They argue that both race and class influence attitudes toward general programs to help the poor, but that race alone explains attitudes on special programs to aid blacks. Their findings suggest that race will continue to be more important than class in American politics.

Ted Jelen traces the alignment of culturally conservative Christians with the Republican Party. He argues that although morally conservative Catholics, as well as evangelical and mainline Protestants, have become more Republican during the past fifteen years, they have done so at different times and for different reasons. He argues that the future of cultural politics may hinge on the ability of the Republicans to win the support of more conservative Catholics.

These chapters establish that race, gender, and religion influence political attitudes. Yet how do Americans form attitudes on new issues? Clearly, they learn the facts about these issues through various media, either directly by watching TV, reading the newspaper, or browsing the Internet, or indirectly by talking with someone who has learned directly from the media. Doris Graber's chapter examines how new media may change the way the public learns about politics and how public opinion functions in American democracy.

2 Gender and Public Opinion

Kristi Andersen

In the last decade of the twentieth century, women's and men's political differences occupy center stage in popular and academic debates. The Year of the Woman in 1992 saw the number of female members of the U.S. House of Representatives increase by two-thirds and the number of female senators double; those numbers remained constant during the Republican takeover of Congress in 1994. Pollsters and politicians attend to the gender gap in voting, for women constitute a majority of the electorate and are more likely than men to support Democratic candidates. With all the recent attention to gender politics, it may seem odd that gender distinctions were barely studied until the 1970s.

Discovering the Difference

For the most part, social scientists, at least until the mid-1970s, denied that men and women held significantly different political beliefs. The prevalent thinking could be described as a convergence model, in which men and women were seen as being subject to similar economic and social forces and thus unlikely to differ significantly in politics. Typically, studies written in the 1950s and 1960s either omitted sex altogether as a classification worth considering or mentioned the comparison only in passing. As one among many examples, James Sundquist in *Dynamics of the Party System* includes a table that delineates "changes in political affiliation of various population groups" between 1960 and 1970. He lists race, region, social class, education, place of residence (urban or rural), religion, and age—but not sex (1973, 348–349).

Later, when sex differences in public opinion and political behavior surfaced, researchers tried to explain them. These difference models can be classified as either essentialist or constructionist. Essentialist arguments assume that biological differences between men and women are the basis of most—if not all—observable differences on political attributes. Within an essentialist approach we can distinguish between arguments that see women as inferior (for example, those made in the nineteenth and early twentieth century opposing women's suffrage) and those that view women as essentially superior to men (such as the recent "woman-centered" brand of feminism). The alternative to essentialism is a constructionist position, which assumes that differences in how women and men perceive and act on their environment are social constructions. That is, there is no such thing as an essential male or female nature; rather, each culture develops assumptions and expectations about the ways men and women think, talk, and act.

While most American political scientists in the 1950s and 1960s used an unstated convergence model, a few scholars did seriously look at the way women's political thinking and behavior differed from men's. These researchers found small gender differences and attributed them to the essential or natural character of the sexes. For example, whenever women's opinions or preferences seemed to differ from men's, the difference was explained by women's "moralistic" or "apolitical" nature. Thus Robert Hess and Judith Torney (1967, 186) in their study of children's political development remark that "there was some tendency for girls to make a higher assessment [than boys] of the influence of rich people and labor unions in determining laws." Rather than interpreting these views of girls as realistic cynicism or political sophistication, the authors attributed such attitudes to "the tendency of girls to personalize governmental processes." The source of this personalization, Hess and Torney suggest, lies in the fact that girls' "experience with their major role model (mother) is a more personal one and [that] authority figures deal with them in more expressive and personalized ways" (Hess and Torney 1967, 193).

Robert Lane, in 1959, described women's votes as moralistic or reformist. Lane concluded that women's political attitudes contained only the "illusion of comprehension" since it is much easier (and therefore less "political") to "compare political acts and statements with moral symbols . . . while it is difficult, indeed, to ascertain causes and estimate results" (1959, 212–213). We should not automatically assume that such stereotypic thinking has disappeared. In 1981, a senior adviser to President Ronald Reagan was quoted in the *New York Times* as saying that the president would have to "develop a compassion issue" because "women don't understand interest rates as well as men" (Bonk 1988, 91).

The view that women have a particular moralistic, reformist, compassionate, or uninterested stance with regard to the political system has been articulated by many men and women for years, certainly at least since the debates surrounding women's suffrage in the early part of this century. Such assumptions tend to essentialize women. Philip Hastings, at the time the director of the Roper Center, wrote a *New York Times Magazine* article in 1960 explaining women's political thinking and political behavior. Hastings essentialized women when he claimed that women "generally are ill-informed about political facts," "distrust the organized political world," "are interested in the candidate as a person," and "have a conservative bent" (14, 80). Hastings went so far as to predict that women's conservatism "may well serve as a decisive force restraining further development of the liberal wing of the Republican party, and bolstering the strength of conservative Democrats" (Hastings 1960, 81).

Table 2-1 Mentions of Gender and Race in Public Opinion Textbooks

Years of Publication	Number of Books	Index References to Sex, Gender, or Women	Index References to Race or Blacks
1964–1981	10	9 (in 4 books)	110 (in 6 books)
1982–1995	10	147 (in 8 books)	226 (in 8 books)

In recent years, social scientists and historians have adopted gender as an important category of analysis.[1] Gender analysis, which now takes a generally social constructionist stance, looks not only at men and women but also at the way language, social interactions, and politics are shaped by assumptions and expectations about feminine and masculine attributes. This research has fundamentally reshaped our understanding of American history, political theory, power, and leadership—just to name a few areas.[2] In studying public opinion, researchers might use the social construction approach to account for observable sex differences in political attitudes by examining the different kinds of familial or work situations in which men and women find themselves. People who study public opinion have, like other scholars, paid more attention recently to the thinking of women and have shifted, in general, from convergence and essentialist models to more social constructionist models.

To get a better sense of the analytical role played by "sex" or—in later years—"gender" in the field of public opinion, I examined twenty public opinion textbooks written between 1964 and 1995, as well as the content of articles appearing in *Public Opinion Quarterly* between 1944 and 1993. For each textbook, I counted references in the index under "sex," "gender," "women," and—for purposes of comparison—"blacks" and "race." Table 2-1 summarizes the findings. Between 1964 and 1981, six out of ten books made no reference to sex, gender, or women in the index. The fact that only nine references were made to gender in the ten books demonstrates the dominance of the convergence model in this time period. Between 1982 and 1995, only two out of ten books failed to include index entries under gender, sex, or women, and the number of total references to gender increased dramatically. Nevertheless, race was more frequently cited than gender in public opinion textbooks in both eras. In the earlier period, race was mentioned about twelve times as frequently as gender. In the latter period, race received one and a half times as many references as sex.

In *Public Opinion Quarterly,* the major journal of the public opinion and survey research community, only four articles dealt with women, sex differences, sex roles, or gender before 1964 (about 0.5 percent of the total number of articles and research notes). Between 1964 and 1981, nine articles, or approximately 1.4 percent, referred to gender, and between 1982 and 1993 the journal contained sixteen articles about women or gender, or about 3.8 percent.

Even when sex differences in public opinion are examined, however, it is often on a limited number of women's or moral issues. In Richard Niemi, John Mueller, and Tom Smith's (1989) useful collection of survey data, the issues on which opinions are broken down by sex are the following: abortion, child care and work, divorce, drinking, euthanasia, extramarital sex, homosexuality, marijuana, nudity, women as politicians, premarital sex, sex education, smoking, suicide, and working. This is an interesting commentary on the extent to which women are still seen as primarily defined by family and by their sexuality—only on these kinds of "family," social, or sexual issues is sex or gender considered a significant category of analysis.

In examining textbooks and journal articles, I counted references to both "sex" and "gender" (as well as to "women"). In fact, often the word *gender* is used interchangeably with the word *sex*. I try in this chapter to use the two terms in distinct and—I believe—appropriate ways. According to our biological differences, we are categorized by sex as either male or female. But gender is a socially constructed set of assumptions and expectations about how these biological differences play out in people's interactions, including political interactions. Unfortunately, the current intellectual fashion to substitute *gender* for *sex* can blind us to the implications of the distinctions between the two.[3] As Sue Tolleson-Rinehart and Jeannie Stanley argue in a recent book (1994, 155–156), in politics we are interested in both sex and gender. For example, we ask questions about how many women senators there are, and also about whether women, because of their particular experiences, bring different perspectives to the policy process. In the first case, we are asking questions that can be answered by categorizing the population in terms of biological sex. In the second case, an answer would need to be shaped by an understanding of gender differences, which we might or might not find among senators.

Should we be interested in questions of sex or questions of gender when we approach the topic of gender and public opinion? I believe the answer is both. When we find differences between men's and women's policy preferences, candidate choices, or party identifications, we will be able to understand those differences if we cast them in the framework of gender. We account for such differences by discovering how men's and women's socialization, structural positions in society, or family relationships affect their politics. But it is also important to understand the political impact of gender differences. Have these differences resulted in the election of more women, changed the policy agenda to be more sensitive to women's issues, meant defeat for some candidates and victory for others, or forced the parties to craft new sorts of appeals? When we ask these questions, we are bringing to the foreground questions about sex differences, that is, women's political behavior and women's representation; questions about gender, though related, recede into the background.

Opinion Differences over Time

Sex differences in public opinion vary by region and over time. The ways that gender affects public opinion (and political behavior) are historically and politically contextual. This chapter focuses on the United States in the 1990s, but we should not lose sight of the fact that the differences we observe now reflect a particular place and time. In this section I examine some of the vast array of data comparing men's and women's opinions on a variety of public issues.

In the past, women were frequently portrayed as having more conservative opinions than men. Writing in 1960, the authors of *The American Voter* found that in the 1952 and 1956 elections women were slightly more Republican than men, although they pointed out that this difference was probably not due to "something unique in female political assessments" but to sex differences in age and education distributions (Campbell et al. 1960, 493). Maurice Duverger's study of women in European political life also found that women's support for right-wing parties tended to be greater than men's (Duverger 1955; and see Lipset 1960, 231). Duverger and other scholars argued that this difference was primarily a result of women's higher level of religiosity (which encouraged them to support conservative religious parties) and the fact that few women belonged to trade unions (as members they would more naturally support labor parties).

In summary, when scholars during this period looked for distinctions between men and women, they focused on electoral behavior, and only at the national level. Researchers reported that women were more conservative than men, were less interested in politics, and were less likely to vote. These patterns were interpreted by means of a scheme that alleged the existence in women of certain "fundamental" characteristics which tended to distance and exclude them from politics. Women were largely invisible to political scientists, who subsumed the evidence of women's somewhat lower level of activity in conventional political activities, such as voting, into a blanket conclusion about women's apolitical nature. These scholars neglected women's history of political participation through social movements and voluntary associations. Because women were viewed as either similar to men or apolitical, sex was typically not a category used to analyze public opinion on issues.

Two trends converged in the 1970s to increase women's visibility and to focus new attention on possible sex differences in public opinion. First, women's rates of participation in electoral politics increased. Although as late as the 1968 elections men outpaced women in voting turnout by 4 to 5 percentage points, by 1980 the relationship was reversed. For the first time women turned out to vote at a higher rate than men. Because women outnumber men in the population, women voters now constitute a clear majority of voters everywhere in the country. Women constituted about 54 percent of the presidential electorate in 1992.

The second trend was the rise of the feminist movement and the dramatic increase in the size and visibility of women's organizations. These organizations worked to move the national political agenda toward concerns for "women's issues," such as reproductive rights, equal opportunity in employment and education, the Equal Rights Amendment, and electing more women to high political office. Suddenly, possible differences between men's and women's opinions took on political meaning. By the end of the decade, pollsters were discovering a gender gap in candidate preference. Gallup polls found that 38 percent of men supported Carter in 1980, compared with 44 percent of women. The discovery of the gender gap in 1980 led to a systematic exploration of gender differences in policy preferences.

Gender Differences on Women's Issues

On most of the issues directly related to women or to women's interests, sex differences have recently been small to nonexistent, but this has not always been the case. Hazel Erskine's 1971 study examined sex differences in opinions about women's roles in politics and society. Until the 1960s, women were much more likely than men to support such things as equal employment opportunities for women or the idea of women in public office. As one example among many, Gallup asked in 1952: "Some people say that if there were more women in Congress and holding important government positions, the country would be better governed. Do you agree or disagree?" Only 31 percent of men agreed, but 47 percent of women did (Erskine 1971, 282). During and after the 1960s, however, such differences were erased or reversed, primarily because men increased their support for sex equality. For example, Gallup poll questions about support of the Equal Rights Amendment, asked seven times between 1975 and 1982, found that an average of 57 percent of the women respondents and 61 percent of the men respondents supported the ERA (Simon and Landis 1989, 275). Similarly, Robert Shapiro and Harpreet Mahajan (1986, 53) found that "on other women's issues [other than abortion, that is] there are few clear and consistent differences." It is worth noting here that black women were more supportive than white women of the ERA in the 1970s, and they were also more supportive of collective and legal action to improve women's status (Wilcox 1990).

When men and women were asked about their thinking on the issue of abortion, in the aggregate their responses looked similar. For example, over a twenty-two-year period (1972–1994), the General Social Survey (GSS) asked this question: "Please tell me whether or not you think it should be possible for a pregnant woman to obtain a legal abortion if there is a strong chance of serious defect in the baby." The approval averaged just over 79 percent for the whole sample, and there was never more than a 4 percentage point difference between the positive responses of men and women (the difference averaged 1.9 points). This pattern is the norm on the so-called traumatic reasons for approving of abortion: the chance of a serious defect in the baby, or pregnancy as a result of rape or incest. To the extent

Table 2-2 Abortion Opinions in 1990

	Men (%)	Women (%)	Difference: Women–Men	Men Aged 18–29 (%)	Women Aged 18–29 (%)	Difference: Women–Men
Favor leaving decision . . . to woman and her physician	69	72	+3	65	80	+15
Should be able to get abortion . . . no matter what the reason	40	45	+5	40	48	+8
Abortion should be legal only in certain circumstances	50	41	−9	52	42	−10
Personally believe having an abortion is wrong	44	50	+6	—	—	—
Abortion should be illegal in all circumstances	18	12	−6	6	10	+4

Source: 1990 General Social Survey.

that there is a difference, men are slightly more favorable to abortion in these circumstances than women.

It is possible that men and women reach similar issue positions through very different routes. Women, not men, confront the possibility of pregnancy because of rape or incest and have to deal most immediately with the reality or the possibility of a severely ill or handicapped child. Furthermore, virtually all women of childbearing age have had to deal intimately with the implications of having a child at a particular moment in their lives—with all the economic, emotional, educational, and career implications associated with such a decision.[4] Consequently, women may tend to have more intensely held views on abortion, to have views based on their own experiences with pregnancy and child rearing, and to make more use of the abortion issue in deciding how to vote.

Opinion polls on abortion, as illustrated by Table 2-2, show that women place themselves at the extremes more often than do men. That is, while women are more likely than men to endorse free access to abortion or to view abortion as a private matter best left to the woman and her physician (the first two questions in Table 2-2), more women than men also believe that having an abortion is wrong. Among eighteen- to twenty-nine-year-olds, more women than men believe that abortion should be illegal in all circumstances. These sex dif-

Table 2-3 Abortion and Voting in 1992 by Age Group (Percentage Saying Abortion Was Important to Their Vote)

	18–29 Years	*30–44 Years*	*45–59 Years*	*60+ Years*
Men	10	9	8	6
Women	21	18	12	8

Source: *American Enterprise,* January/February 1993, 102.

ferences appear to be accentuated among people ages eighteen to twenty-nine, the ages when women are feeling the full force of the choices and constraints represented by their child-bearing capabilities.

In the GSS time series (1972–1994) there are few sex differences in responses to questions on abortion, and when they do occur, men are likely to be more liberal than women. But in thirteen of the sixteen surveys, women aged eighteen to twenty-nine are more likely than men in that age group to endorse abortion in the case of a serious defect in the baby. Furthermore, women are more likely to see candidates' stands on abortion issues as an important component of their voting decisions. In 1992, women in all age groups were more likely than men to say that abortion was important to their vote. Women of childbearing age were twice as likely as men to have used abortion as a factor, as illustrated by Table 2-3.

Gender Differences on Use-of-Force Issues

Polls have found the clearest differences between men and women in the area of force and violence. During the 1970s and 1980s there were consistent differences between the sexes in their responses to questions from all major survey organizations on gun control, capital punishment, military and defense spending, and withdrawal from Vietnam. Men consistently chose the more violent options (such as supporting capital punishment, higher military spending, and less regulation of handguns).

The preferences of both men and women on the appropriate level of defense spending have fluctuated over the years. Both sexes initially approved of Ronald Reagan's plea for the strengthening of American military capabilities. However, over the last twenty-one years, men generally have been more willing than women to have the government spend more on the military, armaments, and defense.

Fairly dramatic differences between men and women were characteristic of public opinion during the Gulf War. For instance, consider two questions asked by Gallup in January 1991. One asked for approval or disapproval of the decision to send U.S. troops to Saudi Arabia, and the other asked, "If the current situation in the Middle East involving Iraq and Kuwait does not change by January 15, would you favor or oppose the U.S. going to war with Iraq

Figure 2-1 Support of U.S. Presence in Gulf and for Possibility of War in January 1991

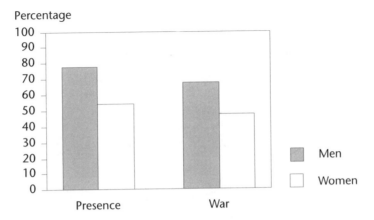

Source: *Gallup Poll Monthly,* January 1991, 14.

in order to drive the Iraqis out of Kuwait?" Figure 2-1 shows clear differences between men's and women's responses, with women showing less support for resorting to war.

Even clearer is the tendency for women to oppose the use of force in situations that arise in the United States. Women are much more likely to endorse stricter controls on firearms. For example, in 1994, 84 percent of female General Social Survey respondents versus 70 percent of male respondents endorsed the idea of requiring a police permit to own a handgun. Women have been consistently less likely to support the death penalty than men, as shown in Figure 2-2. It is also worth noting that more women than men disagreed with the statement on the General Social Survey that "it is sometimes necessary to discipline a child with a good hard spanking."

Gender Differences on Compassion Issues

Compassion issues, such as welfare, care for the elderly, and environmentalism, make up the second area to show consistent gender differences in public opinion. These distinctions, however, tend to be slightly smaller than those found for use-of-force issues. While Shapiro and Mahajan (1986) found an average of 6 percentage points difference between men's and women's responses on force and violence issues, they found an average 3-point difference on compassion issues. Women in the 1970s and 1980s were "more supportive of a guaranteed annual income, wage-price controls, equalizing wealth, guaranteeing jobs, government-provided health care, student loans, and rationing to deal with scarce goods" (Shapiro and Mahajan 1986, 51). They found larger differences in opinion on policies which "regulate and protect consumers, citizens, and the environment." More

Figure 2-2 Percentage Favoring the Death Penalty, 1974–1994

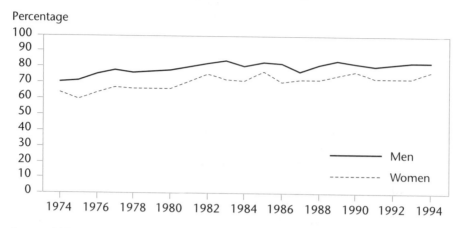

Source: 1974–1994 General Social Surveys.

Note: Question wording is: "Do you favor or oppose the death penalty for persons convicted of murder?"

women than men, in a number of different surveys, opposed cigarette advertising and nuclear power plants. Women were more likely than men to support stiffer penalties for those who drive drunk or fail to wear seatbelts, and to support highway speed limits. Women's greater support for environmental regulation appears to be a product of the 1980s (Shapiro and Mahajan 1986, 51–52). In Figure 2-3 men and women are compared on the GSS time series asking about government spending on health care, welfare, and the problems of big cities. Differences are consistent and minor, and they generally appear to be larger now than in the 1970s.

Gender differences on issue opinions become politically important as they are linked to policy and candidate preferences. Women's more liberal opinions since 1980 have been associated with less positive evaluations of Republican presidents, more positive evaluations of Bill Clinton, and (relative to men) a preference for the Democratic Party. The "gender gap" began when analysts discovered that women's evaluations of Ronald Reagan were significantly less positive than men's. Gallup and other polls during Reagan's first administration found a consistent difference of about 8 percentage points (and sometimes as much as 12 to 14 points) between men and women. Analysis of forty-one Gallup polls through 1983 found that "gender differences existed not only on the national level, but in every major population subgroup as well," including both groups that had many Reagan supporters (for example, Republicans) and groups that were generally less supportive (blue-collar workers, blacks).[5] George Bush also received a lower approval rating from women than from men during his

Figure 2-3   Gender Gaps in Spending on Social Services, 1973–1994

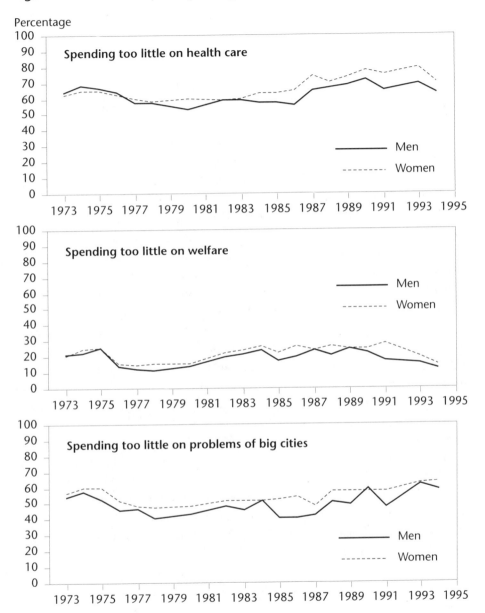

Source: 1973–1994 General Social Surveys.

Note: Question wording is: "We are faced with many problems in this country, none of which can be solved easily and inexpensively. I'm going to name some of these problems, and for each one I'd like you to tell me whether you think we are spending too little money, too much money, or about the right amount. Improving and protecting the nation's health./Welfare./Solving the problems of big cities." Entries are proportion saying too little is spent.

four years in office, by an average of about 6 points on the Gallup polls. Correspondingly, Clinton's ratings have been higher among women (by about 4 percentage points in 1993) than among men.

Bases of Opinion Differences

Just how does gender shape citizens' thinking about politics? Why should the fact that one is male or female, and thus brought up in certain ways and confronted with particular life choices, affect the way one thinks about capital punishment or welfare? Thinking about this question is an important next step beyond identifying gender differences.

Age or generational differences—in addition to work status, education, and race—almost certainly supply different conditions in which gender expectations and ideologies work themselves out for individuals. Political scientists mostly have sought to understand how gender influences opinion as part of a larger effort to explain the gender gap in political opinions. In general, the dependent variables in these analyses have been gender differences in presidential vote (Miller 1988; Carroll 1988) or presidential approval (Frankovic 1982, Carroll 1988), but others have examined differences in issue positions and in basic values (Shapiro and Mahajan 1986; Conover 1988). Virginia Sapiro and Pamela Johnston Conover (1993) tested alternative explanations of gender differences in attitudes toward militarism and war, and particularly toward the Gulf War. One primarily journalistic explanation—that the gender gap in the 1980s was simply a reaction on the part of women to Ronald Reagan's particular "macho" rhetoric and political style—has been disproved by time. As we have seen, the pro-Democratic, liberal bias among women, though not dramatic, has persisted in the post-Reagan era.

When social scientists attempt to explain the gender gap in voting or presidential approval, they have generally sought to identify other demographic factors that might cause men and women to think differently. For example, many studies focus on structural or economic explanations, and attempt to compare men and women with similar levels of income. Although women make less money than men, are economically more vulnerable, and are more dependent on government benefits, these economic differences do not explain voting patterns in 1980 and 1984 (Miller 1988, 261–264; Frankovic 1982, 443–444). Susan Carroll (1988) has suggested a more sophisticated theory which uses psychological as well as economic independence from men to construct a successful explanation of gender differences in voting and Reagan approval in 1980.

A second set of explanations has to do with the women's movement or with feminist ideology. Arthur Miller (1988) found that correlations between feminism and the vote in 1984 were weak and similar for men and women. Kathleen Frankovic (1982) agreed: opinions on ERA or abortion did not predict opinions about Reagan. Conover (1988) finds that feminist identity provides a robust explanation of differences. She writes, "There is not so much a gap between men and women [but] a gap between men and feminist women" (p. 1005). But Elizabeth Adell Cook and Clyde Wilcox (1991) argue persuasively that feminist identity cannot "explain" the gender gap because feminism has a reciprocal relationship with liberal opinions and egalitarian values. When feminism is seen as an ideology that can characterize men as well as women, they show, there remain gender gaps between feminist men and women and nonfeminist men and women. Without some long-term panel data or alternative kinds of research into people's political life histories, our view of causal relationships between feminist attitudes and other political values and opinions remains cloudy.

In searching for an explanation for the gender gap as it manifests itself in vote choice, scholars have focused on issues of war and peace and compassion, arguing that women's typical positions on these issues predisposed them to vote less Republican in 1980 and 1984 (see Frankovic 1982, 444–446; Miller 1988, 272–277). Such issue differences have persisted, widening in some cases, and it may be that women and men construct different political agendas in making up their minds about how to vote (see Miller 1988).

Explaining voting differences in terms of issue differences begs the question of why men's and women's opinion distributions are distinct in the first place. While the structural and feminist mobilization arguments may have some explanatory power here, Conover and Sapiro (1993) address the question of issue differences (in the area of war and violence) directly, offering the contending explanations of "maternalism," feminism, and gender. Maternalism introduces a version of a socialization explanation which others (notably Miller 1988) have rejected. The maternalist hypothesis posits that the practices and experience of mothering foster antimilitaristic attitudes (Ruddick 1980). Though this hypothesis has not been thoroughly tested—there are problems measuring "motherhood"—Conover and Sapiro's (1993) analysis suggests that the maternal model does not explain gender difference. The feminist consciousness hypothesis, according to Conover and Sapiro (1993), is only partially supported. In particular, feminist consciousness led to greater emotional distress over the Gulf War but not to a more negative overall evaluation of the war. The best explanation, in their view, is the "gender hypothesis." In the context of the Gulf War, women were more fearful and concerned about the war than men and more strongly opposed to bombing civilians (though not less supportive of the war in general). The fact that these differences "cannot be eliminated by controlling for the effects of a wide-range of other explanatory elements points to a pervasive, gendered pattern of *early* learning of cognitive and especially affective orientations toward the use of violence" (Conover and Sapiro 1993, 1096). In a nutshell, women are simply different from men and this difference is, though "socially constructed," virtually innate. It seems that we are back to square one.

The Political Impact of Differences: From Gender Gap to Gender Wars?

Gender is socially constructed. It is socially contextual—constructed differently for different generations and races—and it is a complex phenomenon. Over the past fifteen years the differences between men's and women's political attitudes and opinions have received new and vigorous attention. I think it is fair to say that the differences we find are persistent (if still time-bound) and that research into their correlates and antecedents has contributed to our (still partial) understanding of how gender affects politics. Perhaps the questions that now deserve more thought have to do with the political implications of these differences.

When the gender gap became apparent after the 1980 election and was publicized by women's organizations such as the National Organization for Women as a way to drum up support for the Equal Rights Amendment and for the Democrats' nomination of a woman for vice president, it marked an important turning point in the long struggle to reshape the policy agenda to incorporate issues of particular concern to women (Mueller 1988). Today the perception that women have a distinct agenda—or even that citizens as a whole are increasingly embracing aspects of what might be termed a women's agenda—continues to shape candidacies and campaigns. Candidates like one of Barbara Boxer's opponents in her 1992 Senate primary, who declared breast cancer "a state emergency," try to stake out advantageous positions on what have been conventionally described as women's issues. Of course how such issues translate into votes and eventually into policy depends critically on the parties and political leaders who are mobilizing support for them.

The often small differences between men's and women's opinions, as well as the dramatic variance among women, means that women voters are far from a monolithic bloc, despite media oversimplifications to that effect. Karen Paget (1993) argues that "if the pitfall in the past was to assume that women's interests were identical to men's, it is equally misleading today to equate the gender gap with an emergent female voting bloc, let alone a monolithic one" (p. 101). Nonetheless, women's votes are more important than ever, and over time they have had the effect of electing more women to office, increasing the electoral salience of issues that interest women voters, and reshaping the policy agenda. Small differences can be politically significant depending on the media interpretation of the differences, public perceptions of these interpretations, and the actions and goals of the political leaders who make use of them to mobilize resources and supporters.

In this context, the 1990s might be characterized as the era of gender wars rather than of the gender gap. Susan Faludi's 1991 bestseller *Backlash* described a variety of vocal and belligerent antifeminist reactions. What we might consider as opinion differences seem frequently to have escalated into bitter conflicts: violence and killing at abortion clinics, record numbers of sexual harassment grievances, including men's claims against women,[6] an intense focus on domestic violence, and Rush Limbaugh's derogatory term "femi-Nazis" applied to feminists.

Table 2-4 Group Differences in Percentage Approving of Hillary Clinton

Age and Party Groups	Men	Women	Difference: Women-Men
Overall	40	60	+20
Republicans	23	39	+16
Independents	35	60	+25
Democrats	69	75	+6
18–29 years old	32	55	+23
30–44 years old	41	67	+26
45 and over	43	57	+14

Source: Gallup poll, June 1993.

Since the 1992 presidential election, Hillary Rodham Clinton has been a focal point of the gender wars. One of the more interesting public opinion phenomena during the Clinton administration has been the over-time and across-group variation in approval of the First Lady. Over the course of 1992 and the first half of 1993, for example, the proportion of respondents expressing "generally favorable" opinions of Hillary Clinton ranged from a low of 25 percent to a high of 61 percent (Yankelovich/*Time*/CNN polls). In the Gallup poll conducted in June 1993, the overall gender gap (that is, the difference between male and female respondents' favorable opinions) was a substantial 20 points, with 60 percent of women but only 40 percent of men expressing a favorable opinion. Table 2-4 shows how this male/female difference is exacerbated among certain groups. Party and age are important determinants of favorability also. Those women who, we might expect intuitively, would identify most strongly with Hillary Clinton—those who are thirty to forty-four years old and Democrats— are most positive toward her.

The data in Table 2-4, which show a remarkable difference between men and women in the thirty- to forty-four-year-old group of 26 percentage points, suggest that the gender wars are being fought among people in similar situations or close proximity. A few more examples of these striking differences follow. The *Los Angeles Times* surveyed 2,346 enlisted men and women on active duty in February 1993. When asked, "How do you feel about allowing women to take combat roles in the U.S. Armed Forces?" 55 percent of the men and fully 79 percent of the women approved.[7] In 1992, exit polls in four states asked whether the nomination of Clarence Thomas to the Supreme Court should have been confirmed. In all four states men essentially said yes and women said no. This was true in every age group and particularly for younger people. For example, in Pennsylvania, 52 percent of eighteen- to twenty-nine-year-old men backed Thomas, whereas only 31 percent of women in that group did.[8]

A Gallup poll in May of 1992 asked registered voters their opinion of Clarence Thomas. Among the college-educated, 55 percent of the men but only 37 percent of the women had a favorable opinion. Perhaps picking up on this conflictual atmosphere, Gallup asked a national sample in August 1993, "How often would you say that you feel resentful specifically toward men/women because of something they do, or perhaps something they don't do, that you find irritating and just typically male/female?" Twenty percent of men and a substantial 40 percent of women replied "very often" or "often"—virtually no one said "never."

In the 1992 election, the Perot candidacy seemed to bring out gender conflict. Among his strongest supporters in June, according to a Gallup poll for *USA Today*/CNN, were men aged thirty to forty-four (43 percent "considered themselves a supporter"). Women in this age group were much more negative (only 21 percent were supporters). While Democratic men and women were similar to one another in their preferences for Perot, a gender gap of 19 points existed among Republicans, with men much more supportive of Perot than women.[9]

One thing that most all of the explanations of the gender gap have had in common is that they seek understanding by looking at women—that is, they try to explain why women think or behave as they do. Male behavior or opinion is, implicitly, the norm. Why are women more supportive of welfare spending? It must be women's socialization, women's mothering experiences, women's dependence on government benefits. Why are women more opposed to war? It must be women's nurturing, compassionate nature. Why were women less supportive of Reagan? It was something about his message or style of presentation to which women did not respond. Much of the time when journalists and even social scientists say something has to do with gender, they really mean that it has to do with women. This is even more strongly the case with politics, where a deep and hard-to-shake assumption that politics is a male domain means that it is women's behavior that demands explanation.

Looking at the party identification measure in the American National Election Studies from 1952 to 1992, women's preferences have remained quite a bit more stable than men's. Averaging the first four and the last four surveys in the series, the level of Democratic identification among men fell 12 points (from 48 percent to 36 percent) while women's dropped only 5 points (47 percent to 42 percent). Certainly the change in voting behavior from 1992 to 1994 was far greater for men than for women, as illustrated in Figure 2-4. Here we see that men's shift toward the Republicans was about three times the magnitude of women's.

These data suggest that perhaps men's behavior or thinking is just as deserving of explanation as women's, that gender is not just about women. Political discourse should ask how (or whether) men should fulfill their traditional "breadwinner" role; where assertiveness, independence, and other traditionally male attributes fit into an effective leadership style; how men can balance the demands of family with the demands of careers; whether, and in what ways, men or women are better off in present-day American society. The expectations and conflicts of modern American society affect men as well as women.

Figure 2-4   Percentage Shift to Republicans (Between 1992 and 1994 House
Votes) for Age/Sex Groups

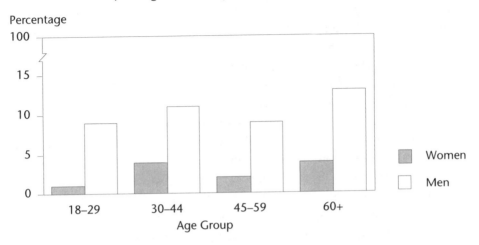

Source: Everett Carll Ladd, "1994 Vote: Against the Background of Continuing Realignment," in *America at the Polls, 1994,* ed. Everett Carll Ladd (Storrs, Conn.: Roper Center, 1995), 48.

In the 1992 election cycle, the media seemed quite taken with the number of women running for and winning office. In 1994, the spotlight shifted away from women candidates (as the *New York Times* announced in October, "In 1994, 'Vote for Woman' Does Not Play so Well") and toward the angry male electorate. In the 1994 elections, fifty-one of sixty-three races covered by Voter News Service exit polls (twenty-four of thirty gubernatorial races, twenty-one of twenty-seven senatorial races, all four of the state attorney general races covered, and both of the at-large House races) were characterized by a gender gap of 4 points or more. In virtually all these situations (forty-nine of fifty-one) women were more supportive of the Democratic candidate.

One of the most striking things about coverage of the 1994 election was that the media began to broaden its understanding of gender. Rather than continuing to try and explain why women again voted more Democratic than men, we saw attempts to explain why men (particularly young white men) voted so heavily for Republicans. *USA Today*'s front page story in the weekend edition of November 11–13, 1994, headlined "Angry White Men: Their Votes Turn the Tide for GOP." As Celinda Lake described it when interviewed for that article, "Women want to change Washington. Men want to torch it." Another pollster suggested that working-class white men are "increasingly convinced society and government aren't making room for them. They feel they are the butt of jokes, condescended to." These men opposed Clinton's attempt to allow openly gay people to remain in or join the military, distrusted and disliked Hillary Clinton and her role, and objected to high taxes and spending on social programs. The gender wars—real conflict over sex roles, rules of discourse, and expectations—combined with the economic insecurity increasingly felt by those in traditionally male jobs (such as assembly-line, heavy industry workers as well as the middle management ranks which many companies are shrinking) to produce a distinctive outlook which can be usefully approached via a gender analysis.

The relationship between gender and public opinion over the past thirty years has been a complicated one. Through the 1970s, women were presumed to be identical to men on one level and different from men on another—a combination that reduced sex to a politically uninteresting distinction. That is, women were seen as essentially and uniquely conservative and apolitical—but to the extent that they did think about politics or vote, their interests were assumed to be identical to men's. When empirical sex differences suggested in the 1980s that the essential attributes of women were perhaps not so fixed, women's organizations took advantage of this change in perception to construct a new picture of women as having distinct political interests. At the same time, the emergence of gender analysis as a way of achieving a deeper understanding of men's and women's political thinking and behavior allowed social scientists and historians to suggest reasons for the observed sex differences. From these perspectives, differences in the opinions held by males and females became both intellectually interesting and politically important. As the 1980s waned, gender itself and gender issues became a focus of political contestation; now, in the 1990s, gender may become a useful tool of analysis to understand both men and women, just as women's issues and women candidates assume an ever more central role in American politics.

Notes

1. Joan Scott's 1986 article, "Gender: A Useful Category of Historical Analysis," is particularly relevant in this context.

2. A few of the books which have had an impact on historians' thinking about various periods in American history include Kerber (1980), Muncy (1991), and Skocpol (1992); on political theory, Susan Muller Okin's two books (1979 and 1991); and on power see Hartsock (1983).

3. If you order clothing from Lands End, for example, the shipping label will be marked with color, size, and "gender." I would argue that Lands End is really talking about biological sex but is (incorrectly) substituting what seems to be a more current term.

4. Klein (1984) also discusses the possibility that while men may come to their stands on abortion through general principles based on rights or liberalism, the issue for women may be more strongly shaped by their personal experience.

5. *Gallup Report* 1983, cited by Kenski 1988, 47–49.

6. The press in February 1995 reported a suit by eight men who had worked for Jenny Craig Inc., a corporation dominated by women, who claimed they had been the target of sexual remarks, been asked to perform demeaning jobs, and denied promotions because of their sex.

7. Data from *American Enterprise,* July/August 1993, 102.

8. Data from *American Enterprise,* January/February 1993, 104.

9. Data from *American Enterprise,* July/August 1993, 98.

3 Race, Class, and Black-White Differences in Social Policy Views

Steven A. Tuch and Lee Sigelman

Few social issues currently being debated in the national political arena generate as much intensity on both sides as government social programs, especially affirmative action. Praised by supporters as an appropriate remedy for past racial injustices and criticized by opponents as unfair reverse discrimination, affirmative action has persisted into the 1990s as an extraordinarily divisive political issue. The outcome of the current debate will be a key to the domestic politics and policy of the United States in the coming years.

It sometimes seems that black and white Americans occupy different worlds, considering their thinking about various aspects of American life (Jaynes and Williams 1989; Schuman, Steeh, and Bobo 1985; Sigelman and Welch 1991). One manifestation of this difference in outlook is the tendency of blacks to hold whites responsible for persisting socioeconomic inequalities between blacks and whites, while whites blame blacks themselves (Bobo and Kluegel 1993; Kluegel 1990; Kluegel and Smith 1986). Another is the steadfast loyalty of blacks to the Democratic Party at a time when more whites are identifying as Republicans or are eschewing party labels altogether (Tate 1993). The races are not always at odds, however; on many important issues there seems to be little or no disagreement between blacks and whites, and on many other issues there seems to be little or no consensus within either race.

As national political leaders invoke more and more intense rhetoric about the proper role of government in a democratic society, this is an especially opportune time to probe the attitudes of black and white Americans toward government social programs, particularly those designed to alleviate race-based socioeconomic inequalities. We pay particular attention to the role that social class plays in the maintenance of these attitudes.

Our starting point is the widespread stereotype of black Americans as politically liberal. Like so many other stereotypes, this one has some basis in fact but is greatly exaggerated. On a seven-point scale ranging from "extremely liberal" to "extremely conservative," blacks fall significantly closer to the "extremely liberal" end of the scale than do whites. But the difference is hardly dramatic. In fact, it amounts to only one-third of a point on the seven-point scale: blacks, on average, fall just to the liberal side of the "moderate, middle of the road" center point, and whites, on average, fall just to the conservative side.[1] Overall, fewer than four blacks in ten consider themselves "extremely liberal," "liberal," or even "slightly liberal," and more than one in four call themselves "slightly conservative," "conservative," or even "extremely conservative"; by comparison, about one in four whites are self-proclaimed liberals, and slightly over one in three are conservatives. As a group, then, blacks are slightly less conservative than whites, but that difference hardly qualifies them as liberals.

The stereotype of blacks as monolithically liberal, then, is simply wrong. The liberal stereotype also ignores a growing body of research that addresses the intersection of race and class and its implications for a wide variety of attitudes and behaviors. This literature highlights the increasing social and economic polarization of the black community, which is associated with two concurrent phenomena: the growth of the black middle class and the entrapment in poverty of the great mass of inner-city blacks (see especially Wilson 1987).

Is this socioeconomic differentiation fostering deeper political cleavages among blacks? According to one school of thought, a conservative black middle class is emerging whose interests are closely aligned with those of middle-class whites—interests, it is argued, that predispose middle-class blacks to adopt perspectives and behaviors generally associated with middle-class whites rather than with lower- and working-class blacks (see, for example, Parent and Stekler 1985; Sowell 1981, 1984; Williams 1982; Wilson 1980). From this perspective, black assimilation into the mainstream of American society heightens class consciousness and decreases racial group identification; thus class is expected to be more important than race in the formation of political views. However, others argue that blacks, as members of a historically subordinated minority group, are likely to maintain their sense of racial group identification despite their increasing social and economic fragmentation (see Dillingham 1981; Huckfeldt and Kohfeld 1989; Jackman and Jackman 1983; Tuch, Sigelman, and Martin 1994; Welch and Combs 1985). According to this view, the political interests and perspectives of blacks continue to cross class lines: blacks still identify, first and foremost, as blacks, and see their interests as bound more closely to their race than to their class. In other words, one school of thought has posited a theory of economic group interests and the other a theory of racial group interests to account for blacks' and whites' views of social policies. Economic group interests cut across racial lines, and racial group interests transcend individual economic circumstances.

Past attempts to disentangle the effects of race and class on policy views have yielded inconclusive results (see Smith and Seltzer 1992 for a review of this literature). Some researchers have concluded that middle-class blacks are more supportive than middle-class whites are of government spending to resolve social problems and to address racial inequities (Seltzer and Smith 1985; Smith and Seltzer 1992). Others have found that middle-class blacks harbor more conservative policy views than working-class blacks do (Gilliam 1986; Gilliam and Whitby 1989; Welch and Foster 1987). Still others have reported mixed results, depending on how they measure class (McDermott 1994; Tate 1993) and on which political attitudes they examine (Smith and Seltzer 1992). For instance, Katherine Tate (1993) reported that although subjective class identification (that is, whether people label themselves as belonging to the middle class or the working class) had no impact on the policy views of blacks, blacks with higher incomes espoused more conservative policy positions than those with lower incomes. Monica McDermott (1994) found larger race than class effects on attitudes toward social welfare spending, but a smaller gap between race and class effects on general beliefs about the fairness of the stratification system.

Our understanding of the factors that shape whites' views on social policy issues, though still incomplete, far exceeds our understanding of how blacks' views are formed. Most researchers have relied on data from national surveys of the general public, and in a typical national survey very few blacks are likely to be interviewed.[2] The small sample size makes it difficult to assess attitudinal differences (class-based or otherwise) among blacks. As A. Wade Smith (1987, 441) recognized, being unable to differentiate among blacks has contributed to the false impression that black Americans all think alike about these issues—an impression that has impeded our understanding of black opinion in general and of black opinion on policy issues in particular.

To analyze blacks' and whites' appraisals of various types of government social programs, we use data from two ongoing national surveys: the 1989–1991 General Social Surveys (GSS) administered by the National Opinion Research Center and the 1988, 1990, and 1992 American National Election Studies (ANES) conducted by the Institute for Social Research at the University of Michigan.[3] Both the GSS and the ANES are national surveys based on full probability sampling designs and are representative of the noninstitutionalized adult population of the continental United States. In each case, we pool respondents from three separate annual administrations of the survey to create a merged sample with enough black respondents to permit us to assess attitudinal differences among blacks as well as differences between blacks and whites. Depending on the particular response item we are analyzing, the number of black GSS respondents falls as low as 128 or rises to 408, while the number of white GSS respondents varies from 937 to 3166; for the ANES, the counterpart ranges are 384–817 and 2094–5125 for blacks and whites, respectively.

Types of Social Programs

The past half century has been a period of enormous change in race relations in the United States. Overt expressions of antiblack and anti-integration sentiments by white Americans—though by no means extinct—have dramatically declined (Jaynes and Williams 1989; Schuman, Steeh, and Bobo 1985). An overwhelming majority of whites now voice strong support for the general principles of racial integration and equality in employment, housing, and education. Even so, most whites disapprove of many of the specific programs that have been devised to implement these principles—especially programs that are "race-targeted" rather than generic or nonracial (see, for example, Kinder 1986; Sniderman and Tetlock 1986).

Generic social programs are "color blind." By generic social programs we mean programs designed to provide a safety net for all Americans who need it, irrespective of race. That is, they seek to deliver government services, for example, to provide programs for better health care, supplemental income, or enhanced job skills, without reference to the race of the beneficiaries of these services. By contrast, race-targeted programs are intended to reduce race-based social, economic, or political inequality. Race is an explicit criterion for eligibility in programs such as busing to achieve school integration or affirmative action programs in education and employment. Recognizing racial distinctions, these programs attempt to overcome the invidious effects that such distinctions have had in the past.

It is sometimes useful to distinguish between two types of race-targeted programs: compensatory programs, such as job training and special education, which are designed to help members of disadvantaged groups compete more effectively in the marketplace; and preferential treatment, such as quotas in college admissions and hiring (see Lipset and Schneider 1978). Most whites and most blacks support compensatory programs (Bobo and Kluegel 1993; Sigelman and Welch 1991). However, most whites reject programs that they view as conferring preferential treatment on members of a particular group, such as blacks, because such programs strike them as violating fundamental principles of fairness. Many blacks apparently share these qualms, although the evidence is far less reliable. Some prominent black conservatives have argued that federal intervention in the race relations arena has perpetuated a social welfare approach to the solution of racial problems that has proven, on balance, to be detrimental to blacks (Sowell 1981, 1984; Williams 1982). Others equate affirmative action with the message that blacks require special help in overcoming obstacles, and thus view these programs as perpetuating racist stereotypes (see Boston 1988 for a review). Black liberals, on the other hand, tend to embrace government intervention as an antidote, albeit a partial and temporary one, to past discrimination.

Relatively few Americans, black or white, seem to object to the mildest types of race-targeted policies, such as special job training programs, but policies that involve quotas evoke heated controversy. Between these extremes lies an array of programs—government spending to improve the social and economic position of blacks, for instance, or federal intervention to assure equal treatment in the workplace. In our analysis of the dual impact of race and class on policy views, we focus on blacks' and whites' attitudes toward programs that lie at points all along this continuum.

The other set of attitudes we examine, orientations toward generic social programs, provides the starting point for our analysis and creates a counterpoint to orientations toward race-targeted programs. Why focus on generic policies? Prior research has suggested that exclusionary programs are unlikely to receive broad-based public support (Bobo and

Kluegel 1993; Burstein 1985; Wilson 1987). Just as most Americans oppose foreign aid because they view it as benefiting "them" rather than "us," many whites who support generic social programs oppose race-targeted programs because they consider such programs a special entitlement for which they themselves are ineligible. By examining blacks' and whites' views toward a range of such programs we hope to shed light on the validity of this interpretation.

In the analysis that follows, we first consider black-white differences in attitudes toward generic social policies, focusing on racial differences in responses to seven questions asked in the 1989–1991 GSS. Then, having assessed the overall extent to which blacks and whites agree or disagree about such policies, we reexamine black-white differences while drawing sharper distinctions among blacks and whites. The primary distinctions in which we are interested are related to social class, which encompasses the interrelated hierarchies of income, education, and occupation. We hope to find out to what extent overall black-white differences in support for generic social policies fall by the wayside when we add class to the picture alongside race. At the same time as we expand the predictors of policy attitudes to encompass social class, we also incorporate a number of demographic and political variables in the model in order to isolate the independent effects of race and class, over and above the effects of other factors to which race and class may be linked. Finally, having established the benchmark of blacks' and whites' attitudes on generic social policies, we repeat the same steps for race-targeted policies, focusing on blacks' and whites' responses to five questions in the 1988–1992 ANES.

Attitudes Toward Generic Social Programs

All seven items on which our analyses of attitudes toward generic social programs focus stem from a single root question in the GSS, in which respondents were asked whether they thought that "on the whole . . . it should or should not be the government's responsibility" to carry out any of a wide range of social services: providing a job for everyone who wants one, health care for the sick, or a decent standard of living for the old and for the unemployed; reducing income differences between the rich and poor; giving financial assistance to college students from low-income families; and furnishing decent housing for those who cannot afford it. In each case, respondents indicated whether a given service "definitely should not be," "probably should not be," "probably should be," or "definitely should be" the responsibility of government.

Table 3-1 breaks down the responses to these questions according to the respondents' race. Comparing the two columns of the table, we can see that blacks were more inclined than whites to endorse government programs in all seven areas. However, the size of the black-white gap varied from program to program. The seven items formed two distinct

Table 3-1 Public Support for Governmental Provision of Generic Social Programs, by Race

	Whites (%)	Blacks (%)
On the whole, do you think it should or should not be the government's responsibility to . . .		
Provide a job for everyone who wants one?		
Definitely should not be	28	6
Probably should not be	32	15
Probably should be	27	34
Definitely should be	14	45
Provide a decent standard of living for the unemployed?		
Definitely should not be	17	4
Probably should not be	32	15
Probably should be	38	43
Definitely should be	13	39
Reduce income differences between the rich and poor?		
Definitely should not be	28	11
Probably should not be	29	20
Probably should be	27	34
Definitely should be	17	35
Provide decent housing for those who can't afford it?		
Definitely should not be	7	2
Probably should not be	23	9
Probably should be	55	41
Definitely should be	16	49
Provide a decent standard of living for the old?		
Definitely should not be	2	2
Probably should not be	12	2
Probably should be	50	34
Definitely should be	36	63
Provide health care for the sick?		
Definitely should not be	3	2
Probably should not be	9	2
Probably should be	51	36
Definitely should be	37	61

Table 3-1 *(Continued)*

	Whites (%)	Blacks (%)
Give financial assistance to college students from low-income families?		
Definitely should not be	3	2
Probably should not be	11	4
Probably should be	60	41
Definitely should be	27	53

Source: 1989–1991 General Social Surveys.

Note: Each entry is the percentage of whites or blacks who offered a particular response; columns may not sum to 100% because of rounding error.

clusters: those on which there were moderate to large racial differences—the first four questions listed in the table—and those on which black-white differences were small—the last three questions.[4]

The first question addressed the government's responsibility to provide a job for everyone who wants one. On this issue a wide gap separated blacks from whites: eight out of ten blacks, but only four out of ten whites, said that guaranteeing a job is probably or definitely the responsibility of government. Substantial racial differences also cropped up with regard to the government's provision of "a decent standard of living" for the unemployed. More than 80 percent of blacks but only 51 percent of whites viewed such support as government's responsibility. On the next two questions, black-white differences were less extreme but still appreciable. The third question, whether it should be government's responsibility to reduce income differences between the rich and poor, elicited approval from only 44 percent of the white respondents, but from 69 percent of the blacks. The fourth question (the final member of this cluster) focused on the provision of housing to those in need. Although large majorities of both blacks (90 percent) and whites (71 percent) considered this a governmental responsibility, the racial gap remains substantial.

On the last three items in the table, which addressed government's responsibility to provide a decent standard of living for the old, health care for the sick, and financial assistance to college students from low-income families, black-white differences were smaller. In each instance, blacks were more emphatic in their support of government's role, as indicated by the preponderance among blacks but not among whites of "definitely should be" rather than "probably should be" responses. Still, all three types of government involvement were overwhelmingly popular among respondents of both races: support levels ranged between 85 percent and 90 percent among whites and between 95 percent and 100 percent among blacks.

In sum, a strong consensus prevailed among blacks and whites alike in favor of an active government role in caring for the aged and the infirm and enhancing the prospects of those from disadvantaged families. But blacks were far more likely than whites to endorse government action to correct a wide range of other social problems.

Now we need to find out whether we can determine the role of socioeconomic factors within each race. The main questions are (1) whether the attitudes of middle-class blacks were distinctive from those of working-class blacks and (2) whether the black-white attitudinal differences we have discussed stemmed largely from interracial differences in income, education, and occupation, which collectively define social class.

To find out, we tested a series of statistical models in which the dependent variables were the seven indicators we have just examined of support for government delivery of generic social programs. The main predictors in the model, besides the race of the respondent, were three separate indicators of social class: education, measured as the number of years of school a respondent had completed; annual family income, measured on a twenty-step scale ranging from less than $1,000 to $60,000 or more; and occupation, defined as upper white-collar, lower white-collar, upper blue-collar, or lower blue-collar.[5] Also included in the model as control variables were a respondent's gender (0 = male, 1 = female); age, in years; region of residence (0 = non-South, 1 = South); party identification, measured on a seven-point scale ranging from 0, for strong Democrats, through 6, for strong Republicans; and political ideology, measured on a seven-point scale ranging from 0, for self-identified extreme liberals, to 6, for extreme conservatives.[6]

The results of these statistical tests are summarized in Table 3-2, which shows the probability that a black or white GSS respondent who was of either lower or higher class standing and had typical scores on the control variables[7] would offer a given answer to a given question. We defined a person of lower class standing as one who had ten years of education and an annual family income of between $10,000 and $12,500 and worked in a lower blue-collar occupation; by contrast, we defined a person of higher class standing as one with sixteen years of education, an annual family income in the $50,000–$60,000 range, and an upper white-collar occupation. Although we measured these three components of social class separately, Table 3-2 summarizes their joint impact on attitudes toward generic social programs.[8]

If race but not class shapes attitudes toward generic social programs, then lower- and higher-class blacks should be clustered together in support of these programs, and lower- and higher-class whites should be clustered together in opposition. On the other hand, if class but not race shapes these attitudes, then lower-class blacks and lower-class whites should cluster together in support of these programs, and higher-class blacks and higher-class whites

Table 3-2 Public Support for Governmental Provision of Generic Social Programs, by Race and Class, Controlling for Demographic and Political Factors

	Probability for Whites		Probability for Blacks	
	Lower Class	Higher Class	Lower Class	Higher Class

On the whole, do you think it should or should not be the government's responsibility to. . .

Provide a job for everyone who wants one?				
Definitely should not be	.14	.30	.03	.11
Probably should not be	.30	.36	.16	.27
Probably should be	.34	.25	.33	.36
Definitely should be	.22	.09	.48	.27
Provide a decent standard of living for the unemployed?				
Definitely should not be	.07	.21	.02	.09
Probably should not be	.25	.37	.14	.28
Probably should be	.47	.35	.45	.46
Definitely should be	.21	.07	.39	.17
Reduce income differences between the rich and poor?				
Definitely should not be	.11	.37	.05	.23
Probably should not be	.25	.34	.17	.32
Probably should be	.36	.23	.35	.31
Definitely should be	.28	.07	.44	.14
Provide decent housing for those who can't afford it?				
Definitely should not be	.01	.06	.00	.01
Probably should not be	.11	.24	.03	.10
Probably should be	.58	.58	.42	.57
Definitely should be	.30	.13	.55	.31
Provide a decent standard of living for the old?				
Definitely should not be	.00	.03	.00	.01
Probably should not be	.04	.14	.01	.06
Probably should be	.39	.56	.23	.46
Definitely should be	.57	.27	.76	.47

(Table continues)

Table 3-2 *(Continued)*

	Probability for Whites		Probability for Blacks	
	Lower Class	Higher Class	Lower Class	Higher Class
Provide health care for the sick?				
Definitely should not be	.01	.03	.00	.01
Probably should not be	.04	.08	.02	.04
Probably should be	.40	.52	.29	.43
Definitely should be	.55	.37	.69	.52
Give financial assistance to college students from low-income families?				
Definitely should not be	.01	.02	.00	.01
Probably should not be	.05	.09	.02	.04
Probably should be	.55	.61	.41	.50
Definitely should be	.38	.28	.57	.46

Source: 1989–1991 General Social Surveys.

Notes: The entries in each column are simulated probabilities, based on a series of ordered probit analyses. Probabilities may not sum to 1.00 because of rounding error. In the simulations, mean or modal values are assumed on the control variables, with gender specified as female, age as forty-five, region as non-South, and liberalism-conservatism and party identification as the midpoints of their respective seven-point scales. Social class is assumed to be either lower (lower blue-collar occupation, no more than ten years of education, and family income in the $10,000–$12,500 range) or higher (upper white-collar occupation, sixteen years or more of education, and family income in the $50,000–$60,000 range). Race is assumed to be either white or black. The probability that a lower- or higher-class black or white GSS respondent with other characteristics as just specified would respond in a particular way to one of the survey questions was calculated from the estimated probit coefficients.

should cluster together in opposition. However, the results in Table 3-2 do not fit either of these patterns. That is, public support for generic social programs did not show through clusters of race or class. Rather, race and class together shape attitudes. For example, on the question of whether government should provide a job for everyone who wants one, higher-class whites stood out from the three other groups. With all the other variables in the model held constant, the probability that a respondent agreed that government "probably" or "definitely" should provide a job for everyone who wants one was only .34 for a higher-class white and at least .56 for members of the three remaining race/class groups. Of those three groups, lower-class blacks stood out as most supportive of government job programs, at .81. Most lower-class whites, like most higher-class blacks, voiced support for such programs.

On the question of whether it is government's responsibility to provide jobs for those who need them, lower-class whites and higher-class blacks occupied an intermediate position between the strong opposition expressed by higher-class whites and the strong support expressed by lower-class blacks. This same general pattern continued to hold for every other set of responses in Table 3-2: lower-class blacks took the most expansive view of governmental responsibilities, higher-class whites took the most restrictive view, and higher-class blacks and lower-class whites fell between the two extremes. To be sure, sometimes (as in opinions about health care for the sick and financial assistance to college students) the intergroup differences were relatively small, while in other instances (as in opinions about reducing income differences and providing a job for everyone who wants one) wide opinion differences were associated with race and class. But higher-class whites always fell at one extreme and lower-class blacks always fell at the other, and lower-class whites and higher-class blacks were generally clustered closely together in the middle.

One partial exception to this pattern emerged. Predictably, the idea that government should oversee a redistribution of income from the rich to the poor was popular among lower-class blacks and unpopular among higher-class whites. On this issue, though, lower-class whites and higher-class blacks were not in close accord. Lower-class whites tended to share lower-class blacks' enthusiasm for income redistribution (albeit to a less extreme degree), and higher-class blacks tended to share higher-class whites' antipathy toward income redistribution (though again to a less extreme degree). As a consequence, when the interests of the rich and poor were explicitly counterposed, the responses of the four groups reflected class distinctions more clearly than their answers to the other questions considered in Tables 3-1 and 3-2.

In sum, when Americans of different racial and social class backgrounds were asked to assess generic social programs, both race and social class shaped their responses. Race and class reinforced one another among higher-class whites and lower-class blacks, and cut across one another among lower-class whites and higher-class blacks. As a consequence, in most instances there ended up being little difference between the attitudes of the two cross-pressured groups (lower-class whites and higher-class blacks); only in the exceptional case of support for income redistribution did the views of the two groups in the middle diverge perceptibly.

Attitudes Toward Race-Targeted Social Programs

Assessments of government programs intended specifically for black Americans were solicited in five ANES questions. Blacks' and whites' responses to these questions are summarized in Table 3-3. Two patterns stand out in the responses. First, both blacks' and whites' expressions of enthusiasm for race-targeted social programs varied widely from question to

Table 3-3 Public Support for Governmental Provision of Race-Targeted Social Programs, by Race

	Whites (%)	Blacks (%)
Some people feel that the government in Washington should make every effort to improve the social and economic position of blacks. Others feel that the government should not make any special effort to help blacks because they should help themselves. Where would you place yourself on this scale . . . ?		
(1) Blacks should help themselves	22	10
(2)	16	9
(3)	16	11
(4)	26	24
(5)	11	9
(6)	5	11
(7) Government should help blacks	4	27
Should federal spending on programs that assist blacks be increased, decreased, or kept about the same?		
Decreased	24	2
Kept about the same	57	29
Increased	19	69
Some people say that because of past discrimination, blacks should be given preference in hiring and promotion. Others say that such preference in hiring and promotion of blacks is wrong because it gives blacks advantages they haven't earned. What about your opinion—are you for or against preferential hiring and promotion of blacks?		
Oppose strongly	68	22
Oppose	18	15
Favor	8	9
Favor strongly	7	53
Some people feel that if black people are not getting fair treatment in jobs, the government in Washington ought to see to it that they do. Others feel that this is not the federal government's business. . . . How do you feel? Should the government in Washington see to it that black people get fair treatment in jobs or is this not the federal government's business?		
Not government's business	50	8
Government should see to it	50	92

Table 3-3 *(Continued)*

	Whites (%)	Blacks (%)
Some people say that because of past discrimination it is sometimes necessary for colleges and universities to reserve openings for black students. Others oppose quotas because they say quotas give blacks advantages they haven't earned. What about your opinion— are you for or against quotas to admit black students?		
Oppose strongly	50	14
Oppose	23	8
Favor	16	12
Favor strongly	12	66

Source: 1988–1992 American National Election Studies.

Note: Each entry is the percentage of whites or blacks who offered a particular response; columns may not sum to 100% because of rounding error.

question. For example, only 15 percent of the white respondents said they were in favor of giving preferential treatment to blacks in hiring and promotion. However, 50 percent of whites considered it the federal government's responsibility to try to ensure that blacks receive fair treatment in jobs. Among blacks, fewer than half agreed that the federal government "should make every effort to improve the social and economic position of blacks"; it seems clear that the self-help theme that resonates throughout the rhetoric of black political leaders strikes a responsive chord in the black public. But at the other extreme, more than nine blacks in ten deemed it the federal government's responsibility to see that blacks get fair treatment in jobs. The lesson is clear: it can be highly misleading to speak in general terms of blacks' or whites' support for or opposition to race-targeted programs. How much support people of either race express for race-targeted programs depends on specific features of the programs they are considering.

Second, on all five questions blacks as a group expressed greater support for race-targeted social programs than did whites as a group. This difference is hardly surprising. After all, we saw in Table 3-1 that blacks were more supportive than whites even of generic social programs, and we would certainly expect a wider black-white gap in assessments of race-targeted programs. Even so, the sheer size of the gap between blacks and whites warrants comment. For example, 69 percent of black ANES respondents, but only 19 percent of whites, said that federal spending on programs to assist blacks should be increased rather than decreased or held at the current level. Black-white differences were no less pronounced

Table 3-4 Public Support for Governmental Provision of Race-Targeted Social Programs, by Race and Class, Controlling for Demographic and Political Factors

	Probability for Whites		Probability for Blacks	
	Lower Class	Higher Class	Lower Class	Higher Class

Some people feel that the government in Washington should make every effort to improve the social and economic position of blacks. Others feel that the government should not make any special effort to help blacks because they should help themselves. Where would you place yourself on this scale . . . ?

	Lower Class	Higher Class	Lower Class	Higher Class
(1) Blacks should help themselves	.16	.12	.04	.03
(2)	.15	.13	.07	.05
(3)	.18	.17	.12	.10
(4)	.29	.31	.30	.28
(5)	.12	.15	.20	.21
(6)	.06	.07	.13	.15
(7) Government should help blacks	.04	.06	.14	.19

Should federal spending on programs that assist blacks be increased, decreased, or kept about the same?

	Lower Class	Higher Class	Lower Class	Higher Class
Decreased	.18	.19	.01	.01
Kept about the same	.59	.59	.28	.28
Increased	.22	.22	.71	.71

Some people say that because of past discrimination, blacks should be given preference in hiring and promotion. Others say that such preference in hiring and promotion of blacks is wrong because it gives blacks advantages they haven't earned. What about your opinion—are you for or against preferential hiring and promotion of blacks?

	Lower Class	Higher Class	Lower Class	Higher Class
Oppose strongly	.63	.68	.18	.22
Oppose	.20	.18	.21	.22
Favor	.09	.07	.18	.17
Favor strongly	.08	.06	.43	.48

Some people feel that if black people are not getting fair treatment in jobs, the government in Washington ought to see to it that they do. Others feel that this is not the federal government's business. . . . How do you feel? Should the government in Washington see to it that black people get fair treatment in jobs or is this not the federal government's business?

	Lower Class	Higher Class	Lower Class	Higher Class
Not government's business	.56	.40	.18	.09
Government should see to it	.44	.60	.82	.91

Table 3-4 *(Continued)*

	Probability for Whites		Probability for Blacks	
	Lower Class	Higher Class	Lower Class	Higher Class

Some people say that because of past discrimination it is sometimes necessary for colleges and universities to reserve openings for black students. Others oppose quotas because they say quotas give blacks advantages they haven't earned. What about your opinion— are you for or against quotas to admit black students?

Oppose strongly	.43	.47	.07	.09
Oppose	.24	.23	.13	.14
Favor	.18	.17	.20	.21
Favor strongly	.06	.13	.60	.57

Source: 1988–1992 American National Election Studies.

Notes: Entries are simulated probabilities, based on the results of a series of probit analyses (ordered in all instances except for the yes/no question about whether the federal government should see to it that blacks get fair treatment in jobs). In the simulations, mean or modal values were set on the control variables, with gender specified as female, age as forty-five, region as non-South, and liberalism-conservatism and party identification as the midpoints of their respective seven-point scales. Social class was assumed to be either lower (lower blue-collar occupation, no more than ten years of education, and family income in the $13,000–$14,000 range) or higher (upper white-collar occupation, sixteen years or more of education, and family income in the $45,000–$49,999 range), and race was assumed to be either white or black. The probability that a lower- or higher-class white or black with other characteristics as just specified would provide a given response to one of the survey questions was calculated from the estimated probit coefficients.

on the questions of preferential treatment in hiring and promotion and of college admissions quotas. And even though half the white respondents considered it the federal government's responsibility to see that black people get fair treatment in jobs, this was far lower than the comparable percentage of blacks (92 percent). In only one instance (the first item in Table 3-3) was there less than majority support among both blacks and whites for a race-targeted social program, and in this instance support among blacks outran support among whites by more than a two-to-one margin.

What happens to these patterns when social class and the various control variables are brought into the picture? Table 3-4 tells the story, which is, for the most part, an extremely simple story to tell. With just one exception, the likelihood that a lower-class white would endorse race-targeted programs is within a few percentage points of the likelihood that a higher-class white would do so. The same statement would hold true for lower- and higher-class blacks. But between a black and a white, irrespective of social class, a wide gulf would be predicted. The lone exception to this pattern emerged for the question about whether the federal government should see to it that blacks are treated fairly in jobs. Of all the race-targeted programs considered here, this would clearly fall the closest to the "compensatory" end of a scale that stretched from compensatory programs, at the one extreme, to preferential treatment, at the other. Clearly, higher-class whites were more committed to fair treatment of blacks on the job than lower-class whites were. But no less clearly, this difference did not extend to programs that fell closer to the preferential treatment end of the scale.

Conclusion

In this chapter we have examined the views of black and white Americans toward race-targeted and generic social programs, with a particular focus on the confluence of race and class in shaping these views. Amid heightening economic fragmentation within the black community, many analysts see political cleavages among blacks as inevitable. Is a conservative black middle class emerging whose political attitudes and interests are more closely aligned with those of middle-class whites than of working-class blacks? Our analysis of data from two series of national surveys has suggested that the answer to this question depends on whether the program is race-targeted or not as well as on specific features of the program itself.

Analyzing attitudes toward government sponsorship of generic social programs, we observed a strong black-white consensus in favor of providing a safety net for the elderly and the infirm and financial assistance to college students from low-income families. But in terms of a government role in solving such ills as unemployment and inadequate housing, whites were considerably less likely than blacks to support intervention. Moreover, on most generic issues, lower-status blacks were most strongly in favor of government intervention to remedy social problems and higher-status whites most strongly opposed to such intervention; lower-status whites and higher-status blacks were intermediate between the two. Thus, both race and class jointly shaped Americans' views of these programs.

The story was different with respect to the race-targeted policies. There was wide variation in the degree of support for race-targeted programs among both whites and blacks, depending on the particular program being considered. For instance, most blacks and most whites endorsed the idea that ensuring blacks equal treatment in jobs falls within the purview of government responsibility. Programs that raise the specter of preferential treatment, however, were very unpopular among whites and received far from unanimous support among blacks. Moreover, when class was introduced into the analysis of race-targeted programs, views diverged markedly along racial, not class, lines. We uncovered no evidence of political cleavages between higher- and lower-status blacks, nor between higher- and lower-status whites, in their evaluations of race-targeted programs.

As long as race continues to be a fundamental basis of cleavage in American society, blacks are likely to retain a strong sense of racial group solidarity that transcends class lines. Many middle-class blacks were not born to middle-class parents, and their political views may spring more from the circumstances in which they grew up than from the circumstances in which they currently live. In light of the continuing discrimination reported by many middle-class blacks, particularly in the workplace (see, for example, Feagin 1991), racial group identification is unlikely to be replaced by class awareness in shaping blacks' policy views.

Notes

1. The data are from the 1989–1991 GSS; see below for a description of this data source. The question was: "We hear a lot of talk these days about liberals and conservatives. I'm going to show you a seven-point scale on which the political views that people might hold are arranged from extremely liberal—point 1—to extremely conservative—point 7. Where would you place yourself on this scale?" The black mean was 3.80 and the white mean was 4.14 (F = 27.3, p < .001).

2. The small number of blacks in most national surveys is a function of two factors: blacks constitute approximately 13 percent of the U.S. population, and most academic surveys have approximately 2,000 respondents. If blacks are proportionally represented in the survey, they will constitute only 260 respondents.

3. For descriptions of GSS and ANES sampling procedures, see Davis and Smith (1991) and Miller et al. (1992). The most recent years in which the generic social policy questions were asked in the GSS were 1989–1991, and the ANES is conducted only in even-numbered years. Notwithstanding minor procedural differences in data collection procedures, the GSS and ANES can be considered functionally equivalent (Martin 1983; see also Smith 1978).

4. This is not the order in which the questions were asked; they were asked in the order given in the preceding paragraph.

5. Upper white-collar workers were defined as incumbents of the "managerial and professional specialty occupations" in the 1980 census classification, plus nonclerical incumbents of the "technical, sales, and administrative support occupations." Lower white-collar workers were clerical incumbents of the "technical, sales, and administrative support occupations," plus incumbents of protective service occupations in the "service occupations" category. Upper blue-collar workers were incumbents of the "precision production, craft, and repair occupations" category. Lower blue-collar workers were incumbents of private household occupations and of service occupations, except protective, in the "services occupations" category, plus incumbents of the "operators, fabricators, and laborers" category. Excluded were members of the armed services and incumbents of the "farming, forest, and fishing occupations" category.

6. Because the dependent variables were measured at the ordinal level, ordinary least squares regression techniques were inappropriate. We employed an ordered probit model to estimate the effects of race, class, and the remaining predictors on support for the various policies considered here. The coefficient estimates in probit models lack the substantive interpretability of the unstandardized coefficients in ordinary least squares regression. To conserve space, we do not present the coefficient estimates per se; instead we proceed directly to estimating the substantive impacts of race and social class.

7. We defined a "typical" score as the mean or mode of a variable. By that definition, a respondent with typical scores on the control variables would be a forty-five-year-old woman living outside the south who scored 3 on both the party identification and political ideology scales.

8. We set education, family income, and occupational category at particular values solely for purposes of the impact assessments in Tables 3-2 and 3-4. In the underlying probit analyses, each varied as described earlier in the text. The statistical results all derive for additive models. To determine whether class differences might have had different effects on blacks' and whites' attitudes, we also tested models that contained a full set of race-class interaction terms. In none of the models summarized in Tables 3-2 and 3-4 did an interactive specification provide a better fit to the data.

4 Religion and Public Opinion in the 1990s: An Empirical Overview

Ted G. Jelen

In the aftermath of the 1994 midterm elections, political scientists were faced with a puzzling anomaly. Despite the fact that the first two years of the Clinton administration had been characterized by a growing, prosperous economy and a relatively peaceful international environment, the Republican Party made enormous gains in the midterm elections. Republicans regained control of the U.S. Senate for the first time since 1986, and, more important, won control of the U.S. House of Representatives for the first time in a generation. The GOP made substantial inroads at the state level as well. Democratic losses, which far exceeded the losses usually incurred by the party of an incumbent president at midterm, resurrected speculation that a partisan realignment would permanently establish the Republicans as the majority party in the United States (see Ladd 1995).

Clearly, the causes of the 1994 Republican surge are quite complex and will occupy the attention of political scientists for some time to come. One possible explanation for increased Republican strength relates directly to the political role of religion. In recent years, several analysts have argued that the economically based New Deal party system is giving way to a new alignment based primarily on cultural issues, especially matters of personal morality. This "culture war" is thought to pit the religiously "orthodox" against "progressives" (Hunter 1991) or the religious against the not so religious (Kellstedt et al. 1994a, 1994b). In this morally dualistic polity, "family values" become the dominant axis of political conflict (Hammond, Shibley, and Solow 1994; Reed 1994), and degree of religiosity supersedes divisions based on religious doctrine or denominational preference (Kellstedt et al. 1994a, 1994b; Guth and Green 1993). The politicization of issues of personal morality is thought to result from major cultural changes (lowered standards of sexual morality, less decorous behavior, increased drug use, and other issues) which took place in the 1960s and 1970s. This view can be expressed as the culture wars hypothesis: a belief that American public opinion increasingly exhibits a dualistic structure, with competing factions and political parties organized around issues of moral traditionalism or lifestyle conservatism.

The purpose of this chapter is twofold. First, I will offer a brief summary of research on the relationship between religion and public opinion. Second, I will offer empirical evidence relating to the culture wars hypothesis. Are American political parties in fact realigning among the religiously observant? Is partisan change related to the values of cultural traditionalism? Are these effects (if they exist at all) uniform across religious groups?

Measuring Religion in Surveys

Since the highly visible rise of the New Christian Right in the 1980s, the study of religion and politics has attracted a great deal of scholarly attention. A lack of agreement on the conceptual or empirical meaning of the independent variable—religion—has been a source of continual frustration among scholars who conduct research in this area.

In general, there are three approaches to the measurement of religious variables in American politics. One approach simply measures the extent of religious intensity or observance. According to proponents of the culture wars thesis, the main axis of political competition in the United States in the immediate future will be between religious and less religious Americans, and the particular type of religion will become increasingly irrelevant for political purposes. If this is the case, then it is important to measure church attendance (the main behavioral manifestation of religiosity), religious salience (the importance a person attaches to religious values), or religious intensity (see Wald, Kellstedt, and Leege 1993; Guth and Green 1993).

Such a general approach does not take into consideration the variety of religious doctrines and experiences to which American citizens might be exposed. Thus, a second approach to the measurement of religious phenomena uses denominational affiliation. The denomination, after all, is the basic social unit of American religion. This approach is relatively simple, and it is likely to be meaningful to most Americans. Moreover, denominational questions have been asked in surveys for more than forty years, providing good longitudinal data on religious affiliation.

Yet simply measuring denominational affiliation is at once too broad and too narrow. Denomination is too broad in that such a measurement strategy does not take into account differences between individuals or congregations within a single denomination. Some large denominations (such as Baptists) are much more decentralized and committed to congregational autonomy than others are (such as Roman Catholics). Denomination is too narrow to use as the sole measurement in that the U.S. population encompasses a bewildering variety of affiliations. In the average sample survey, few Protestant denominations will contain enough cases for meaningful data analysis. Therefore, several analysts (Smith 1990a; Kellstedt and Green 1993) have suggested ways of classifying Protestant denominations into denominational families or traditions. A very common division is to classify denominations into the broad categories of "mainline" (those denominations that view scriptural authority less stringently) and "evangelical" (those denominations which hold an authoritative view of the Bible). Examples of mainline denominations are Methodists, Presbyterians, and Episcopalians, while a list of evangelical denominations might include Baptists, Assemblies of God, and Nazarenes. For some research purposes, it is necessary to divide evangelicals further into groups such as "charismatics" or "fundamentalists" (Smidt 1988).

A third approach to the measurement of religious phenomena addresses the respondent's beliefs directly. A common survey item, often used to distinguish evangelicals from mainline Protestants, is the respondent's view of the Bible (Kellstedt 1989; Wilcox 1986; Kellstedt and Smidt 1993; Smidt 1989). Some Christians believe that the Bible is literally true, word for word; others hold that the Bible has no errors but is not literally true; and still others believe that the Bible is the inspired word of God but contains human error. Such a measure appears to tap directly into the doctrinal sense of evangelicalism and appears to be meaningful to most Americans (see especially Jelen, Smidt, and Wilcox 1990). Another measure, often used in conjunction with the respondent's view of the Bible, is the respondent's "born-again" status (see Dixon, Levy, and Lowery 1988; Jelen, Smidt, and Wilcox 1993). Being born again refers to a personal decision or experience involving the acceptance of Jesus Christ as a personal savior; most often, people report that the experience was very specific.

Thus, the state of research in the relationship between religion and public opinion in the United States remains complex. Religion is clearly an important variable in understanding the manner in which Americans think about politics, but specifying which aspects of religion have political relevance in particular contexts requires the use of multiple methods and approaches.

Measuring the Effects of Religion

Individual religious characteristics can account for variations in attitudes and behavior that are of interest to political scientists. Indeed, the large body of research on the relationship between religious beliefs and political attitudes has borne out the general hypothesis that religion is one source of political values.

It is logical that religion might affect attitudes toward political issues. However, the evidence to date suggests that the impact of religion on attitudes toward issues of public policy is generally limited to matters of personal morality, despite the attempts of religious leaders to take positions on a variety of issues (Berke 1995; Falwell 1980; Reed 1994).

Even when pastors in local congregations attempt to take positions on specific issues, congregations are often unresponsive (Jelen 1993; Welch et al. 1993; Hadden 1969). Studies of the effects of religious variables on attitudes toward foreign policy suggest that such effects are erratic and idiosyncratic (Jelen 1994), or rather short-lived (Wald 1992). Similarly, despite the efforts of some evangelical leaders to promote an economically conservative agenda (Falwell 1980; Reed 1994), empirical research at the mass level shows that the relationship between theological conservatism and economic conservatism is quite weak (Iannaccone 1993). Indeed, a few studies (Jelen 1991; Tamney, Johnson, and Burton 1989; Hart 1992) demonstrate that white evangelicals are slightly more liberal on economic issues than other Americans.

Thus, religion appears to have its greatest effect on issues involving lifestyle preferences, sexual morality, and traditional standards of behavior. These issues are the stuff of a possible culture war, and they may have become increasingly salient during the past generation. (For an overview of the research, see Jelen 1990, 1991.)

Some research reports that religion influences political participation. Turnout rates of evangelical Christians increased in 1976 as a result of the candidacy of Jimmy Carter, a born-again Southern Baptist. More generally, church participation has a positive effect on a variety of forms of political participation, and this effect is somewhat stronger among members of theologically conservative congregations (Wilcox 1989; Peterson 1992).

Finally, religion increasingly affects partisanship and voting behavior. Despite changes in socioeconomic status across generations, Roman Catholics remain among the most loyal members of the Democratic coalition (Kellstedt et al. 1994b; Kenski and Lockwood 1989). Conversely, white evangelicals are shifting to the Republican Party, and in recent years such voters have been among the most loyal members of the Republican electorate (see especially Kellstedt et al. 1994a, 1994b). Moreover, this apparent realignment does not appear to be fragmented by the effects of religious particularism—that is, the belief in the superiority of one's own religious tradition (Jelen 1991). The party system appears to aggregate the preferences of a theologically diverse group of evangelical Protestants.

The empirical analyses which follow are intended to address two questions. First, to what extent can the apparent realignment of white evangelicals be attributed to the social conservatism of such voters? Does the increasing Republican share of the evangelical vote support the culture wars thesis? Second, is a shift to the Republican Party occurring solely among evangelical Protestants, or are other socially conservative Americans being recruited into the Republican coalition? In other words, does the scope of the culture war extend beyond the ranks of evangelical Protestants?

Data and Methods

Data for this study were taken from the General Social Surveys (GSS), 1972–1993. These data are quite appropriate for this study for several reasons. First, the series begins in 1972, a year regarded by many as a watershed for the political mobilization of cultural conservatives (see Lopatto 1985).[1] Second, the surveys have been administered virtually every year since 1972 (omitting only 1979, 1981, and 1992). This feature enables researchers to combine years to obtain a large number of cases for rather precisely defined subgroups (for example, evangelical Christians who attend religious services at least once a week). Finally, the GSS contains a number of questions regarding social or lifestyle issues, which are of primary interest here.[2]

For purposes of this study, the GSS were divided into four periods: 1972–1976 (the Nixon-Ford administration), 1977–1980 (the administration of evangelical Jimmy Carter), 1981–1985 (the first Reagan administration, which Matthew Moen [1992, 1994] argued corresponds to the "expansionist period" of the New Christian Right), and 1986 to the present (which Moen characterizes as the "institutional period" of the Christian Right).[3] This procedure allows the researcher to monitor attitudinal changes over the span of two decades while it provides an adequate number of cases at each observation point.

The analyses presented in this study are limited to white Christians. The religious basis of the political behavior of African-Americans and Jews, though quite interesting, is beyond the scope of this chapter—both groups appear to have religious and cultural traditions that are quite different from those of white Christians (Wilcox 1991; Sigelman 1991). Moreover, to assess the impact of religious socialization on political behavior, the study is confined to respondents who report attending religious services at least once a week. Church attendance is a behavioral measure of religious salience, as well as an indicator of exposure to religious communications (Wald, Kellstedt, and Leege 1993). It is less likely that religious values will have a strong effect on those whose religious commitments are intermittent or casual (Kellstedt 1989).

The principal independent variable in this study is religious preference, measured by denominational affiliation (for the precise coding scheme, see Smith 1990a). Although using denominations to measure religious variables may not be an ideal strategy, denominational preference is the only religious variable measured across the entire GSS.[4] Respondents are divided into evangelical Protestants, mainline Protestants, and Roman Catholics.[5]

Three sets of dependent variables are considered in this study. First, attitudes toward several different social issues are considered. These include attitudes toward traditional sexual morality, homosexuality, abortion, tolerance of nonconformists (see Wilcox and Jelen 1990), pornography, and school prayer. Also examined are "public feminism," tapping attitudes toward gender roles in public settings such as politics, and "private feminism," which measures gender-role attitudes in family settings. (See Jelen 1988 and Wilcox and Jelen 1991 for theoretical and empirical analyses of the different forms of feminism; for details of question wording and index construction, contact the author.) A second set of dependent variables consists of self-reported presidential votes for each presidential election since 1972.[6] Finally, the effects of religious preference and issue attitudes on the respondent's party identification are considered. Ultimately, the political effects of religion should be manifested at the ballot box.

Table 4-1 Mean Social Issue Attitudes over Time, by Religious Affiliation (Frequent Church Attenders Only)

	1972–1976	1977–1980	1981–1985	1986–1993
Sexual morality				
Evangelical	1.70	1.78	1.73	1.72
Mainline	1.44	1.49	1.41	1.37**
Catholic	1.31	1.22	1.19	1.16**
Homosexuality				
Evangelical	1.86	1.92	1.94	1.89
Mainline	1.48	1.69	1.70	1.63*
Catholic	1.32	1.24	1.19	1.16*
Private feminism				
Evangelical	—	1.77	1.66	1.59*
Mainline	—	1.68	1.57	1.50*
Catholic	—	1.71	1.57	1.47*
Public feminism				
Evangelical	1.49	1.56	1.41	1.34*
Mainline	1.36	1.38	1.33	1.24*
Catholic	1.28	1.34	1.24	1.21*
Abortion				
Evangelical	1.49	1.52	1.60	1.61*
Mainline	1.35	1.36	1.41	1.41**
Catholic	1.54	1.57	1.55	1.56
Tolerance				
Evangelical	1.65	1.69	1.63	1.53*
Mainline	1.52	1.52	1.51	1.42**
Catholic	1.45	1.44	1.44	1.38*
Pornography				
Evangelical	1.66	1.69	1.70	1.76*
Mainline	1.49	1.59	1.52	1.59*
Catholic	1.51	1.52	1.50	1.50
School prayer				
Evangelical	1.23	1.19	1.28	1.24
Mainline	1.28	1.26	1.39	1.31
Catholic	1.28	1.36	1.35	1.19

Table 4-1 *(Continued)*

	1972–1976	*1977–1980*	*1981–1985*	*1986–1993*
Party identification				
Evangelical	2.94	2.80	3.18	3.51*
Mainline	3.44	3.22	3.52	3.69**
Catholic	2.14	2.30	2.34	2.69*

Source: 1972–1993 General Social Surveys.

Note: Higher scores indicate greater conservatism, greater Republican identification.

*Difference between 1972–1976 (or 1977–1980) and 1986–1993 significant at .01 level.
**Difference between 1972–1976 and 1986–1993 significant at .05 level.

Findings

Table 4-1 displays issue attitudes for frequent church attenders in each denominational group over time. Listed are the mean positions for each religious group on a series of issues. Higher values indicate more conservative opinions. These data suggest few changes in issue attitudes over time. For example, Catholics and mainline Protestants became more permissive with respect to sexual morality over time, but no corresponding change occurred among white evangelicals. Similarly, Catholics became more liberal on the issue of homosexuality during the period studied. On both public and private feminism, a liberalizing trend developed across all denominational groupings, but religiously observant Protestants of both evangelical and mainline denominations became somewhat more conservative on the issue of abortion. Evangelicals tend to be more conservative than other white Christians, but, except on the issues of homosexuality and sexual morality, most religious groups moved in the same direction. No general trend developed, since on some issues (abortion, pornography) attitudes have shifted in a conservative direction, while on others (feminism, tolerance, homosexuality, and sexual morality) the churchgoing public has become more liberal. Thus, there has been no conservative mobilization of religiously observant Christians in general.

The last entries in Table 4-1 show a Republican shift within all three religious groups during the past two decades. The shift has been most pronounced among evangelicals (Kellstedt, Smidt, and Kellstedt 1991; Kellstedt et al. 1994b) and Catholics, although Catholics as a group retain their Democratic allegiance (Kellstedt and Noll 1990; Kenski and Lockwood 1989). Across all four time periods, mainline Protestants are the most Republican group of regular church attenders, Catholics are the most Democratic. For both groups of Protestants, a very slight shift in the direction of the Democrats occurred during the Carter administration.

Table 4-2 Mean Party Identification over Time, by Age Cohort and Religious Affiliation (Frequent Church Attenders Only)

	1972–1976	1977–1980	1981–1985	1986–1993
Evangelical Protestants				
Depression	3.17	2.88	2.76	2.68
World War II	3.03	3.10	2.87	3.07**
Postwar	2.67	2.36	3.03	3.52*
Baby boom	3.03	2.85	3.07	3.62**
1970s	2.77	3.12	3.83	3.93*
Reagan	—	—	3.76	4.06
Mainline Protestants				
Depression	3.53	3.51	3.43	3.97
World War II	3.64	3.20	3.44	3.55
Postwar	3.31	3.45	3.46	3.76**
Baby boom	3.21	3.45	3.47	3.76
1970s	3.32	2.88	3.60	3.86
Reagan	—	—	4.14	3.67
Catholics				
Depression	1.94	2.06	2.16	2.34
World War II	2.04	2.18	2.24	2.51**
Postwar	2.41	2.28	2.19	2.65
Baby boom	2.11	2.62	2.41	2.67**
1970s	2.15	2.54	2.75	2.86**
Reagan	—	—	2.61	3.36

Source: 1972–1993 General Social Surveys.

Notes: Higher mean scores indicate greater Republican identification. Depression: Born before 1916. World War II: Born between 1916 and 1926. Postwar: Born between 1927 and 1942. Baby boom: Born between 1943 and 1951. 1970s: Born between 1952 and 1961. Reagan: Born 1962 or after.

*Difference between 1972–1976 and 1986–1993 significant at .01 level.
**Difference between 1972–1976 and 1986–1993 significant at .05 level.

The dynamics of this general shift to the Republican Party can be clarified through an examination of the partisanship of different age cohorts over time. Table 4-2 presents (for each denominational group) mean partisanship by age cohort and time period. (Higher values indicate Republican identification.) Data in Table 4-2 suggest that Republican gains in aggregate partisanship have resulted from a combination of generational and period effects. (See Abramson [1976, 1979], Converse [1976, 1979], and Claggett [1981] for analyses of generational, life-cycle, and period effects.) That is, it is generally the case that younger cohorts are more Republican than older cohorts; thus it is likely that part of the observed aggregate partisan change is attributable to generational replacement (although this tendency is least pronounced among mainline Protestants). Moreover, the younger cohorts tend to move more rapidly in a Republican direction over time. For example, evangelicals of the World War II cohort (born between 1916 and 1926) exhibit a mean partisan identification of 3.03 during the Nixon-Ford years and 3.07 during the most recent historical period studied. By contrast, evangelical baby boomers (born between 1943 and 1951) move from 3.03 to 3.62 during the same time span.

Thus, across all three religious traditions, younger voters are somewhat more likely to enter the electorate as Republicans, and to strengthen their ties to the Republican Party as they age. It is perhaps noteworthy that most evangelical cohorts shifted slightly in a Democratic direction during the Carter administration, suggesting that Carter's public profession of his evangelical roots temporarily slowed the evangelical shift into the Republican camp (see especially Wilcox 1989). Nevertheless, the data suggest that changes in the age composition of the electorate together with individual party conversions may account for partisan change.

It is unlikely, however, that the general shift to the Republican Party is the result of the increased salience of cultural issues among the religiously devout. When a similar analysis was conducted among white Christians who do not regularly attend religious services (data not shown), there was a significant shift toward the Republicans among the postwar, baby boom, and Reagan cohorts as well. Thus, churchgoing white Christians do not appear to be particularly distinctive in their partisan leanings; they are more likely part of a larger national trend.

To what extent does the shift to Republicanism reflect the increased salience of cultural or social issues among religiously devout white Christians? The increase in Republican identification among white, churchgoing Christians can be attributed to a renewed attention to family values or traditional morality only if the relationship between these issues and party identification has increased over time. In other words, the culture wars hypothesis can be correct if respondents perceive that the relationship of cultural values and partisanship has strengthened over time. Such a finding would be quite consistent with the hypothesis that religious political mobilization is in large part a defensive reaction to social trends and government policies that make maintaining a religiously based traditional lifestyle difficult (see Reed 1994). This possibility is tested in Table 4-3, which shows the correlations between issue positions and party identification over time for each religious tradition. Positive correlations indicate that conservative positions on the issue are associated with Democratic identification, and negative correlations indicate that conservative positions are associated with Republican partisanship. In each case, the greater the absolute value of the correlation (that is, the farther the number is from zero), the stronger the relationship.

Table 4-3 suggests that, prior to the Reagan administration, issues of traditional morality were not generally related to partisanship among frequent church attenders. One interesting exception is that the issue of school prayer seems to have been salient in all religious groups during the Nixon-Ford era, although, among Catholics, support for school prayer has been consistently related to identification with the Democratic Party. However, none of the other coefficients attain statistical significance among either group of Protestants in the earlier time period.

Among evangelicals, the issues of abortion, school prayer, and tolerance toward nonconformists first had a significant impact on party identification during Ronald Reagan's first term. For evangelicals, then, a realignment in the Republican direction was well under way during the early 1980s (the period Moen [1992] has described as one of strong mobilization on the part of the Christian Right). Bruce Nesmith (1994) offers similar evidence. During the most recent period, Republican identification among evangelicals was significantly related to conservative positions on abortion and tolerance, as well as on issues of public feminism, sexual morality, and homosexuality. While the magnitude of these coefficients is moderate, all are statistically significant and in the expected direction.

By contrast, social issue attitudes (with the exception of public feminism) have not been significantly related to partisanship among mainline Protestants until the most recent period. For this group, the cultural component of a pro-Republican realignment did not occur until late in the 1980s.[7] In this most recent period, conservative positions on both forms of feminism, as well as on homosexuality, abortion, and pornography are associated with Republican identification among mainline Protestants. Indeed, the coefficients are slightly stronger for mainline Protestants than for evangelicals.[8]

The findings suggest that the culture wars thesis has become increasingly credible with the passage of time among American Protestants. In the early stages of Christian Right mobilization, the cultural component of partisan realignment appears to have been confined to evangelicals. As time has passed, the partisan effects of traditional values on issues of sexual morality and lifestyle have penetrated the Protestant mainline. To this extent, the assertion seems plausible that it is the extent rather than the type of religious observance that has political relevance (Kellstedt et al. 1994a, 1994b).

However, the hypothesis that the parties are realigning around an axis of cultural conflict must be qualified by the responses of Roman Catholics. With the aforementioned exception of school prayer in the early 1970s and pornography in the most recent period, the only social issue that exhibits a significant relationship with party identification is tolerance toward nonconformists. In one sense, this finding is not surprising, since issues of intellectual freedom have long been quite important to American Catholics (see Jelen 1996; Jelen and Wilcox 1990; McNamara 1992). However, since the partisan effects of tolerance are virtually constant for the past two decades (indeed, the tolerance-partisanship relationship is

Table 4-3 Correlations Between Social Positions and Partisanship over Time, by Religious Affiliation (Frequent Church Attenders Only)

	1972–1976	1977–1980	1981–1985	1986–1993
Evangelical Protestants				
Sexual morality	−.03	−.01	−.07	−.08**
Homosexuality	−.04	−.01	−.09	−.11*
Private feminism	—	.09	.04	.04
Public feminism	.08	.09	.01	−.10**
Abortion	.00	.08	.12*	−.08**
Tolerance	−.07	−.07	−.19*	−.13**
Pornography	.02	.02	−.03	−.09**
School prayer	−.12**	.04	−.11**	−.03
Mainline Protestants				
Sexual morality	.01	.05	.01	−.04
Homosexuality	.01	.05	−.01	−.23*
Private feminism	—	−.04	.02	−.11**
Public feminism	.01	.07	.11**	−.14**
Abortion	−.06	−.06	.06	−.14*
Tolerance	−.05	−.01	−.02	.02
Pornography	−.03	−.02	.09	−.11**
School prayer	−.16**	−.02	.06	.11
Catholics				
Sexual morality	.03	−.00	.03	−.04
Homosexuality	−.02	.09	.04	−.03
Private feminism	—	−.07	−.04	.08
Public feminism	−.05	.01	−.02	−.04
Abortion	−.01	.02	.05	.03
Tolerance	−.09**	−.19*	−.11**	−.11**
Pornography	.02	.03	.04	−.08**
School prayer	.12**	−.03	.03	−.01

Source: 1972–1993 General Social Surveys.

Notes: Entries are Pearson's r.

*Statistically significant at .01 level.
**Statistically significant at .05 level.

somewhat stronger during the Carter administration), it is unlikely that tolerance can account for partisan change among American Catholics. Thus, it is difficult to maintain that Catholics (even those with high levels of religious observance) are likely to be a component of an orthodox, traditionalist, Republican coalition.

When the effects of social issue attitudes on presidential vote choice are examined, the distinctiveness of Roman Catholics again becomes apparent. These data (not shown) suggest that, for both evangelical and mainline Protestants, a variety of social issue attitudes are significant predictors of Republican presidential voting in 1984, 1988, and 1992, with attitudes toward homosexuality and abortion consistently having the strongest effects. By contrast, the effects of cultural issues on presidential voting among Catholics are much weaker. Tolerance is related to Republican presidential vote among Catholics in 1976 and 1980, and conservative attitudes on the private feminism index are related to voting for George Bush in 1988. Aside from these scattered exceptions, none of the social issues considered here exhibits a statistically significant effect on voting for president among Catholics.

Conclusion: An Incomplete Realignment?

The task of itemizing the deductions from the Democratic coalition is well beyond the scope of this chapter. The rise of the Republican Party among religiously observant white Christians is a complex phenomenon which defies simple explanation. The data presented here suggest that the increased political salience of issues involving traditional morality cannot be the complete story. The shift to a Republican identification applies across all three groups of white Christians, and it may have begun for two of the groups before the effects of family values on party identification attained statistical significance. Moreover, even among church-going white evangelicals, the relatively low magnitude of the relationships between issues and party identification suggests that a complete explanation of evangelical realignment will likely involve considerations other than social issues.

Nevertheless, the evidence presented here also suggests that the observed Republican shift among observant white Christians contains elements of a values-based realignment. Although issue positions have been relatively stable among regularly attending evangelicals, Catholics, and mainline Protestants, the effects of these issue positions on partisanship have varied across time and across religious tradition.

The political mobilization of evangelicals based on social issues appears to have begun during the early years of the Reagan administration. While Carter's candidacy in 1976 may have prompted increased turnout among evangelicals (Wilcox 1989), an increase in the relationship between conservative positions on social issues[9] and party identification (and presidential voting) appears to have coincided with the rise of the Christian Right. While Christian Right organizations themselves were generally quite unpopular (Buell and Sigelman 1985; Jelen 1991;

Sigelman, Wilcox, and Buell 1987), it is possible that the activity of such groups (along with the Reagan candidacy) caused the political relevance of such issue attitudes to increase.

With respect to mainline Protestants, the partisan salience of social issues has occurred more slowly and appears to have involved a two-step process. While social issues were significantly related to presidential vote in the 1984 election, the relationship between conservative positions on family values and underlying partisanship did not occur until the very end of the decade. Again, it is possible that the religious identification of George Bush (perhaps a less religiously divisive figure than Reagan, Falwell, or Robertson) facilitated such a transition. Regardless of the reasons for the transition, it is clear that, by the 1990s, socially conservative Protestants (either evangelical or mainline) are more likely to identify with the Republican Party than Protestants who take more permissive positions on lifestyle issues.

Nonetheless, a culture wars realignment, based on the mobilization of religious and social conservatives, remains incomplete, since the relationship between moral-cultural conservatism and Republican identification has not strengthened among devout Roman Catholics. While churchgoing Catholics do tend to take conservative positions on some social issues (especially on abortion), Catholic social conservatives are no more Republican than their more liberal counterparts. While the data do suggest that Catholics are becoming more Republican (although they remain the most Democratic group of white Christians), these partisan shifts are not related to any increase in the salience of moral traditionalism.

The lack of mobilization of Roman Catholics in support of traditional moral values is an important finding. Most analysts who argue for a value-based realignment (Falwell 1980; Hunter 1991; Reed 1994) suggest that Catholics are an important component of a traditionalist political coalition.[10] Roman Catholicism is the single largest denomination in the United States, and the Church's centralized, hierarchical structure suggests that the Church has substantial political resources (see especially Segers 1995). The failure of even culturally conservative Catholics to be drawn toward a traditionalist Republican Party represents an important question mark for the future of religiously based politics in the 1990s. Indeed, it may well be that the future political success of the orthodox, or religious, side in the culture war depends upon the recruitment of Roman Catholics to an increasingly traditionalist Republican Party.

The data also suggest that Catholics are realigning in a Republican direction. The causes of this partisan shift (which is also to be observed among infrequent churchgoers) may lie in economic issues, as succeeding generations of Catholics become increasingly prosperous. Conversely, the salience of racial issues may have increased among white Catholics, who are slightly more likely than Protestants to live in urban areas. Thus, a coalition of culturally conservative Protestants and Roman Catholics may well form in the near future. However, such a diverse GOP coalition would not reflect one side of an intense culture war, but would involve the more traditional politics of compromise, bargaining, and accommodation between groups with different values and priorities.

Notes

1. House Speaker Newt Gingrich's occasional characterization of some Democrats as "McGovernite elitists" suggests that George McGovern's 1972 presidential candidacy remains a salient symbol.

2. The use of the GSS posed some limitations as well. The fact that different issue questions were asked during different years renders it difficult to perform genuinely multivariate analyses for certain subgroups. Moreover, the GSS contains relatively few questions on economic issues and virtually no questions on attitudes toward political figures such as presidential candidates.

3. Experimentation with subdividing the most recent period (second Reagan term, Bush administration, first year of Clinton presidency) reveals little difference in the results of the bivariate analysis.

4. The American National Election Studies suffer from the same limitation prior to the 1980s.

5. For the most recent period (during which doctrinal variables were measured in the GSS) evangelicals were much more likely to report a highly authoritative view of the Bible than either mainline Protestants or Catholics. They were also much more likely to report a "born-again" experience. There were 573 churchgoing evangelicals in the study for 1972–1976, 359 in 1977–1980, 580 in 1981–1985, and 967 in 1986–1993. For mainline Protestants, the equivalent figures were 572, 296, 428, and 601, respectively; for Catholics, the respective numbers were 827, 457, 604, and 853.

6. In this study, analysis is limited to the division of the two-party vote in presidential elections. Thus, the candidacies of John Anderson in 1980 and Ross Perot in 1992 are not considered here. Gilbert, Johnston, and Peterson (1994) have shown that third-party candidates generally draw very little support from religiously observant voters.

7. To make this finding somewhat more precise, the correlations were run for each year of the 1986–1993 era. Although the pattern is somewhat erratic (due to the small number of cases of white mainline Protestants who attend church frequently for each year), the data suggest that the relationship between social issue attitudes and partisanship began to strengthen in 1989. It is possible that the strengthening is at least partly attributable to a perceived decline in the influence of the Christian Right. In 1988, Pat Robertson's presidential campaign was quite unsuccessful, and televangelists Jim and Tammy Bakker and Jimmy Swaggert were publicly embarrassed by scandals. In 1989, the term of Ronald Reagan (a president with whom many in the leadership of the Christian Right sought to identify) ended, and Jerry Falwell dissolved his Moral Majority organization. It is possible that the social agenda of the Christian Right became more attractive to mainline Protestants when less attention was paid to these leaders. Similarly, the presidency of Episcopalian George Bush may well have made a conservative social issue agenda more acceptable to mainline Protestants. For accounts of the unpopularity of the Christian right, and of general mainline dislike of fundamentalists, see Jelen (1993); Buell and Sigelman (1985, 1987); Wilcox (1987); and Sigelman, Wilcox, and Buell (1987).

8. The relatively late cultural mobilization of traditionalist mainline Protestants may also account for the surge in the importance of family values in explaining presidential votes in 1992, as reported by Hammond, Shibley, and Solow (1994).

9. There is no general tendency among any religious group to take more consistently conservative positions across social issues. I computed an index of internal consistency, based on individual standard deviations across the issues of abortion, tolerance, public feminism, pornography, homosexuality, sexual morality, and school prayer, after recoding all issues to a common range and direction (see Jelen 1990). Over the twenty-year period under investigation, this variable was virtually constant for all three religious groups. Thus, there is no evidence that even respondents who base their partisanship on social conservatism perceive a common thread in their positions on discrete issues.

10. Ralph Reed (1994), in his book *Politically Incorrect*, devotes substantial space to arguing that anti-Catholic prejudice on the part of evangelical Protestants is a thing of the past and that Catholics are welcome to participate in a culturally conservative political movement.

5 Media as Opinion Resources: Are the 1990s a New Ball Game?

Doris A. Graber

A study of public opinion trends over a fifty-year time span leads political scientists Benjamin Page and Robert Shapiro to conclude that ordinary Americans are capable of forming sound political opinions if they receive adequate information about public policies. The authors express some doubts about the availability of good political information, noting that "the information presented to the public through the mass media has certain persistent biases, slants, or value tendencies that may distort the public's picture of the world and lead its policy preferences astray." Hence, "there is reason for concern that democracy in the United States may be undermined to some extent by systematic distortions in the information that is provided to the public" (Page and Shapiro 1992, 394–396).

Page and Shapiro's concerns about the deficiencies of news stories in American mass media are based on the widely shared assumption that average Americans depend on the mass media for information as they form opinions about politics. It does not matter whether people expose themselves directly to news stories or learn about them from others; most of their current information about political events originates in newspapers, television and radio programs, and news magazines. Television reaches the largest audience; daily newspapers are next. Though used less widely than television, they are often considered the second most important source of information because they offer the largest amount of news. Information available from the media includes descriptions of people and events, as seen either through the eyes of journalists or through the eyes of their sources from public and private life. Irrespective of the audience's appraisal of the quality of these news and opinion reports, and irrespective of the credibility accorded to journalists, news stories are the basic and most widely used way to learn about current political events.

During the 1990s a variety of new technologies, such as the Internet, electronic bulletin boards, and CD-ROMs, enable citizens to gather news information from many additional sources. The proponents of these new media claim that they enable citizens to access news events directly, without the filter of journalistic prejudices, and to search more widely for stories that interest them. This chapter will evaluate the quality of news provided by traditional outlets such as television and newspapers and then assess newer technologies and their implications for opinion formation in a democracy.

The Quality of Political News

Significance, Breadth, and Depth

Page and Shapiro are not alone in complaining about the quality of news. The mass media have been accused frequently of providing an inadequate information base for understanding the political challenges faced by the nation. Periodic content analyses of print and television news carried out since the mid-1970s show that roughly half the stories in major daily newspapers deal with political issues. The rest cover sports, entertainment, and miscellaneous other topics. On local television, "political" news, broadly construed, encompasses two-thirds of the offerings; on national television, it is close to 90 percent. That sounds impressive until one considers the small number of stories (twenty-three or twenty-four) that make up the average news broadcast. Political stories thus are by no means the dominating concern of American news media (Graber 1980, 1984, 1989, 1993). Table 5-1 provides illustrative data from national and local television news and Chicago area newspapers. Such data raise the question whether the political news diet of average Americans is adequate to allow them to be intelligent political observers, let alone participants, in the affairs of their government.

The media have been criticized for according privileged status to the views of public officials, who are journalists' preferred sources of political news. News stories are presented almost exclusively from a mainstream perspective if elites agree on the issues that should head the political agenda and the context into which these issues should be embedded. The technical term for placing news into particular perspectives is *framing*. Political scientist Lance Bennett refers to the heavy reliance on information framed by official sources as "indexing" news to the behavior of political elites (Bennett and Paletz 1994).

Table 5-1 Distribution of News Story Topics, July 1990–August 1991 (in Percentages)

News Topics	Newspapers		National Television			Local Television		
	Sun Times (N=6,323)	Tribune (N=5,668)	CBS (N=168)	NBC (N=138)	ABC (N=172)	CBS (N=287)	NBC (N=228)	ABC (N=210)
Governmental affairs	20	22	57	54	47	32	33	35
Economic issues	13	16	13	14	17	5	6	6
Social issues	13	14	26	22	26	30	23	29
Sports and entertainment	51	42	2	7	10	25	31	24
Miscellaneous	4	6	3	3	1	8	8	6

Table 5-2 Distribution of Soviet News Story Topics in the *New York Times,* January 1945–January 1991 (in Percentages)

News Topics	Press Conference Themes (N=2,636)	Editorial Themes (N=5,310)
Soviet foreign relations	23	14
Soviet military policy	18	9
U.S. attitude about U.S.S.R.	21	33
U.S./U.S.S.R. meetings	14	5
U.S. military policy	5	6
Soviet attitudes about U.S.	4	7
U.S./U.S.S.R. comparisons	5	4
Human rights issues	3	11
Soviet leaders' quality	2	4
Communism as ideology	2	3
U.S. policy about U.S.S.R.	1	2
Soviet technology	1	1

Critics also complain of the narrow range of political topics that are covered extensively by the news media; many important political events and issues get no coverage. Furthermore, even relatively extensive media coverage is not thorough enough to allow the public to evaluate and understand policy options.

Table 5-2 presents the results of a content analysis of information about the Soviet Union in the American press during the cold war (Graber 1991). The analysis focused on presidential news conferences over a forty-six-year time span, ranging from the Truman administration to the Bush administration. News conferences generally reflect the topics and themes that reporters representing the country's major news media subsequently cover in news stories. The same holds true for *New York Times* editorials and Gallup poll questions, both of which were also analyzed. The editorials covered the same array of topics as the news conferences, but often diverged in the slant of coverage and appraisal of the significance of particular developments. Scrutiny of the Gallup poll questions, in addition to indicating which topics received press attention, provided an indirect gauge of agenda-setting effects because pollsters' questions address topics that they believe to have caught the public's attention (Dearing 1989).

Overall, the information provided by the American press, as reflected in *New York Times* press conference and editorial coverage during the entire cold war period, did not provide readers with sufficient background to appraise the merits of U.S. policy toward the Soviet

Union, even though U.S.-Soviet relations were unquestionably of vast importance to Americans and the rest of the world.

Table 5-2 shows that official American attitudes regarding the USSR, such as fears about Soviet intentions or the possibility for cooperation (21 percent), were broadly covered; specific events, such as summit meetings (14 percent), also got solid attention. But only 6 percent of the press conference themes dealt with the actual status of U.S.-Soviet relations, mostly with military affairs such as agreements on arms control and nuclear testing. Matters such as trade relations or scientific cooperation or the major weaknesses of the Soviet economy (which ultimately led to its stunning collapse) were largely ignored. Only 8 percent of the news conference themes covered Soviet internal affairs at all, despite their importance for assessing the country's economic and political strength. Editorial coverage was equally sparse.

The political influence and power of the Soviet Union were assessed primarily in terms of Soviet relations with other countries, including Vietnam, China, and Poland, or regions like Western Europe and the Persian Gulf (23 percent); or in military terms (18 percent), including defense spending, weapons systems, and troops stationed in satellite countries. In line with the pattern of highlighting only a few topic areas, the range of internal matters that were discussed was extremely narrow. Comparisons between the United States and the Soviet Union were infrequent (5 percent), even though they would have been useful in putting the balance of power into perspective. Though U.S. attitudes toward the Soviet Union were amply discussed (21 percent), there was little reciprocal analysis of Soviet attitudes and fears concerning the United States (4 percent).

Interestingly, the Soviet press covered the United States more broadly. Soviet citizens benefited accordingly. Soviet viewers saw a large number of stories about many aspects of the United States, including economic and cultural features (Mickiewicz 1991).

American journalists have also been reproached for emphasizing trivial information at the expense of more significant data. Much of the news has been characterized as "infotainment" because it emphasizes entertaining aspects and human interest appeals over serious political concerns. The desire to maximize audience size has led to a one-size-fits-all journalism that produces large numbers of mismatches. Audience comprehension suffers when journalists fail to accommodate the interests and intellectual skills of diverse populations.

Uniformity

Collectively, the news media have been taken to task for the lack of diversity of news despite a multiplicity of news-dispensing enterprises. This shortcoming has been blamed on pack journalism. Pack journalism means that the huge chorus of media voices echoes a small group of elite media so that all sing the same tune, rather than presenting a variety of distinct political tunes from which audiences can choose their favorites.

Pack journalism aside, there are several additional reasons for conformity and the other news problems already mentioned. The commercial nature of American mass media is a prime factor. To maximize profits, media are organized to serve mass markets which, in turn, requires that stories be dramatic and entertaining to attract large audiences. Because most audiences are not interested in complex political issues, many stories about politics are sensationalized or trivialized to make them entertaining. When major political events compete for attention and coverage with the activities of a major entertainment figure or with a natural or manmade disaster, the political story invariably loses out. In 1994, for example, the ABC, NBC, and CBS networks featured more prime time news stories (431) about the murder case involving sports idol O. J. Simpson than about major developments in Russia (412) or the extraordinary midterm congressional elections (409). Stories about crime, disasters, and the Clinton scandals (2,648) accounted for a third (34 percent) of the stories on the early evening national news (Center for Media and Public Affairs 1995).

The consolidation of media enterprises is another factor that contributes to uniformity. Most news transmission channels are controlled by huge conglomerates, so that the number of independent voices competing for attention in the marketplace of ideas has been sharply reduced. Many conglomerates control not only the means of transmission but also the content of the news. Several giant transnational corporations enjoy vast influence over the substance and framing of news received by people all over the globe. Homogenization of mass-mediated political information now has a worldwide reach. It has become as easy to move news stories across political barriers and national borders as across physical barriers of space and forbidding terrain.

The Growth of the "New" Media

Considering the main complaints about the news media, and granting the debatable premise that ordinary people are willing, able, and obligated to form their own political opinions based on information obtained from the news media, does the proliferation of media types and outlets in the 1990s provide a larger data base for opinion formation (Popkin 1991; Stimson 1991; Sniderman et al. 1991; Bartels 1993)? Do the new media broaden the scope of topics and enhance the depth and breadth of available information? Do they make more policy-relevant information readily available? Does the information cover a broad spectrum of diverse views, so that the public is alerted to the wide range of policy options that need to be discussed by interested citizens? Do the new media customize the information in substance and format, so that heterogeneous audiences can form sensible opinions about the issues of the day?

To answer these questions, I will briefly survey the salient features of the evolving media scene, commenting on the nature of political information presented to the public and on the suitability of the new media as information bases for the formation of public opinion. I will also point out advantages and disadvantages of various formats in serving as information bases for forming individual and collective opinions. Finally, based on recent studies of the capabilities and predilections of average people in selecting and processing political information, I will assess the likelihood that twenty-first century Americans will be better informed about their political world than their twentieth-century forebears.

What's New About "New" Media?

The "new" media include a growing list of computerized information sources such as E-mail, tens of thousands of bulletin boards, the Internet, CD-ROMs, on-line library services, and on-line newspaper extensions. They include service enhancements by older media, such as daily newspapers, that now provide their readers the opportunity to supplement information in print news stories by accessing an electronic data base. Users of the Internet and various on-line computer services, such as America Online, CompuServe, MCI Mail, and Prodigy, can download the full texts of major political speeches and news conferences, including pictures, into their home computers, and peruse them at their convenience.

New technologies allow audiences to edit prepackaged information, such as a news story, to their taste by adding, combining, or deleting data. Teletext can deliver virtually unlimited amounts and types of data from satellite or television signals directly to home computers or television screens. Videotext provides a direct two-way link between home television sets and a central computer. Electronic publishing on home computers has vastly boosted the numbers of newsletters that various social, professional, and trade communities can distribute. People can also buy CD-ROMs, each small disk carrying voluminous amounts of information.

Computer search capabilities have made it easier for journalists to assemble essential background facts for breaking stories. For instance, when the political limelight suddenly falls on a previously obscure politician or when the nation's economy takes an unexpected turn, computerized searches can quickly and cheaply assemble masses of relevant information from earlier sources. The displacement of film by videotape has greatly increased the number and timeliness of scenes that can be featured on television, since tape is less expensive and enables broadcasters to bypass the film developing stage. Hence people, including young children, are becoming much more familiar with events remote from the surroundings in which they live. Familiarity with the world beyond their physical reach increases their receptiveness to news about these distant people and places.

The new media also include a variety of novel television offerings produced by recent entrants to the field and transmitted through an expanding variety of technologies. Cable television systems can offer broadcasts from hundreds of separate channels. Satellites can relay a vast number of radio and television programs which can be received over the air or via cable

Figure 5-1   Availability of New Technologies in American Households, 1994

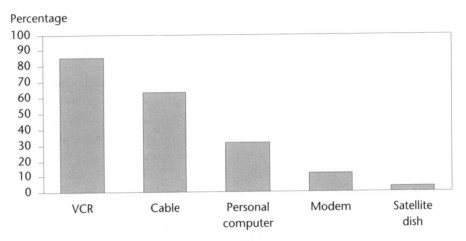

Percentage

Source: Adapted from Times Mirror Center for the People and the Press, "Technology in the American Household," May 1994, 17.

television. Individual consumers can tap directly into these offerings through backyard satellite dishes. Space for various types of transmissions can be rented by public and private parties from the satellites' owners. Individual television stations can even use satellites to supply other stations with live videos of stories that the station has covered locally. These opportunities expand television programming options and vastly reduce viewers' dependence on network programming.

Twenty-four-hour news radio and television channels are multiplying. Eighty-five percent of America's households have at least one videotape recorder to selectively tape their own programs or play rented tapes. Videotapes, laser discs, and CD-ROMs store electronic fare, allowing people to watch what they want when they want it. Pay TV provides special entertainment at a moderate cost; people pay solely for programs they choose to watch. Figure 5-1 provides data on the availability of various new technologies in America's households.

This wealth of material, including news sources, provides mass audiences with more ways to get information than ever before. There no longer is any excuse for missing the news because of timing problems. The ability of the new breed of technologies to furnish information on demand, responding to the needs of the audience rather than those of the message supplier, is an extremely important advance. Until fairly recently print and electronic media presented their packets of information at predetermined regular intervals. Audience members who missed a particular offering could not readily retrieve it at a later time. That obstacle has vanished. Widely available new technologies now permit prospective audiences to receive broadcasts at any time, preset a machine to record them, and then watch them when convenient. Timing has become even less important as newspapers and magazines have put out electronic versions of their printed offerings ahead of the scheduled publication date.

One may argue that these "new" developments are merely new uses of old formats. A presidential speech recorded on teletext is still a written version of an oral event, and a television program captured on tape and played back later is still television. Minimally edited presentations like the live telecasts presented by CNN (the Cable News Network) or C-SPAN (Cable Satellite Public Affairs Network), the chronicler of congressional action, are still televised news stories. Nonetheless, I will argue that the new media really are different from their predecessors in important ways. I will also argue that what looks like a wealth of new information is a mixed blessing.

Who Should Frame the News?

A major feature of many of the new media is their tendency to shift control of framing away from journalists. For example, the live telecasts about political events that have become routinely available on CNN and C-SPAN allow media audiences to be virtual eyewitnesses to history. The public can form conclusions based on observing entire events, rather than witnessing only brief excerpts and relying heavily on journalists to present the news from particular perspectives.

This change has advantages as well as disadvantages. On the plus side, curbing the scope of journalistic framing is good because these frames are frequently one-sided or flawed. As I have mentioned, journalists rely heavily on political elites, particularly public officials. Furthermore, their need for drama often propels journalists to present caricatures of the political world that overemphasize sensational features and thereby distort reality. For example, journalists typically put accounts about politicians' activities into a "base motivations" frame even when that is not warranted. Reporters routinely paraphrase politicians' pronouncements to fit their preferred framing. This deprives the public of the actual messages of the politicians. During the 1992 presidential campaign, for instance, sound bites from presidential candidates' speeches averaged less than eight-and-a-half seconds on regular news broadcasts. That is one-fifth of the time granted to candidates some thirty years earlier and represents a steady trend toward paraphrasing.

Gaining more control over framing has costs, however. Audiences have to make much larger time investments when they view entire events, rather than listening to brief summaries. Since the supply of free time is inelastic, most people are unwilling and unable to watch or listen to broadcasts of lengthy events in their entirety. Moreover, drawing one's own conclusions about a broadcast event can be daunting, particularly for people who are politically unsophisticated. Eyewitnesses who lack sufficient knowledge about the situations that they are witnessing may not grasp their full significance, or they may misjudge the people and events. Politicians, who are experts in manipulating the unwary, may deceive them. On balance, whether broadcasts of entire events or brief reports and interpretations by journalists are preferable depends on who is likely to be a better judge of a given situation—the trained but often biased professional journalist or the average person, who is apt to be politically naive.

Radio and television talk shows present another example of shifting control of the framing of news. Talk shows have become a major medium that bypasses strict journalistic control. The interactive format of many of these shows allows citizens to feed their opinions into the marketplace of political ideas with relative ease. Audiences, who are tired of the near-monopoly of journalists and officials, relish such shows, which provide them with a public forum (Herbst 1995). In 1993, 42 percent of the respondents to a Times Mirror Center for the People and the Press survey reported that they often listened to talk shows. Eleven percent had tried to call in (Times Mirror Center 1993). Political scientist Susan Herbst, in another survey, asked respondents who had placed calls to talk shows why they had done so. Thirty-eight percent said that they wanted to pass on facts or express opinions, while 36 percent wanted to engage in dialogue or broaden the discourse to correct views they deemed mistaken. Five percent had called for advice or information; the remainder had reasons unrelated to the substance of the talk show.

Politicians like talk shows because they provide an opportunity to interact directly with ordinary folk, and because talk show hosts often allow them to present their arguments, largely unchallenged, in their own words and from their own perspectives. The 1992 presidential campaign established talk shows as important election information channels. All major candidates used them, appearing on *Larry King Live, Arsenio Hall,* and even rock-music-oriented MTV. The practice of using talk shows for important political pronouncements by major political figures has continued since then, as has the publicity given to such shows by pundits and the standard mass media. This mainstream media echo effect has raised the profile and political significance of talk shows.

Talk shows, by creating a readily accessible, widely disseminated public forum for political exchanges between political leaders and average citizens, enlarge the opportunities for citizens' participation in the public dialogue. However, some would say that this advantage is outweighed by the danger that the forum may be misused. Disgruntled citizens or unprincipled ideologues may mislead an unsophisticated public. Talk show detractors argue that journalists using conventional channels are more likely to feel external and internal constraints to stick with the truth and allow for airing of opposing views. Talk show defenders counter this claim by accusing journalists of deflecting attention from the substance of political issues to irrelevant questions about politicians' psyches and motivations (Ridout 1993). At this point, it is not clear where the balance of truth lies in these conflicting appraisals.

Computers make it relatively easy for computer-literate citizens to talk back to public officials, from the president on down, providing them with a citizens' perspective on political events that is unmediated by journalists or pollsters. Would-be participants in the public debate are likely to find it less daunting to contact a computer "comments line" to record their reactions to political issues than to go to the trouble of writing and mailing letters to public officials or to news outlets which are unlikely to publish them. Consequently, the feedback of unmediated comments to top decision makers has increased. Unfortunately, the views of people who talk back to public officials often differ markedly from those of the majority of ordinary citizens.

The Impact of Narrowcasting

The impersonal nature of mass media messages has long been considered a major deterrent to information transmission. Is this barrier shrinking? If so, what are the consequences for opinion formation? With the proliferation of media it has become possible to serve the specialized needs of even tiny or ephemeral population groups—hence the term *narrowcasting*. In the past, small groups sharing esoteric interests or united by support or opposition to a current public policy or activity had relatively few media that catered narrowly to their interests. That has been changing steadily, and the pace of change has sharply accelerated in the age of new media. Computer networks and bulletin boards, electronic mail and faxes, now make it easy and relatively cheap to collect, edit, and distribute customized information packages widely.

Many local news outlets, regardless of the size of their audiences, can tap into satellite transmissions for locally relevant information. Major newsmakers can be interviewed directly by local reporters about issues that interest only small groups of individuals. Interactive communication channels allow news consumers to query journalists about matters that concern them. Even mass-circulation news magazines now offer their subscribers a variety of customized editions. Some newspapers are experimenting with transmitting individualized news packages to their subscribers (Garry 1994).

Advantages. Tailoring news to the experiences and interests of specific audiences makes the transmission of information more effective. Besides concentrating on news that addresses the interests and needs of specific audiences, journalists can cast stories into formats suited to the capabilities and tastes of the users of the information. For example, based on audience surveys, entire newspapers can be constructed to address the interests of specific communities such as a single small town or a school district or retired people who enjoy trout fishing or families with triplets (Charity 1995). Language complexity can range from grade-school levels to the specialized lingo of experts.

Making use of opportunities for one- and two-way communication between officials and selected audiences can enhance the fit between people's needs and government action. Most local governments, including local school systems and police and fire departments, have been eager to use cable channels to exchange information with their publics. In fact, many thousands of hours of community programming are aired each week on community access channels. The impact of these channels is difficult to assess without accurate and complete audience data. Current information indicates that audience sizes are quite modest. Assuming at least modest interest by a community's citizens, broadcasts by local governments could increase their influence and could lead to better performance. Similarly, the opportunity to inform citizens about the ways in which their government functions has been increased through broadcasts of court proceedings, as well as of legislative sessions at all levels of government. In theory, the new communications media allow many political organizations to stay in close touch with their constituencies, but these offerings have found few consistent takers among the public.

Narrowcasting has other potential political consequences. The ability to target messages more precisely to groups of people can change power equations and political opinions in important ways. The electoral chances of minority candidates and minority parties may improve when they can tailor their messages to the concerns of selected audiences, provided that these people are listening. Single-interest groups, such as opponents of a particular pending law or petitioners for mercy for a death-row inmate, may become more powerful because computer networks, especially the Internet, make it easy to aggregate people with shared interests who are widely dispersed. Consequently, the already substantial influence of such groups on public opinion and governmental activities may be greatly enhanced. In fact, the computer lanes of the information superhighway can be used by very small, yet highly persuasive, groups, or even by single individuals, to win support for their ideas. In that sense, these lanes are great equalizers of power (Williams and Pavlik 1994).

Drawbacks. The chief danger inherent in customizing news presentations is the potential for developing communication ghettos where people are exposed to a limited number of voices, often only those that reinforce their own perspectives. They may no longer be exposed to the point-counterpoint dialogue that more generalized media, at their best, feature. Audiences who limit themselves to small ethnic media, or computer software news, or music videos, to mention just a few specialized areas, may become isolated from the currents of information that shape the opinions of mainstream folk. Many citizens may become prisoners of their special political interests and may miss out on important events in the broader culture to which they also belong. Attention to politics may actually decline when attractive customized nonpolitical information is plentiful, because politics has never been a priority for average Americans. If narrowcasting leads to a narrowing of the intellectual focus of many people, well-rounded citizens, who have varied interests and some knowledge of the nation's major concerns, may become a rarity.

Excessive specialization may also make it more difficult to build the bridges across interest and opinion cleavage lines which are necessary to sustain an integrated nation. When news becomes fragmented, people are likely to be exposed and socialized in disparate ways. The national political consensus, supported by common news fare, may become fragmented. A nationally shared dialogue then might be replaced by many specialized dialogues that never converge. This prospect seems frightening, but, judging by the past, the fears may be exaggerated. The national consensus was not seriously ruptured, for example, when alternative media were used extensively during the early days of the nation and during the political turmoil of the 1960s. It may well be that fragmented interests create the demand for fragmented media rather than the reverse. The causes of the fragmentation of political consensus, rather than its symptoms, should be the focus of concern. Moreover, many people do not find fragmentation objectionable, believing that pluralism is preferable to the traditional melting-pot ideals.

In fact, to a certain extent, increasing specialization is unavoidable, irrespective of the degree of narrowcasting, because available information about societal problems has increased geometrically. However, it seems unlikely that narrowcasting will replace broadcasting entirely. The fact that the major television networks have held their own after an initial steep drop in audiences for their news programs may suggest that there is a threshold level below which general information media are unlikely to decline. Political scientist W. Russell Neuman reaches the same conclusion (1991) after an extensive study of narrowcast media, the communications industry, and the psychology of media use.

Cementing Worldwide Social Bonds

Global Village Trends. Another pathbreaking feature of the new technologies is the ease with which they leap across national boundaries and put the entire world within electronic reach of average Americans. Americans of all ages are becoming vicarious world travelers. The magic carpet of television allows them to visit the world electronically and to develop background information that makes their global environment more familiar than ever before. Television newscasts, with their visual information, are far more effective and memorable than radio news, with its reliance on text alone. Pictures allow even semiliterate or illiterate populations to comprehend information that was previously unavailable to them. American cable television networks, such as CNN (owned by Atlanta-based Turner Communications) or the Colorado-based Tele-Communications, Inc. (which owns over six hundred cable outlets worldwide), are examples of information distributors who reach audiences around the globe (Aufderheide 1992; *Television and Cable Fact Book* 1992).

Still, Marshall McLuhan's vision of a global village, where humanity would share a culture via television, has not come to pass (Office of Technology Assessment 1988). Even when people around the world are exposed to the same information, they still interpret it differently because of their cultural differences. In fact, people's inability to place information from strange cultures into appropriate contexts can lead to dangerous misperceptions, rather than helpful insights.

The Internet. One of the largest carriers of information with a global reach is the Internet. This decentralized computer network was created to facilitate communication between U.S. defense research centers, but now allows users worldwide to send as well as receive messages, potentially linking them to millions of other individuals and institutions. The system, which can be reached through ordinary computers equipped with modems, carries an amazing array of personal, professional, political, and even entertainment messages. This medium could promote in-depth discussions of current political issues based on unparalleled access to expert information sources, but that promise thus far has barely materialized. As it turns out, when citizens interact on computer networks, they spend much of their time gossiping with likeminded people over the electronic backyard fence of cyberspace or browsing through electronic bulletin boards that carry trivial information. They rarely attend to genuinely important political issues. In fact, there is much garbage on the Internet, often inserted by people who fail to identify themselves. Unwary consumers of this type of misinformation may learn a lot that is wrong and misleading, thereby impairing the accuracy of their perceptions of their world and hampering critical thinking.

By mid-1994, more than 25 million people were connected to the Internet, either through commercial computer networks, such as Prodigy and CompuServe, or through local area networks (Lewis 1994). Initially, the only barrier to access was lack of equipment or expertise. There were no tolls because the network was built by tax money. However, the rapid growth of the system has led to a variety of charges, and these create additional access barriers for low-income users. The commercial networks, which have been sprouting rapidly, charge for the use of their system.

Although a mind-boggling array of information resources is made available to the public by the Internet and other new outlets, there are political costs. The overuse of electronic connections could be as detrimental to the political process as underuse. To develop sound opinions interested citizens must have forums where they can test the merits and acceptability of their ideas and discover what their peers think and why (Barber 1984; Dahl 1989; Rucinski 1991). Newspapers can be a good basis for consensus building, as scholars have acknowledged. The information provided by newspapers becomes the starting point for citizens' discussions of public issues (Schudson 1995). When most social contacts no longer take place in person, and when these contacts occur between faceless, nameless partners whose sociopolitical environments are unknown, people lose opportunities for developing the shared understandings that make them a public. Discussing politics in computer forums or

Table 5-3 Personal Computers, Modems, and Cable Television in American Households, 1994 (Prevalence of Technology in the Home, by Education and Family Income, in Percentages)

	$50,000+		$30,000–$50,000		< $30,000	
	College grad	Non-grad	College grad	Non-grad	College grad	Non-grad
Has a personal computer in home	68	48	47	30	30	15
Uses a modem	21	12	14	4	10	2
Subscribes to cable television	76	74	61	64	50	57

Source: Adapted from Times Mirror Center for the People and the Press, "Technology in the American Household," May 1994, 8.

registering one's views electronically generally does not serve the interactive, opinion-shaping functions that these activities entail when they are conducted face-to-face. Though individual or small group opinion formation may thrive, widely dispersed opinions shared by large segments of the population are unlikely to emerge (Rucinski 1991; Golding 1990; Lenart 1994).

The Human Bottleneck

Information-Processing Hurdles

The impact of the new media on the body of information used by average Americans as they form political opinions is fairly small because most average Americans use these media irregularly or not at all. There are several reasons why electronic media have not taken over. Most important, the new technologies must compete with established, easier to use sources of information, such as radio and network television. Even print information sources, such as newspapers, books, and magazines, despite the literacy hurdles, are comparatively simple to master, besides being cheap and portable.

When access to major information sources requires even moderate intellectual effort, large numbers of Americans will be left out because they lack the necessary training or even the intellectual basis for such training. The bottom line, as Table 5-3 illustrates, is that many of the important new information resources are accessible mainly to people who are educationally and economically privileged. Consequently, a knowledge and gullibility gap divides the public into "haves," whose opinions are apt to be influential and discriminating, and "have-nots," whose political life and influence is more marginal and who can be more easily

Table 5-4 Newspaper, Television, and Radio Use by Americans (Attention to Common News Sources, January–February 1994, in Percentages)

	30 minutes or more	Less than 30 minutes	None
Paper	35	23	42
TV	62	12	26
Radio	22	25	52

Source: Adapted from Times Mirror Center for the People and the Press, "Technology in the American Household," May 1994, 75–77.

Questions: About how much time did you spend reading a daily newspaper yesterday? About how much time did you spend watching the news or any news program on TV yesterday? About how much time, if any, did you spend listening to any news on the radio yesterday or didn't you happen to listen to the news on the radio yesterday?

manipulated by demagogues. As technology continues to evolve, the knowledge and gullibility gap is likely to widen.

In fact, the gap is already evident. By 1993, it was estimated that 12 million Americans had the equipment and know-how to tap into major computer networks. Although that figure represents more than a tenfold rise in ten years, the total still amounts to less than 5 percent of the total population (Times Mirror Center for the People and the Press 1994). Most adults who grew up without exposure to computers are unlikely to have the opportunity to catch up. The chances for children and adolescents will not be much better. The nation's school systems and public libraries still lack the capacity to make the majority of their clients computer literate. Optimistically, one may view this as a temporary condition and expect many of the young to eventually join the ranks of the information-rich (Negroponte 1995). Realistically, the fact that millions of American adults, despite compulsory education, still are functionally illiterate when it comes to reading printed materials does not support a prediction of 90 percent computer literacy in the future (Segal 1994; Warf 1995).

Simplifications of existing technologies or totally new technologies could lower these barriers and make it as easy to get on the information superhighway as it is to turn on a television set. Yet, even if the new technologies become much simpler to use, learning to cope with them will be an ongoing task that many citizens may be unwilling or unable to master. People have a natural tendency to resist change. Moreover, the expense of new technologies may be beyond the budgets of large numbers of citizens.

Even assuming that most people gain access to new media, there will remain a ceiling to the demand for political information. Most people are not seeking new ways to learn about political matters. As Table 5-4 makes clear, the public spends relatively little time consum-

Table 5-5 Magazine and News Broadcast Use by Americans (Attention to Specialized News Sources, May 1993 and May–June 1992, in Percentages)

	Often	Rarely	Never
Magazines			
Personality *(People, US)*	31	22	47
News *(Time, U.S. News & World Report, Newsweek)*	47	23	30
General *(Atlantic, Harpers, New Yorker)*	8	14	78
Business *(Fortune, Forbes)*	21	17	62
Broadcasts			
Magazine *(60 Minutes, 20/20)*	81	11	8
General *(MTV, VH1)*	27	12	60
Discussion *(MacNeil-Lehrer)*	22	11	66
Tabloid *(A Current Affair)*	53	18	29
NPR *(Morning Edition, All Things Considered)*	22	12	66
Cable news (CNN)	63	8	29
Government (C-SPAN)	27	15	56

Source: Adapted from Times Mirror Center for the People and the Press, "Technology in the American Household," May 1994, 81–83.

ing news, especially when it is published in newspapers, which carry the largest amount of information. Among specialized news sources, except for CNN, the most informative sources—such as the news magazines, the *McNeil-Lehrer Report*, C-SPAN, and National Public Radio—all attract less than half the public as frequent audiences. Table 5-5 tells that story.

Most people do not have the time or the mental capacity to absorb the massive amounts of information now available to them, even in areas of knowledge that concern them greatly. Moreover, some of the hurdles to information processing have remained in place. The complexity of most newspaper texts has remained at the twelfth-grade reading level, despite evidence that many citizens find this level too difficult. Television news stories continue to be too brief to cover news items adequately. One-third of the stories on the nightly news are less than one minute long, and half range from one to three minutes. All are overloaded with pictures and lack stopping points to permit the audience to assimilate the audio-visual information. There is no indication that the audiences are becoming more willing to learn. In fact, the public may become increasingly cynical and less willing to learn as the credibility of politicians and journalists continues to fall.

Increasing the supply of political information is likely to be useless (Entman 1989). Daily newspapers and news broadcasts already offer a great deal more than most people seem to want and will use. For example, in areas where more than a hundred television channels are available to cable users, average consumers routinely use less than a dozen. Sources comparatively rich in political fare, such as C-SPAN, NPR, and public television, normally attract less than 10 percent of the national news audience. Thus, while the potential for universal access to all of the new facilities exists, most Americans, by choice, will remain unconnected to these rich lodes of information.

Barring developments that would sharply reduce the time most Americans now spend sleeping, working, maintaining their bodies, and engaging in recreational activities, the total time available for exposure to information is likely to remain fairly constant. However, some redistribution in attention to particular information resources may occur. For example, time invested in newspaper reading may decline and time spent in vicarious trips via television or computer to strange places and familiar and unfamiliar realms of knowledge may increase.

The Prospects for Direct Democracy

Do interactivity and narrowcasting make direct democracy more feasible? Scholars have hailed electronic interactivity as the gateway to genuine direct democracy and a sound basis for the formation of opinion, especially at the local level (Abramson 1988; Arterton 1987; McLean 1989). They have forecast that much future public business will be conducted in front of television sets. Citizens presumably will watch proceedings of governmental bodies, interact with participants and fellow audience members, and cast votes of approval or disapproval of proposed government action. Ross Perot, whose candidacy for the U.S. presidency in 1992 was announced on a television talk show, promised to hold electronic town meetings to develop public consensus on controversial issues. He even promised to resign if the public demanded it with their faxes and phone calls. President Bill Clinton, although he has not gone quite as far, has used the electronic town-meeting approach.

The unstated, questionable assumption behind these forecasts of the imminent arrival of a new age of direct democracy is that the technical difficulties of becoming informed, joining the public debate, and voting have squelched citizens' desires to participate directly in governance. When hurdles to participation have been removed, the disappointing results suggest that the desire to take part is much weaker than anticipated. Most people have neither the time nor the inclination to engage in direct democracy. Sustained public debates and collective deliberations have been the exception rather than the rule when opportunities for direct democracy have been offered.

In San Jose, California, for example, school board meetings were televised and fully reported in local newspapers. All sides of controversial school issues were aired so that people could indicate their approval or disapproval of policy suggestions through two-way cable television or through ballots printed in the local newspapers. Not unexpectedly, in San Jose, as in most other places where "televote" projects have been tried, most votes came from middle-class people and overall participation was sparse. Similar results obtained when General Telephone and Electronics Corporation (GTE) tested the popularity of direct democracy in the prosperous suburban community of Cerritos, California. Despite the installation of sophisticated two-way cable communication enabling residents to access most public institutions from home with the push of a button, the experiment failed miserably (Grossman 1994).

The chances for making government more democratic through interactive communications also have been hurt by the reluctance of public officials to adopt policies supported by televotes. There are several reasons for their reluctance. Most important, electronic voting raises serious constitutional issues. The Constitution of the United States did not provide for direct democracy exercised through plebiscites. The Founders feared that an ignorant, impetuous public would make ill-informed governmental decisions. They provided for a representative democracy where, ideally, decisions are made by the best and the brightest, chosen in periodic elections and acting as surrogates for their constituents. Plebiscites would disrupt this system, which was designed to guard against mob rule.

Quite aside from the crucial legal questions, Americans disagree about the advisability of direct democracy at various government levels in the United States. Critics of the concept point to the unrepresentativeness of the participants in electronic debates and televotes and the complexity of most political debates, which require more information than average citizens are likely to amass. They also warn that political leaders are adept at packaging policy proposals so expertly that ordinary citizens may be unable to detect their flaws. The new technologies have made it vastly easier to manufacture deceptive stories, and law and ethics are lagging in these areas. In view of such objections, the widespread adoption of electronic plebiscites, with or without extensive prior information campaigns and public discussions, is unlikely in the foreseeable future.

The Balance Sheet: For Better or for Worse?

In his book *The Future of the Mass Audience* (1991), W. Russell Neuman visualizes a world in which all media modalities are interlinked and public and private communications form a nearly seamless web. "The new media will be—a single, high-capacity, digital network of networks that will bridge what we now know as the separate domains of computing, telephony, broadcasting, motion pictures, and publishing" (p. x). Yet the overall effects on circulating information throughout the body politic will be minimal. The reasons, as Neuman sees them, are the structure of the communications industries, which drives them toward economies of scale (that is, the mass media produce information for large audiences), and the nature of the mass audience. The "economies of scale in production and promotion will not be changed by the new technologies" (p. 13). Neuman sees the mass audience as "semi-attentive, entertainment-oriented." Because of the public's lack of interest, politics is going to remain a very small part of public communication, overall, and diversity is not likely to increase.

My crystal ball reveals a similar picture. Just as airplane travel has made the entire world accessible to human exploration, so are the new channels of information transmission opening up new worlds of knowledge. But the vast majority of the benefits will be reaped by the socially and educationally privileged. They can draw on a greater diversity of information sources than ever before. Interactivity technologies allow them to engage in dialogues and debates with experts and laypeople throughout the world. Just as world travelers have always shared their experiences with stay-at-homes, thereby giving them vicarious glimpses at some of the information that the less privileged cannot obtain directly for themselves, so the travelers on the world's information superhighways are going to share some of their insights with the multitudes living on the information margins. Journalists, in particular, will help disseminate the newly accessible information riches. There will be some direct and indirect benefits—as well as disadvantages—for everyone.

But enhancements in the information supply will not create the democratic utopia of government by well-informed average citizens that appears in the rosy dreams of some futurists. The growth in the public's base of knowledge about political personalities and issues is likely to be incremental rather than geometric. That means that opinion formation will continue to be based primarily on established core beliefs and intellectual shortcuts, rather than on extensive analysis of the available information. Advances in levels of education have done little to increase civic knowledge. Similarly, advances in information technology are unlikely to bear rich fruit for opinion formation as long as the public remains politically passive.

The greatest political impact of the new media may well come from the powers they confer on political elites, including special interest groups. These elites will be able to collect plentiful information to further their goals faster and more efficiently and effectively than ever before. Whether they will use these powers for good or ill remains to be seen.

Part 2   The Organization of Public Opinion

Republicans in 1995, having taken over Congress for the first time in forty years, began dismantling the welfare state in the name of a conservative revolution that they claimed was mandated by voters in the 1994 elections. The congressional struggle over this legislation has been fought in terms of ideology and party.

Whether the public intended to send such a message will be debated for many years. What is clear is that ideology and party are vitally important to the way the American political system structures its political debates. For many Americans, ideology and partisanship serve a similar function and help them organize their political opinions. Faced with a new political issue on which they have no opinion, many citizens turn to party leaders or to leading ideological figures to provide them with cues about which position they should take. Theoretically, both ideology and party identification shape our viewpoints on specific issues and candidates. Yet much of the early political science research questioned the meaning of ideology for the American public, while more recent works question the meaning of party identification in an era in which candidates dominate elections.

The classic studies of ideology, based on surveys from the 1950s, concluded that the American public was incapable of abstract ideological thought (Campbell et al. 1960; Converse 1964). Most Americans conceived of politics in terms of which groups benefit or lose, or in terms of "the nature of the times"—whether they thought that things were getting better or worse. Very few American voters seemed to use ideology to shape their opinions and influence their candidate choices.

Public opinion researchers in the 1980s began to question the classic interpretation of ideology. Perhaps social scientists were looking for the wrong type of ideology. One group of scholars began to suggest that ideological labels had more to do with symbolism than with specific issue positions (Conover and Feldman 1981; Levitan and Miller 1979). Americans' definitions of conservatism are shaped by linking this label to feelings about the police, military, and business; definitions of liberalism are influenced by reactions to the challenges that women, students, and minority groups made to the 1950s traditional lifestyle (Conover and Feldman 1981).

Other scholars argued that the search for ideology in the American public should not be limited to identifying liberals and conservatives (Maddox and Lilie 1984). Other possible ideologies include populism—a preference for expanded social welfare programs and stricter governmental controls to maintain social order—and libertarianism, the rejection of government intervention in the economy and in social issues. Both populists and libertarians would appear to be inconsistent on the traditional liberal-conservative scale. The American public may be equally divided into liberals, conservatives, populists, and libertarians (Janda, Berry, and Goldman 1995, 26, 165).

Kathleen Knight and Robert Erikson's chapter fits in with the final group of scholars who accept the classical definition of ideology but recognize its usefulness for only a portion of Americans (see also Jacoby 1986, 1991). Knight in an earlier article (1985) demonstrated that ideologues efficiently use liberal and conservative labels to evaluate candidates. Citizens lacking the ability to use these cues select candidates by summarizing a variety of issue positions and candidate qualities. Knight and Erikson continue this investigation into the varied use of ideology as they try to explain the growth of conservatism in the American electorate.

The classical voting behavior studies from the 1950s viewed party identification as the key to understanding the American electorate. Party identification influenced whether people voted and which candidate they voted for. Partisans were more likely to vote than independents, and partisans voted overwhelmingly for their party's candidates, especially for lower-level offices. Partisanship was vastly more stable than any other attitude. The New Deal generation had strong partisan preferences and passed these identifications on to their children. Yet beginning in the 1960s the dominant role of party identification in elections began to decline. More people adopted an independent identification, more split-ticket ballots were cast, partisans defected more often from their party's candidate, and more citizens began to develop negative attitudes toward both parties. (See Gant and Luttbeg 1991 for a summary and explanation of these changes.)

Barbara Norrander's chapter continues the investigations into the relationship between issue positions and party identification. She asks three questions: How much consensus on the issues exists within each party? Who belongs to each party's more conservative and liberal factions? Do strong party attachments mean greater consistency in issue positions?

6 Ideology in the 1990s

Kathleen Knight and Robert S. Erikson

Electoral politics is often depicted as a battle between the ideological forces of liberalism and conservatism. For instance, when Republicans gained control of Congress in the historic 1994 midterm elections, many attributed the Democratic defeat to a public clamor for the more conservative policies offered by the Republicans. Yet the ideological meanings of elections are generally ambiguous, and other interpretations may explain results as well. Still, the ideological positions of parties and candidates, and the electorate's reactions to them, are important in U.S. elections.

Even scholars who study public opinion and elections have not been able to identify the exact influence of ideology on electoral politics. On the one hand, a well-developed body of theory articulates how the ideological tastes of the electorate can determine party positions and electoral choice. On the other hand, political scientists who study individual voters find that much of the electorate is unresponsive to ideological cues. The apparent disjuncture between theory and reality can be resolved, however, if we keep in mind that ideology as a cue, or the ideology schema (Conover 1991; Kuklinski, Luskin, and Bolland 1991), is invoked by only an identifiable subset of the American public (Knight 1985; Knight and Lewis 1992; see also Palfrey and Poole 1987). This assumption moves the focus of attention from questions of whether the "ideology glass" is half empty or half full (Levitan and Miller 1979) to questions about how many ideological voters there are in the American public and whether more voters have become ideological over time.

For some citizens, the liberal versus conservative ideological spectrum is a central part of political life. Naturally, it is among ideological voters that we are likely to find liberal or conservative "extremists." But many ideological voters are moderates, who prefer centrist politics over ideological extremes. Ideologically oriented voters generally identify with the party that is more compatible with their vote (Democrats for liberals, Republicans for conservatives). In general elections, their vote is usually consistent with their party identification (just like most others), but they may defect temporarily when the other party runs a candidate who takes the preferred ideological position.

For the remainder of the electorate, however, the ideological debate draws little attention. Nonideological citizens do vote, but their choices are more often based on other consider-

Figure 6-1 Distribution of Voters and Candidates in Ideological Space
(Hypothetical)

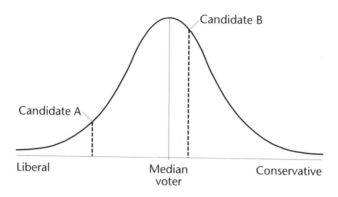

Note: The curve represents a distribution of voters on a liberal-to-conservative scale. Candidate B is closer to more voters than Candidate A and wins this hypothetical election.

ations. Like the ideologically oriented, they develop party identifications based on their perception of their political interests. But their party loyalty has little to do with ideological distinctions. Nonideological voters are not restricted to partisanship as a basis of choice, however. More so than ideological voters, nonideological voters select candidates based on qualities such as perceived likability and leadership capability (Lau 1986; Pierce 1993). In empirical research nonideological motivations are often more important than ideological voting as a way to explain election victories and losses (Miller and Shanks 1982; Hamill, Lodge, and Blake 1985).

Ideological Voting in Theory and Reality

Suppose that all voters were motivated by ideology, choosing the candidate whose ideology is closest to their own. Rational choice theorists have developed a model of electoral politics under such circumstances. In its basic form, the model is readily understandable. In this section we present the rational choice model of the vote and discuss its relevance for understanding the ideological behavior of actual voters. The version of the model we use was presented by Anthony Downs (1957) in his classic book, *An Economic Theory of Democracy*.

Theory: The Downs Model

Downs presents a simple model of one-dimensional ideological space. Voters are arrayed on this left-right dimension, perhaps according to the normal distribution of the bell curve, but the exact shape is unimportant (see Figure 6-1). The key assumption is that ideological voters will choose a party or candidate closest to themselves ideologically. In a two-party contest, then, the candidate or party closer to the greater number of voters wins the election. For instance, within the hypothetical setup of Figure 6-1, Candidate B, whose ideological position is closer to that of the average voter than that of Candidate A, will win the election.

The second part of the Downs theory addresses the behavior of parties or candidates (here we will use *party* and *candidate* interchangeably). If the candidate who is ideologically closest wins, the equilibrium candidate position is the position of the median voter at the 50th percentile of liberalism or conservatism. This position is in equilibrium because if either candidate takes the median position while the opponent takes a different position, the candidate at the median wins because that candidate is closer ideologically to more voters.

This logic propels both candidates toward the median. One feature of this result is that the winning ideological position is the median voter's position, so that government policy will usually be near the electorate's collective preferences. A second feature is that because both candidates take positions near the center, they may look almost alike to voters; in such a case voters may feel they have no reason to vote. Finally, when both parties take positions in the center, the election outcome should be very close—in theory, a tie vote. Thus, when the Downs model works perfectly, the winning candidate in a close election has promised to work for policies representing voters in the middle, but voters have little reason to care which of two nearly identical candidates wins.

Reality: A Partially Ideological Electorate

The Downs model is useful as a general guide to what candidates must do to win elections: move toward the center. But the model's predictions fail. Republican and Democratic candidates do not converge at the center of the spectrum. And elections generally do not end in ties. The Downs model is logical, based on its premises. The interesting complications are that voters are only partially motivated by ideology and candidates are only partially motivated by electoral victory. In addition, neither voters nor candidates hold the perfect information that the Downs model assumes. The following paragraphs describe five caveats to the Downsian model.

First, voters care about ideological location to varying degrees and also consider other aspects of an election besides simple ideological positioning. Thus, for instance, an electorate might reject the most ideologically compatible candidate in favor of an opponent who is more attractive based on nonideological considerations such as leadership, character, or simple likability. Or an electorate might reject the most ideologically compatible candidate because of loyalty to party attachments formed long in the past. Thus, to determine the role of ideology in elections, one must sort out ideological responsiveness from other motivations. By selecting for observation those voters who are ideologically more sensitive, it is possible to observe an approximation of Downsian voting, but the model does not hold for nonideological voters.

A second limitation of the Downsian premises is the assumption that parties or candidates care solely about winning elections. Candidates and their most loyal followers care both about winning and about the ideological direction of policy outcomes. While candidates are pulled toward the center by the median voter logic, they are pushed away by their own ideology and the ideology of their supporters. However, to win a party's nomination, a candidate must satisfy the party's median voter in the primary election.

Thus, Democrats are almost always committed to policies that are more liberal than the median voter would support, while Republicans are almost always committed to policies that are more conservative than those preferred by the median voter. In practice, elections are often won by candidates who, although their position is farther from the center than that of the median voter, are still closer to the center than the opponent. Earning the votes of moderates is often the key to winning U.S. elections.

Third, the Downs model assumes that candidates are perfectly informed regarding the voters' positions and especially the median voter position. This assumption is far from true. Despite the frequent public opinion polls that accompany every campaign, the exact center of the ideological spectrum is never known with certainty. At any moment, ideological positions represent the composite of voter preferences over a variety of specific issues that fade in and out of awareness. These preferences and their importance to voters cannot be precisely measured by polls.

If public preferences were easily discovered, politicians would respond smoothly to changing public tastes, and there would be few electoral surprises. In fact, interpretations about the preferences of the median voter generally are made only after the voters' verdict comes in. Similarly, candidates do not know for sure how the voters perceive them ideologically. In light of such uncertainty, candidates often make strategic mistakes.

Fourth, the basic Downs model assumes that voters accurately assess the candidates' ideological positions.[1] This assumption, too, as one might expect, is often false. Even ideologically attentive voters often are ignorant of candidates' exact positions and must guess from such cues as the candidates' party affiliations. This ignorance increases as one moves down the ballot from the presidential contest. When one considers races for the U.S. Senate and the U.S. House, for instance, only very well informed voters (such as those who contribute money to campaigns) know much about a candidate's position beyond what can be inferred from the party label (Powell 1989).

Finally, in theory, parties and candidates can move fluidly along the ideological spectrum. In practice, for a politician to change his or her ideological reputation is both difficult and risky. Politicians' reputations are quite strongly tied to their past behavior and their party identification. If a candidate shifts noticeably, voters may see ideological flexibility as a symptom of unreliability or opportunism (Hinich and Munger 1994).

In practice, then, what can be said about ideological voting? In contrast with the assumptions of the Downs model, ideological voting accounts for only part of the outcome of an election. And although candidates gain some votes by approaching the ideological center, the winning candidate is not always the one who is the nearest ideologically to the median voter. In the following pages we examine the role of ideology among actual voters using nationally representative surveys conducted by the American National Election Studies (ANES).

Ideological Identification and Sophistication

We will focus on two important ideological attributes of ANES respondents: ideological preference, or self-identification; and ideological sophistication, or understanding. Identification represents the individual's preferred position on the liberal-conservative continuum. Sophistication refers to the voter's ability to understand electoral information cast in liberal and conservative terms. Sophistication might be thought of as a basic working knowledge of the ideological continuum.

Measuring Ideological Identification

Beginning in 1972, in its biennial election surveys the ANES has measured ideological preference by offering respondents seven choices ranging from 1 ("extremely liberal") to 7 ("extremely conservative"), with the midpoint 4 labeled "moderate/middle of the road." For most of our analysis, we collapse these responses into the familiar alternatives of liberal (1, 2, 3), moderate (4), and conservative (5, 6, 7). In addition, a significant minority, between 20 and 30 percent in ANES surveys, do not classify themselves on the liberal-to-conservative scale.

Measuring Ideological Sophistication

We measure ideological sophistication based on the respondent's understanding of the two major parties' ideological positions. Since 1972 the ANES has asked respondents not only to supply their personal ideological preference, but also to estimate the positions of the Democratic and Republican parties on the same seven-point scale.

The exact placement of the parties is not important for our purposes; rather the relative positioning is what counts. Respondents who rate the Democratic Party as more liberal than (to the left of) the Republican Party are scored as ideologically sophisticated, or attuned to party differences along the ideological spectrum. Respondents who rate the Democrats to the right of the Republicans, who rate the two parties the same, or who fail to rate at least one of the parties are all scored as ideologically naive. Respondents who do not give self-

Table 6-1 Major Party Vote by Ideological Identification, 1992 Presidential Election (in Percentages)

	Liberal (23%)	Moderate (23%)	Conservative (33%)	No Preference (21%)
Bush (Rep.)	8	38	73	31
Clinton (Dem.)	92	62	27	69

Source: 1992 American National Election Study.

Note: Number of reported major party voters in survey = 1,357.

ratings on the ideological scale are also scored as unsophisticated.

Our measure of ideological sophistication is similar to the test Philip E. Converse (1964) used to measure "recognition and understanding" of the ideological terms (see also Luskin 1987; Luttbeg and Gant 1985). His terms are useful to describe the gulf between those who are equipped to follow policy debates involving ideological rhetoric and those who do not know what the key words of the debate actually mean. We assume that for behavior to be goal directed—that is, rational—the voter must have the same understanding of the ideological positions of the parties as the parties do themselves. Some people may be able to rationalize an idiosyncratic understanding of the relative positions of the parties. But voting on the basis of this understanding (for example, voting for the Democratic candidates because they are seen to be more conservative than the Republicans) cannot get them the result they desire.[2]

An interesting question is why some people maintain an ideologically based understanding of politics and others do not. Political interest, the costs (in time, energy, and so on) of being informed, and cognitive ability all play some role. Later in this chapter we explore trends in ideological identification and ideological sophistication. But first, we illustrate the importance of these variables in the context of the 1992 presidential election.

Ideology, Ideological Knowledge, and Presidential Voting

When we examine the relationship between ideological identification and presidential vote choice, we find voting consistent with ideology—but only if the voter is ideologically sophisticated. We illustrate with ANES data from the 1992 election.

Table 6-1 shows a statistical relationship between ideological identification (liberal, moderate, conservative) and 1992 presidential vote choice. Perot votes are deleted from this table in order to clarify the presence of ideological voting.[3] Table 6-1 demonstrates that most "lib-

Table 6-2 Major Party Vote by Ideological Identification, 1992 Presidential Election, Among Ideologically Sophisticated and Ideologically Naive Voters Separately (in Percentages)

| | Ideologically Sophisticated Voters (61%) | | | |
	Liberal (33%)	Moderate (25%)	Conservative (42%)	No Preference
Bush (Rep.)	4	39	84	—
Clinton (Dem.)	96	61	16	—
	Ideologically Naive Voters (39%)			
	Liberal (8%)	Moderate (19%)	Conservative (20%)	No Preference (53%)
Bush (Rep.)	36	36	38	31
Clinton (Dem.)	64	64	62	69

Source: 1992 American National Election Study.

erals" voted for the more liberal candidate, Democrat Bill Clinton, and a smaller majority of "conservatives" voted for the more conservative candidate, Republican George Bush. More moderates chose Clinton than chose Bush. Obviously, ideology played a role, but the Democratic leanings of moderates and the considerable resistance to Bush even among conservatives suggests that Clinton may have won the election for nonideological reasons. Note too that Clinton did particularly well among voters who did not rate themselves ideologically.

To sharpen our understanding of the role of ideology, Table 6-2 depicts the vote-ideology relationship separately for the ideologically sophisticated and ideologically naive. Among the 61 percent who placed the parties correctly, the vote-ideology relationship is even stronger than before. But among the remaining 39 percent, who did not display a conventional understanding of the ideological distinctions between the parties, voting did not vary by ideological identification. Among these voters, Clinton won a bit over 60 percent from each self-identified ideological group. Among these uninformed voters, the most pro-Clinton of all were those who failed to venture an ideological identification.

These results lead us to conclude that there are two types of voters. One group understands the conventional ideological distinctions and votes as if in response to ideological location. The other group does not understand the ideological terms, even if they are willing to label themselves, so any self-identification does not influence their vote.

Table 6-3 Major Party Vote by Ideological Identification, 1992 Presidential Election, Among Ideologically Sophisticated Voters (in Percentages)

| | Conservative Minus Liberal Responses, Three Panel Waves | | | | | | |
| | Always Liberal | | | Balanced, Moderate | Always Conservative | | |
	(−3)	*(−2)*	*(−1)*	*(0)*	*(+1)*	*(+2)*	*(+3)*
Bush (Rep.)	3	0	4	32	50	69	95
Clinton (Dem.)	97	100	96	68	50	31	5
Number of cases	(57)	(16)	(28)	(34)	(30)	(35)	(79)

Source: 1990–1992 American National Election Study Panels.

Note: Ideological responses summed over three interviews (panel waves), 1990, 1991, and 1992.

To sharpen our standard of sophistication, suppose we include only those who correctly characterize the parties in each of a series of interviews in which they are asked to rate the parties ideologically. A "lucky" but uninformed respondent might "guess" correctly that the Republicans are to the right of the Democrats and thus be falsely scored as ideologically sophisticated. However, few uninformed voters would guess correctly, say, in three interviews in a row. We refine our measurement instrument this way by observing 1992 respondents' ratings of the parties in interviews conducted in 1990 and 1991. Approximately half of the 1992 respondents were part of this ANES panel study.

Table 6-3 shows the vote-ideology relationship for the ideologically sophisticated voters who placed the Democrats to the left of the Republicans three times out of three. We can likewise refine our measure of ideological identification by consolidating the three responses on the seven-point scale. Of the 101 ideologically sophisticated liberals (those in the three left categories), all but 3 reported voting for Clinton. Likewise, all but 4 of the 79 voters who called themselves conservative in all three surveys voted for Bush. Mildly conservative voters (those who said they were moderate, or even liberal, one time out of three) reported voting for Bush, but not lopsidedly. Those who correctly located the parties all three times but claimed a conservative identification in only one of the three interviews were evenly divided.

From Tables 6-1, 6-2, and 6-3 we have seen evidence that ideological identification is an important determinant of voting, but only among the ideologically sophisticated. On the other hand, a large minority of voters (and close to half of all citizens) are not ideologically sophisticated. Interestingly, many nonideological voters offer ideological responses when asked, but their responses are unrelated to voting behavior (or to any other political attitudes).

Table 6-4 Ideological Identification of the U.S. Electorate, 1972–1994 (in Percentages)

	Liberal	Moderate	Conservative
1972	25	37	37
1974	28	36	36
1976	24	38	38
1978	26	37	37
1980	25	31	44
1982	23	35	42
1984	26	33	41
1986	24	37	39
1988	23	31	45
1990	25	37	38
1992	27	31	42
1994	20	33	47

Source: American National Election Studies Cumulative File, 1972–1994.

Notes: Liberals are scored as 1, 2, or 3 on the ANES 7-point Liberal-Conservative Scale. Conservatives are scored as 5, 6, or 7. Moderates placed themselves at 4. Nonidentifiers are excluded.

Ideological Trends from the 1970s to the 1990s

The Conservative Surge

When asked to place themselves on the liberal-conservative scale, the American public has a clear and well-known preference for the conservative over the liberal label. Since at least the early 1970s, more voters call themselves conservatives than liberals. And this tendency has clearly been growing.

Table 6-4 and Figure 6-2 illustrate this preference, using ANES data for the years 1972–1994. Table 6-4 shows the distribution of liberals, moderates, and conservatives among those who ventured an ideological preference in ANES surveys. Figure 6-2 graphs a simple trend line to illustrate the growth in conservative identification. The line represents the percent of respondents who chose the conservative label among all who identified as either liberal or conservative. This graph reveals a mild trend toward conservatism from a 1974 nadir (a 56 to 44 percent conservative-liberal division) to 1988 (a 66 to 34 percent division). In 1990 and 1992, conservative identification dropped to just above 60 percent of ideological identifiers as if a liberal comeback were in progress. But 1994 presented a decisive conservative upsurge: 73 percent of the ideological identifiers placed themselves on the conservative side of the ideological continuum.

Figure 6-2 Ideological Identification, 1972–1994

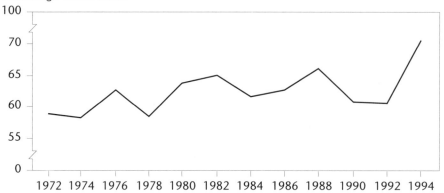

Source: American National Election Studies Cumulative File, 1972–1994.

Note: Percentages represent percentage conservative among conservative and liberal identifiers.

Growing Ideological Sophistication

Coinciding with the growth in conservative identification is an increase in ideological sophistication. Figure 6-3 presents the time series for ideological sophistication, as measured by the frequency with which ANES respondents as a whole place the Democrats to the left of the Republicans. Ideological sophistication increased from a low of about 38 percent in 1972 to 55 percent in 1994.[4]

As if the evidence were not already stacked in favor of conservatives, some observers (mainly of the conservative persuasion) see a causal link between the electorate's growing ideological sophistication and its increasing attraction to conservatism. According to this argument, as voters become newly awakened ideologically, they start to act according to their latent conservatism. As we demonstrated earlier, ideologically sophisticated liberals vote Democratic and ideologically sophisticated conservatives vote Republican. Thus, if greater ideological sophistication means an increase in the number of ideologically informed conservatives, the electoral result is positive, to say the least, for the conservative Republican Party.

Convergence of Ideology and Partisanship

Another important bit of evidence apparently supports this argument. Over the twenty-two years of the ANES time series, the public has increasingly connected conservatism with Republicanism. In particular, the correlation between ideological identification and party identification has noticeably increased. Conservatives have become more closely associated with partisan Republicanism (and liberals with Democratic partisan-

Figure 6-3   Political Sophistication, 1972–1994

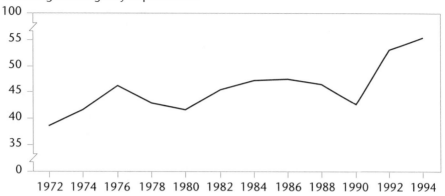

Percentage Ideologically Sophisticated

Source: American National Election Studies Cumulative File, 1972–1994.

Note: Sophisticates rate Democrats to the left of Republicans and place themselves ideologically.

ship). What is more, this growing correlation is most pronounced among the ideologically sophisticated.

Table 6-5 shows the relevant correlation evidence. Note in particular the distinct difference in the correlation patterns for the ideologically sophisticated and for the ideologically naive. The sophisticated groups demonstrate the correlation pattern we described. Among the ideologically naive group, the correlation between partisanship and ideology stays close to 0 throughout the time period. In other words, these self-labeled but naive "liberals" and "conservatives" show equal frequencies of Republican and Democratic identification as if there existed no connection between ideology and party.

A proponent of conservative causes could argue, in addition, that recent gains in Republican Party identification have been caused by the electorate's growing conservatism. Whereas once the Republicans were clearly the minority party, by the end of 1994 they were about even with the Democratic Party in polls of party identification. The electorate, in other words, was at one time both Democratic and conservative. (For more lengthy discussion of this logic see Levitan and Miller [1979] and Miller [1991].) Ideological awakening allowed conservatives to make a partisan correction. If this view is accurate, then the ideological correction represents a major change in American politics.

As we will see, the trends in liberalism and conservatism among the electorate are open to other interpretations. For instance, we do not know that newly ideological voters behave any more conservatively than they had before they became ideological. But one causal argument does seem incontrovertible from the evidence: people are increasingly choosing party

Table 6-5 Correlation Between Party Identification and Ideological Identification of the U.S. Electorate, 1972–1994

	Ideologically Sophisticated	Ideologically Naive	All Respondents
1972	.43	.03	.32
1974	.50	.05	.33
1976	.53	−.08	.38
1978	.54	−.00	.35
1980	.60	−.11	.39
1982	.59	−.15	.42
1984	.62	−.15	.41
1986	.58	−.09	.36
1988	.58	−.05	.41
1990	.57	−.19	.34
1992	.61	−.12	.44
1994	.68	−.02	.52

Source: American National Election Studies Cumulative File, 1972–1994.

Note: Coefficients are Pearson product moment correlations (r).

identification consistent with ideological considerations. Whatever the consequences, there is a pattern of ideologically based partisan realignment.

A Conservative Electorate? The Possibility of Overinterpretation

From our discussion so far, it might seem that election outcomes and policy outcomes in the United States have been more liberal than the clearly conservative electorate might wish. Some argue that a conservative correction is under way. In this section we offer some reasons for skepticism as we consider these questions: What should we make of the electorate's preference for the conservative label? Do people really want to press politics in a more conservative direction?

Philosophically Conservative but Operationally Liberal?

It is by now a cliché that U.S. public opinion may be philosophically conservative but it is operationally liberal (Free and Cantril 1968). The argument is that people may support the conservative ideal of less government in the abstract, but they will back specific spending proposals when given the choice. Along the same lines, John Zaller and Stanley Feldman (1992) note that while most Americans believe in individualism in the abstract, many also support social welfare programs because they see that people are not always able to support themselves despite their best efforts. Sympathy for the disadvantaged leads these Americans to support social welfare programs while favoring limited government in the abstract. The preference for an active government makes people operationally liberal.

It is difficult to find a clear conservative trend with regard to specific policy issues. According to Tom W. Smith's (1990b) analysis of political and social issues, preferences became steadily more liberal for decades, until reaching a plateau in the 1970s. In the conservative 1980s, polls show that, if anything, the public became decidedly more liberal on specific spending issues (Erikson and Tedin 1995). James A. Stimson (1991) documents this trend as part of a pattern of ideological "mood" cycles. It can be argued that these mood cycles come about because the electorate opts for more government spending when it is believed that policy has become too conservative and for less when policy has become too liberal (Wlezien 1995). For 1993 and 1994, Stimson's mood indicators show increasing conservatism, perhaps as a signal that Clinton's policies were perceived as too liberal.

Ideological Sophistication and Ideological Preference

We have assumed in this discussion that the conservative edge in ideological identification is based mainly on the responses of the ideologically sophisticated. To evaluate the significance of the conservative side's ideological lead, it is instructive to compare the responses of the ideologically sophisticated with those of the ideologically naive, who seemingly offer ideological preferences without comprehending the implications of those preferences for party choice. One might expect that the ideologically naive would not venture ideological preferences on a subject they know so little about. But one interesting problem that plagues survey research is that people often offer "doorstep" opinions on subjects, even when they lack any real knowledge of the subject (Converse 1964). Typically in ANES surveys, slightly over half of the ideologically naive do decline to rate themselves ideologically. Of the remainder, close to half choose the "moderate" midpoint. Thus, the responses of the ideologically naive tend to be neutral and do not seriously bias assessments of the electorate's ideology. Of special interest here, however, is the fact that about a quarter of those who are ideologically naive do identify themselves as liberals or conservatives on the ANES seven-point scale.

Figure 6-4 tracks ideological preferences of the two sophistication groups, measured by the net difference between the percent of all identifiers calling themselves conservative and the percent calling themselves liberal. Some may find the results surprising. If we compare the conservative-liberal balance of the ideologically sophisticated and ideologically naive, we find that the strongest conservative tilt is among the naive, those who presumably do not understand the ideological labels well enough to translate their preferences into meaningful votes.

Figure 6-4 Ideological Identification by Sophistication Level, 1972–1994

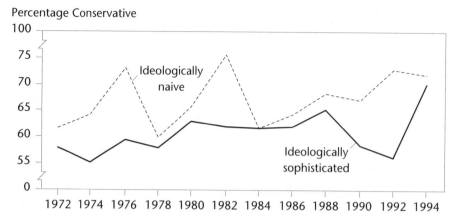

Source: American National Election Studies Cumulative File, 1972–1994.

Note: Percentages represent percentage conservative among conservative and liberal identification.

There is no question that the ideologically sophisticated prefer the conservative label, and that their conservatism is growing rather than receding. Still, the ideologically naive are more strongly conservative than the ideologically sophisticated are.[5]

Claims about the electorate's conservatism must be balanced by the realization that some (but far from all) of the conservative edge in the opinion polls is a result of the responses of "doorstep conservatives" whose ideological preferences have no impact on their vote. A full answer to why people who are not properly attuned to ideological differences show the strongest tendency to choose the conservative label is beyond the scope of this chapter. At least part of the explanation must involve social desirability—the people we have classified as ideologically naive are aware that something defined as "conservatism" is more in vogue than "liberalism."[6]

Citizens' Perceptions of the Parties' Ideological Positions

The imbalance in ideological identification is of no particular electoral significance unless voters perceive themselves as closer to the Republican Party than to the Democrats. As a new frame of reference, Figure 6-5 presents the time series for mean voter ideology (using the full seven-point ANES scale) along with the electorate's mean perceptions of the two parties' positions on the same scale. The public does not rate the parties symmetrically around the scale midpoint of 4. Instead, voters place Republicans farther from the center than Democrats, with the Republicans on the right (up in Figure 6-5), and the Democrats on the left (down in Figure 6-5). As a result the Democrats and Republicans are placed at about the

Figure 6-5   Average Ideological Location of Voters and Average Perception of Parties, 1972–1994

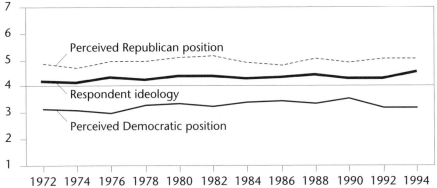

Ideological Location

Source: American National Election Studies Cumulative File, 1972–1994.

Note: The ideological location is the mean position on the seven-point ideological scale.

same distance from the mean voter position, although even by this standard the Republicans hold a slight edge.

Figure 6-6 depicts relative ideological distances between voters and parties in a still more detailed fashion for those respondents who order the parties correctly on the ideological continuum—the ideologically sophisticated. This figure tracks the cumulative frequencies of seven categories of respondents, based on their relative ratings of themselves and the two parties. These relative positions are, from left to right, as follows:

1. Respondent rates self to the left of both parties.
2. Respondent rates self and Democrats at exactly the same position.
3. Respondent rates self in between parties, but closer to Democrats.
4. Respondent rates self exactly at midpoint between Democrats on left and Republicans on right.
5. Respondent rates self in between parties, but closer to Republicans.
6. Respondent rates self and Republicans at exactly the same position.
7. Respondent rates self to the right of both parties.

Generally, about one-quarter of respondents rate themselves either to the left or to the right of both parties (groups 1 and 7). Of the rest, about half claim to share the position of one of the two parties (groups 2 and 6). The remainder (roughly 35 percent of all the ideologically sophisticated) place themselves between the two parties.

Figure 6-6 Relative Ideological Position of Ideologically Sophisticated Voters, 1972–1994

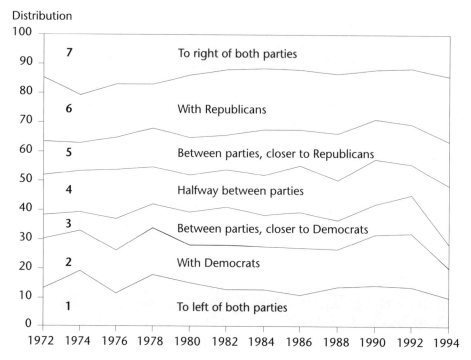

Source: American National Election Studies Cumulative File, 1972–1994.

Note: Cumulative percent, numbered areas refer to categories described in the text.

This figure illustrates why the parties struggle to both win elections and satisfy their ideological constituencies. Voters in the center reward and punish candidates based on their proximity to the center. Voters at the extremes will usually vote for their party as long as it is closer to their position than the opposition, but they still try to pull their party as far in their own ideological direction as possible.

By this more detailed measure, Republicans usually enjoy a modest edge (about 55 to 45 percent) in terms of perceived ideological proximity to (ideologically sophisticated) potential voters. Republicans held their biggest lead by this measure in 1994, the year of the generally unexpected Republican congressional "revolution." Yet the Democrats held their best (slight) lead according to this measure in 1992, the very election before. It may not be wise to declare a trend. It remains to be seen where the ideologically attuned part of the electorate will equilibrate.

Figure 6-7 Party Identification by Level of Sophistication, 1972–1994

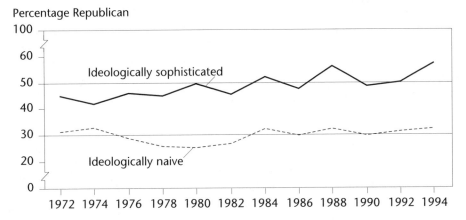

Percentage Republican

Source: American National Election Studies Cumulative File, 1972–1994.

Note: Percentages represent percent Republican among Republican and Democratic identifiers.

Ideological Sophistication and Party Identification

Recalling that the ideologically sophisticated tend to choose a party identification consistent with their ideology but that the ideologically naive do not, we examine the party identification of the two groups separately. Figure 6-7 presents the two time series, using the same measurements as Figure 6-4.

It is worth noting first in Figure 6-7 that both ideological sophistication groups were predominantly Democratic in identification prior to 1984 (below the 50 percent threshold in the figure). Since 1984, the ideologically sophisticated have tended to be balanced in their party identification, with a small, and gradually increasing, Republican tilt. This result reflects the slight Republican edge in ideological proximity, as illustrated in Figure 6-6. The ideologically naive, on the other hand, decidedly favor the Democratic Party.

Ideology and the 1994 Congressional Vote

Recall, as well, that research we presented in Table 6-2 indicated that ideological identification did not affect vote choice in 1992 among those who did not share a conventional understanding of the ideological positions of the parties. Tables 6-6 and 6-7 update this analysis for the 1994 congressional elections. Table 6-6 simply illustrates the division of the two-party vote by ideological identification. The vote preferences of liberals and conservatives are mirror images of each other. The Republican electoral victory in 1994 (53 percent

Table 6-6 Major Party Vote by Ideological Identification, House Elections, 1994 (in Percentages)

	Liberal (17%)	Moderate (23%)	Conservative (44%)	No Preference (16%)
Democratic	76	56	24	64
Republican	24	44	76	36

Source: 1994 American National Election Study.

Note: Number of reported two-party voters in survey = 936.

Republican over all House seats) results from the disproportionately conservative identification in 1994. Note, however, that the majority of moderates, and an even greater percentage of those who did not identify with any ideological position, report voting Democratic.

Table 6-7 divides House voters by ideological sophistication. In 1994 ideologically sophisticated conservatives voted Republican in slightly greater proportions than ideologically sophisticated liberals voted Democratic. Ideologically sophisticated moderates still favor the Democratic Party. Taken as a whole, the ideologically sophisticated reported a 60 percent Republican vote in 1994.

Reported vote among the ideologically naive overall is, however, 60 percent Democratic. Among the ideologically naive, liberals, moderates, and even conservative identifiers report majority votes for Democratic House candidates. And, as was the case in Table 6-2, nonidentifiers are even more likely to vote Democratic than ideologically naive liberals are. In sum, even though the ideologically naive are more conservative than the ideologically sophisticated, their apparent conservatism has not done much to shake them from their Democratic Party identification.

Ideology at the Crossroads?

Much of the story of conservative success in the 1990s is told in Figure 6-4. The impressiveness of the 1990s surge in ideological sophistication can draw attention away from the slower change since the 1970s. It is very likely that this gradual change is more profound than the upturn of conservative sentiment accompanying the Republican takeover of Congress in 1994.

The increasing ideological sophistication of the American electorate makes the logic of the Downs model more relevant to political campaigns than it has been in the past. But it is important to remember that we are still dealing with a public that is only partially ideologically sophisticated. Moreover, even among the ideologically sophisticated, the voting deci-

Table 6-7 Major Party Vote by Ideological Identification, House Elections, 1994, Among Ideologically Sophisticated and Ideologically Naive Voters Separately (in Percentages)

	Ideologically Sophisticated Voters (67%)			
	Liberal (22%)	Moderate (23%)	Conservative (56%)	No Preference
Democratic	80	54	17	—
Republican	20	46	83	—
	Ideologically Naive Voters (33%)			
	Liberal (7%)	Moderate (25%)	Conservative (19%)	No Preference (48%)
Democratic	52	58	58	64
Republican	48	42	42	36

Source: 1994 American National Election Study.

sion may be only partially motivated by ideological influences (Erikson and Romero 1990).

The model we presented at the beginning of this chapter assumes that parties are motivated by both winning and ideology and that voters are only partially motivated by ideological considerations. This model can aptly depict the normal state of American politics, where the parties are moderately distinct ideologically and ideological proximity plays a modest role in deciding elections. We could imagine this model remaining in equilibrium until there is a shift in the motivations or preferences of the parties or the electorate.

Our analysis of ideological trends leading into the 1990s points to the possibility that major change will push the ideological balance out of equilibrium. More people are becoming attuned to the ideological debate; consequently, they are increasingly aligning their ideology and partisanship in a consistent fashion. Moreover, we see evidence of shifts in the balance of public opinion. The electorate of the mid-1990s is more conservative than those of the recent past, despite a modest shift in the liberal direction just a few years earlier.

What will be the next turn in ideological direction? Conservatives can hope that the ideological "awakening" is the prelude to greater conservatism in the electorate. Liberals can hope that increasing ideological sophistication among voters will bolster voters' beliefs that their interests are best served by the liberal policies of the Democratic Party.

Much depends on the behavior of the parties as well. As of this writing, contemporary political discussion focuses on the novelty of a Republican Congress, with its vigorously conservative agenda. Will the ideological reaction of the public be favorable, or will a basically moderate electorate see the Republicans as going too far? We will know more by the end of the 1990s.

Notes

1. Downs (1957) himself modifies his model for imperfect information. In fact, he demonstrates that it is irrational for a voter to be perfectly informed.

2. The conceptual meaning of sophistication has been "thoroughly muddied by diverse uses" (Converse 1964, 207) and particularly by differences in the operationalization of empirical indicators. However, the alternative terminologies have their own problems. Several of the simpler pairs of terms have acquired meaning in other disciplines. For example, in social psychology the terms *expert* and *naive* commonly refer to the presence or absence of particular schemata whether they have been instilled through experimental manipulation or acquired by natural social processes (see Fiske and Taylor 1984 or Lau 1986). Other possible pairs of terms have even more pejorative implications than *naive*—for example, literate/illiterate, competent/incompetent. Terms like *sophisticated, knowledgeable*, or *expert* may imply substantially greater facility with ideological concepts than we mean. Nonetheless, for ease of presentation we will generally use the terms sophisticated and naive. Our empirical operationalization most closely resembles Converse's "recognition and understanding" (1964, 224) and Luskin's variable RU (1987). We wish to stress that the criterion for ideological sophistication is minimal: if the common relationship of the parties on the liberal-to-conservative continuum is misunderstood (for example, if Democrats are viewed as more conservative than Republicans), a vote cast on this basis will produce a result that is opposite of what was intended.

3. Voters who supported independent candidate Perot were located all along the ideological spectrum. Perot's appeal did not involve ideological placement in the traditional sense.

4. Note that these numbers represent citizens and not reported voters, as was the case for our earlier analysis of ideology in the 1992 election.

5. Because ideologically naive voters tend to choose the moderate category, their greater "conservatism" becomes muted if we measure each group's net ideology as a percentage difference, percent conservative minus percent liberal. Even so, for most years the naive show up as the more conservative group by this standard too.

6. In Figure 6-4, the "gaps" between the sophisticated and naive in terms of ideological preference appear to spread in Democratic years and narrow in Republican years. We suspect that this pattern arises because marginally sophisticated voters are more likely to call themselves liberals in Democratic years and conservative in Republican years. Neither the sophisticated nor the naive appear more responsible for ideological trends. In the ANES 1992–1993–1994 panel, respondents who saw party differences in each of the three surveys showed the same net ideological movement as the other respondents.

7 Partisanship and Issues in the 1990s

Barbara Norrander

Before the Republicans' Contract with America, electoral choices offered by the political parties to the American voter were often depicted by journalists and some scholars as no more different than tweedledum and tweedledee. Such a characterization was overstated, for in recent elections the two parties' presidential candidates have differed on taxes, the abortion issue, government regulation of business, and defense spending. Since the early 1980s, the two parties in Congress have become more distinctive in their policy positions, and voting along party lines has become more common. If the parties operating in the government have moved apart, we might ask if the voters have kept pace? Have they followed this trend toward a greater separation between Democrats and Republicans when it comes to the issues?

Traditionally, scholars have described the distinctions between Democratic and Republican voters as small, except perhaps on social welfare questions (Erikson and Tedin 1995, 83). The two parties were loose coalitions of various groups in society, rather than more cohesive ideological groups. People's attachment to the parties, in the form of party identification, was molded by their cultural context and family backgrounds—having experienced the New Deal, coming from an urban ethnic background or suburban prosperity, having a family tradition strongly in favor of one party, and so on. Partisan attachments strongly influenced voting behavior through the 1950s.

In the 1960s and 1970s, new issues—such as civil rights, the Vietnam War, and women's rights—came to the forefront. These issues often divided the political parties within themselves. As issues became more important in elections, partisanship appeared to decline. More Americans began viewing themselves as independents. While in the 1950s about one-fifth of Americans chose the independent label instead of identifying with a party, by the 1970s over one-third called themselves independents. Even among Democrats and Republicans, increasing numbers defected from their party to vote for the other party's candidate in a presidential election or to vote for a congressional incumbent of the other party. These defections, coupled with the increasing numbers of independent voters, led to a rise in split-ticket ballots, where many voters supported one party for one office and the other party for another office.

In the 1960s and 1970s, political scientists focused on the decline of partisanship, but in the 1980s a newer story began to emerge from social research. Partisans were becoming more distinctive on political issues. Democratic voters were becoming more consistently liberal, while Republican voters were becoming more consistently conservative. These changes were most noticeable in the South and among younger voters.

The South had been overwhelmingly Democratic since the Civil War; at the same time, southern Democrats had traditionally been quite conservative. In the 1960s, particularly during the Johnson administration, the national Democratic Party in Washington strongly backed the extension of civil rights to black Americans. Some southern Democratic voters felt alienated from the national party. Their disillusionment grew as Johnson extended the welfare state with his Great Society programs. Conservative white southern Democrats began voting for Republican presidential candidates but continued to vote for conservative Democrats for state and local offices. Gradually the Republican Party grew stronger in the South, fielding better and more competitive candidates. Southern whites, particularly younger residents, began to move to the Republican Party. Racial attitudes (Carmines and Stimson 1989), ideology (Carmines and Stanley 1990), and economic positions (Nadeau and Stanley 1993) shifted more conservative southern voters into the Republican Party.

Voters outside the South also began adopting party allegiances along issue lines, particularly voters who entered the electorate after 1964. Racial attitudes (Carmines and Stimson 1989), opinions on the welfare state (Luskin, McIver, and Carmines 1989; Abramowitz 1994), national security views (Abramowitz 1994), evaluations of the Vietnam War, and opinions on school prayer (Niemi and Jennings 1991) shaped the partisan preferences of new voters. In the North and the South, Republicans became more consistently conservative and Democrats more consistently liberal (Carmines and Stanley 1990). As the parties' positions became clearer, some older partisans adopted the issue stance of their party's leaders. However, other older Americans retained lifelong party affiliations without switching issue positions. The continued presence of these voters in the electorate prevents perfect consistency between party and issue preferences for American society as a whole (Carmines and Berkman 1994).

This chapter will examine the issue positions held by Democrats and Republicans in 1992 to determine the level of consistency within each party. We will ask three questions about the relationship between party preferences and issue positions for the public as a whole. First, how much consensus on the issues exists within each party, and how much do Democrats and Republicans disagree? Second, which groups of Democrats and Republicans tend to disagree with their party's average position? Finally, are those voters with strong attachments to political parties more consistent in their issue positions than independent voters?

Studying the Issue Positions of Partisans

To examine the relationship between issue positions and partisan affiliations we will use the 1992 American National Election Study (ANES) survey of 2,400 Americans. The survey asks a variety of issue-oriented questions, many on a 1–7 scale. For instance, in answering the question on health insurance, those who felt "there should be a government insurance plan which would cover all medical and hospital expenses for everyone" were told to place themselves at 1. Respondents who believed "that all medical expenses should be paid by individuals, and through private insurance plans like Blue Cross or other company paid plans" would choose 7. Individuals whose opinion fell between the extremes could select any point from 2 through 6. A score of 4 represents a neutral or moderate position on the issue.[1] A total of twelve issue questions was adopted for this study. These issues represent a broad spectrum including economic, defense, and social issues. In a few cases response categories were recoded so that in all questions a higher score would indicate a more conservative answer.[2] A few questions had fewer than seven categories. For these questions the category numbering was stretched out to fit the 1–7 scale format.[3]

To illustrate the position of each party's adherents on these issues, the median and frequency of responses for each party are charted. The median response reflects the "average" position taken within each party. It is the value on the issue scale where an equal number of respondents fall to the left and right of this point. By comparing median responses we can tell if the average Democrat holds a different issue position than the average Republican.

The frequency of distributions shows a different part of the story. A tight distribution within a party indicates agreement among party members. An elongated distribution indicates disagreement. Extensive overlap between the Democratic and Republican distributions blurs the issue preferences of both parties.

The shape of each distribution also matters. A bell-shaped or normal distribution (similar to an upside-down *U*; see Appendix Figure A-1) indicates that a majority of party members take a middle-of-the-road position, with equal numbers trailing off to the right or left of the median position on the issue. With this distribution a moderate position taken by party leaders will please most members. A *J*-shaped distribution indicates considerable consensus within a party, but on a more extreme position. Once again party leaders can please most of their followers but the position that they adopt is no longer a centrist position. A *U*-shaped distribution represents the most divisive format for partisan opinions. In this format large numbers of partisans take an issue position to the right or left, and very few are in the middle. This distribution leaves little room for compromise on an issue and fails to provide party leaders with an obvious position to adopt, inviting instead an intraparty struggle between adherents of the two positions.

Democrats and Republicans were identified in the ANES by a seven-point partisanship scale. Based on their responses to a series of questions, respondents are classified as strong Democrats, weak Democrats, independents leaning toward the Democratic Party, pure independents (having no leanings), independents leaning toward the Republican Party, weak Republicans, and strong Republicans. Because this chapter seeks to examine differences between Democrats and Republicans, all those who strongly or weakly identify with a party have been combined with those who initially identify as independents but then indicate that they lean toward that party.

This means that Democrats include those who strongly identify as Democrats, those who weakly identify as Democrats, and independents who lean toward the Democratic Party. Although it might initially seem odd to classify these "independent leaners" as partisans, research has shown that they often vote more loyally for their party's candidates than weak partisans, and they often hold issue positions similar to those held by weak partisans (Keith et al. 1992, chap. 7).

Issue Consensus and Conflict Within and Between the Parties

Is there a consensus on issues within the parties and disagreement between them? Consensus within each party and divergence between parties would be expected to occur in a system characterized by highly ideological parties. Traditionally, the viewpoints of Democrats and Republicans have been characterized as overlapping and diverse, but some have argued recently that the parties are evolving into two distinct, polarized groupings.

Figure 7-1 shows median positions and distributions of opinions for Democrats and Republicans on ideology and on three issue questions. For each question, Democratic and Republican preferences overlap. Nevertheless, the average Democrat was more liberal than the average Republican. In all but one case, preferences for the remainder of party adherents either clustered closely and evenly around the party's average position, or were slightly lopsided in the direction of the average position.

The first of the questions asked about preferences for overall government spending. People were asked whether they felt that "it is important for the government to provide many more services even if it means an increase in spending" (coded as 1) or whether they believed "the government should provide fewer services, even in areas such as health and education in order to reduce spending" (coded as 7). The second issue concerned defense spending, whether it should be decreased greatly (1) or increased greatly (7). The third issues question asked whether people strongly agreed (1) or strongly disagreed (7) that homosexuals should be allowed to serve in the military.

The patterns of opinion on the government spending and defense questions are mirror images. On government spending the average Democrat adopts the moderate posi-

Figure 7-1 Differences Among and Between Democrats and Republicans on Four Issues

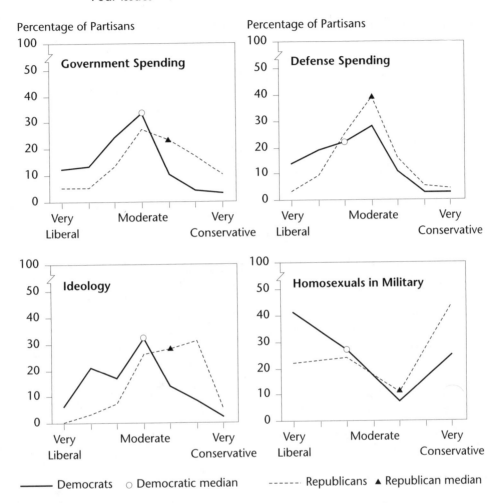

Percentage of Partisans

Government Spending

Percentage of Partisans

Defense Spending

Ideology

Homosexuals in Military

——— Democrats ○ Democratic median ----- Republicans ▲ Republican median

Source: Data from 1992 American National Election Study.

tion while the average Republican leans toward reducing spending levels somewhat. On defense matters, the average Republican prefers no change in spending, while the average Democrat preferred a slight cut in defense spending. On both issues the distribution of opinion within each party is basically bell shaped. The Republican consensus is pulled off slightly to the conservative side on government spending, while the Democrat distribution is pulled toward a slightly liberal position on defense. Nevertheless, tight dis-

Figure 7-2 Issues on Which Each Party's Members Show Consensus but the Parties Differ

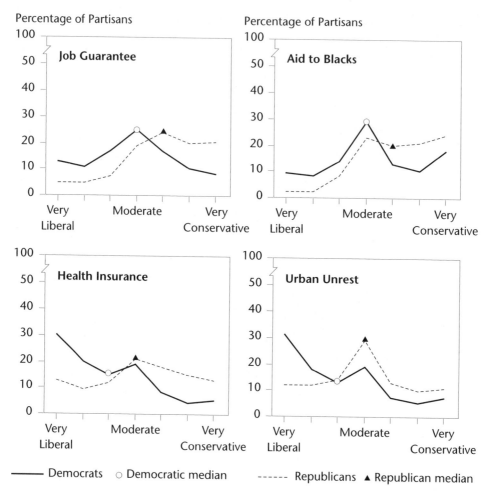

Percentage of Partisans

Percentage of Partisans

Source: Data from 1992 American National Election Study.

tributions around median party positions indicate considerable intraparty consensus on these two issues.

Partisan positions on ideology are not as tightly aligned. Most of the Republicans span a three-point range between moderate and conservative, and there were few at either extreme. Democrats coalesce around two peaks in the distribution: one at a liberal position and a second at the moderate position. Few Democrats adopt a conservative identification. The bimodal distribution (that is, having two peaks) suggests that there is more ideological conflict among Democrats than among Republicans. Republican Party leaders can appeal to their supporters by adopting the conservative label, but Democratic leaders have to please both liberal and moderate supporters.

The issue of gays serving in the military provokes the most intraparty disagreement. The U-shaped curves mean that both of the parties is divided.[4] The average Democrat agrees that homosexuals should be allowed to serve in the military, with another 41 percent strongly approving, but 27 percent of Democrats strongly disapprove. On the Republican side, the median position is one of opposing gays in the military, with 44 percent expressing this viewpoint; yet 46 percent of the Republicans approve of allowing homosexuals to serve in the military. This divisiveness within both parties makes it difficult for leaders of either party to choose an issue position that would please most of the party's voters.

Figure 7-2 presents graphs for four issues on which both parties demonstrate considerable consensus, with tight bell-shaped or J-curve distributions. Occasionally one party's members take a slightly wider range of positions. Democrats demonstrate consensus around a moderate position on the issue of whether the government should "see to it that every person has a job and a good standard of living," or whether "the government should just let each person get ahead on their own." In contrast, Republican positions on this issue span a range from moderate to very conservative. Similar partisan patterns emerge on the question of whether the government should aid blacks to improve their social and economic position or whether blacks "should help themselves." On this question, however, 18 percent of Democrats join 24 percent of Republicans in selecting the most conservative position.

Republicans coalesce around a middle-of-the-road position on two other issues: whether the government or private industry should provide health insurance, and whether urban unrest is best solved by maintaining law and order through the use of force or by solving the problems of poverty. A plurality of Democrats adopt the most liberal response on these two issues, with another group selecting the moderate position. Few Democrats choose the conservative option. If it were not for the tendency of people with less firm opinions to select the neutral position, then the Democratic distribution would be J-shaped, indicating consensus at the liberal position on these two issues.

Figure 7-3 presents four issues on which most Democrats and most Republicans fall on the same side. Two of the issues have J-shaped distributions, indicating consensus for each of the parties at one end of the political spectrum. Both Democrats and Republicans overwhelmingly approve of capital punishment for those convicted of murder; however, in the Democratic Party nearly one in five opposes capital punishment. Similarly, most Republicans and Democrats agree that women should have an equal role in business and government, but the Republican average is pulled slightly to a more moderate position by the number of respondents who choose the neutral position. Nevertheless, on these two issues most Repub-

Figure 7-3   Issues on Which Democrats and Republicans Hold Similar Opinions

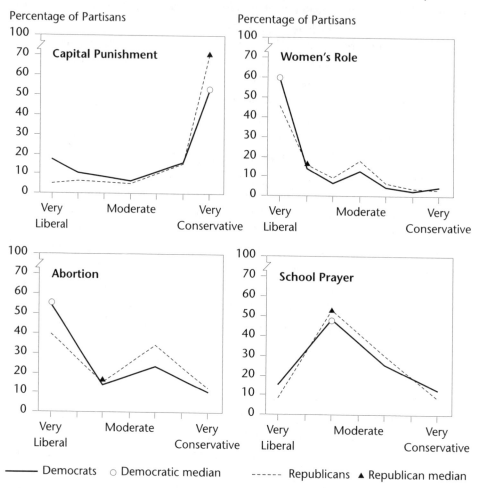

Source: Data from 1992 American National Election Study.

licans and most Democrats come down on the same side of the issues: approving of capital punishment and supporting an equal role for women in society.

On abortion, 54 percent of Democrats and 39 percent of Republicans believe a "women should always be able to obtain an abortion as a matter of personal choice." About 15 percent of Democrats and Republicans would allow abortion in cases of rape, incest, to save the woman's life, and other reasons, but "only after the need for the abortion has been clearly established." In the third category, one-third of Republicans and a smaller group of Democrats believe that abortions should be permitted only in the case of "rape, incest, or when the woman's life is in danger." About one in six of each of the parties believes that abortion should be illegal. The public disagrees on abortion. This disagreement is not between the two parties but within each of them. There are prolife Democrats and prolife Republicans, prochoice Democrats and prochoice Republicans, and many Democrats and Republicans who fall between the two positions. On school prayer a majority of Republicans and 48 percent of Democrats believe that public schools should observe a moment of silence for optional prayer. A tight bell-shaped distribution indicates considerable consensus within and across the two parties on this issue.

We have seen that the issue orientations of Democratic and Republican voters often follow a pattern in which Democrats adopt a slightly liberal bent to their generally moderate positions and Republicans set a slightly conservative tone to their moderate stances. On the social welfare issues examined, Democrats and Republicans agreed among themselves and differed from one another slightly. Democrats are somewhat divided on ideology—there are moderate and liberal rank-and-file members. Republicans see themselves as conservatives. On two social issues (capital punishment, women's roles) Democratic and Republican supporters' preferences fell on the same end of the policy question. On the other two social issues (gays in the military, abortion), Democrats and Republicans disagreed among themselves. The newer social issues do not distinguish the two parties from each other. The consensual social issues unite both parties; the contentious social issues divide both parties.

Issue Factions Within the Parties

On every issue some party followers disagree with their fellow partisans. We refer to distinctive issue groups within parties as factions. Often these factions are enduring groups within the party, and some have existed for many years. Traditionally, eastern Republicans have been more liberal, more supportive of aid to minorities and environmental protection. Black Americans often hold more liberal positions than other Americans, and thus may be part of the more liberal wing of the Democratic Party. If women are less willing to support the use of force at home or abroad, and more willing to support government spending on social security and aid to the poor, then they may constitute an identifiable liberal faction in both parties. Evangelical Protestants are depicted as the heart of the Christian Right, a sizable Republican faction (Rozell and Wilcox 1995).[5] Jewish Americans are usually liberal. Union members as part of the older New Deal coalition may now be part of the conservative Democratic wing. Finally, income and education influence attitudes on many issues and may play a role in party factionalism. To investigate these possibilities, liberal, moderate, and conservative Democrats and Republicans will be identified and analyzed for their demographic traits.

The makeup of the ideological wings of the two parties was determined by counting the number of times each partisan's responses were located to the left or right of the responses

Table 7-1 Distributions on Party Factionalism Scales (in Percentages)

	Democrats	Republicans
Most liberal faction (–6 or lower)	11	9
Liberal faction (–5, –4)	8	12
Somewhat liberal faction (–3, –2)	14	16
Party core (–1, 0, 1)	30	28
Somewhat conservative faction (2, 3)	16	16
Conservative faction (4, 5)	14	11
Most conservative faction (6 or more)	7	8
Number of cases	(1,176)	(913)

Source: 1992 American National Election Study.

Note: Entries represent percentage of Democrats and Republicans that fall into each faction group, based on respondents' issue positions.

of the party's median member. The number of times each respondent gave an answer that was more liberal than the party's median was subtracted from the number of times each respondent gave an answer that was more conservative than the party's median. The resulting scale varies from a score of –11, where a partisan always fell to the left of the party's median, to a score of 11, where the partisan always fell to the right of the median.[6] A score of 0 could be obtained either by always adopting the party's median position or by having the number of liberal positions match the number of conservative positions.

Table 7-1 lists responses on this party factionalism scale. Most partisans fall in the party core (scores of –1 to 1) or in the somewhat liberal or somewhat conservative groupings (scores of –3, –2, 2, or 3). General consensus within both parties is demonstrated by the smaller number of partisans in the more extreme categories. In 1992, large numbers of partisans adopted similar issue positions. Those who disagreed with their party's position did not consistently do so, and their more liberal beliefs on some issues were canceled out by their more conservative attitudes on other issues.

It is important to note that the party factionalism scale could have looked quite different. If the same individuals always adopted a more conservative position than the party median, the percentage of partisans in the most conservative category would increase. The same would be true on the liberal side. Also, if we had seen more issues with *U*-shaped distributions, the number of extreme Democrats and Republicans on the party factionalism scale would be greater. But most of the issue distributions were bell-shaped or *J* curves, indicating consensus within each party. As a result, approximately 60 percent of partisans agree on most issues, falling in the party core or taking a slightly ideological position. Nonetheless,

Table 7-2 Party Factions and Demographic Characteristics

	Democrats			Republicans		
	Beta	b	t-ratio	Beta	b	t-ratio
Higher age	.07**	.02	2.38	.18*	.04	5.34
South	.04	.30	.92	.09**	.80	2.25
East	−.07**	−.70	−2.06	−.08**	−.82	−1.98
West	−.11*	−1.08	−2.96	−.06	−.57	−1.51
Black	−.20*	−2.05	−6.42	−.04	−1.02	−1.01
Hispanic	.04	.67	1.49	−.08**	−1.53	−2.37
Female	−.10*	−.85	−3.69	−.24*	−1.91	−7.09
Evangelical Protestant	.16*	1.37	3.04	.08	.69	1.51
Mainline Protestant	.05	.54	1.17	−.12**	−1.06	−2.37
Catholic	.04	.41	.95	−.08	−.80	−1.71
Jewish	−.04	−.82	−1.13	−.02	−1.03	−.55
No religion	−.09**	−1.01	−2.15	−.17*	−2.10	−3.89
Union member	.08*	.75	2.61	.01	.14	.36
Higher income	.08**	.05	2.40	.04	.03	1.13
More education	−.31*	−.46	−8.94	−.07	−.11	−1.73
R^2		.23			.18	
F		19.41*			10.98*	
Number of cases		(1,010)			(783)	

Source: 1992 American National Election Study.

Notes: Entries are standardized regression coefficients (Beta), unstandardized regression coefficients (b), and t-ratios, which test for levels of statistical significance. Negative coefficients indicate membership in the party's liberal faction and positive coefficients indicate membership in the party's conservative faction.

  * Statistically significant at the .01 level
** Statistically significant at the .05 level.

40 percent of the partisans belong to one of the wings of their party, either conservative (scores of 4 or higher) or liberal (scores of −4 or lower).

To identify those who occupy the liberal and conservative wings of the two parties, the statistical procedure of multiple regression was employed. Multiple regression allows us to examine a variety of characteristics simultaneously to ascertain which factors are linked with the liberal or conservative wing.[7] Two identical regression models were used to explain factionalism, one for Democrats and one for Republicans. With the coding scheme for the party factionalism scale, a positive coefficient indicates membership in a party's conservative faction and a negative coefficient indicates membership in the liberal faction. Membership of each group in the liberal or conservative factions is best designated by the magnitude of the standardized regression coefficients (in the "beta" column) and whether these coefficients are statistically significant (designated by asterisks). Variables that are not statistically significant (no asterisks) cannot be considered to influence membership in the liberal or conservative wings of the two parties.

We see in Table 7-2 that older Democrats and Republicans form the conservative wings of both parties. Although conservative young Americans may be choosing the Republican Party in greater numbers, older Republicans remain more conservative than younger Republicans. The growing Republican strength in the South has reversed the historical distinctiveness of that region in party politics. Traditionally the conservative wing of the Democratic Party, southerners now form the conservative wing of the Republican Party. Meanwhile, easterners form the liberal branch of both parties. Westerners join easterners in the liberal branch of the Democratic Party.

Women and minorities belong to the liberal factions of both parties. Democratic and Republican women fall in the liberal camp, and the pattern is strongest in the Republican Party.[8] In other words, the gender gap on issues is greater in the Republican Party than in the Democratic Party. African Americans, as expected, belong to the liberal wing of the Democratic Party. Too few blacks identify with the Republican Party for any pattern to emerge.[9] Hispanics who are Republicans belong to the liberal wing.

Among the various religious denominations, evangelical Protestants stand out as the strongest component of the conservative Democratic wing. In the more conservative Republican Party, evangelicals fall within the party's mainstream. In contrast, mainline Protestants, once the mainstay of the Republican Party, now form the liberal faction of the Republican Party. Catholics fall in the mainstream of both parties. Americans claiming no formal religious ties belong to the liberal faction of both parties. The percentage of Jewish Americans in the sample is too small to show a pattern. The three socioeconomic factors play a role in Democratic Party factionalism. Both union members and those with higher incomes fall in the conservative camp of the Democratic Party. Democrats with high levels of education are the most liberal group.

Recapping these findings, we see the liberal wing of the Democratic Party composed of those with higher education, African Americans, westerners, women, those with no formal religion, and easterners. Among the conservative Democrats are evangelical Protestants, union members, those with high incomes, and older Americans. The liberal Republican wing is composed of women, those without religious ties, mainline Protestants, Hispanics, and easterners. Conservative Republicans tend to be older or from the South. If party leaders always adopt the median issue position for their party, they risk alienating these groups of Americans. At the same time, party leaders would please the bulk of their members by adopting such positions. Demographic distinctions compound the tug of war over each party's policy positions.

Partisanship and Issue Consistency

The final question about issues and partisanship is whether partisanship can help bring consistency to each individual citizen's issue positions. It is often assumed that ideology helps people structure their attitudes by providing a constraining framework, and partisanship may serve the same function. It is possible that party leaders establish consistent issue positions which are then adopted by rank-and-file members: in this scenario the consistency is provided by elites and adopted by party adherents. Alternatively, those with consistent issue positions may find that their positions fit one party's platform, and those whose positions are most consistent with the party's platform become strong partisans. Citizens with less consistent opinions may feel mismatched with both parties and adopt an independent identification.

The consistency of each respondent's issue positions was measured by a technique developed by Allen H. Barton and R. Wayne Parsons (1977). With this technique, consistency means giving similar answers to all questions relating to one general area of politics. The coding scheme was restructured so that higher scores indicate more consistency. Two consistency scores were calculated: one for economic issues (that is, questions of government aid to individuals) and one for social issues (that is, civil rights and lifestyle questions). The economic issues included government spending, health insurance, guaranteed jobs, aid to blacks, and how to address urban unrest. Social issues included abortion, women's role in society, gays in the military, and school prayer.

Those who score high on these consistency indices adopt consistently liberal or consistently conservative positions on all issues in a given domain, and those with lower scores may have some attitudes that are liberal and some that are conservative within a given issue area. Once again regression analysis was used to sort out the demographic traits as they relate to consistency. Besides the fifteen demographic groupings used in the factionalism analysis, two additional variables were added as possible explanations. The first of these is the intensity of partisan attachments: strong, weak, independent but leaning toward a party, and pure independent.[10] The second variable measures use of ideology: high, middle, or low.[11]

As shown in Table 7-3, those with stronger attachments to the political parties do have more consistent opinions on the economic issues. However, for social issues those with the strongest party attachments are less consistent. On these newer social issues the positions of the political parties may not be as clear, or partisans may not consider addressing social issues to be part of their party's role. Thus it is the older New Deal economic issues that continue to distinguish the two parties and their strongest supporters.

An ideological identification, in contrast, results in greater consistency for both economic and social issues. The influence of ideology is slightly greater than that of party identification. The other variable that has a strong effect in producing more consistency in issue posi-

Table 7-3 Issue Consistency and Demographic Characteristics

	Economic Issues			Social Issues		
	Beta	b	t-ratio	Beta	b	t-ratio
Intensity of party identification	.05**	.02	2.10	−.05**	−.02	−2.11
Higher use of ideology	.08*	.05	3.31	.08*	.05	3.41
Higher age	.01	.00	.49	−.10*	−.00	−4.28
South	−.02	−.02	−.77	.02	.01	.58
East	−.08*	−.06	−2.99	.07**	.05	2.46
West	.01	.01	.43	.03	.03	1.19
Black	−.06**	−.06	−2.48	−.01	−.01	−.31
Hispanic	−.05**	−.06	−2.06	−.06**	−.08	−2.51
Female	−.01	−.01	−.57	.06**	.04	2.55
Evangelical Protestant	−.00	−.00	−.13	.04	.02	.95
Mainline Protestant	.09*	.07	2.60	.05	.04	1.62
Catholic	.04	.03	1.11	.04	.03	1.15
Jewish	.02	.05	.89	.03	.08	1.42
No religion	.03	.03	.89	.09*	.09	3.04
Union member	−.01	−.01	−.30	.04	.03	1.72
Higher income	.04	.00	1.57	.11*	.01	4.25
More education	.16*	.02	5.95	.15*	.02	5.84
R^2		.08			.12	
F		10.27*			14.43*	
Number of cases		(1,923)			(1,867)	

Source: 1992 American National Election Study.

Notes: Entries are standardized regression coefficients (Beta), unstandardized regression coefficients (b), and t-ratios, which test for levels of statistical significance. Negative coefficients indicate less consistency in issue positions. Positive coefficients indicate more consistency in issue positions.

  * Statistically significant at the .01 level.
** Statistically significant at the .05 level.

tions is greater education. In fact, education has the strongest effects on consistency for both economic and social issues.

On social issues, women hold more consistent positions than men, perhaps because two of these issues (equal role for women and abortion) directly affect women's lives. Easterners, those with no formal religion, and those with higher incomes also demonstrate more consistency on social issues. Groups demonstrating less consistency on the social issues include older Americans and Hispanics.

On economic issues, mainline Protestants are unusually consistent. Revealing less consistency on economic issues are easterners, African Americans, and Hispanics. Less consistency will occur if a group sees specific issues in the consistency scales as representing fundamentally different phenomena. For African Americans in the survey, the two questions on government aid to blacks and the solution to urban unrest may be viewed more as racial issues than economic questions.

In summary, the intensity of partisan attachment leads to greater consistency only on the types of economic issues associated with the two parties since the New Deal. On newer social issues, party identification does not lead to consistent positions. Generally two other traits of individuals are much more likely to explain the presence or lack of consistent positions on the issues. These two factors are the use of ideology and the level of education.

Conclusions

We have seen that each party's supporters demonstrate considerable consensus on social welfare issues. Democrats coalesce around an option slightly to the left of center and Republicans form a consensus slightly to the right. On the newer social issues the patterns are not consistent. When we consider all types of issues together, those who disagree with their party tend to do so on only a few issues. Only a minority of each party consistently falls to the left or right of the average member of the party. People who do fall in their party's liberal or conservative camp tend to belong to clear demographic subgroups. Party identification helps people organize opinions on economic issues. Party identification, however, does not lead to consistent opinions on social issues. For all the types of issues, ideological identification and educational attainment were associated with holding consistent opinions on the issues.

As others have reported, adherents of the two parties may be increasingly distinctive in their issue positions. But the gap between the two parties is not large. Party leaders who adopt polarized positions risk losing their own party members. On social welfare issues slightly off-center moderate positions appeal to each party's core constituency. And the most strongly identified partisans will hold consistent attitudes across the range of social welfare issues. The new social issues do not yet clearly divide Democrats from Republicans. The issues of abortion and homosexual rights divide both parties. Whether partisans become distinctive on these newer social issues and become more polarized on the traditional social welfare issues will depend on the actions of both the party elite and rank-and-file members. If Republican and Democratic leaders in Washington, D.C., and the nation's statehouses continue to espouse and enact distinctive legislation, such as many elements of the Republicans' Contract with America, the public may follow by moving either their partisanship or their issue preferences to match those of the party leaders. Not all partisans or independents will do so, however. The relationship between party identification and issue preferences in America will never be perfect due to generational, regional, and demographic partisan traditions.

A party system with a congruence between issues and partisanship may not be workable in the American system of democracy. Back in the 1950s a group of political scientists advocated a model of "responsible" parties, in which the two parties would adopt and be accountable for clearer, more distinct issue positions. Voters would then make a well-informed choice between the parties. The responsible party model was fashioned after the British party system. Yet in Great Britain's parliamentary system one party controls both the legislative and the executive branches of government. In the U.S. system separate elections are held for Congress and the president; divided government, where Democrats control one branch and Republicans the other, often results. Under divided government, two strongly distinctive party positions can lead to stalemate, as occurred during the federal budget impasse of 1995–1996. The framers of the U.S. Constitution set up a political system that requires compromises. The looser fit between partisanship and issue positions in the American public allows elected leaders to seek compromises to solve America's political problems.

Notes

1. The neutral option sometimes is selected by respondents who do not have well-developed opinions on the issue. Even though most of the ANES questions have an option for admitting one has not thought much about the issue, some respondents prefer to give a "doorstep" opinion to please the interviewer or to avoid looking ill informed.

2. The codings on government spending, abortion, gays in the military, and the death penalty were reversed to have high values indicate conservative responses.

3. The coding for the questions on abortion, gays in the military, and the death penalty was stretched from four categories to seven. On the death penalty question (v5934), those who had responded to the first question on the death penalty (v5933) with the "depends" answer were entered at the neutral position of 4.

4. Some of this divisiveness may be an artifact of the question format. No neutral position was given as an option. Respondents had to select an agree or disagree option.

5. Categorizations for evangelical and mainline Protestants were provided by Ted Jelen and are based on denominational membership.

6. When the party median was the most extreme category, such as for Democrats and Republicans on the death penalty, this question could not be counted for membership in the liberal (or conservative) wing. To preserve a more representative sample, respondents who failed to provide an answer to a specific question were assigned their party's median position. Respondents who failed to answer at least six of the twelve issue questions were eliminated from the analysis.

7. The excluded categories from the dummy variable series included: Midwest for region; other Christian and other religions for religion; and whites, Asians, and Native Americans for race and ethnicity. For the race and ethnicity classification, all African Americans were coded as black, leaving only white Hispanics in the Hispanic category.

8. This is demonstrated by the unstandardized regression coefficients.

9. Regression is sensitive to the marginals. This means that when there are only a few individuals belonging to one group, regression cannot find the linear pattern it is seeking between this classification and the dependent variable.

10. The seven-point ANES partisanship scale was folded in half to obtain four groups with different

levels of partisan attachments. Strong Democrats and strong Republicans were combined to form the strongest attachment group. Weak Democrats and weak Republicans formed the second group; independents leaning toward the Democratic or Republican Party formed the third group. Pure independents were the group showing the least partisan attachment.

11. Those most comfortable with the ideological terms of liberal, moderate, or conservative will label themselves when first asked. These individuals are coded as high users of ideology. Some survey respondents will select a label if asked a second time. These are coded as moderate users of ideology. Finally, some respondents indicate that they do not use such terms even after the second question. These people are coded as low users of ideology.

Part 3   The Content of Public Opinion

Surveys of political opinion typically include questions on a wide range of topics. Major national academic surveys may include over a hundred questions on public policy issues and scores of others on topics that might be thought of as in some way political. Yet during election campaigns, one or more of four types of issues is always emphasized: economic issues, social or moral issues, foreign policy issues, and race issues. Within these broad categories, of course, there are countless political issues. Economic issues can include tax rates, welfare payments, business regulation, and health care; social issues include abortion, gay rights, equal rights for woman, school prayer, home schooling, and divorce laws; and foreign policy issues include spending on bombers and submarines, giving aid to foreign countries, imposing trade sanctions on other countries, and even going to war.

Of course, many issues fall into more than one category. Foreign trade, for example, involves both foreign policy and domestic economic policy. Equal pay for equal work laws, designed to eliminate wage discrimination against women, involve both social and economic policy. And policies that deny funding for international agencies that advocate abortion are at the intersection of foreign and social policy.

Scholars who study public opinion in a particular policy area ask many different questions. They may describe how opinion on racial discrimination has changed over the past several decades, or how an event like the Bosnian conflict has changed foreign policy views. They may study the changing sources of opinion on gay rights, or the way certain groups such as highly religious blacks are torn on these issues between their religious views and their strong belief in equality. They may investigate the impact of economic attitudes on vote choice or on the outcome of congressional elections.

In this section, we include a chapter by Elizabeth Cook investigating the sources of opinions on abortion. She finds that opinion on abortion has been remarkably stable for more than twenty years, but that the politics of the issue has changed as political events have energized the activists on one or the other side of the issue.

In the next chapter Barbara Bardes investigates public opinion on foreign policy in the post–cold war world. Earlier research had shown that Americans' attitudes on foreign policy were largely centered on containment of communism and the Soviet threat. The breakup of the Soviet Union left many Americans without this strong anchor to their opinion. This leaves American presidents with the ability to mobilize the public behind moral imperatives, at least as long as the policy does not involve major American casualties.

Finally, William Jacoby is interested in attitudes on economic policy. He shows that individuals' economic attitudes vary according to their perception of the economy, their political orientation, and their economic self-interest.

8 Public Opinion and Abortion Law in the Post-*Webster* Era

Elizabeth Adell Cook

Abortion has been at the forefront of American politics for more than two decades. In 1973, the U.S. Supreme Court ruled in *Roe v. Wade* that states could not restrict abortion in the first trimester (three months) of pregnancy and could regulate abortion in the second trimester "to the extent that the regulation reasonably relates to the preservation and protection of maternal health." This ruling nullified virtually all state laws regulating abortion, and legal access to abortion became the law of the land.

While feminists and others heralded the Court's opinion, those opposed to legalized abortion formed a large and active prolife movement and worked to make abortion illegal again. In the 1970s, the prolife movement sought to pass the Human Life Amendment, a proposed constitutional amendment that would have declared that life begins at conception and that would have granted fetuses (or unborn children) the rights of U.S. citizens. Such an amendment would have banned abortion in all fifty states, but this tactic failed. The Human Life Amendment was not passed by either house of Congress, the first step in the amendment process.

In the 1980s, the prolife movement realized that the Human Life Amendment was not likely to be passed in the near future. If the Constitution could not be amended, they reasoned, then *Roe* could be reversed by carefully chosen justices on a future Supreme Court. Prolife groups began to work within the Republican Party to gain influence over future Court appointments. Beginning in 1980, the Republican Party adopted a prolife plank in its presidential platform. Abortion became a litmus test for both parties, as Democrats sought candidates with prochoice credentials, and Republicans sought those with prolife stands.

Although state legislatures attempted to limit access to abortion after *Roe,* the Supreme Court consistently struck down their laws. After Ronald Reagan replaced three retiring justices on the Court, however, the story changed somewhat. In 1989 the Court upheld a Missouri law that prevented state hospitals from performing most abortions, that required tests of fetal viability before abortions could be performed, and that included a preamble stating that life begins at conception. In *Webster v. Reproductive Health Services,* the Court ruled that all of these requirements passed constitutional muster. Moreover, the ruling did not let the states know which types of regulations would be considered unconstitutional; thus the Court seemed to invite states to experiment with new restrictions on abortion.

From the point of view of the prolife groups, the most encouraging part of the *Webster* decision was that four of the nine justices indicated a willingness to overturn the *Roe* decision. Speculation flourished that *Roe* would eventually be overturned. If a single justice who supported *Roe* retired and was replaced by one who opposed *Roe*, there would be enough votes to overturn the landmark 1973 decision. In 1989 and in the early 1990s, this seemed likely to occur. President George Bush had record approval ratings in March 1991, and many expected him to be reelected in 1992 and to continue to appoint to the Supreme Court justices who opposed *Roe*. Indeed, during the 1993–1996 presidential term, two seats on the Court became vacant. Bush would presumably have appointed two opponents of *Roe*; instead, Clinton named two prochoice justices.[1]

The *Webster* decision changed the politics of abortion. Suddenly actions of state legislatures and governors had more than symbolic meaning: they had real policy implications. For some time abortion policy had been decided by the courts, and thus had been somewhat insulated from the political process; now the issue of abortion rights became even more important and controversial as it moved back into the arena of elections and politics.

Just as the *Roe* decision had mobilized the prolife movement, *Webster* mobilized the prochoice movement. From the 1973 *Roe* decision until the *Webster* decision in 1989, prochoice Americans had believed that the right to abortion was secured by the Court; therefore, they were free to base their voting decisions on other issues. During the 1970s and 1980s prochoice citizens frequently supported prolife candidates. Their prolife counterparts, however, were far more likely to base their vote solely on the abortion issue and were more likely to volunteer their time and money for the cause (Luker 1984; Wilcox 1988). All of this changed in 1989. The *Webster* decision stimulated fund raising by prochoice political action committees (PACs) and encouraged prochoice voters to look first at the candidates' views of abortion (Wilcox 1995).

The Supreme Court reaffirmed the rights of states to regulate abortion in 1992. The Court upheld in *Planned Parenthood of Southeastern Pennsylvania v. Casey* several restrictions on abortion enacted by Pennsylvania, including waiting periods, parental consent, and viability tests, but struck down the requirement that married women notify their husbands before undergoing abortions. In addition, the *Casey* decision specified that states cannot place an "undue burden" on women who seek abortions.

The *Webster* and *Casey* decisions elevated the importance of the abortion issue in state and national elections. Abortion was an important issue in the 1992 election to the benefit of Bill Clinton (Abramowitz 1995). Some of Clinton's first actions as president were to exercise his executive power to reverse some of the policies of the Bush administration on abortion, such as the "gag rule" that prohibited anyone at a federally funded family planning clinic from discussing abortion with patients. When Justice Byron White (who had consistently opposed *Roe*) retired in 1993, Clinton appointed Ruth Bader Ginsburg, who was expected to vote to uphold *Roe*. When Justice Harry Blackmun (who authored the *Roe* decision) retired, Clinton appointed Stephen Breyer, who also was presumed to support *Roe*.

In the wake of *Webster* and *Casey,* Republican leaders have begun a debate on their party's position on the abortion issue. Because prochoice Americans outnumber their prolife counterparts by a wide margin, Republican candidates have lost a number of elections at least in part because of their prolife position (Cook, Jelen, and Wilcox 1994, 1995; Cook, Hartwig, and Wilcox 1993; Dodson and Burnbauer with Kleman 1990). Some prominent Republicans have urged the party to jettison the prolife language from the party platform. Nevertheless, all major candidates for the Republican nomination in 1996 maintained a prolife stance.

As the prochoice side was mobilized and as some Republican leaders have begun to rethink their ties with the prolife movement, more radical prolife activists have escalated their extralegal activity. In the late 1980s and early 1990s, members of Operation Rescue took to the streets to try to stop women from having abortions. They blockaded clinics to keep patients from entering and used Super Glue to jam door locks so that even the staff could not enter. Their supporters have likened them to supporters of civil rights who demonstrated and held sit-ins at lunch counters to bring about racial integration. Their opponents have likened them to opponents of civil rights who threw rocks at buses of black children who were trying to exercise their constitutionally guaranteed right to attend integrated schools. Protests against abortion also have been quite violent. In the early 1980s a series of bombings of abortion clinics occurred. And the 1990s have witnessed the assassinations of doctors who performed abortions.

Thus, in the 1990s, abortion continues to be an issue that inspires intense reaction and political action. Both sides have experienced some victories. The *Webster* and *Casey* decisions were partial victories for the prolife movement in that they were the first decisions since *Roe* that allowed significant state regulation of abortion. But the election of Bill Clinton in 1992 led to the appointment of two prochoice justices to the Supreme Court, and that body is expected to continue to uphold *Roe* for the foreseeable future. The issue will continue to occupy a prominent place on the public agenda.

Trends in Public Opinion on Abortion

Although the relative fortunes of the prolife and prochoice movements have waxed and waned over time, attitudes toward abortion have remained quite stable. The General Social Survey (GSS) has asked samples of Americans in most years since 1972 whether abortion should be allowed under various circumstances. Specifically, respondents have been asked:

Figure 8-1 Support for Legal Abortion over Time

Mean number of circumstances supported (out of 6)

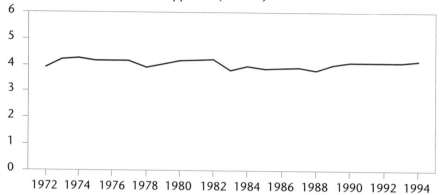

Source: General Social Surveys, 1972–1994.

Note: No data were available for 1979, 1981, 1986, and 1992.

Please tell me whether or not you think it should be possible for a pregnant woman to obtain a legal abortion . . .

    If there is a strong chance of serious defect in the baby?

    If she is married and does not want any more children?

    If the woman's own health is seriously endangered by the pregnancy?

    If the family has a very low income and cannot afford any more children?

    If she became pregnant as a result of rape?

    If she is not married and does not want to marry the man?

One simple way to measure support for legal abortion is to count the total number of circumstances under which respondents would allow abortion. Figure 8-1 shows that support for legal abortion has remained remarkably steady since the GSS began asking this question in 1972. Support increased slightly after the *Roe* decision in 1973, then declined during the 1980s, only to rise again at the time of the *Webster* decision in 1989. The rest of this chapter will focus on abortion attitudes in the post-*Webster* period, from 1989 through 1994.

Table 8-1 shows the percentage of respondents to the General Social Survey during this period who would allow abortion under each circumstance, and the average number of circumstances under which respondents indicate that abortion should be allowed. Note that the circumstances are ordered according to the percentage who support abortion for that reason. Not surprisingly, the most compelling reason to justify an abortion is to protect the woman's health; the vast majority of Americans favor allowing abortion in this circumstance. Large majorities also support allowing abortion when pregnancy is a result of

Table 8-1 Support for Legal Abortion

	Percentage
Supporting abortion under particular circumstances	
Woman's health	91
Rape	84
Fetal defect	82
Poor family	49
Single woman	46
Married, wants no more children	46
Accepting abortion for given number of reasons	
No reasons	7
1 reason	5
2 reasons	9
3 reasons	22
4 reasons	8
5 reasons	6
6 reasons	43
Mean: 4.1 reasons	

Source: 1989–1994 General Social Surveys.

rape and when there is a strong chance of a serious defect in the baby. These three circumstances are sometimes referred to as traumatic circumstances. The next three circumstances have the support of slightly less than half of the public: poverty, unmarried woman, or a family that wants no more children. These three situations are sometimes referred to as elective circumstances.[2]

As Table 8-1 shows, only 7 percent would have the law forbid abortion under all of the six circumstances. Forty-three percent would allow abortion under all six circumstances. Half of respondents take positions that fall between these two absolutes and would allow abortion in some but not all circumstances. The mean number of circumstances under which abortion would be allowed is just over four of the six possible.

Both the prolife and the prochoice movements have argued that public opinion is on their side. From the point of view of the prochoice movement, most Americans lean prochoice because they oppose the Human Life Amendment and do not want abortion made illegal. From the point of view of the prolife movement, most Americans lean prolife because they oppose abortion in at least some circumstances and would like to see access to abortion restricted in some way. Both claims are true, but they also provide a misleading portrait of public opinion.

Instead, the public is ambivalent about abortion, for many value both individual liberty and fetal life. Half of Americans are neither entirely prochoice nor entirely prolife; they would instead allow abortions in some but not all circumstances. Although tremendous support exists for legal abortion for traumatic reasons (about three-fourths would allow abortion in all three traumatic circumstances), considerably less support is found for abortion for elective reasons (nearly one-half would not allow abortion in any of these elective circumstances).

Kristin Luker (1984) studied activists in the prolife and prochoice movements in California in the early 1980s. She characterized the differences in their attitudes toward abortion as "the tip of the iceberg."[3] By this she meant that those who so strongly supported or opposed abortion that they became actively involved in the issue differed in many ways besides their attitudes toward abortion. The majority of activists she studied in both movements were women. Prochoice activists were better educated, had higher family incomes, were more likely to be employed, and had fewer children than the prolife activists. Further, the two sets of activists differed substantially in their world views. Prolife activists were highly religious, held more traditional sex roles and sexual morality values, and often saw abortion as part of a larger set of issues that devalued human life, such as euthanasia. Prochoice activists, on the other hand, were less religious, held feminist views about sex roles, viewed sexual morality as part of overall morality, and saw access to abortion as an important part of women's freedom and autonomy.

In the remainder of this chapter, we will examine how some of the differences between prochoice and prolife activists observed by Luker predict abortion attitudes in the mass public. Despite the stability of abortion attitudes over time, abortion attitudes vary across the population. Not all citizens are equally likely to take a particular position on abortion. This chapter will examine three sets of predictors of abortion attitudes: demographic characteristics; religious affiliations, beliefs, and behaviors; and attitudes toward sex roles, sexual morality, and life-and-death issues.

Demographic Characteristics and Abortion Attitudes

Demographic characteristics are basic background information about people: for example, their sex, race, age, education, income, and part of the country in which they grew up and in which they currently live. People who are from different backgrounds or who live in different circumstances have different life experiences. These experiences may lead them to view political issues differently. Thus, our background, circumstances, and life experiences influence how we view the world.

Several demographic characteristics influence attitudes toward abortion. Whenever I ask students what demographic variables will predict attitudes toward abortion, one of the first that they mention is sex. Most students are convinced that women are more supportive of abortion than men because it is women who become pregnant, although prolife students often argue that women should be more likely to oppose abortion because of their unique maternal role. In fact, only very small differences between men and women occur on attitudes toward abortion, and to the extent that there is a difference, men are more supportive of legal abortion than women. Table 8-2 shows the mean number of circumstances under which respondents from various demographic groups think abortion should be allowed. Men are slightly more supportive of legal abortion than women.

Previous research demonstrates that women who are homemakers are less supportive of legal abortion than men and working women (Cook, Jelen, and Wilcox 1992). However, when we look at respondents under age sixty-five who are married, we see that women who are homemakers and men who are married to homemakers are both less supportive of abortion rights than women who are employed and men who are married to employed women.

Race is another demographic characteristic that might be expected to influence attitude toward abortion. Despite years of social change, the United States is still very much a segregated society, and people of different races live in different neighborhoods, work in different occupations, and attend different churches. Race is one of the most important predictors of attitudes on a wide variety of political issues. However, as we see in Table 8-2, whites and blacks are almost equally likely to support legal abortion. In earlier years sizable racial differences in abortion attitudes were found, with blacks substantially less likely to support legal abortion. Black support for legal abortion began to increase in the mid-1980s, primarily because of generational turnover: younger people were replacing a generation that had been much more religious and prolife (Cook, Jelen, and Wilcox 1992).

Age can influence people's views in two ways. Age differences can reflect changes in attitudes across the life cycle, for people at different ages are at different points in the life cycle and thus differ in their circumstances. Age differences can also reflect a generational effect, in which the members of each generation, or cohort, bear the imprint of the period in which they grew up. There is no evidence that attitudes toward abortion change over the course of the life cycle; however, evidence exists of generational differences (Cook, Jelen, and Wilcox 1993). Table 8-2 shows that support for abortion declines with age, with the exception of the youngest group. Longitudinal analysis (not shown) reveals that in the 1973 to 1982 period, the youngest Americans were the most supportive of abortion rights, but after 1983, the youngest age group—aged eighteen to twenty-nine—was slightly less supportive of abortion than those who were thirty-one to forty-five. Although the youngest Americans are somewhat less supportive of legal abortion than those who are slightly older, they are still far more liberal in their views on abortion than the oldest cohorts. Thus, the process of generational replacement will continue to create a more strongly prochoice public.

Table 8-2 Mean Support for Legal Abortion by Demographic Variables

	Mean Support
Total	4.1
Sex	
Male	4.2
Female	4.0
Married, under age 65	
Male, wife in labor force	4.2
Male, homemaker wife	3.6
Female, in labor force	4.1
Female, homemaker	3.5
Race	
White	4.1 (n.s.)
Black	3.9 (n.s.)
Age	
18–30	4.1
31–45	4.2
46–60	4.0
61+	3.8
Education	
Less than high school graduate	3.4
High school graduate	4.0
Some college	4.3
College graduate	4.4
Graduate degree	4.6
Income	
Bottom 20%	3.6
Second 20%	3.9
Middle 20%	4.2
Fourth 20%	4.1
Top 20%	4.4
Region where grew up	
South	3.8
Non-South	4.2
Region of current residence	
South	3.9
Non-South	4.2

Source: 1989–1994 General Social Surveys.

Notes: Entries are the average number of circumstances respondent would allow abortion out of six possible. Differences in means are statistically significant at the .01 level, except where "n.s." is specified.

Education exposes people to a diversity of ideas. Formal education in the United States socializes students to values of civil liberties and political tolerance. As Table 8-2 shows, support for abortion increases uniformly with education. Those with postgraduate education are far more likely to support legal abortion than those whose formal education ended short of a high-school degree. The effect of education is striking, but it is not surprising. Those with more education are more supportive of civil liberties in a variety of areas.

Closely linked to education is income. Often, the term socioeconomic status is used to indicate the combined effect of income and education. Although income and education are distinct concepts, increased education often leads to increased income. But even on noneconomic issues, income and education often have independent influences. Table 8-2 shows that support for abortion increases with income. The association between abortion attitude and income is not due entirely to education; when education is controlled, the relationship between income and support for abortion is weakened but does not disappear. The women in high-income families are often in the labor force. It follows that people in these circumstances may especially value the ability to limit the size of their families and to time pregnancies so that the woman's career and the family's income are optimized.

Region of the country in which we grew up or in which we live also influences our view of the world. Different states and regions have different cultures. Southerners, for example, often profess distinctive values. The South is more conservative than the rest of the country on a variety of issues. Table 8-2 shows regional influences on attitudes toward abortion. People from the South and people currently living in the South are less supportive of legal abortion than those in the rest of the country.

Of course, many demographic variables are associated with each other: the South has more African Americans than the Midwest, and older Americans have lower average levels of education than younger cohorts. Regression analysis (not shown) reveals which of these variables are important predictors when we hold constant all of the other demographic factors. When all factors are simultaneously controlled, education is by far the most important predictor, and age, income, and region of current residence are not significant predictors. Yet these demographic variables combine to explain only 6 percent of the variance in attitudes on abortion. Thus, while demographics may be the first variables we look at to explain differences in abortion attitudes, we need to look to other variables to more fully explain these differences.

Religious Variables and Attitudes Toward Legal Abortion

It is obvious to any observer of American politics that religion is the source of most opposition to legal abortion. Various religious denominations have taken official positions on the issue, most notably the Roman Catholic Church, which has staked out a strong prolife position and invested important resources in an attempt to get lawmakers to ban abortions. Catholics are less supportive of abortion than Protestants, Jews, and those with no religion. As Table 8-3 demonstrates, Catholics favored abortion for an average of 3.8 circumstances, less than the 4.0 for Protestants, 5.0 for those with no religious affiliation, and 5.6 for Jews.

The figure for Protestants may be misleading. A large number of Protestant denominations coexist in the United States, and these churches have taken a variety of positions on abortion. When all Protestants are put into the same category, many of the differences between these groups are obscured. Evangelical, pentecostal, and fundamentalist Protestant churches stress the authority of scripture and personal religious experience, and generally oppose abortion.[4] This is especially true of the pentecostal Assemblies of God, which is the most strongly against legal abortion of all religious groups in the United States (Cook, Jelen, and Wilcox 1992). Mainline Protestants such as United Methodists, Episcopalians, and Presbyterians, in contrast, take more moderate positions on abortion, and pastors in many of these churches tell their members that abortion is a matter of personal choice (Jelen 1993).

As Table 8-3 reveals, when Protestant denominations are divided into those that are fundamentalist, pentecostal, or evangelical versus those that are mainline, it is the first three groups that are the most strongly against legal abortion. Catholics are more supportive of abortion rights than the conservative Protestants but less so than members of mainline Protestant churches. Mainline Protestants are in turn less supportive of abortion rights than Jews or those with no religious affiliation.

The prolife views of evangelical, fundamentalist, and pentecostal Christians are tied to their religious doctrine and experience. Those who say they have been "born again" are less supportive of legal abortion than those who have not had this experience. Similarly, those who believe that the Bible is literally true come out more strongly against abortion than those who take a less orthodox view (see Table 8-3).

Although these religious groups take different positions on the abortion issue, the intensity of religious practice has the same effect among those associated with each group. Table 8-3 reveals that for all religious groups, those who consider themselves strong members of the denomination and those who attend religious services more frequently are less supportive of legal abortion.

Religion has a somewhat different effect on attitudes of whites and blacks. Among whites, regression analysis shows that these religious variables combine to explain about one-fourth of the variance in support for legal abortion, and thus provide a far better explanation than demographic factors.[5] The denominational differences shown in Table 8-3 are statistically significant, with fundamentalists, pentecostals, evangelicals, and Catholics less supportive than mainline Protestants, and Jews more supportive. Holding denomination constant, strength of attachment to one's denomination is a predictor of abortion attitudes, so that those who are more strongly attached are less supportive of legal abortion. Although the denomina-

Table 8-3 Mean Support for Legal Abortion by Religious Variables

	Mean Support
Religious identification	
Catholic	3.8
Protestant	4.0
Fundamentalist	3.1
Pentecostal	2.5
Evangelical	3.6
Mainline	4.4
No religion	5.0
Jewish	5.6
Frequency of church attendance	
Never	4.9
Less than once per year	4.6
Once or twice per year	4.7
Several times per year	4.5
Once per month	4.3
2–3 times per month	4.1
Nearly every week	3.5
Every week	3.2
Several times per week	2.2
Religious attachment	
Strong	4.1
Somewhat strong	4.6
Not strong	5.0
View of Bible	
Literal word of God	3.1
Inspired word of God	4.2
Ancient book	5.1
Born again	
No	4.5
Yes	3.3

Source: 1989–1994 General Social Surveys.

Notes: Entries are the average number of circumstances respondent would allow abortion out of six possible. All entries are statistically significant at the .01 level.

tional variables are significant predictors of support for legal abortion in the multivariate analysis, they do not predict as well as view of the Bible and frequency of church attendance. These two variables are much stronger predictors of abortion attitudes than denomination. Thus, among whites it is not so much which church a person belongs to as how often the person attends and how literally the person interprets the Bible that predict attitudes toward abortion.

Among blacks, denominational differences are not a significant predictor of abortion attitudes, although frequency of church attendance and view of the Bible are important sources of attitudes. Black churches in different religious traditions frequently preach the same mix of social gospel and charismatic doctrine, thus muting the effects of denomination.

Sources of Attitudes Toward Legal Abortion

Demographic and religious characteristics are useful predictors of abortion attitudes, but it is also likely that they are a source of other types of attitudes that in turn influence abortion attitudes. It seems especially likely that attitudes on feminism, sexual morality, and the sanctity of life will be sources of beliefs about abortion.

Abortion rights have been on the feminist agenda almost since the inception of the modern feminist movement in the 1960s. Many national feminist organizations have made abortion rights their central issue for the 1990s, and some feminists and academics have even defined feminism as support for legal abortion. Luker (1984) found that among activists in the prolife and prochoice movements, one of the biggest differences was in their views of sex roles: prolife activists held far more traditional views of the appropriate roles for men and women than prochoice activists did.

The General Social Survey includes a number of questions that measure attitudes toward women's roles, and these items have been combined to form two distinct indexes. The first measures "public feminism"—support for women's participation in public life. Respondents were asked to agree or disagree with two statements:

1. Women should take care of running their homes and leave running the country up to men.
2. Most men are better suited emotionally for politics than are most women.

The second index measures sex role attitudes on "private feminism," and focuses more on sex roles in the family. Respondents were asked whether they strongly agreed, agreed, disagreed, or strongly disagreed with the following statements:

1. A working mother can establish just as warm and secure a relationship with her children as a mother who does not work.

Table 8-4 Mean Support for Legal Abortion by Sex Role Attitudes

	Mean Support
Public feminism	
Low	3.1
Medium	3.8
High	4.2
Private feminism	
Low	3.6
Medium	3.8
High	4.3

Source: 1989–1994 General Social Surveys.

Notes: Entries are the average number of circumstances respondent would allow abortion out of six possible. All entries are statistically significant at the .01 level.

2. A preschool child is likely to suffer if his or her mother works.
3. It is much better for everyone involved if the man is the achiever outside the home and the woman takes care of the home and family.

As Table 8-4 shows, both public and private feminism are related to attitudes toward abortion, with those who are more feminist in their views exhibiting more support for legal abortion. Note also, however, that those who are low on the feminism indexes are not strongly prolife; they support legal abortion in about three circumstances on average. In fact, those who score low on the feminism indexes are more likely to take a strict prochoice position (support abortion in all six circumstances) than to take a strict prolife position (oppose abortion in all six circumstances). In the post-*Webster* period, 18 percent of those who scored low on public feminism and 13 percent of those who scored low on private feminism took an extreme prolife position, compared with 24 percent and 33 percent, respectively, who took an extreme prochoice position.

Similarly, those who score high on these indexes of feminism are not universally prochoice: they oppose abortion in almost two circumstances on average. Nonetheless, feminists are more supportive of abortion rights than nonfeminists. Only about 5 percent of those who scored high on each index of feminism took an extreme prolife position on abortion. Nearly one-half who scored high on each index took an extreme prochoice position.

Despite these differences, public and private feminism are not strong predictors of support for abortion. The two indexes together explain 4 percent of the variance in support for abortion in the 1989 to 1994 period, and private feminism was a slightly stronger predictor

Table 8-5 Mean Support for Legal Abortion by Attitudes Toward Sexual Morality

	Mean Support
Premarital sex	
Always wrong	2.6
Almost always wrong	3.5
Wrong only sometimes	4.3
Not wrong at all	4.8
Teenage sex	
Always wrong	3.6
Almost always wrong	4.8
Wrong only sometimes	5.0
Not wrong at all	4.6
Homosexual relations	
Always wrong	3.6
Almost always wrong	4.6
Wrong only sometimes	4.9
Not wrong at all	5.2

Source: 1989–1994 General Social Surveys.

Notes: Entries are the average number of circumstances respondent would allow abortion out of six possible. All entries are statistically significant at the .01 level.

than public feminism. Thus, while attitudes toward sex roles and attitudes toward abortion are related, they are by no means one and the same, and sex role attitudes do not predict support for abortion nearly as well as religious variables.[6]

Attitudes toward sexual morality have also been found to be related to abortion attitudes. In the eyes of many Americans, abortion is an "easy" solution to pregnancies that result from sexual promiscuity, and they oppose abortion as part of a more general conservatism on matters of sexual morality. Table 8-5 shows mean support for abortion by attitudes toward sexual morality. The General Social Survey included questions asking whether sexual relations between a man and a woman before marriage, between unmarried teenagers aged fourteen to sixteen, and between two adults of the same sex were wrong. As Table 8-5 demonstrates, those with more conventional values on sexual morality are less supportive of legal abortion. On each of the three items, those who indicated that such relations are always wrong were the least supportive of legal abortion.

When we compare those who indicated that sexual relations under each of these three circumstances were always wrong with those who indicated that these acts were not wrong at all, we see large differences (not shown in table). Among those who were highest in conventional sexual morality, 13 percent took an extreme prolife position and 26 percent took an extreme prochoice position. Conversely, among those who were lowest in conventional sexual morality, only 4 percent took an extreme prolife position and 76 percent took an extreme prochoice position. These three measures of conventional sexual morality together explain about one-fourth of the variance in support for legal abortion in the 1989 to 1994 period. Attitude toward premarital sex between a man and a woman is the strongest predictor.

The last set of attitudes to be examined consists of attitudes toward life-and-death issues. Specifically, we will look at attitudes toward suicide for people with an incurable disease and toward capital punishment. Two questions were asked about suicide:

1. When a person has a disease that cannot be cured, do you think doctors should be allowed by law to end the patient's life by some painless means if the patient and his family request it?
2. Do you think a person has a right to end his or her own life if this person has an incurable disease?

The issues of suicide for those with an incurable disease and capital punishment do not initially appear to have much in common. Yet when people argue about these issues, they often make claims about the sanctity of human life, the question of whether life is worth living, and whether humans or God should decide who shall live and die, much as many opponents of abortion invoke the sanctity of unborn life.[7]

As Table 8-6 confirms, those who favor allowing suicide for people with an incurable disease, whether doctor assisted or by their own hand, are more supportive of legal abortion. Those who are opposed to suicide for someone with an incurable disease would allow abortions for most of the traumatic reasons, but not for the elective reasons. Those who favor allowing suicide for someone with an incurable disease would allow abortions for all of the traumatic and some of the elective reasons as well. Among those who would allow neither type of suicide under consideration, one-fourth take an extreme prolife position and only 13 percent take an extreme prochoice position. Among those who would allow both types of suicide, only 2 percent take an extreme prolife position and a majority, 58 percent, take an extreme prochoice position. An index created from the two suicide items explains about one-fourth of the variance in support for legal abortion.

Position on capital punishment is not significantly associated with support for legal abortion, despite the connection between these issues made in Catholic "seamless garment" theology. Those who favor capital punishment are only slightly more supportive of legal abortion than those who oppose it. Similar percentages of supporters and opponents of capital punishment take an extreme prolife position, and similar percentages take an extreme prochoice position.

Table 8-6 Mean Support for Legal Abortion by Attitude Toward Suicide for Someone with an Incurable Disease

	Mean Support
Doctor-assisted	
Yes	4.6
No	2.6
Self	
Yes	4.8
No	2.8

Source: 1989–1994 General Social Surveys.

Notes: Entries are the average number of circumstances respondent would allow abortion out of six possible. All entries are statistically significant at the .01 level.

Multivariate Model of Abortion Attitudes

It is not surprising that many of the sets of variables discussed above are interrelated. For example, those with the highest levels of education are the least likely to hold orthodox religious views and the most likely to take liberal positions on issues of sexual morality. A multivariate regression equation was therefore estimated to help sort out the independent impact of each of these variables. For the final multivariate analysis, support for abortion is regressed on all of the items from each set which were statistically significant in earlier equations.

The demographic variables sex, race, region of residence at age sixteen, and education are included. The religious variables include: conservative Protestant (fundamentalist, pentecostal, or evangelical), Catholic, Jewish, strength of attachment to denomination, frequency of church attendance, and view of the Bible. An index of sexual morality, the two feminism indexes, and the suicide index are included. Table 8-7 shows the results of this analysis. The fourteen independent variables together explain 39 percent of the variance in support for abortion. If we compare the standardized regression coefficients we can determine the relative importance of each independent variable in predicting support for legal abortion.

The most important independent variable is the index of attitudes toward suicide for someone with an incurable disease, and the next most important variable is the index of sexual morality. Thus, the most important sources of opposition to legal abortion in the 1990s appear to be beliefs about the sanctity of human life and the desire to curb nonmarital sexual behavior.

Table 8-7 Regression Analysis Explaining Support for Legal Abortion

	Unstandardized Regression Coefficients	Standardized Regression Coefficients
Demographic variables		
Sex	.06*	.02
Race	.37	.06
Southern residence at age 16	.02	.00
Education	.06*	.09
Religious variables		
Conservative Protestant	−.22**	−.04
Catholic	−.41*	−.09
Jewish	.35	.02
Strong attachment	−.03**	−.05
Frequency of church attendance	−.10*	−.14
View of Bible	.22*	.08
Attitudes		
Sexual morality	−.50*	−.20
Private feminism	.06	.01
Public feminism	.17	.03
Suicide for incurable disease	1.54*	.32
Constant	4.39*	
R^2	.39	

Source: 1989–1994 General Social Science Surveys.

Notes: Conservative Protestants included fundamentalists, evangelicals, and pentecostals. N = 2,283.

* Statistically significant at the .01 level.
** Statistically significant at the .05 level.

Neither of the feminism indexes is a statistically significant predictor in the equation. Once other factors are controlled, the weak relationship initially observed disappears. Despite the strong prochoice position of most feminist organizations, feminism as measured here is not a significant predictor of abortion attitudes in the mass public once other factors are controlled.

Religious factors also are significant predictors of attitudes. Catholics and conservative Protestants are significantly less supportive than mainline Protestants, and frequency of church attendance, strength of religious attachment, and view of the Bible are also important sources of attitudes. Jews are not significantly different from mainline Protestants in the equation.

Finally, of the four demographic variables—sex, race, region of residence at age sixteen, and education—only race and education are significant predictors of abortion attitudes. Although in bivariate analysis blacks were slightly less supportive of legal abortion than whites, once the other factors are held constant, as in this equation, whites are less supportive than blacks. That is, once we take into account that whites are less religious and have more formal education than blacks, for example, we find that whites are less likely to support legal abortion than we would expect based on the patterns of blacks.

Conclusion

Abortion attitudes are primarily explained by attitudes toward the sanctity of life and sexual morality, and by religious affiliations, beliefs, and behaviors. This finding is not surprising; the same pattern occurred in the 1970s and the 1980s as well as the 1990s. Indeed, the only change in the sources of abortion attitudes during this period is the reversal of the racial gap as older, prolife black cohorts are replaced by younger, more prochoice ones. Thus the sources of public opinion have been fairly constant over time.

The distribution of abortion attitudes has remained fairly stable as well. In the immediate aftermath of *Roe,* public support for legal abortion increased somewhat. During the Reagan administration in the 1980s, support declined, only to increase again around the time of the *Webster* decision. Yet these changes have been quite minor: from 1972 to 1994 respondents approved of abortion in just over four of the six circumstances listed in the GSS.

If the sources and distribution of attitudes have remained constant, why have the politics of the issue changed so dramatically over this period? In 1973, *Roe* seemed to signal the ultimate victory of the prochoice forces. By 1981, a prolife Republican president seemed bent on replacing liberal justices with those who shared his abortion views, and the Republican Party had firmly embraced the prolife position in its platform. By 1992, it was evident that prolife Republicans were scrambling to stake more moderate positions, and in 1996, the abortion issue would remain divisive for the GOP.

Quite simply, the changing politics of abortion demonstrates the importance of political institutions in translating opinion into policy. The *Roe* decision effectively removed abortion from the control of elected officials and mobilized prolife forces. Republican candidates felt free to stake rather extreme prolife positions, for prochoice voters were unlikely to vote the abortion issue while they felt that abortion rights were protected by the Court. When *Webster* gave the states additional authority to regulate abortion and made it evident that the accumulation of new Republican appointments had nearly created a prolife majority on the Court, the prochoice side mobilized and began to vote on the issue. Although prochoice voters remain less likely than prolife voters to base a vote solely on abortion, there are many more prochoice than prolife citizens. A strong prolife position became a difficult one to defend in a close election. Of course, since most Americans favor some restrictions on abortion, a rigid prochoice position would also be a liability for a candidate.

In the 1990s, both the prolife and the prochoice forces are mobilized, and their interest groups are well funded and have many volunteers. It seems likely that abortion will continue to play a major role in the political debate for some time to come.

Notes

1. Overturning *Roe* would not automatically make abortion illegal. Instead, it would allow states to regulate abortion. States could choose to guarantee access to abortion, enact restrictions on abortion, or make it illegal. Undoubtedly, each of these options would be exercised by one state or another.

2. Note that the distinction between these two types of reasons for abortion is based on statistical analysis. In addition to the difference in the percentage of the public supporting abortion for various reasons, factor analysis confirms that these are two distinct dimensions.

3. Many of the differences observed by Luker, who studied activists in California, also were observed by Granberg, who studied activists in Missouri (Granberg 1982a, 1982b).

4. In fact, the Bible does not specifically proscribe abortion and biblical references cited in opposition to abortion are subject to interpretation. See Cook, Jelen, and Wilcox (1992), 98–100.

5. Data from the 1989 to 1994 studies were included in this analysis. The measure of support for abortion was the dependent variable. Independent variables in multiple regression included a dummy measure for fundamentalist or pentecostal or evangelical denomination, a dummy variable for Catholic, a dummy variable for Jewish, a dummy variable for no religion (mainline Protestant was the excluded category), a three-point item measuring strength of attachment to one's denomination, a measure of frequency of church attendance, and a measure of view of the Bible. The born-again item was not included because it was asked in only one year. There were 2,056 cases in the equation, and the R-squared was .25. All variables were significant predictors of abortion attitudes except no religion.

6. The comparison of variance explained is not entirely fair, in that there were more measures of religious characteristics included in that equation than there were measures of sex role attitudes included in the current equation. However, at the bivariate level each religious variable was more strongly associated with attitude toward abortion than each index of feminism.

7. Interestingly, these two issues are more strongly associated with one another among Catholics than among non-Catholics. This makes sense because of the Catholic doctrine of the "seamless garment" of life-and-death issues. Official Catholic doctrine is opposed to suicide, capital punishment, and abortion. However, while attitudes toward suicide and toward capital punishment are more closely associated among Catholics than among non-Catholics, they are not better predictors of abortion attitudes for Catholics than for non-Catholics. Separate regression equations for Catholics and non-Catholics using an index of suicide for those with an incurable disease and position on capital punishment to predict support for legal abortion look remarkably similar, and the variance explained also is similar for the two groups.

9 Public Opinion and Foreign Policy: How Does the Public Think About America's Role in the World?

Barbara Bardes

The Persian Gulf War of 1991 was a thoroughly modern military event. It was the first military conflict to begin "live" on cable television, with Cable News Network (CNN) correspondent Bernard Shaw reporting from a hotel in Baghdad, Iraq. As the first post–cold war military engagement, the Gulf War provided a public showcase for testing the newest and best in American weaponry, including the Stealth class of aircraft and all of the computer-directed bombs and artillery. Operation Desert Storm gave President George Bush an unexpected opportunity to almost rescue his flagging presidency by demonstrating his leadership in the international community while also demonstrating that a multilateral force could be assembled to stop aggression. Finally, the made-for-TV war provided an unparalleled opportunity for pollsters to track public opinion about the wisdom of marshaling the troops and, in the end, of engaging in combat. No definitive count exists of the number of polls taken between August 1990 and June 1991 focusing on the Persian Gulf situation, but the number was certainly in the hundreds.

The Persian Gulf War can be seen as a relatively unimportant military action that was very successful in attaining its primary objective—the defeat of the Iraqi forces and their removal from the nation of Kuwait. Certainly, the conflict did little in the long run for George Bush, who was defeated eighteen months later despite the enormous popularity of his decisions in the Gulf situation. Why, then, was so much scholarly and media attention paid to the attitudes of the American public in this circumstance? One way to explain the excess of polling that went on is to note again that this war was a media event. The media wanted to acquire data on how the public viewed the possibility of war as much as they wanted to gather information on the buildup of armaments and difficulties of putting American troops into Saudi Arabia. Both the weaponry and the polls made good news stories.

Another reason for this extensive polling effort was the renewed interest in the impact of public opinion on U.S. foreign policy since the Vietnam War era. Although, as we shall see, the need to build public support for military action is not a new idea, the Vietnam conflict brought home to politicians and the media that the American public, if not supportive of the efforts of its political leaders, can deal out political punishment as easily as it can provide support. In this chapter, we will look more closely at the increasing attention paid to public opinion on foreign policy issues and how that attention is linked to the polling data available. We will see that the availability of data and the historical context in which they are collected both affect our theories about how people think about these issues.

Public Opinion and Foreign Policy: The Linkage of Consent

At the core of democratic theory is the presumption that public policy should reflect the desires of the citizens, either as expressed directly or as interpreted by formally designated representatives of the voters. Although it is never easy to translate the desires of the electorate into public policy, the arena of foreign policy is especially problematic. Rarely can a foreign policy issue under debate be decided by a simple vote of the legislature. Foreign policy encompasses a wide range of policy decisions and postures, including the nation's overall foreign policy stance, negotiations about delicate matters of trade and immigration, and the arcane matters of daily diplomacy. Foreign policy decisions often depend on detailed intelligence reports gathered from overt and covert sources.

The need for secrecy, speed, and high-level judgment in foreign policy is so great that many commentators have suggested that the public should not play an important role in foreign policy decision making. During the 1920s, the journalist Walter Lippmann was one of the first to carefully articulate the reasons why the opinions of the public should not play an important part in deciding matters of international import. Lippmann (1922, 1956) portrayed the electorate as too enmeshed in its own parochial interests to be able to pay attention to the details of international affairs and certainly too influenced by emotion to be able to make reasoned judgments on these complex matters. Lippmann's pessimism about the public was shared by many members of the realist school of foreign policy, including Hans Morgenthau (1978, 558), who felt that the public was too likely to be swayed by emotion, thus jeopardizing the stability needed to conduct effective foreign policy.

The framers of the Constitution were not entirely clear about their intentions. In a few brief phrases, they vested certain important diplomatic powers in the office of the chief executive: the power to recognize foreign nations and to negotiate treaties. These grants of executive power underline the framers' understanding of the need for a single voice for the nation in international affairs. In addition, the Constitution gives the power to command the armed forces to the chief executive. In light of the miserably weak military capacity of the United States in the early years as well as the clear national desire to avoid entanglements in European politics, it is possible that the framers did not believe that the chief executive would garner much power from these constitutional powers. However, the framers were creating a "balanced" government, one that could operate effectively in the face of varied conditions yet would rest on the consent of the people. Their techniques for keeping the chief executive under democratic control included congressional control over the budget, senatorial ratification of treaties, and most important, the congressional prerogative in declaring war. These checks make it clear that the framers expected the president and Congress to be responsive to the public will in foreign affairs.

Many times throughout American history presidents or Congresses have sought to build public support for their military actions, beginning with James Madison's failures during the War of 1812. The American psyche carries the image of the Alamo, a historic battle waged in part to increase American support for the war against Mexico in 1848. The Spanish-American War in 1898 was also a creation of Congress. One of the major campaign issues in 1916 was the U.S. role in World War I, followed by President Woodrow Wilson's unsuccessful attempt to build public support to convince the Senate to ratify the League of Nations treaty.

We can examine the efforts of President Franklin D. Roosevelt in the 1930s to convince the American public of the need to oppose the Nazi threat, using two sources of data: the historical record and the results of the fledgling public opinion enterprise. As explained by Benjamin Page and Robert Shapiro (1992), the president and his administration moved very cautiously in the period between 1936 and 1941 to lead voters to support American involvement in World War II. Early polling data from Gallup in the late 1930s showed large majorities opposed to entering another European conflict, yet polling also revealed support for increased spending on the U.S. military. As German aggression increased, the public still opposed war, but in 1940 and 1941, "large majorities of about 70%-75% told Gallup and OPOR [Office of Public Opinion Research] that the United States should 'do everything possible' to help England (and, in the case of Gallup, France) 'except go to war'" (Page and Shapiro 1992, 185).

During the election year of 1940, Roosevelt continued his cautious but steady leadership of public opinion in support of England and France. Page and Shapiro, while criticizing FDR for manipulating opinion by withholding information, evaluate his actions as extremely effective. They conclude that "Roosevelt showed great skill . . . at interpreting foreign policy polls and at tailoring his political strategy and his messages accordingly" (Page and Shapiro 1992, 192). Roosevelt never got too far ahead of opinion but used other leaders and groups to initiate publicity in favor of military involvement.

In *The Rational Public* (1992), Page and Shapiro carefully document the interaction between presidential leadership, media coverage of events, and the changes in public opinion on foreign policy issues from the 1930s through the 1980s. Their work casts doubt on the conclusions of those who see the public as ignorant and uninterested in world affairs and supports the view of a public that holds mostly stable and reasonable views about all public issues.

There are, however, many other schools of thought about how the public views America's role in the world and other foreign policy questions. Gabriel Almond (1950) and, later, Frank Klingberg (1983) have suggested that Americans exhibit "mood swings" toward the nation's role in world affairs. John Mueller (1973, 1994) has focused on the public's support for the use of force and the correlation of support for the use of force with support for the president as commander in chief. Other scholars have investigated the public's understanding of foreign policy issues in terms of psychological traits, predispositions, information frameworks and cognitive processing, and media influence.

Our understanding of the formation and dynamics of public opinion on foreign policy issues is still evolving, and it lags far behind our understanding of the influences on public opinion on domestic issues. There are a number of factors that account for the difference in the development of the two fields. Perhaps the most important factor is that domestic political issues and the corresponding sources of public support have been structured along the same social and economic cleavages for many generations: the distribution of opportunity and wealth among classes of Americans continues to dominate political debate. Other dimensions with historic roots include the role of government in American life, the role of religion in public life, and the definition of the private sphere. Although our understanding of the components of liberalism and conservatism (and some other minority positions) is continually being refined through more sophisticated scholarship and research, the basic questions about the distribution of rights and resources have defined the parameters of research, especially research that uses public opinion data.

The only issue that seems to have a historical base in the study of public opinion on foreign policy issues is the question of whether the United States should play an active role outside of its own borders or focus solely on domestic issues. Washington's farewell address, which warned the nation of "foreign entanglements," set the stage for a continuing debate over America's role in the world. As we shall see, the field of scholarship and, perhaps, political understanding of this public opinion arena have been greatly influenced by three factors: the events and dynamics of affairs among nations, the historical and political interpretation of those events, and the availability and methodology of public opinion polling during a particular time period. What follows is an examination of three periods of scholarship on public opinion and foreign policy: the post–World War II consensus era, the post-Vietnam destruction of consensus, and the post–cold war struggle for a new consensus. In each time period, we can look at the relationship between the external factors that constructed U.S. policies, at the types of polling data that became available, and at the changes in our understanding of public opinion that came through new scholarship.

The Internationalist Consensus

As the United States approached the end of World War II and the allied leaders began to discuss the creation of another world security organization, political leaders and commentators feared that the American public would oppose such an organization with the vehemence with which it had opposed the League of Nations. True, Franklin Roosevelt had carefully led the public to support the United States' entry into the war and had maintained that support to the end of his life. However, the commitment of the American public to an era of international involvement seemed doubtful in light of the events that had followed World War I.

While diplomats and politicians framed the United Nations Charter and laid the groundwork for a new international order, scholars turned their attention to understanding the American public. In a most influential work, Gabriel Almond pictured the American public as basically uninformed about foreign policy and fairly indifferent to international events. According to Almond's "mood theory," the public reacts to crises and threats from other nations but does not hold stable, consistent views on international issues. Instead, public opinion shifts from internationalism to isolationism under the influence of events, exhibiting a "mood, a superficial and fluctuating response" (Almond 1950, 53, 73, 76). Almond's analysis of the formation of public opinion on foreign policy issues complemented the doubts of Walter Lippmann on the potential usefulness of public involvement in foreign policy decision making. Other analysts of public opinion on foreign policy also have found patterns in public behavior that support mood swing theories (Holmes 1985; Klingberg 1983).

There can be little doubt that polling data available by the 1950s contributed to these interpretations of the public's inconstancy of opinion. Within the first twenty years of public opinion polling, Gallup and others documented the extreme reluctance of the American public to enter the second European war, the buildup of support for American military intervention in Europe, and then, after the war, strong support for taking a position of world leadership. The first election polls, conducted in 1944 and 1948, provided a portrait of a public that was fairly ignorant of political issues, inconsistent in its domestic policy preferences, and unduly influenced by group identities. Given these types of data and the scholarship that reported them, it is not surprising that few writers placed great faith in the public's view of foreign policy issues.

Out of this postwar analysis came two important developments for the study of the public's views: first, Gallup developed a survey question that has become the standard measurement of public support for international involvement, and second, that question, together with the "mood theory" of public opinion, constructed a one-dimensional scheme for understanding public opinion on foreign policy issues.

The Gallup survey question, "Do you think it would be best for the future of this country if we take an active part in world affairs or if we stay out of world affairs?" has been asked almost continuously since 1943 by Gallup, by the National Opinion Research Center, in media polls, or, in some form, by the American National Election Study. Often the question has been embedded within a political or social survey that asks almost no other questions on foreign affairs. Analysis of the public's views on this issue domain was thus constrained to a dichotomous choice usually interpreted as isolationist or internationalist.

Not only did this become the single measurement of the public's views but, over the years, any fluctuation in the public's support for an internationalist foreign policy was said to have signaled the beginning of a "mood" change and the potential reassertion of America's isolationist tradition. During the post–Vietnam War debate over the future foreign policy direction of the United States, the decline in the proportion of Americans who agreed to an "active role" for the nation to 61 percent in 1975 suggested to many that the United States was entering a dangerously isolationist period.

Fortunately, the same data can be read in another way. After analyzing this question and many others from the 1940s to the present, Shapiro and Page render a quite opposite conclusion: "The notion of a capricious public is a myth" (1988, 213). They view the public as at least reasonable or sensible on foreign policy issues and provide considerable data to support their conclusion. Indeed, results of the isolationist/internationalist question itself, when viewed over more than forty years, suggest that the public's views on this single measure are quite consistent. As shown in Table 9-1, the proportion of the American public that has supported an active role for the United States in the world has ranged from 79 percent at the very beginning of the Vietnam conflict in 1965 to lows of 61 percent in 1975 and in 1982. Never has that support fallen below 60 percent in the history of the question. It is amusing to compare the stability of these responses with the extreme instability of presidential approval ratings, which, in the case of George Bush, fluctuated about 40 points in one short year.

The Vietnam Difference

The Vietnam War forever changed the way presidents and political leaders consider the use of American troops abroad. The growth of the opposition to the war and its ultimate impact—forcing Lyndon B. Johnson to drop his bid for reelection to the presidency—changed the way that the public was regarded as well. Americans came to believe that U.S. efforts in Southeast Asia were clearly a mistake and to strongly prefer U.S. withdrawal from the conflict. Public opinion polls during the Vietnam era tracked the evolution of public views while underlining the complexity of public opinion on the war.

Public Opinion During the War

During the Vietnam conflict, public opinion followed a completely different path than it had in World War II. Recall that President Roosevelt very carefully built support for the American efforts on behalf of the allies before the attack on Pearl Harbor. By the time he sought a declaration of war on Germany and Japan, the American public was strongly supportive of having the United States enter the war.

Table 9-1 U.S. Role in the World, 1943–1991 (in Percentages)

Question: Do you think it will be best for the future of this country if we take an active part in world affairs, or if we stay out of world affairs?

Year	Take Active Role	Stay Out
1943	76	14
1944	73	18
1945	71	19
1946	78	19
1947	66	26
1948	67	25
1950	66	25
1952	68	23
1953	71	21
1954	69	25
1955	72	21
1956	71	25
1965	79	16
1973	66	31
1975	61	36
1976	63	32
1978	64	32
1982	61	34
1983	65	31
1984	65	32
1985	70	27
1986	65	32
1988	65	32
1989	68	28
1990	69	27
1991	73	24

Source: Adapted from "Sensible Internationalism," *Public Perspective,* March/April 1993, 95. Reprinted with permission of the Roper Center.

Notes: The question was asked from 1947 to 1991 by the National Opinion Research Center; Gallup used different wordings during World War II (1943–1946 data). Percentages for each year do not add to 100 due to "not sure" or "don't know" responses. The question was not asked every year.

Table 9-2 Percent Approving and Disapproving of the Vietnam Conflict

Question: In view of the developments since we entered the fighting in Vietnam, do you think the United States made a mistake sending troops to fight in Vietnam?

Date	Made Mistake (%)	Did Not Make Mistake (%)
September 1965	24	60
November 1966	31	52
December 1967	45	46
October 1968	54	37
September 1969	58	32
May 1970	56	36
May 1971	61	28
January 1973	60	29

Source: "Vietnam," *Public Perspective*, March/April 1993, 101.

Note: The question was asked from 1965 to 1973 by Gallup. Percentages for each date do not add to 100 due to "not sure" or "don't know" responses.

As shown in Table 9-1, in 1965, 79 percent of the American people believed the United States should play an active part in the world. After the 1964 Gulf of Tonkin incident, Americans supported the introduction of U.S. military forces in South Vietnam, and in 1965 they supported the bombing of North Vietnam to hasten the end of the conflict. As Table 9-2 reveals, only one-quarter of Americans thought the initial commitment of U.S. troops to Vietnam was a mistake. Only after the Tet offensive in 1968 did a majority of Americans begin to express the view that American involvement in Vietnam was a mistake. Not until 1970 did polls show that Americans believed that the U.S. should withdraw its troops regardless of the consequences to South Vietnam (Levering 1978, 130).

Public views toward American involvement in Southeast Asia were always more complicated than it appears from the retrospective judgment that the war was a mistake. Cleavages over the war existed within almost every generation and within social classes and political parties. Levering interpreted the situation in this way: "Large segments of the public maintained contradictory goals: a strong desire for peace combined with unwillingness to accept an American defeat . . . or a wish to support the President in wartime combined with distrust of his credibility" (1978, 128).

The New Meaning of Public Opinion to Foreign Policy

In the decade following the end of the Vietnam conflict, scholars and political leaders puzzled over how Americans had come to understand the war and what that understanding meant for the future of American foreign policy. As a consequence, research institutions, the media, and polling organizations became far more interested in public opinion on foreign policy issues. If public opinion about Vietnam could topple a sitting president with an extraordinary record of domestic policy leadership, how would public opinion constrain presidents in the future? The Chicago Council on Foreign Relations began a series of national polls on foreign policy issues in 1974, while others focused on foreign policy elites or on more specialized issues. The availability of comprehensive surveys, essentially created to understand the public's view of America's future role in the world, stimulated scholars to consider new models of public opinion, models that replaced the old isolationist/internationalist continuum.

Public opinion had become important to the nation's foreign policy. Post-Vietnam studies focused attention on the citizen or on elite decision makers in an attempt to discover how individuals respond to foreign policy events, including presidential decisions, military actions, and other crises. Using the many sources of survey data that had become available, scholars began to explore how individuals process information about international affairs and how their belief systems or core values shape their attitudes on specific issues. For the most part, the characterization of Americans as either internationalist or isolationist was discredited. It is worth noting, however, that the historic "active role" question continues to be asked, even within some of the most prestigious national studies.

New Patterns of Public Support for Military Intervention

The complexity of the public's response to the Vietnam War led scholars to propose a number of schemes for understanding how people form attitudes about foreign policy decisions and events. John Mueller (1973), who was intrigued by the pattern of responses to the Vietnam conflict, added the first new understanding of public opinion through his study of the rise and decline of American support for the Vietnam War. Mueller found that public support for the war was high in its early years but fell precipitously after the Tet offensive. After studying the events of the war itself and noting the rising cost of the war in American lives, he posited the "rally-round-the-flag effect" to explain the early public support for the country's military adventures. In addition to the Vietnam conflict, Mueller studied the Korean conflict and other military actions; he found that American support rallied at the beginning of each action due to innate patriotism and support for the presidential decision to use force and then declined as the number of American casualties rose.

Since Mueller's study, the pattern has continued: presidential approval ratings generally rise quickly after the initial use of military force and then return to a lower level at the conclusion of the crisis or as the intervention continues. Perhaps the most extraordinary illustration of this phenomenon occurred during the Persian Gulf War when, at the time of the military engagement, President Bush's approval ratings climbed to a post–World War II high and then a year later fell to exactly where they had been before the conflict.

Another approach to studying public opinion on foreign policy was greatly influenced by new insights into how people process information. Scholars in many different fields, including psychology and information sciences, suggest that most individuals are bombarded by far more information and stimulation than they can possibly react to. To conserve energy and to be able to make day-to-day decisions, people behave as "cognitive misers." Thus, they form opinions only when necessary. Once they have developed a predisposition toward something (a political party, another nation, or any other object or concept), they use that predisposition and its associated information as a kind of mental file folder or schema. When they receive new information about something or are asked to react to a survey question about a topic, people are likely to use the previously stored information and predisposition to create a response. Only when they are confronted with striking new information or experience a change in the emotional content of the schema are they likely to change their basic pattern of responses.

New Questions, New Models

After the Vietnam era, most students of public opinion on foreign policy began to search for the mental conditions, predispositions, underlying principles, or other mental attributes that people rely on to form attitudes toward international affairs. Mark Peffley and Jon Hurwitz (1992) proposed that people hold certain "core values," including patriotism and traditional morality, that "structure" the attitudes and responses of individuals toward foreign policy events. They also investigated the impact that images of foreign nations have on the shaping of opinions. In a series of studies, Peffley and Hurwitz first found that negative images of the Soviet Union as an enemy nation constrained or structured people's attitudes toward a number of foreign policy issues. After the Soviet Union under Gorbachev and the United States concluded a series of agreements that would lead to a reduction in nuclear arms and a lowering of tension between the two superpowers, Peffley and Hurwitz looked at the possibility that a changing image of the Soviet Union could change the mental constructs that Americans used to evaluate foreign policy events. As they suggest, "Once a person becomes convinced that the Soviet Union is not the menace of yesteryear, he or she may also question the wisdom of a more militant foreign policy designed to counter the Soviet threat" (1992, 439). Their research, drawn from a panel study of citizens polled in 1987 and 1988, showed that opinions do shift and that those shifting opinions were based in revised appraisals of the Soviet Union. The work of Peffley and Hurwitz provides strong support for the existence of dynamic mental constructs that influence foreign policy opinions. There are, however, other ways to think about those constructs.

Using data from the first general foreign policy survey sponsored by the Chicago Council on Foreign Relations, Barbara Bardes and Robert Oldendick (1978) investigated the possibility that the mass public responded to foreign policy events on the basis of policy arenas or policy dimensions. Their analysis of the multitude of foreign policy questions included in the 1974 Chicago Council survey produced five dimensions or continua that captured the structures underlying the questions. For example, on the militarism dimension opinions could be arrayed on a continuum from opposing military force to strong support for using military action to solve world problems. Their research suggested that an individual responds to a foreign policy issue first in terms of the arena or dimension that it relates to and second in terms of his or her predisposition or position along that dimension. Subsequent analyses of the 1978 and 1982 Chicago Council surveys showed that the most predominant dimensions—internationalism and militarism—were stable in meaning, while other, less powerful dimensions, such as the role of the United States in solving world problems and support for foreign aid, showed some changes in response to world events and political leadership.

It is worth repeating that both the availability of survey data and the impact of world events shape our understanding of how members of the public formulate opinions on foreign policy issues. By the mid-1980s, the Chicago Council had conducted and published data from three national surveys of the public and smaller surveys of elites. Media polls and other national survey organizations were tracking U.S. relations with the Soviet Union, the public's support or lack thereof for U.S. involvement in Nicaragua, views of committing U.S. troops in Grenada, and other Reagan initiatives. Thus, most scholarship came to focus on American opinion in a time that was dominated by the relationship between the United States and the Soviet Union.

In 1990, Eugene Wittkopf published the summary of his studies of foreign policy opinions in a book entitled *Faces of Internationalism: Public Opinion and American Foreign Policy*. Drawing on all of the Chicago Council data and looking carefully at other sources, Wittkopf and several colleagues developed a portrait of the American mass public that differed from that of Bardes and Oldendick (1978). Wittkopf believed that a two-dimensional scheme captures the basic predispositions of Americans toward U.S. involvement in world affairs. The two dimensions—militant internationalism and cooperative internationalism—structure the basic attitudes of Americans toward foreign policy. Militant internationalism is a dimension that measures the degree to which Americans support the use of military force to achieve American objectives in the world. Cooperative internationalism measures the degree to which Americans believe that the United States should engage in collaborative, nonmilitary action in the world. As Wittkopf puts it, "The dimensions themselves . . . demonstrate that a sin-

Figure 9-1   Model for Evaluating Foreign Policy Beliefs

Source: Adapted from Eugene R. Wittkopf, *Faces of Internationalism: Public Opinion and American Foreign Policy* (Durham, N.C.: Duke University Press, 1990), 49. Reprinted with permission.

gle internationalism-isolationism continuum of the sort characteristic of the presumed Cold War foreign policy consensus does not describe adequately the attitudes of the American public" (1990, 50). Wittkopf's dimensions make the point that Americans are concerned not only about whether the United States is involved in the world but also about how that action is implemented.

As shown in Figure 9-1, Wittkopf goes further with his analysis, using the two dimensions to define four types of foreign policy beliefs. He then used the Chicago Council data to estimate the percentage of the mass public that would fit into each of the types. The four types are characterized as follows: internationalists support an active role for the United States in the world, including both economic and military action to achieve the nation's goals; isolationists oppose any type of involvement whether peaceful or militaristic; accommodationists support peaceful or economic action by the United States but reject the use of force; and hardliners believe that unilateral military force is appropriate but other forms of involvement should be opposed (1990, 24).

Over the span of four surveys and more than a decade of research, Wittkopf finds very consistent proportions of the mass public to fall into each type. Internationalists number about 28.5 percent, accommodationists about 26 percent, hardliners about 23 percent, and isolationists about 22 percent (1990, 25). Thus about three-quarters of the public supports an

American role in the world and less than one-quarter could be counted as true isolationists. Wittkopf's consistent findings over the period from 1974 to 1990 led him to assert not only that the two-dimensional scheme is the best way to understand foreign policy attitudes but also that the scheme is extremely stable and does not change with events in the post-Vietnam era (1990, 50). As we shall see, the breakup of the Soviet Union and the end to the cold war raise new questions about how the public views war.

Changes Among Political Elites

Political elites (including political leaders, corporate executives, and church leaders) and citizens do not always think alike about foreign policy. But the Vietnam War divided American society at many levels. Researchers became interested not only in mass opinion but also in elite opinion. From the end of World War II until the Vietnam conflict, American elites seemed to be in agreement about the role the United States should play as a global leader. Within the halls of Congress, bipartisanship on foreign policy issues was the norm at least until the late 1950s. In general, bipartisanship and internationalism characterized the views of the economic and political elites of the nation. Then as the Vietnam War dragged on, elite opinion shattered over the wisdom of American intervention there and over the future role of the nation in world affairs.

The impact of the Vietnam era was the subject of a sustained research effort by Ole Holsti and James Rosenau (1984, 1986). After several extensive surveys of American elites, Holsti and Rosenau concluded that the Vietnam War did have a serious impact on how elites view the American role, but not along the generational lines they had expected. The cleavages were along ideological, partisan, and professional lines. William Chittick and Keith Billingsley's (1989) work, which builds on that of Wittkopf, also explores elite opinion. Although they agreed with the earlier researchers that there are identifiable dimensions of elite policy opinion, Chittick and Billingsley warned against developing a limited number of opinion types too quickly. Their work suggests that there are at least three distinct dimensions to elite thinking on foreign policy and that individuals may take polar or moderate positions on each of the three. They concluded that there is not much agreement among elites on foreign policy issues. As they note, "Even if individuals could agree on priorities to be given to these various goals, they might express strong differences over the means chosen to implement these goals in specific circumstances" (1989, 220).

The Growing Gender Gap

As scholars analyzed the new data made available during the 1970s and 1980s, another group of Americans came into focus as distinctive. The "gender gap," which had become evident among voters in the 1980 presidential election, was also evident in many surveys on foreign policy. As best described by Kathleen Frankovic (1982), women seemed to be more opposed to the use of force and to taking risks with the environment than men. Frankovic believed that women's aversion to the use of military force contributed to their greater support of Jimmy Carter in the 1980 election over the hawkish Ronald Reagan. The work of Robert Shapiro and Harpreet Mahajan (1986) demonstrates that the gender gap on the use of force, including opposing the death penalty and other forms of violence, goes back several decades, but the gender gap on foreign policy issues appears to be growing. Early studies of the Chicago Council surveys found little evidence that women held distinctive opinions about foreign policy. Since the 1970s the number of issues on which women are likely to hold different opinions has increased. The work of David Fite, Marc Genest, and Clyde Wilcox (1990) confirmed the persistence of the gender gap but did not find that it was linked to work force participation or other demographic differences between men and women. Further work by Elizabeth Adell Cook and Wilcox (1991) explored the link between the gender gap and feminist views but found only a weak linkage which works for both men and women. As Cook and Wilcox speculate, differences between men and women in political opinions, including foreign policy views, may be more linked to differences in how men and women reason politically than to other factors.

Public Opinion Since the Cold War

In 1989, the world watched with amazement as the Berlin Wall came down and the Soviet Union's hold over Eastern Europe relaxed. Since that time, most of the former Eastern bloc nations have become democracies in one form or another, the two Germanies have become one, and the Soviet Union itself has fragmented into separate republics, most of which have reconvened as a commonwealth. We watched a failed palace coup in the Russian capital, the downfall of Gorbachev, and the emergence of multiple political factions within the Russian parliament. Former enemies, the Soviet Union and the United States, are working to destroy their nuclear weapons and delivery systems. Meanwhile, South Africa has become a full democracy, electing Nelson Mandela as president, and the Middle East has seen the creation of Palestinian entity and real progress toward peace.

Where international change occurs, polls follow close behind. Pollsters have tracked opinion on all of the changes in the world situation mentioned here as well as in smaller "hot spots" throughout the world. Many questions are asked about particular situations, but there is no guiding framework to help polls get to the sources of people's opinions. Researchers would probably not be able to give pollsters a framework if they asked. The Wittkopf typology will no longer suffice: it is heavily dependent on survey questions about the Soviet Union as the enemy and about the need for the United States to maintain its position as a military superpower. All schemes for understanding public opinion that start with military internationalism are put in doubt by the evolution of a world that, depending on your viewpoint, has many militarily powerful nations, has one major power (the United States), is driven by economics, or is basically unstable and at the mercy of terrorist and outlaw regimes. The looming question for research is to find ways to measure change in the underlying premises of public opinion—if there is any—and to define, if possible, the cognitive structures that help people understand the new world order and shape public opinion.

Almost all students of public opinion on foreign policy agree that the isolationist-internationalist framework has been discredited. Most analysts view the cognitive world of the citizen as structured or ordered by major concepts such as internationalism, cooperative or unilateral action, use of military force, foreign aid, U.S. vital interests, or preservation of democracy. Whether these are numerous dimensions on which people hold opinions or whether these can be grouped into a two-dimensional scheme like Wittkopf's is debatable. The information-processing school of thought might suggest that looking for a specific list of dimensions is misguided: we should be trying to identify core principles and then look for beliefs related to those principles. Meanwhile, the citizenry and politicians are trying to absorb and understand at least some of the staggering amount of data coming in from around the world.

Several attempts have been made to sort out this situation. Ronald Hinckley (1994), starting from the Wittkopf (1990) typology, proposes that the major dimensions of public opinion will not change; in response to the changing world, Americans are becoming more supportive of "multilateral" solutions to world problems, more concerned about the impact of foreign policy on domestic issues (concern for jobs, the economy), and more aware of the importance of global environmental issues. As he states, "Foreign policy ends or goals appear more like domestic issues—single items with little coherent structure for public coalition from item to item" (1994, 11). Another longtime watcher of public opinion, Al Richman (1994), has observed Americans' struggle to define the nation's role in the world. He suggests that the United States is beginning to set out the "rules of military engagement" in the world, a refinement of the American internationalist tendency. Richman's analysis of poll data outlines key decision points that may influence American support for military intervention: the critical factors include the nature of the threat, the source and target of the threat, the means proposed to answer the threat, and the calculus of costs of the operation and its benefits. Richman portrays public opinion as situation-specific, influenced by many factors, and almost too complicated for political leaders to anticipate.

Yet Americans are able to make decisions about whether they support American policies and actions in the world. If we accept the consistent finding of Wittkopf that 75 percent or more of Americans believe that the United States should participate in the international community, we need to identify the influences and factors that come into play in the discrete policy situations that seem to be the norm in the post–cold war world. Bruce Jentleson (1992) was principally interested in the conditions that lead Americans to support the use of military force abroad. As he points out, knowing the degree of support among the public for broad general goals, such as protecting American vital interests, is not very helpful in predicting public support for action in the kinds of situations that seem to becoming more prevalent: the invasion of Panama, the invasion of Grenada, support for Contras in Nicaragua, bombing Libya, and the Persian Gulf War. Jentleson hypothesizes that the public is deeply influenced by the principal policy objectives of the nation, whether cultivated in advance by the president and political leadership or explained after the fact. Americans, in Jentleson's view, are far more likely to support action to enforce "foreign policy restraint," meaning keeping another nation from being an aggressor or threatening American interests, than they are to support action intended to bring about "internal political change" within another nation (1992, 53). In Jentleson's view, the means for internal political change could be using military action, sending aid, or intervening through counterintelligence means. Jentleson tested his hypothesis against eight cases and found that the highest support for military action occurs, as he predicted, when the intervention was intended to stop an aggressor or to restrain another nation.

The Persian Gulf War provided yet another opportunity to investigate public opinion toward foreign policy and toward the use of military force. Jentleson's (1992, 67) analysis of polling data gathered during the Persian Gulf operation finds that support among the public was highest for objectives such as defending Saudi Arabia or forcing Iraq out of Kuwait, objectives that meet his definition of foreign policy restraint. Support was very low for those objectives that could be defined as internal intervention in Iraqi politics: assassinating Saddam Hussein and invading Iraq to change the government. John Mueller (1994) also completed an extensive study of survey data gathered during the Persian Gulf War with the goal of studying the rally-round-the-flag effect in that situation. In some ways, the Persian Gulf War was too short and too successful to fit in with Mueller's earlier work. There were far too few casualties and the success of the venture was too great for the public to stop supporting the effort.

Most recently two cases of American involvement in overseas situations have provoked considerable ambivalence on the part of the American public. Keeping the broader dimensions of foreign policy in mind and using Jentleson's (1992) policy objectives, it is instructive to look at American public opinion in support of using U.S. troops in Somalia and Haiti.

Just a few of the results from the extensive polling on the use of troops in Somalia are shown in Table 9-3. Throughout the period from the arrival of troops through the attack on the Army rangers in early October, the American public continued to support the worthiness of the enterprise. In a clear statement of cooperative internationalism, the public's support for the use of troops in this humanitarian situation was fairly steady. However, after the attack on the Army rangers, public support for keeping the troops in Somalia became much more guarded. By December 1993 an overwhelming majority (see question IV c of Table 9-3) believed

Table 9-3 Public Opinion on the Use of U.S. Troops in Somalia, December 1992 to December 1993 (in Percentages)

I. Do you approve or disapprove of Bush's decision to send troops to Somalia?

	Dec. 1992	Sept. 1993	Oct. 1993
Approve	76	43	56
Disapprove	21	46	38

II. Do you think the United States is doing the right thing to send U.S. troops to Somalia to try and make sure shipments of food get through to the people there or should U.S. troops stay out?

	Dec. 1992	Oct. 1993	Dec. 1993
Right thing	81	64	62
Should have stayed out	14	32	33

III. Given the possible loss of American lives, the financial costs, and other risks involved, do you think sending the troops to make sure food gets through to the people of Somalia is worth the cost or not?

	Dec. 1992	Oct. 1993	Dec. 1993
Worth the cost	70	45	48
Not worth it	21	45	44

IV. a. Do you think the U.S. troops should stay in Somalia only as long as it takes to set up supply lines to make sure people don't starve or should they stay there as long as it takes to make sure Somalia will remain peaceful?

	Dec. 1992	Sept. 1993	Oct. 1993	Dec. 1993
Set up supply lines	48			
Stay until peaceful	44			
Not be there	3			

b. Should troops disarm warlords or deliver food?

Disarm warlords	22
Only deliver food	69
Not sure	9

c. Keep troops until civil government restored or pull out?

			Oct. 1993	Dec. 1993
Keep troops in			28	33
Pull troops out			64	61

Sources: ABC News/*Washington Post* poll (questions I, IV c); CBS News/*New York Times* poll (questions II, III, IV a); *Time*/CNN poll (question IV b).

that troops should not be committed to restoring a civil government. Polls showed increasing ambivalence about the humanitarian task from October 1993 on. In this situation, the public seems to be lending support to an international role for the United States but, as Jentleson predicts, support is limited and drops greatly if there is a hint of intervention in the local political situation.

Turning to the deployment of troops in Haiti in September of 1994, selective poll results given in Table 9-4 suggest the public's continued discomfort with the goal of returning a democratically elected government to the island nation. From the earliest discussion of sending troops into Haiti to restore democracy in May of 1994 up to the day before the troops arrived, the public overwhelmingly rejected that policy alternative. For a very brief period after the agreement with the military leaders on September 19, 1994, the public gave modest support to the presence of troops in Haiti and, in mid-October, expressed some optimism about the outcome of the operation. However, at no time during the seven months of polls on the topic did Americans express the belief that the nation had a vital interest in Haiti. If we are looking for some evidence of internationalist sentiment in these data, it is hard to find. The public has steadily refused to accept the idea that the United States has the responsibility of intervening in Haiti to restore its democracy. Instead, the public seems to perceive the use of troops in Haiti as an extremely risky venture that falls under the category of intervening in another nation's affairs.

If Americans disapprove so strongly of the venture, why wasn't there more of an outcry against the American presence in Haiti? First, to consider Mueller's (1973) thesis, virtually no American casualties have occurred, so we would not expect active resistance to the operation. Second, there was a brief period of public support for the policy immediately after the troops landed, a "blip" on the opinion screen that should be regarded as the rally-round-the-flag effect. President Clinton's approval ratings on his handling of the situation in Haiti also show the rally effect, rising from 31 percent in May 1994 to more than 50 percent in September.

Thinking About Public Opinion in a Changing World

In this changing world, which of the models and hypotheses put forth since the Vietnam era can guide our understanding of the public's role in foreign policy? Clearly, a continuing need exists to search for fundamental principles or dimensions that structure the cognitive process for most Americans.

With the end of the cold war, the militant internationalism/cooperative internationalism dimensions seem less relevant. We do not know which core values provide cues to average citizens as they process information from around the world. The response to new information or to a survey question is affected by other forces as well, among them demographic fac-

Table 9-4 Public Opinion on the U.S. Role in Haiti, May to December 1994
(in Percentages)

I. a. Do you agree or disagree that the United States should take all action necessary, including the use of military force, to restore a democratic government to Haiti?

	May	July	Sept. 18
Agree	36	36	30
Disagree	58	58	63

b. Do you approve or disapprove of the presence of U.S. troops in Haiti?

	Sept. 20	Oct. 16	Dec. 6
Approve	54	48	40
Disapprove	45	47	51

II. Do you think that America's vital interests are at stake in Haiti or not?

	May	July[a]	Sept. 18	Sept. 19-20
Vital	30	38	45	31
Not	58	54	51	57

III. Do you think the U.S. has a responsibility to do something to restore democracy in Haiti or doesn't the U.S. have this responsibility?

	May	July	Sept. 18
Does	40	36	41
Does not	50	56	53

IV. a. After the troops were sent: Do you approve of the presence of U.S. troops in Haiti?

	Oct. 11
Approve	55
Disapprove	39

b. Do you think the U.S. will be successful in restoring democratic rule to Haiti?

Successful	57
Not successful	30

Sources: ABC News/*Washington Post* poll (questions I a, II); CBS News/*New York Times* poll (question III); *Time*/CNN poll (questions I b, IV a and b).

[a] Wording different.

tors, partisanship, ideology, and, it would seem, a measure of patriotism that shows up in the rally effect.

Finally, in today's world of microcrises in strange and seemingly unimportant places, Jentleson's (1992) hypotheses about how Americans react to the use of military force are helpful. The public does acknowledge moral imperatives in the world and, if convinced, will follow presidential leadership in the use of troops. But sustained support is much more likely if the purpose of using troops is to stop an aggressor nation or defend clear American interests rather than to intervene in the affairs of another nation. Defining the relationship between these situational responses and the guiding values or dimensions behind them is the task for future scholars and will await new surveys that investigate underlying constructs as well as the crisis of the moment.

10 Public Opinion and Economic Policy in 1992

William G. Jacoby

An often repeated story about the 1992 presidential campaign holds that there was a sign placed on the wall of Bill Clinton's national headquarters proclaiming "It's the Economy, Stupid!" This sign was supposed to provide a constant reminder to the candidate's strategists about the single most important issue facing the American public. The truth of the sign's message is, perhaps, supported by the outcome of the 1992 election. But it is important not to take too narrow a perspective: citizens do not view different facets of the social world in isolation from one another, and their ideas about the national economy are inextricably linked with their political outlooks. The relationship between individual political orientations and economic beliefs is this chapter's central focus.

Citizens' reactions to the national economy are of obvious importance for understanding mass political behavior in the United States. Economic considerations place constraints on what individuals can do with their own lives (Hamilton and Wright 1986; Schlozman and Verba 1979). Voters hold the government responsible for the state of the economy, and they often vote on that basis (Lewis-Beck 1988; Stimson 1991). Political leaders clearly recognize this responsibility. Proposed governmental policy initiatives are routinely weighed for their economic implications, while candidates for public office almost always make economic concerns a central focus of their campaign rhetoric (Page 1978). At a more general level, popular feelings about capitalism constitute a central theme in American political culture (McClosky and Zaller 1984). In this capacity, citizens' broad feelings about the predominant economic system exert an important influence on a wide variety of more specific political beliefs and attitudes. Many of the issues that come to the forefront of American public opinion crystallize around explicitly economic phenomena such as inflation, unemployment, and the like.

Although the subject matter is clearly important, public opinion toward the national economy and government economic policy remains unclear or contradictory. When we consider aggregate policy preferences (that is, the proportion of the public that feels or acts a certain way), the public appears to be capable of making rational assessments of economic events and policies. But when we consider individual policy preferences (that is, the beliefs and attitudes maintained by specific people), the public appears far less able to understand economic affairs.

Ample aggregate-level evidence demonstrates that the public reacts to economic trends and events in predictable, rational ways. For example, when the economy is performing poorly, the party of the president loses seats in Congress, and when the economy is booming the president's party is often rewarded (Kramer 1971). Similarly, aggregate public support for economic policies such as government-guaranteed jobs and income supports parallels statistics on unemployment and changes in income (Page and Shapiro 1992). Even more generally, it appears that public expectations about the economy exert a strong impact on broad policy preferences within the American electorate (Durr 1993). Thus, the overall contours of public opinion seem to be nicely consistent with the nature and content of the economic environment (Hibbs 1987; Mayer 1992).

Despite the apparent coherence of the aggregate relationship between public opinion and economics, a very different picture often seems to emerge at the individual level. For example, there is little evidence that individuals vote their personal pocketbooks in elections (Kiewiet 1983). Moreover, many people simply do not seem to recognize the nature of fundamental economic policy choices, such as the tradeoff between policies aimed at dealing with unemployment and those trying to curb inflation (Aldrich et al. 1982; Peretz 1983). Indeed, there are many studies demonstrating that outright inconsistencies and internal contradictions exist within mass attitudes toward economic phenomena (Free and Cantril 1967; Sears and Citrin 1985). Based upon this kind of evidence, it is very easy to conclude that public opinion toward economic policy is just one more potent indicator of the shallow and unsophisticated nature of citizens' thoughts on important aspects of modern society.

Many scholars have rebutted these negative conclusions about the public's capacity to deal with economic matters. For example, some analysts point out that a strong ethic of self-reliance in American culture leads most individuals to take personal responsibility for their own economic circumstances; that ethic explains the failure of the public to blame the government for their own unemployment (Sniderman and Brody 1977). In a similar vein, Stanley Feldman (1982) has shown that once people make the connection between governmental policies and their own economic condition, then they are more likely to vote their personal pocketbook. The problem is that most people simply fail to make this connection.

Another line of argument holds that it is individual judgments about collective, or society-wide, economic conditions, rather than personal economic circumstances, that are important for understanding political behavior. Such sociotropic judgments have been shown to affect voting behavior and political attitudes in a variety of contexts (Kinder and Kiewiet 1979, 1981). Pamela Johnson Conover and Stanley Feldman (1986) argued that public reactions toward the economy are often emotional, rather than cognitive, in nature. If this is the case, then much of the economic "content" of public opinion will be missed by typical survey questions. Thus, a variety of explanations try to deal with the "economic innocence" of the American public.

The basic objective of this chapter is to provide a middle ground interpretation of public opinion toward government economic policies. People generally react to the national economy in a very reasonable manner. However, public orientations toward economic phenomena are based more upon subjective assessments and personal experience than upon "objective" external conditions. Once this basic feature is recognized, then opinions about economic conditions and policies do, in fact, seem to be rationally conceived. In order to provide empirical support for this relatively optimistic assessment, I will use data from the 1992 American National Election Study (ANES) to analyze citizens' orientations toward economic conditions and policies. Specifically, I will examine three distinct, but closely related, topics: citizens' perceptions about economic conditions, their evaluations of the government's economic policy performance, and their attitudes toward economic policy choices.

Perceptions of Economic Conditions

How do people perceive their own financial situations and the current state of the national economy? The 1992 American National Election Study includes a number of items that address respondents' perceptions of economic conditions. Two of these are aimed specifically at personal circumstances. The first item asks about respondents' family finances over the preceding year. The second asks whether family income has kept up with the cost of living over the previous year. Responses to these two survey questions have been combined to create a scale of beliefs about personal financial conditions.[1] Responses to the items that comprise this scale suggest that most people are moderately satisfied with their personal financial situations, with slightly more people dissatisfied than satisfied.

Five questions are aimed at respondents' perceptions of the national economy. Three of them elicit evaluations about economic performance over the preceding year. One question asks about the economy in general, while the others specifically mention inflation and unemployment, respectively. Two remaining questions ask about the national economy's performance over somewhat different time frames, with one asking about the previous few months and the other asking about the economy over the preceding four-year period. Individual responses to these five questions tend to be highly consistent, so they are combined to create a scale measuring beliefs about national economic conditions.[2] Although most individuals were moderately satisfied with their personal financial situation in 1992, most were moderately unhappy with the state of the nation's economy.

The two summary scales of beliefs about personal economic conditions and the national economy will be used as dependent variables for this part of the analysis. We can expect individual evaluations of personal economic conditions to vary with objective personal circumstances, such as income and employment status, but it will also be interesting to determine whether and how social and political factors impinge on evaluations of personal economic conditions.

Beliefs about national economic conditions also provide an interesting situation because citizens are all judging a common stimulus—the national economy itself. Since individuals differ in their evaluations of the national economy, it will be useful to see how individual biases, predispositions, and information sources combine to create the observed variability in economic judgments.

I hypothesize that perceptions of economic conditions are affected by three sets of explanatory factors.[3] The first set is composed of personal economic circumstances. I will consider two aspects of these personal circumstances: objective measures of an individual's position within society—including family income, age, race, gender, and employment status—and subjective behavioral measures of personal economic circumstances—including personal concern over employment status, the extent to which a person reports having to cut back on his or her expenditures, and reliance on public assistance.

The second set of influences on economic judgments is composed of contextual factors within the external environment. These variables include the 1992 unemployment rate in each person's state of residence, the state-level change in personal income from 1991 to 1992, and the change in the regional consumer price index over the same time period. The last two variables are both measured in constant 1987 dollars in order to gauge the true, rather than perceived, effects of inflation on individual economic judgments.

The third set of influences on economic judgments is composed of symbolic political orientations, specifically party identification and ideological self-placement. Following standard practice, party identification is coded 1–7, ranging from strong Democrat, through independent, to strong Republican. Similarly, ideological self-placement is coded into seven categories from extremely liberal to extremely conservative. In both cases, larger values of the variables indicate more Republican or more conservative self-placements. These two variables are usually regarded as long-term predispositions which are developed early in life, remain relatively stable over a person's political life span, and tend to exert broad, pervasive influences over a variety of other beliefs, attitudes, and behaviors. In the present context, these factors are particularly interesting because we are examining their possible effects on matters that would appear to be nonpolitical in nature.

Finally, beliefs about personal economic situations will be used as an independent variable for beliefs about the national economy. This decision represents an assumption that individuals use their own personal economic conditions as cues for more abstract evaluations about the national economy. Personal economic conditions are immediate, vivid, and tangible in their nature and consequences and are likely to color any judgment about the overall economy.

Ordinary least squares regression is used to estimate the independent variables' effects on the two sets of economic beliefs. Results are presented in Tables 10-1 and 10-2. In each table (and in all those to follow), the leftmost column of figures contains the unstandardized regression coefficients, and statistically significant coefficients are noted with asterisks. The rightmost column contains standardized coefficients, which are useful for comparing the effects of independent variables that are measured in different units. It is important to remember that larger values of the dependent variables indicate more pessimistic beliefs about personal and/or national economic conditions.

The influences on personal economic perceptions are shown in Table 10-1. All three sets of explanatory variables do seem to have some effect on economic perceptions. First, consider personal economic circumstances. Among the demographic background variables, age, female gender, and unemployed status all have statistically significant effects. Younger people are relatively optimistic about their personal economic situations (as indicated by the negative coefficient for the age under twenty-one variable), while older Americans, women, and people who are currently unemployed give relatively pessimistic assessments (shown by their positive regression coefficients). These results make good sense: young people are just beginning to enter the labor force, so their personal incomes and economic circumstances should be steadily improving. In contrast, the elderly, the unemployed, and women are all in economically disadvantaged positions relative to much of the rest of society; therefore, their negative beliefs about personal economic conditions probably reflect quite realistic assessments.

All three behavioral measures of personal circumstances exert significant effects on economic beliefs. Job worries, cutbacks in family spending and consumption, and reliance on public assistance all lead to more negative assessments of personal financial conditions. It is particularly interesting to juxtapose the effects of these behavioral variables with the null results obtained for income and race. This pattern of effects and noneffects suggests that it is an individual's relative position with respect to the economy, rather than his or her race or absolute standing within the income hierarchy, that determines beliefs about personal conditions. In other words, people seem to ask themselves, "How have I had to change my spending lately?" rather than "Where do I stand in relation to other Americans?"

Only one of the variables measuring external economic conditions show a significant influence on beliefs about personal economic circumstances. The state unemployment rate shows a fairly weak, but still nonnegligible, effect. Those who live in states with high levels of unemployment are more pessimistic about their personal financial situations, regardless of their objective circumstances.[4]

Only one of the political orientations, party identification, has a significant impact. The coefficient for this variable is negative, showing that Democrats were more likely to give pessimistic assessments of personal economic conditions than Republicans in 1992. What is a bit surprising is the fact that party identification shows an impact on a psychological orientation that has no ostensible partisan content whatsoever. People do seem to incorporate

Table 10-1 Influences on Beliefs About Personal Economic Conditions

Independent Variable	Unstandardized Regression Coefficient	Standard Error	Standardized Regression Coefficient
Demographic characteristics			
Income	−.00	.00	−.04
Age less than 25	−.22**	.07	−.07
Age greater than 60	.34**	.08	.12
Black	−.07	.08	−.02
Female	.08**	.05	.04
Unemployed	.28**	.10	.07
Economic behavior variables			
Personal cutbacks	.18**	.01	.38
Income assistance	.06**	.02	.06
Job worries	−.09**	.02	−.12
Economic conditions			
State unemployment	.04**	.02	.06
Disposable income	−.00	.00	−.01
Consumer prices	−.04	.05	−.02
Political predispositions			
Party identification	−.04**	.01	−.09
Ideology	.00	.02	.00
R^2		.24	
Intercept		3.07	
Number of cases		(1,417)	

Source: 1992 American National Election Study.

** Statistically significant at the .05 level (one-tail test).

a political twist into beliefs about personal economic circumstances. This confirms the pervasive effects of party identification as a potent mechanism for structuring a wide variety of social and economic, as well as political, opinions.

Finally, we can determine which variables have the strongest influence on beliefs about personal economic conditions by examining the standardized regression coefficients shown in the right-hand column of Table 10-1. One variable clearly stands out for its strong effects: those who have personally cut back on spending or consumption are markedly more pessimistic about their economic fortunes. The remaining independent variables all have much smaller effects. The second-largest coefficient is that for worries about personal employment status, followed closely by the variable for older respondents. This pattern of coefficients shows that personal economic behavior has a more pronounced effect on evaluations than either age or concern about future employment status. Interestingly, the effects of party identification follow closely after age and concern about employment, with a standardized coefficient of −.09. All of the remaining explanatory variables have even smaller effects than these four variables. The empirical results in Table 10-1 show that beliefs about personal economic conditions seem to reflect relatively accurate assessments of an individual's current economic circumstances, tempered somewhat by partisan political considerations.

The data in Table 10-2 clearly show that the influences on beliefs about the national economy are quite different from those on personal economic conditions. First, income, black racial status, and female gender all have significant regression coefficients, while the age variables and unemployed status do not show any effect. This result indicates that an individual's place within the status hierarchy of American society does shape evaluations about the nation's economic health. As one would expect, blacks and women provide relatively negative evaluations. But somewhat surprisingly, the coefficient for income is positive, indicating that wealthier people actually believe the national economy is in worse shape than people with lower incomes.

Three of the four variables measuring psychological and behavioral aspects of personal economic situations show significant effects: an individual's general belief about his or her economic condition, worries about employment status, and cutbacks in personal spending and consumption. Apparently, people use relevant personal economic concerns and experiences as tangible indicators of the external economic environment. As such, these indicators are employed within the public as evidence to create overall assessments of the nation's economy.

The measures of economic conditions also show a very different pattern of influences for beliefs about national economic conditions than for beliefs about personal economic conditions. In Table 10-2 changes in disposable personal income and the consumer price index have significant coefficients, while the state unemployment rate does not. Clearly, people are relying on very different kinds of external evidence when they factor objective conditions into their beliefs about personal and national economic conditions, respectively. This finding contradicts some of the more pessimistic assessments of the public's capacity to deal with the technical aspects of economic issues. For example, some analysts have argued that ordinary citizens simply do not understand the nature of inflation (Peretz 1983); others suggest that unemployment has a relatively strong effect on subsequent evaluations because it is a more visible and easily communicated issue, capable of more personalized interpretations (Behr and Iyengar 1985). The present evidence suggests that neither of these arguments is entirely accurate, at least when people are making explicit judgments of collective economic conditions. The factors influencing economic perceptions may not be very sophis-

Table 10-2 Influences on Beliefs About National Economic Conditions

Independent Variable	Unstandardized Regression Coefficient	Standard Error	Standardized Regression Coefficient
Demographic characteristics			
Income	.00**	.00	.05
Age less than 25	.05	.05	.02
Age greater than 60	.03	.05	.01
Black	.15**	.05	.07
Female	.12**	.03	.09
Unemployed	.02	.06	.01
Economic behavior variables			
Personal cutbacks	.02**	.01	.05
Income assistance	.03	.02	.04
Job worries	−.04**	.01	−.09
Economic conditions			
State unemployment	.02	.01	.04
Disposable income	−.00**	.00	−.08
Consumer prices	.09**	.03	.07
Political predispositions			
Party identification	−.08**	.01	−.27
Ideology	−.02**	.01	−.05
Beliefs about economic conditions			
Personal conditions	.17**	.02	.25
R^2		.30	
Intercept		3.19	
Number of cases		(1,417)	

Source: 1992 American National Election Study.

** Statistically significant at the .05 level (one-tail test).

ticated in scholarly terms, but they are certainly quite reasonable. When income goes down and/or prices go up, people judge that the national economy is worse off, and vice versa.

Party and ideology are significant influences on perceptions of national economic conditions. Democrats and liberals make relatively negative assessments, while Republicans and conservatives take a more positive view. Of course, these effects undoubtedly reflect the specific political conditions that existed when the 1992 ANES interviews were made. The nation had experienced twelve years of Republican presidencies, and it was in the middle of a presidential campaign focused on a theme of economic distress in American society. For these reasons, it would be more surprising if we did *not* observe political effects on judgments of national economic conditions. Still, the fact that political effects do exist reinforces our finding that political orientations color citizens' judgments about ostensibly nonpolitical aspects of American society.

Turning to the relative magnitudes of the various influences, we find that two variables stand out prominently: party identification and beliefs about personal economic conditions. The standardized regression coefficients for these two variables are almost three times larger than the next largest coefficient, and they greatly outdistance those for all of the remaining variables. These results underscore the highly subjective nature of economic perceptions among the mass public. Although sophisticated observers might consider "the economy" to be a distinctive component of the external environment of Americans, ordinary citizens apparently do not feel that way. Their beliefs about the national economy are formed largely as a composite of personal experiences and partisan predispositions.

Evaluations of Economic Policy Performance

The 1992 ANES contains four questions that are relatively direct measures of retrospective policy evaluations, that is, government performance in the recent past. Survey respondents were asked whether they approved of President Bush's handling of the economy; whether the federal government's economic policies had done anything to make them or their family better or worse off during the previous year; whether the federal government's economic policies had made the national economy better or worse off; and whether the Bush administration, the Democratic Congress, or both should be blamed for the federal budget deficit. Responses to these four items have been combined into a single scale measuring citizens' generalized reactions to the national government's economic policies.[5] The responses to these items reveal that in 1992, the American public was relatively dissatisfied with the government's economic policies. Yet opinion was varied as people evaluated these policies: some citizens were very satisfied and some were very dissatisfied.

The model that will be used to analyze individual evaluations of governmental policy performance closely parallels the one that was used for beliefs about economic conditions. The dependent variable is the summary measure of retrospective policy judgments just described; note that larger values of this scale correspond to more pessimistic evaluations of economic policy performance. The independent variables can be divided into five sets. First, there are the demographic background variables, income, age, black racial status, female gender, and unemployed status. Second, there are the three behavioral measures of personal economic circumstances—family financial cutbacks, reliance on public income assistance, and worry about losing or finding a job. Third, there are the three contextual factors, state unemployment rate, changes in per capita disposable personal income within the state, and the change in the regional consumer price index. Fourth, there are the two political predispositions, party identification and ideology. The fifth category is comprised of the summary measures of beliefs about personal and national economic conditions. If people use their own financial experiences and their perceptions of economic conditions as evidence of the effectiveness of governmental economic policies, then the variables from these last two categories should exhibit significant effects.

The various independent variables' effects on the summary scale of evaluations of policy performance are estimated with ordinary least squares, and the resultant coefficients are shown in Table 10-3. This large set of explanatory variables accounts for 57 percent of the variance in evaluations of economic policy performance.

Which factors explain evaluations of economic performance? The entries in the table show that variables from all five categories have an effect. Among demographic groups, wealthier individuals, young people, and men were relatively dissatisfied with the government's economic initiatives. It is interesting that the young, who were optimistic about their own economic future, are more dissatisfied than the elderly with the government's attempts to shape the economy.

Two of the three variables measuring behavioral economic responses exhibit influences on citizens' evaluations of economic policies. Those who had cut back on their spending and consumption were significantly more pessimistic, while those who relied on public income supports were more optimistic. These relationships make sense: those who have experienced a negative change in their circumstances are less satisfied with economic policy, while people who get more money from the government are more supportive of the government's economic performance record.

Not surprisingly, economic perceptions have pronounced effects on evaluations of governmental performance. When people are asked how the government is doing with respect to economic affairs, they look to the most readily available sources of evidence—their own perceptions of economic conditions, at both the personal and national levels.

Although perceptions of the national economy affect evaluations of economic policies, objective economic indicators have virtually no effect on policy evaluations. Among the three variables in this category, only changes in the regional consumer price index achieves statistical significance (and then, just barely). Apparently, there is a very slight tendency for people to hold the government accountable for price stability, but beyond this, external realities have virtually no additional impact on public judgments of economic policy performance. This result reaffirms the subjective nature of economic opinion.

Finally, the two political orientations both affect judgments about economic performance. As one would expect, self-identified Democrats and liberals are both more likely to take a critical stance toward the economy in 1992 than Republicans or conservatives.

Table 10-3 Influences on Evaluations of the Government's Economic Policy Performance

Independent Variable	Unstandardized Regression Coefficient	Standard Error	Standardized Regression Coefficient
Demographic characteristics			
Income	.00**	.00	.05
Age less than 25	.14**	.05	.05
Age greater than 60	−.01	.05	−.00
Black	.00	.05	.00
Female	−.10**	.03	−.06
Unemployed	−.10	.06	−.03
Economic behavior variables			
Personal cutbacks	.03**	.01	.08
Income assistance	−.03**	.02	−.04
Job worries	−.01	.01	−.02
Economic conditions			
State unemployment	−.01	.01	−.01
Disposable income	.00	.00	.01
Consumer prices	.05**	.03	.03
Political predispositions			
Party identification	−.15**	.01	−.37
Ideology	−.08**	.01	−.14
Beliefs about economic conditions			
Personal conditions	.10**	.02	.11
National conditions	.50**	.03	.39
R^2		.57	
Intercept		1.83	
Number of cases		(1,417)	

Source: 1992 American National Election Study.

** Statistically significant at the .05 level (one-tail test).

This is very reasonable, given the overt political content of government economic performance.

When we move from the question of which variables affect evaluations to a consideration of how strong their various effects are, a relatively simple picture emerges from the empirical results. The standardized regression coefficients in the right-hand column of Table 10-3 clearly show that the process of retrospective economic policy evaluations is dominated by just two variables. Beliefs about national economic conditions have the strongest impact, followed closely by party identification. It is interesting to note that the next largest effects are those associated with ideological self-placement and beliefs about personal economic conditions. Indeed, these two variables form a sort of secondary plateau in the relative sizes of effects. All of the other independent variables have meager impacts that pale in comparison with these four.

Although individual evaluations of economic policy performance are largely based upon subjective evaluations, this should not, in itself, lead to pessimistic conclusions about the abilities and capacities of the American public. I believe that a much more positive interpretation is suggested by the data. On the one hand, people are forming their judgments on the basis of two sets of criteria: (1) certain performance indicators—their own perceptions about the kinds of economic conditions in existence—and (2) several symbolic predispositions—specifically, party identification and ideology—that imply rather unambiguous reactions toward the people, institutions, and parties that are currently involved in setting economic policy. Taken together, these seem to constitute a reasonable set of evaluative standards for thinking about the government's economic policies.

Attitudes Toward Economic Policies

A third logical area of study is public attitudes toward different possible governmental economic policies. Notice that these represent a fundamentally different aspect of public opinion from the material covered in the previous two sections. Individual perceptions of economic conditions and retrospective judgments about policy performance are both examples of beliefs; they represent individual understandings about the current state of the external environment (and one's own place within it, in the case of personal financial perceptions). In contrast, citizens' attitudes toward economic policies represent preferences about the courses of action that government should take in dealing with the economy. Given the overall salience of the economy and economic concerns to everyday life and political rhetoric alike, it seems reasonable to suppose that economic attitudes would occupy a central position in citizens' orientations toward the political world.

In light of the potential importance of economic attitudes, it is surprising to find that the standard sources of public opinion data contain very few measures of mass attitudes toward specific economic policies.[6] The 1992 ANES contains only two items that seem to be direct measures of economic policy attitudes. One question asks respondents to choose between two statements: (1) "We need a strong government to handle today's complex economic problems"; or (2) "The free market can handle economic problems without government being involved." This item measures feelings about government's overall role in the economy, without specifying any particular policy or economic problem. Public sentiment is strongly in favor of the government over the free market, by a margin of nearly three to one.[7]

The second item is a seven-point scale, upon which respondents locate themselves according to their feelings about the following two statements: "Government should see to it that each person has a job and a good standard of living"; and "Each person should get ahead on their own." On this question, more than half of the respondents place themselves within the three middle categories (out of a total range of seven categories).[8] Among those who do take a stand on this issue, sentiment clearly favors individual responsibility over governmental action to provide jobs for those who need them.

Public opinion on the two economic policy items seems to point in opposing directions. The American public recognizes the need for government action but simultaneously supports individual (rather than governmental) responsibility for employment and living conditions. What can account for this apparently contradictory result? To address this question, we must examine the sources of attitudes toward economic policies. The independent variables in this analysis are largely the same as those employed in the earlier parts of the chapter. There are several variables measuring demographic characteristics, behavioral indicators of personal economic situations, perceptions of economic conditions, objective economic indicators, and symbolic political predispositions. The summary scale of policy performance evaluations also will be included as an explanatory variable for both of the policy attitudes. Retrospective judgments about the effectiveness of policies already in effect should have an impact on one's preferences about future courses of action with respect to the economy. And finally, an individual's choice between government and the free market represents a rather fundamental decision that could be expected to have far-reaching consequences for many of that person's more specific political orientations. Therefore, the government/market choice will be included as an explanatory variable for attitudes toward the narrower question of government-guaranteed jobs.

The influences of the various independent variables are once again estimated using ordinary least squares, and the resultant coefficients are shown in Tables 10-4 and 10-5.[9] The factors that affect citizens' choices between the government and the free market for dealing with economic problems (Table 10-4) are straightforward and very reasonable in nature. There are a number of fairly predictable demographic influences. The income variable has a significant positive coefficient, showing that wealthier people favor market solutions to economic problems. The coefficients for the young age group and women are both significant and negative, indicating that people in these categories are more favorable to governmental economic initiatives. Of these variables, only income and female gender really seem to have any pronounced effect, as measured by the standardized coefficients in the rightmost column of the table.

Apart from the demographic variables, only three other independent variables show any effect whatsoever. These are the two political predispositions and the retrospective evaluations

Table 10-4 Influences on Attitudes Toward Government Versus the Free Market

Independent Variable	Unstandardized Regression Coefficient	Standard Error	Standardized Regression Coefficient
Demographic characteristics			
Income	.00**	.00	.08
Age less than 25	−.26**	.15	−.04
Age greater than 60	.10	.16	.02
Black	.00	.05	.00
Female	−.43**	.10	−.12
Unemployed	−.07	.21	−.01
Economic behavior variables			
Personal cutbacks	−.01	.03	−.01
Income assistance	−.06	.05	−.03
Job worries	−.02	.04	−.02
Economic conditions			
State unemployment	−.04	.04	−.03
Change in disposable income	−.00	.00	−.02
Change in consumer prices	.06	.10	.02
Political predispositions			
Party identification	.11**	.04	.13
Ideology	.17**	.04	.13
Beliefs about economic conditions			
Personal conditions	.06	.06	.03
National conditions	−.08	.10	−.03
Political evaluations			
Retrospective policy judgments	−.24**	.08	−.11
R^2		.16	
Intercept		2.34	
Number of cases		(1,268)	

Source: 1992 American National Election Study.

** Statistically significant at the .05 level (one-tail test).

scale. Both self-identified Democrats and liberals come down on the side of governmental action, while Republicans and conservatives prefer the free market. At the same time, people who evaluate previous economic policies favorably are more likely to support continued governmental action. The standardized coefficients for these three variables are all quite large, showing that they have stronger effects than virtually all of the other independent variables.

The combination of effects found in Table 10-4 suggests some interesting conclusions about the factors that influence attitudes toward governmental economic intervention versus the free market. The strong impacts of party identification and ideology confirm the importance of symbolic political orientations for understanding the basic economic attitudes of American citizens (Sears and Funk 1990). But the effects of affective political predispositions are tempered by empirical evidence. Retrospective judgments about economic policy performance also have a strong effect in Table 10-4, indicating that people evaluate the nation's prior experiences when determining their own reactions toward government and the free market as economic actors. And it is important to emphasize that this phenomenon is not a simple reflection of current economic conditions. The three objective economic indicator variables have no significant impact at all. Nor do subjective perceptions of national economic conditions. Thus, people really do seem to be responding to their beliefs about the past effectiveness of governmental economic initiatives and not simply to their perception of the state of the current economy.

The situation is very different when we examine public attitudes on the more narrowly defined issue of government-guaranteed jobs (Table 10-5). Once again, there are some expected, but relatively modest, demographic effects reflected in the significant coefficients for income, the young age group, and blacks. In addition, several indicators of economic self-interest show an impact. The variables measuring concern over losing or finding a job, perception of personal financial condition, and reliance on public assistance all have significant regression coefficients. In every case, as personal economic stress increases, so does support for government-guaranteed jobs, and vice versa.

Symbolic political orientations exhibit their typical pronounced effects in Table 10-5. Party identification and ideology both have significant coefficients, and their standardized values are the largest in the table, suggesting that they have the strongest impact on this particular issue attitude. These two explanatory factors are joined by the dependent variable from the previous equation. Exactly as hypothesized, an individual's generalized orientation toward government versus the free market has a strong effect on more specific attitudes about economic policies like guaranteed employment. And one more explicitly political variable—evaluations of economic policy performance—has a significant effect, although it is somewhat weaker than those of the more symbolic predispositions. Still, it is the case that people who have positive reactions to the results of past governmental initiatives favor further action to guarantee jobs to those who need them.

Table 10-5 Influences on Attitudes Toward Government-Guaranteed Jobs

Independent Variable	Unstandardized Regression Coefficient	Standard Error	Standardized Regression Coefficient
Demographic characteristics			
Income	.00**	.00	.07
Age less than 25	−.32**	.15	−.06
Age greater than 60	.15	.16	.03
Black	−.41**	.16	−.07
Female	−.14	.09	−.04
Unemployed	−.10	.06	−.03
Economic behavior variables			
Personal cutbacks	−.02	.03	−.02
Income assistance	−.09**	.05	−.05
Job worries	.07**	.04	.05
Economic conditions			
State unemployment	.02	.04	.02
Disposable income	.00	.00	.05
Consumer prices	−.03	.09	−.01
Political predispositions			
Party identification	.10**	.03	.12
Ideology	.14**	.04	.12
Beliefs about economic conditions			
Personal conditions	−.19**	.06	−.11
National conditions	.04	.09	.02
Political evaluations			
Retrospective policy judgments	−.16**	.08	−.08
Government versus free market	.10**	.03	.11
R^2		.21	
Intercept		3.96	
Number of cases		(1,192)	

Source: 1992 American National Election Study.

** Statistically significant at the .05 level (one-tail test).

What kind of general conclusions can be drawn from the results in Table 10-5? On the one hand, attitudes toward guaranteed jobs have a strong symbolic component. On the other hand, the symbolic nature of these attitudes is offset by the clear, separate impact of self-interest. As people perceive themselves to be in greater economic peril at a personal level, they are more strongly supportive of governmental action to promote jobs. And it is important to emphasize that the impact of self-interest does not seem to be affected very much by empirical evidence about the external environment. In summary, attitudes toward government-guaranteed jobs are largely symbolic in nature, but they are also strongly affected by the ways people perceive their own problems and potential personal benefits from public policies.

Let us now return to the question posed at the beginning of this section. Why do public attitudes on these two economic issues exhibit apparent inconsistencies? It seems that individuals use different decision-making routines in answering these two questions, for the two economic issues evoke different considerations. The distinction between government and the free market involves a judgment about collective economic matters. The question of guaranteed jobs raises personal concerns about employment and financial situations. Different ways of thinking about public issues naturally produce somewhat different conclusions.

Conclusions

In this chapter, I have examined public opinion with respect to the national economy and governmental economic policies. Careful consideration of the empirical evidence suggests that individual reactions to economic phenomena are fairly coherent in content and structure. They are grounded in reality, based upon reasonable evaluative criteria, and consistent with other psychological predispositions. The results reported in this chapter have several important implications for our understanding of the ways that citizens react to the political world in the 1990s.

First, this analysis underscores the importance of subjectivity in public opinion. Stated simply, people do not react very strongly to the objective components of the external environment. Instead, it is their own perceptions of this environment that are important. To be sure, these perceptions are at least partially based upon economic realities such as unemployment and inflation, but they also are tempered by party identification and ideology. Some observers might conclude that individual economic judgments are simply partisan rationalizations. I contend that this judgment is unnecessarily harsh. Instead, the subjectivity in citizens' economic judgments probably just reflects the variability in the sources of information and behavioral cues that are employed within the mass public.

Second, this analysis has shown unambiguously that personal economic situations affect individual orientations toward the social and political aspects of society. This finding is important because it shows that an individual's immediate life circumstances do affect his or her broader reactions to society. The gulf between these two types of concerns is apparently not as wide as some previous studies have suggested (Brody and Sniderman 1977). A long line of research asserts the primacy of symbolic orientations over self-interest in the formation of political attitudes (Sears and Funk 1990). And the literature on economic voting almost uniformly stresses that personal economic circumstances have no effect on electoral choice (Kinder and Kiewiet 1981; Lau and Sears 1981). The analysis presented in this chapter is not directly at odds with these earlier results, but it does offer a very important caveat. Personal economic circumstances certainly do exert an indirect effect because they serve as strong determinants of the sociotropic judgments that influence vote choice.

A third implication to be drawn from this analysis is that public opinion toward the economy and economic policies is rational in nature. This is not to say that public opinion is the product of sophisticated, abstract thinking about economic causes and effects, or that its content involves a great deal of detailed information about economic conditions. But it is based upon reasonable kinds of evidence, drawn from the sources of information that are likely to be readily available to citizens—personal economic perceptions and experiences, as well as evaluations of past governmental policy activities. Furthermore, the conclusions that people reach about economic conditions and policy alternatives are quite consistent with their own social situations. Citizens rely on available evidence to arrive at decisions about and an orientation toward society and governmental policies that tend to maximize their self-interest. It would be difficult to come up with a more effective operational demonstration of rationality within the mass public than this (Chappell and Keech 1990).

The final conclusion to be drawn from this chapter concerns the political nature of citizens' economic orientations. Stated simply, public opinion toward economic policy is composed in large part of political beliefs and attitudes: party identification, personal ideology, and evaluations of governmental economic policies (which are, themselves, heavily based upon political considerations). For this reason, I believe that it is appropriate to modify Bill Clinton's 1992 campaign slogan to say "It's not just the economy, stupid—it's *politics*, as well."

Notes

1. The reliability for this scale is .71 (coefficient alpha). The scale scores range from 1 to 5, with larger values indicating more pessimistic assessments of financial circumstances. The mean score is 3.32 with a standard deviation of .93.

2. The reliability for this scale is .78 (coefficient alpha). The scale scores range from 1 to 5 (with larger values indicating more pessimistic assessments). The mean is 3.94 and the standard deviation is .65.

3. All of the demographic, attitudinal, and behavioral variables used in this analysis are created from items included in the 1992 American National Election Study. Variables measuring objective economic conditions are created from information contained in the *1992 Statistical Abstract of the United States*. Details about all of the variables are available from the author.

4. The previous literature confirms that individual judgments do seem to be more strongly related to unemployment (Conover, Feldman, and Knight 1986), and a variety of mechanisms have been proposed to account for this phenomenon, including the amount and nature of media coverage, the operation of interpersonal communications networks, and lower public understanding about the nature of inflation (Behr and Iyengar 1985; Katona 1975; Peretz 1983). Nevertheless, the result remains intriguing. After all, unemployment has direct effects on only a relatively small proportion of the population, while changes in income and prices affect everyone. And yet, measures of the latter show no effect whatsoever on beliefs about personal economic well-being. Evidently, the economic climate against which individuals compare their own situations is defined in terms of how many people are working, rather than personal income purchasing power and consumer prices.

5. The reliability for this scale is .60 (coefficient alpha). The scale scores range from 1 to 5, with larger values indicating more negative retrospective evaluations. The mean score is 3.52, with a standard deviation of .82.

6. The scarcity of specific economics-related questions on academic public opinion surveys has already been noted by Mayer (1992).

7. The values on this variable are coded 1 for people who prefer governmental solutions, 5 for those who select the free market, and 3 for people who refused to choose or said both. The mean value is 2.10, and the standard deviation is 1.74.

8. The values are coded as successive integers from 1 (for guaranteed jobs) to 7 (people should get ahead on their own); the intermediate points on this variable are not labeled. The mean value is 4.30 and the standard deviation is 1.79.

9. Because the dependent variable is trichotomous, ordinary least squares is not, strictly speaking, appropriate for this analysis. But, replication with other techniques (designed explicitly for ordinal dependent variables) produces identical results to those presented here. Therefore, I will use the OLS results in order to facilitate interpretation and comparison with the other findings in this analysis.

Part 4   The Consequences of Public Opinion

Commentators who tried to explain the Republicans' victories in the 1994 elections inevitably based their explanations largely on political attitudes. Sometimes attitudes were evoked directly, as when some pollsters referred to 1994 as the year of the angry white male or when they argued that many Republican voters were especially dissatisfied with Clinton's handling of the presidency. At other times commentators implied that attitudes were involved. For example, some suggested that the election represented a rejection of big government or of government as usual. This explanation suggests (1) that voters changed their attitudes about the value of big government; (2) that voters who disliked big government decided that in 1994 they were definitely going to the polls to vote; and/or (3) that voters decided to vote Republican because they felt they shared the party's attitudes toward big government.

Professional pollsters are especially interested in the behavioral consequences of public opinion in the electoral arena. They need to know what kinds of people are likely to vote in a given election and which of their attitudes are most likely to influence their vote. They also seek to determine which existing attitudes might be activated to help the candidate who hired them, which attitudes might be changed, and in some cases whether a new attitude might be developed. For example, in 1996 President Clinton's pollsters could be expected to formulate a strategy to activate attitudes of social justice and fairness in the electorate, as a way to rally opposition to Republican cuts in programs to aid the poor. Dole's pollsters could be expected to try to figure out how to lessen voters' worries about the candidate's advanced age. Steve Forbes's pollsters presumably tried to determine how they might build support for their candidate's flat tax proposal.

Political scientists are not interested in manipulating public opinion, but they do want to study the impact of public opinion on political behavior. They generally ask two questions: How do attitudes and opinions influence the decision to engage in political behavior? and How do they influence citizens' behavior?

The first question is essentially one of political participation. In recent years the definition of participation has broadened considerably, and scholars have begun to explore the role of opinions and attitudes in shaping contributions to candidates (Brown, Powell, and

189

Wilcox 1995), voluntarism in communities (Verba, Schlozman, and Brady 1995), and the blocking of entrances to abortion clinics (Maxwell 1995). But the vast majority of research remains centered on the individual's decision whether to vote in caucuses, primary elections, and especially in general elections.

Turnout in American elections is quite low by international standards, and it has been declining since 1960. In the first chapter in Part 4, John Hughes and Margaret Conway examine the attitudinal sources of the decision to vote in presidential elections from 1964 to 1992. Their innovative analysis allows them to examine the impact of increasing education, which makes the public more likely to vote, and increasing cynicism and distrust, which make people less likely to vote.

The second question is one of political choice. To whose campaign does a citizen contribute? What candidate does the voter choose to vote for? What kinds of political groups will a citizen join? Once again, the vast majority of research focuses on elections—specifically on vote choice. In Chapter 12, Alan Abramowitz examines the role of peoples' attitudes on social issues in their voting decisions in 1992. Although there is a large and well-developed literature that traces voting decisions to economic factors, scholars have only recently begun to explore the role of cultural identities and attitudes on electoral decisions. Abramowitz demonstrates that attitudes on abortion and gay rights had a major impact on vote choice, even in an election widely characterized as a referendum on Bush's handling of the economy.

11 Public Opinion and Political Participation

John E. Hughes and M. Margaret Conway

Relative to other industrialized democracies, the United States has very low voter turnout; only in Switzerland does a smaller proportion of the citizenry vote. During the last half of the twentieth century, turnout in U.S. presidential elections peaked in 1960 at 62.8 percent and began a decline that lasted until 1992, when it increased slightly. Why has turnout declined? Did the turnout increase in 1992 reverse the trend, or was it just a reaction to conditions that affected citizens' attitudes and beliefs about that election?

In this chapter we examine the impact of political attitudes and beliefs on patterns of political behavior. We present evidence that suggests that turnout has declined largely as a result of changes in attitudes and beliefs toward the political system. We do not discount the impact of other factors, however. Resources brought to the political process—such as socioeconomic status, experience, and social involvement—and the legal and political context of the election also shape patterns of voter turnout and other forms of election-related political participation, both directly and indirectly, through their influence on attitudes, beliefs, and values.

We shall focus on three aspects of the relationship between public opinion and political participation. First, we examine how selected political attitudes and beliefs have changed from 1964 to 1992. Second, we examine the extent to which those attitudes and beliefs are related to political activity. Although many different types of political activity could be examined, here we will focus only on participation through voting in presidential elections. Finally, we combine the first and second parts in order to determine how changes in attitudes have affected political participation over time. As the distribution of attitudes and beliefs changes, and to the extent that these attitudes and beliefs influence political actions, we expect patterns of political participation to change.

Potential Influences on Turnout

Several types of attitudes and beliefs could affect the decision to engage in political activity. We divide them into two groups. First are the psychological orientations toward the political system and evaluations of the potential for political activity to influence the system. Those who see no probable benefit from participation are unlikely to take part in politics. It is also likely that people who believe that no one in the system listens to them or cares about their views will be less likely to vote. For example, we would expect individuals to be less likely to vote if they believe that voting is an ineffective means for controlling the government, see the government as unresponsive to citizens, or perceive themselves to have no influence on politicians or government (Abramson and Aldrich 1982; Teixeira 1992).

It is also possible that some attitudes toward the political system may affect the underlying motivations for voting more than political participation in general. For example, we might expect trust in government to influence rates of voter turnout, with those less trusting of government being less likely to vote. Yet research suggests that individuals with different levels of trust participate, but for different reasons. The more trusting engage in political activity to support leaders they trust, while the less trusting act to rid the political system of leaders they do not trust or to change aspects of the system they dislike (Bennett and Resnick 1990; Hill and Luttbeg 1983; see also Craig 1993, chap. 6; Luttbeg and Gant 1995, chap. 4). In short, attitudes toward the political system are expected to shape participation within that system in complex ways.

The second group of attitudes focuses on actors in the political system, and these attitudes may differ from one election to another. The extent to which candidates and political parties are salient to the electorate varies. In some elections, candidates and political parties confront the issues of greatest public concern. In these elections, voters may ultimately care more about who wins the election, follow the election more closely, and be more interested in the campaign. In other years, candidates fail to excite the electorate.

The influence of groups on individual behavior will also vary from one election to another. Mobilizing constituents to vote is a goal of many groups, including candidate organizations, political parties, interest groups, and community-based organizations such as churches, civic clubs, and other local organizations (Huckfeldt 1979; Leighley 1990; Verba and Nie 1972; Weilhouwer and Lockerbie 1994). These groups may bring people into the political process through personal influence (for example, when group members ask others to participate) or by activating, reinforcing, or changing some of the beliefs and attitudes through contact with voters (Dalton 1988; Harris 1994; Rosenstone and Hansen 1993).

In the next section we examine changes in political attitudes between 1964 and 1992. Next we examine how each of these is related to voter turnout and how these relationships have changed over time. Finally, we estimate the extent to which changes seen in the first two sections altered turnout between 1964 and 1992. Some attitudes changed dramatically over time, leading to changes in turnout (Miller 1992). Other attitudes may simply have become unrelated to participation patterns (Bennett 1991; Schlozman, Burns, and Verba 1994).

Changes in Beliefs and Attitudes, 1964 to 1992

From 1964 to 1992 significant changes occurred in basic attitudes that we have hypothesized would influence political participation. To document these changes we use data from the American National Election Studies (ANES) surveys conducted in presidential election years from 1964 through 1992. Each of these nationwide surveys asks around 2,000 respondents about their political activity and beliefs.

Table 11-1 shows that during this period the electorate voiced increasingly negative opinions about government and politics. For example, trust in the government in Washington declined: fully 63 percent indicated that they trusted the federal government "most of the time" in 1964, while only 26 percent voiced that sentiment in 1992. Those who reported that they trusted the government "just about always" dropped from 5 percent to 3 percent.

People are more likely to participate if they perceive the government to be responsive to citizens. Many fewer Americans in 1992 believed that the government pays a good deal of attention to people like them than in 1964. The proportion of the electorate who believed that elections are very effective in making government pay a good deal of attention to what people think also declined significantly over the twenty-eight-year period.

Over the last three decades, substantial increases occurred in the proportion of Americans believing that people in the government waste a lot of money, that many government officials are crooks, and especially that the government is run for the benefit of a few big interests. For example, although only 31 percent believed that the government was run for a few big interests in 1964, fully 79 percent voiced that view in 1992.

The proportion of the electorate that has low external efficacy—the belief that the political system does not respond to people like them—also increased. In Table 11-1 efficacy is measured by one item: government officials don't care about "what people like me think." From 1964 to 1992, responses to that statement fluctuated from election to election, but a substantially larger proportion of citizens agreed with the statement in 1992 than in 1964.

One culprit in citizens' increasingly negative orientations toward government might be its increased complexity. However, during the twenty-eight-year period, the proportion agreeing with the statement that "sometimes politics seems so complicated that a person like me can't really understand what's going on" ranged between 68 and 74 percent of those responding. The public does not appear to find politics more complex in the 1990s than in the 1960s.

Overall, however, most attitudes toward the political system have become more negative. Compared with 1964's respondents, citizens in 1992 were less trusting, more cynical, more likely to perceive the government as being corrupt, and less likely to believe that the government is responsive to ordinary citizens. Each of these changes seems likely to produce a decline in voter turnout.

Table 11-1 Political Attitudes over Time, 1964–1992 (in Percentages)

	1964	1968	1972	1976	1980	1984	1988	1992
Trust the government in Washington								
None of the time	0.1	0.2	0.6	1.2	4.1	1.2	2.5	1.9
Some of the time	22.2	37.1	45.3	64.5	70.2	53.9	56.4	68.7
Most of the time	63.2	55.3	48.8	30.9	23.6	41.2	36.9	26.1
Just about always	14.5	7.5	5.4	3.6	2.1	3.7	4.2	3.2
Government pays attention								
Not much	25.4	30.9	24.7	33.5	41.4	30.2	28.7	26.4
Same	40.6	44.5	57.6	55.7	49.9	54.8	58.2	61.1
A good deal	34.0	24.6	17.8	10.8	8.5	15.0	13.1	12.5
Elections make government pay attention								
Not much	6.8	8.7	7.7	10.4	12.8	20.2	17.6	11.6
Some	25.7	29.5	36.5	36.4	35.4	37.1	44.9	41.4
A good deal	67.5	61.8	55.8	53.0	51.8	42.7	37.5	47.0
Government is run								
For the benefit of all	69.1	56.4	41.4	26.8	23.1	41.4	32.7	21.3
By a few big interests	30.9	43.6	58.6	73.4	76.9	58.6	67.3	78.7
People in government waste money								
A lot	48.1	60.6	67.0	76.5	80.0	66.2	64.0	68.2
Some	45.2	35.2	30.6	20.6	17.9	30.1	33.5	30.0
Not very much	6.7	4.2	2.4	2.9	2.0	3.7	2.5	1.8
Government officials are crooked								
Quite a few	30.0	26.3	37.7	44.1	48.5	33.4	41.8	46.6
Not many	51.0	54.0	47.5	42.4	42.7	51.6	46.6	44.4
Hardly any	19.0	19.6	14.8	13.3	8.8	15.0	11.6	9.0
Public officials don't care what people like me think								
Agree	37.0	43.7	50.1	53.7	54.5	42.6	51.0	58.1
Disagree	63.0	56.3	49.9	46.5	45.5	57.6	42.5	41.9
Politics is too complicated								
Agree	67.9	71.3	73.9	72.7	71.4	70.9	70.4	70.7
Disagree	32.1	28.7	26.1	27.7	28.6	29.1	23.3	29.3

Sources: 1952–1988 American National Election Studies Combined File; 1992 American National Election Study.

The second group of attitudes—attitudes toward political actors—have not changed as dramatically or consistently, as Table 11-2 shows. Some scholars have pointed to the decline in party activities as a major cause of changes in turnout from 1964 to 1988 (Rosenstone and Hansen 1993). If parties are less active and therefore less salient to the public, lower voter turnout may follow.

The salience of political parties can be measured by the number of comments survey respondents make about them when they are asked open-ended questions. The average number of comments about the political parties varies by year but produces no trends; however, the proportion with no comments about either party increased from 17 percent in 1964 to 34 percent in 1980.[1] In 1992, 29 percent of survey respondents indicated that the political parties were not salient to them. Yet note also that there is no clear trend in the proportion of the potential electorate contacted by the political parties (as shown in Table 11-2).

Strength of partisan identification is another factor associated with levels of turnout. Significant changes have occurred in party identification, most notably a sharp increase between 1964 and 1992 in the proportion of the electorate that reported no party identification. Accompanying this trend was a decrease in the proportion of Americans identified with a party strongly or weakly. Together, the low level of party salience and declining levels of party identification provide evidence that the public is becoming increasingly detached from the current political parties (Wattenburg 1990).

However, not all the news is bad for the parties. Despite declines in party salience and identification, during the 1980s and in 1992 more survey respondents perceived policy differences between the two major political parties than survey respondents had during the 1960s and 1970s. Opinions on whether one party was more capable of handling our most important problems, however, remained stable during this period.

As people have shifted their attention away from the parties, they have increasingly turned to the candidates themselves. Throughout the twenty-eight-year period under examination candidates were more relevant to the citizens than political parties were (Wattenburg 1991). The proportion of respondents who made no mentions of candidates increased from 4 percent in 1964 to a high of 16 percent in 1988, then dropped to almost 10 percent in 1992.[2] As Table 11-2 reveals, the average salience, however, peaked in 1992, with people mentioning over five specific things they liked or disliked about the major party candidates. This is nearly two mentions higher than the 1992 mean for mentions of the two parties. No trends are evident, however, in the average number of mentions of likes and dislikes about either political parties or the presidential candidates.

Trends in other measures of political engagement also would lead us to expect participation to decline after 1964. Table 11-2 shows that the proportion who are very interested in the campaign declined, as did, to a lesser extent, the proportion who follow politics most of the time. In contrast, however, in 1992 the percentage of respondents reporting they cared

Table 11-2 Attitudes Toward Political Actors and Political Campaigns, 1964–1992 (in Percentages)

	1964	1968	1972	1976	1980	1984	1988	1992
Strength of party identification								
Independent	8.7	11.9	14.6	15.5	15.1	12.7	12.2	12.7
Leaner	15.0	18.5	21.6	21.5	21.7	23.2	25.1	26.7
Weak	38.4	39.9	38.8	39.3	37.0	34.8	31.5	31.6
Strong	37.9	29.6	25.1	23.7	26.2	29.3	31.2	29.1
How close the presidential election will be								
Close	49.4	74.9	36.2	83.9	83.4	50.7	73.5	81.9
Not close	50.6	25.1	63.8	16.1	16.6	49.3	26.5	18.1
Parties differ on most important problem								
Yes	55.4	54.3	51.4	53.1	63.3	67.9	63.3	63.4
No	44.6	45.7	48.6	46.9	36.7	32.1	36.7	36.6
One party is better able to handle most important problem								
Yes	—	—	53.6	50.4	54.0	56.2	45.7	52.4
No	—	—	46.4	49.6	46.0	43.8	54.3	47.6
Contacted by a political party								
Yes	23.7	21.7	12.0	24.8	21.3	20.4	20.5	18.2
No	76.3	78.2	88.0	75.2	78.7	79.6	79.5	81.8
Political party salience								
Mean	3.32	4.02	2.99	3.21	2.71	3.20	3.71	3.50
Standard deviation	2.64	3.12	2.83	3.15	2.87	3.38	3.57	3.45
Candidate salience								
Mean	5.02	5.17	4.39	4.77	5.00	5.20	4.49	5.46
Standard deviation	2.86	3.10	2.90	3.17	3.12	3.56	3.58	3.60
Interested in campaign								
Not much	25.1	20.8	27.4	20.5	26.0	24.8	25.0	38.8
Somewhat	36.6	40.4	41.4	42.3	44.2	46.8	47.2	43.8
Very	38.2	38.9	31.5	36.5	29.8	28.4	27.8	17.4
Care who wins the election								
Don't care	34.5	34.9	39.6	42.6	44.1	35.2	39.0	24.3
Care a great deal	65.5	65.1	60.4	57.4	55.9	64.8	61.0	75.7
Follow politics								
Hardly at all	11.2	17.6	11.4	11.7	15.3	14.0	15.2	—
Only now and then	16.9	18.7	15.9	18.0	23.4	23.1	25.5	—
Some of the time	41.6	30.7	36.2	31.6	34.9	36.4	36.9	—
Most of the time	30.3	33.0	36.6	38.0	26.4	26.4	22.4	—

Sources: 1952–1988 American National Election Studies Combined File; 1992 American National Election Study.

Notes: Salience entries are the sum of the number of mentions by respondents of things they liked or disliked about a party or candidate. Totals ranged from 0 to 20.

who won the election was at its highest level in twenty-eight years. This jump probably can be attributed to the unique candidacy of Ross Perot. The proportion who believed that the division of the vote between the two presidential candidates would be close varied over time, reaching its highest levels in 1976, a low turnout election, and 1992, a high turnout election.

Although there are few obvious trends in the salience of parties and candidates, overall interest in campaigns and politics has declined. Coupled with increases in cynicism and distrust of government, these trends suggest that people have become less willing to invest the time and energy required to register and vote. In the next section we examine whether or not each of these variables is related to turnout and how that relationship may have changed over time.

Beliefs, Attitudes, and the Turnout Decision

Although we have hypothesized that the attitudes we discussed influence the decision of whether to vote, we can investigate that question more directly by correlating these attitudes with voter turnout. Table 11-3 reports the bivariate relationships between turnout and the attitudes we examined. Interest in the campaign, caring who wins the election, and following politics are moderately related to turnout. Because the electoral context changes with each election, the strength of these relationships varies over time: relationships are slightly stronger in the 1980s and 1990s than earlier. Candidate and party salience are moderately related to turnout, and they, too, show a tendency to be more strongly related to turnout in recent elections.

Several attitudes are, at best, only weakly related to turnout. These include believing that public officials do not care what people like them think and viewing politics as too complicated for someone like them to understand. In a candidate-centered age, attitudes toward the parties are often only weakly related to participation. A person's strength of party identification, perceived policy differences between the parties, and being contacted by the party have relatively small relationships to turnout. This is true for many of the other attitudes as well, as Table 11-3 shows. Trust in the federal government, perceiving government to be run by a few big interests, believing that government wastes money, and perceiving public officials to be dishonest have almost no relationship with turnout.

The data in this table clearly show that attitudes vary in their influence on turnout. The relationship between these attitudes and turnout also varies across elections, in part because of election-specific events. To more fully test the impact of these variables on turnout over this twenty-eight-year period, we must resort to multivariate analysis.

To determine the influence of particular variables we first divided the variables into two categories—attitudes toward the system and attitudes toward political actors. We then combined the surveys from 1964 to 1992 into a single dataset to compute the average increase

Table 11-3 Bivariate Correlations Between Voting Turnout and Independent Variables

	1964	1968	1972	1976	1980	1984	1988	1992
Interested in campaign	.21	.26	.28	.27	.36	.29	.39	.32
Care who wins the election	.20	.16	.23	.21	.20	.19	.29	.32
Follow politics	.21	.25	.33	.34	.29	.29	.36	—
Trust the government in Washington	.01	.03	.06	.03	.00	.01	.09	.03
Government run by a few big interests	.03	.02	.04	.01	.02	.02	.04	−.05
People in government waste money	−.03	−.01	−.01	−.03	−.03	−.08	−.02	−.07
Government officials are crooked	.02	.03	.03	.06	.04	.03	.08	.01
Public officials don't care what people like me think	.14	.24	.18	.20	.18	.16	.20	.16
Politics is too complicated	.09	.12	.14	.18	.11	.12	.16	.15
Strength of party identification	.14	.14	.18	.18	.21	.20	.25	.19
Government pays attention	.05	.07	.11	.10	.06	.08	.12	.06
Elections make government pay attention	.05	.09	.11	.12	.07	.09	.13	.10
Net candidate salience	.17	.23	.29	.27	.32	.28	.40	.32
Presidential election will be close	−.04	−.00	−.03	.07	.05	−.04	.06	.08
Party salience	.22	.24	.23	.26	.28	.26	.35	.30
Parties differ on most important problem	.21	.17	.12	.14	.19	.22	.23	.21
One party is better able to handle most important problem	—	—	.16	.11	.15	.14	.14	.10
Contacted by a political party	.19	.15	.13	.20	.18	.18	.22	.18

Sources: 1952–1988 American National Election Studies Combined File; 1992 American National Election Study.

Notes: Cell entries are tau$_b$ and tau$_c$ correlation coefficients.

in turnout associated with each variable.[3] This operation does two things. First, it controls for the changes shown in Table 11-3 by taking into account the different relationships between turnout and attitudes. Second, it compares the variables relative to each other so that we see which variables have the largest and smallest influences on turnout.

Table 11-4 shows the relationship between turnout and attitudes toward the political system. Each entry in the table is interpreted as the percentage increase in the probability that a person will vote when he or she is one step (1 standard deviation) above average for that

Table 11-4 Effect of Attitudes Toward the Governmental System upon Probability of Turnout, 1964–1992 Presidential Elections

Variable	Percentage Change in Probability of Voting
Interested in campaign	9.7**
Care who wins the election	4.8**
People who don't care should not vote (1972–1992 only)	6.4**
People in government waste money	−3.5**
External efficacy: Public officials don't care . . . and people like me have no say	5.9**
Internal efficacy: Politics is too complicated	1.9**
Government pays attention to what people think	1.1**
Elections make government pay attention	1.1**
Presidential election will be close	0.9**

Sources: 1952–1988 American National Election Studies Combined File; 1992 American National Election Study.

Notes: Cell entries represent the predicted difference in turnout associated with each variable. This is computed by calculating the probability that a respondent who is one standard deviation above mean for that variable will vote and subtracting the probability of voting for respondents at the mean while leaving all other variables constant. N = 10,931.

** Significant at the .05 level.

particular variable. Some people will be more than one step above or below average on each variable, so the percentage changes presented here, and throughout this chapter, represent a minimal effect of the given variables.

The analysis shows that some attitudes have considerable influence upon turnout. A person who has above average interest in a presidential race is nearly 10 percent more likely to vote than a person whose interest is average for the sample. While no other variable has as much influence on turnout as interest, several others are quite important. For example, those who care more about the contest are about 5 percent more likely to vote than the average person. People who think that you should not vote if you do not care about the election are in fact less likely to vote by 6 percent. Cynicism plays a role also, but in a peculiar manner. Those who think the government wastes a lot of money are over 3 percent more likely to vote—presumably in an effort to end that waste.

Other attitudes focus more directly on whether the system responds to the public. External efficacy, or the degree to which people perceive themselves as capable of influencing government, also has a large impact on turnout. More efficacious people are 6 percent more likely to vote than those with lower feelings of external efficacy. By contrast, the sense that you as an individual can understand the political process has a more modest influence on

Table 11-5 Effect of Attitudes Toward Political Actors upon Probability of Turnout, 1964–1992 Presidential Elections

Variable	Percentage Change in Probability of Voting
Strength of party identification	5.3**
Political party salience	4.7**
Parties differ on most important problem	2.4**
Candidate salience	7.7**

Sources: 1952–1988 American National Election Studies Combined File; 1992 American National Election Study.

Notes: Cell entries represent the predicted difference in turnout associated with each variable. This is computed by calculating the probability that a respondent who is one standard deviation above mean for that variable will vote and subtracting the probability of voting for respondents at the mean while leaving all other variables constant. N = 11,346.

** Significant at the .05 level.

turnout: 2 percent. Other attitudes, such as the perceived closeness of the election, belief that the government pays attention to the public, and attitudes toward whether elections make the government pay attention to the public, all have relatively small effects on turnout. In short, all attitudes toward the system have some level of influence, but those associated with the importance of or need for participation are consistently the most influential.

What, then, of attitudes toward the political actors? The American National Election Studies surveys provide fewer measures of attitudes toward candidates and parties, but the ones available demonstrate considerable influence. Table 11-5 shows that an increase in strength of partisanship, for example, makes a person over 5 percent more likely to vote than average, while persons for whom parties are more salient are almost 5 percent more likely to vote. Perceived differences between the parties, however, have a modest influence on turnout—just over 2 percent. But while partisan attachment and party salience are influential, the strongest effect stems from candidate salience. When a person expresses many likes or dislikes in conversation about the two major candidates, he or she is almost 8 percent more likely to vote. Candidate salience has increased in influence in recent years. These results underscore the dramatic shift from a party-centered electoral system to a more candidate-centered one. If this trend is not reversed, and a reversal does not appear likely, then candidates will continue to overshadow parties in the minds of voters. This means that, in part, people vote when they are motivated by the presence of particularly liked or disliked candidates, something we will examine in more detail below.

One problem with Tables 11-4 and 11-5 is that they treat attitudes toward political actors and the government system as if they are independent of each other. We know, however, that some of the variables in Table 11-4 are closely related to those in Table 11-5. For example, people who are more strongly partisan are generally more interested in politics. In addition, many demographic variables such as age, education, and income are related to participation and many of them are related to political attitudes as well. For example, people with more education are more likely to be interested in politics and to have high levels of internal efficacy. Thus, to estimate the effects of political attitudes on political participation we must compare them with each other while including demographic information. Table 11-6 shows how each variable influences turnout while taking into account the effect of the other variables.

Many of the demographic variables have a strong impact on turnout, even controlling for some of the attitudes that these variables may also affect. Age has the single largest effect: people who are older than average by 1 standard deviation are 3 percent more likely to vote than those of average age. Higher education and higher income both increase participation, even when we control for attitudinal variables. The power of socioeconomic factors is evidence that resources such as money, time, and experience encourage people to vote. In addition, social groupings facilitate participation. People who regularly attend church or are members of a union are more likely to be mobilized into political action. Residential stability can be viewed as both a resource and a social variable. The longer people stay in an area, the more time they have to register to vote and the more likely they are to be socially connected. The parties and candidates themselves also encourage people to vote. Being contacted by a political party increases the likelihood that a person will vote by about 2 percent. In addition, as Steven Rosenstone and John Mark Hansen (1993) point out, political contact is related to a person's demographic characteristics—employed, well-educated, higher-income individuals are contacted more often. This fact, combined with the evidence that education and income are among the most influential variables also gives rise to potential bias in political participation, as we discuss later in the chapter. For now, it is simply appropriate to note that demographics can play a large role in a person's decision to vote.

Demographics are not destiny. Some of the attitudes toward the system, such as whether the government wastes money, internal efficacy, and the government's attention to the public, are no longer significant predictors of turnout once we hold constant demographic factors. But several attitudinal variables do continue to have an influence on turnout. Above average interest in the presidential contest increases the likelihood by more than 2 percent that a person will vote. In addition, caring about the outcome causes more than a 1 percent increase. Perceiving the system as responding to people like oneself increases a person's probability of voting by over 1 percent as well. Finally, a sense of civic duty—the idea that people should vote whether or not they care about the outcome—increases the probability of voting by approximately 2 percent.

Table 11-6 Effect of All Variables upon Probability of Turnout, 1964–1992 Presidential Elections

Variable	Percentage Change in Probability of Voting
Age	3.0**
Education	2.7**
Income	1.9**
Union membership	0.9**
Church attendance	2.0**
Home ownership	1.5**
Married	—
Mobility (1968–1992 only)	1.3**
Contacted by a party or campaign	1.9**
Interested in campaign	2.1**
Care who wins the election	1.3**
People in government waste money	—
External efficacy: Public officials don't care . . . and people like me have no say	1.5**
Internal efficacy: Politics is too complicated	—
People who don't care should not vote (1972–1992 only)	1.9**
Government pays attention to what people think	—
Elections make government pay attention	—
Presidential election will be close	—
Strength of party identification	1.7**
Political party salience	—
Candidate salience	1.5**
Parties differ on most important problem	0.7**

Sources: 1952–1988 American National Election Studies Combined File; 1992 American National Election Study.

Notes: Cell entries represent the predicted difference in turnout associated with each variable. This is computed by calculating the probability that a respondent who is one standard deviation above mean for that variable will vote and subtracting the probability of voting for respondents at the mean while leaving all other variables constant. N = 7,193.

— Nonsignificant.

** Significant at the .05 level.

While our datasets have measures for only a few attitudes toward the political actors, those that are available show an impact on turnout. People who are more partisan than average are almost 2 percent more likely to vote, and people who see significant differences between the parties are also somewhat more likely to vote. But in an era of candidate-centered campaigns, we once again find that candidate salience has a fairly large effect on turnout. This is especially noteworthy considering that party salience has no discernible effect, further proof that this is a candidate-centered age in politics. In all, demographics combine with attitudes to show that a large number of factors influence the decision to vote.

Changes in Attitudes and Turnout

As we have seen, the overall level of turnout is at least partially dependent upon the way attitudes and resources are distributed within society. That is, an electorate that is older, more educated, wealthier, and interested will have a higher rate of turnout than a younger electorate with fewer resources. Thus, if education levels in the United States were to rise, we would expect turnout to rise, but if the public should withdraw support from the system and become uninterested in the elections, we would expect turnout to decline. In reality, both of these situations have occurred. Educational levels have risen, and some supportive attitudes have declined. Thus, some trends favor increased participation, while others foster turnout decline.

To untangle these trends, we hypothetically transformed 1992 respondents into 1964 voters. To do this, we first estimated the probability that each 1992 respondent would vote, based upon his or her scores for all of the variables discussed so far. We then systematically substituted the average traits and attitudes of 1964 respondents for those of 1992 respondents. For example, we gave each respondent the mean, or average, level of education for 1964 while leaving all other variables constant. Then we subtracted the probability that he or she would vote under the simulated condition from the original odds that he or she would vote. The result, when averaged across the entire 1992 sample, tells us how changes in a particular variable have influenced participation. Thus, we can examine whether changes since 1964 caused an increase or decrease in 1992 turnout.[4]

The results of this simulation are shown in Table 11-7. We can test the accuracy of the model by predicting how many 1992 voters should vote based on the changes in attitudes and demographics. In 1964 voter turnout was 61.9 percent, but only 55.2 percent voted in 1992, for a decline of 6.7 percent. This model predicts a total decline in turnout of 6.9 percent, or 0.2 percent more than occurred.

Some factors that help explain who votes are less useful in explaining changes in turnout over time. The changing age composition of the electorate, for example, does not have a significant influence on changes in turnout. Indeed, only a few variables help explain changes in participation.

For the most part, socioeconomic variables had a relatively small effect upon the change in turnout from 1964 to 1992. Rising levels of education led to a modest turnout increase of about one-quarter of a percent. The decline in family incomes in 1992, however, more than offset those modest gains. Whereas Table 11-6 shows demographics to be strongly related

Table 11-7 Predicted Change in Turnout for 1992 Respondents Using 1964 Characteristics, 1964 versus 1992 Presidential Election

Variable	Percentage Change in Probability of Voting
Age	.23
Education	.23*
Income	−.81**
Union membership	−.49
Church attendance	−.17
Home ownership	−.28
Married	.12
Mobility (1968–1992 only)	.60
Contacted by a party or campaign	−1.02**
Interested in campaign	−1.23*
Care who wins the election	.11*
People in government waste money	.66
External efficacy: Public officials don't care . . . and people like me have no say	−2.95*
Internal efficacy: Politics is too complicated	.82**
People who don't care should not vote (1972–1992 only)	−.80
Government pays attention to what people think	.44
Elections make government pay attention	.54
Presidential election will be close	.92
Strength of party identification	−1.46*
Political party salience	−.39
Candidate salience	−.07
Parties differ on the most important problem	.00
Predicted change in turnout by complete model	−6.9%
Actual change in turnout from 1964 to 1992	−6.7%

Sources: 1952–1988 American National Election Studies Combined File; 1992 American National Election Study.

Notes: Cell entries represent the average percentage change in turnout for 1992 respondents after adjusting them to represent 1964 means for that particular variable. This yields the average increase or decrease in turnout caused by the changing distribution of those variables from 1964 to 1992. N = 932.

 * Significant at the .01 level.
** Significant at the .05 level.

to turnout in any given year, Table 11-7 shows that the demographic characteristics of the potential electorate in the United States have not changed enough to have a major effect upon turnout.

But attitudes toward the system were more influential than demographic changes in explaining the decline in turnout. Generally these changing attitudes have produced declining turnout, although a few attitudes have mitigated that trend by increasing participation. The decline in external efficacy led to nearly a 3 percent drop in voting turnout, by far offsetting the modest increase associated with the increase in internal efficacy.[5] The second most important attitudinal source of declining turnout is the electorate's decreasing partisanship. Declining interest has produced a 1 percent decline in turnout, as have the reduced efforts by parties to contact potential voters. The increase in concern about the outcome of the election in 1992, spurred in part by the candidacy of Ross Perot, accounted for a one-tenth of 1 percent increase in turnout.

Although Table 11-6 showed socioeconomic variables to be more important than attitudes in determining turnout in a specific election, attitudinal variables are the principal explanation for the decline in turnout over time. For example, note that external efficacy and partisanship are not that important in Table 11-6 but are quite important in Table 11-7. Table 11-6 compares the likelihood of voting for a person with the average level of that variable with the likelihood of voting for a person with a higher score. Table 11-7, by contrast, measures how actual changes in the electorate for that variable have influenced total turnout. For example, external efficacy and partisanship may have small individual influences on turnout in any given election, but the massive changes in these variables over time have been a major contributor to the decline in voting since 1964.

Overall, the distribution of attitudes has shifted far more than the distribution of demographic characteristics. Income and education rose, but not by much. On the other hand, party identification, efficacy, and other attitudes changed more rapidly. Thus, changes in attitudes affected turnout patterns more dramatically over time than demographics.

Differences in Group Representation

The changes we have seen in education and income lead us back to a point suggested earlier. If wealthier and better educated individuals vote more often, is there a class bias in political participation? That is, are the people who vote not representative of the eligible population? The question is compounded by the fact that political parties and candidates find it easier to contact and mobilize people who are employed, are more educated, and have higher incomes (Rosenstone and Hansen 1993). Thus, higher resources lead directly to greater participation. In addition, higher resources increase the likelihood of being contacted by political campaigns, which in turn leads to still greater participation. This combination

Figure 11-1 Racial Bias in Turnout, 1964–1992

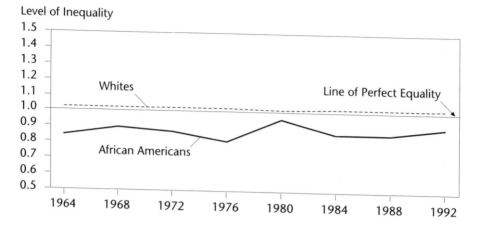

suggests that some groups of people may be overrepresented in elections while others are underrepresented.

To test the level of bias in turnout we calculate whether a group is over- or underrepresented. This calculation has two steps. First, using the surveys of the American National Election Studies, we determine what percentage of voters are in a particular group. Next we calculate the percentage of the population in that group. The ratio of these two percentages is a measure of the equality of representation. A ratio of 1 means perfect representation, ratios over 1 mean that a group is overrepresented, and ratios under 1 mean the group is underrepresented.

For example, one concern may be that African Americans are less represented than whites. To test this we first calculate the percentage of voters who were African American and then the percentage of African Americans in the total population. In 1992, 11.5 percent of voters were African American while 12.8 percent of the total sample was African American. The ratio is 0.89, meaning African American voters were somewhat underrepresented in 1992. For each election between 1964 and 1992 we calculate these ratios for six groups—whites and African Americans, college graduates and those with high school degrees or less, and the top and bottom third in income level.

Figure 11-1 shows the level of racial bias in turnout from 1964 to 1992. Whites are consistently overrepresented while African Americans are consistently underrepresented, although African American representation varies substantially across elections. African Americans were slightly better represented in 1992 than in 1964, but there is no clear pattern of gain in representation. In short, racial bias in turnout has declined somewhat over the twenty-eight years studied here but there remains a persistent level of inequality.

Figure 11-2   Educational Bias in Turnout, 1964–1992

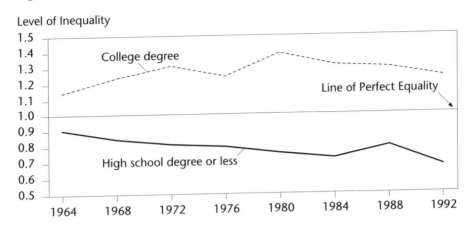

Figure 11-2 shows that not only are those with a college education consistently overrepresented but the inequality has increased over the last three decades. In 1964 the college educated were about 11 percent overrepresented in the electorate, a discrepancy that increased to about 23 percent (a 1.23 ratio) by 1992. Far more than race, education provides a consistent basis for bias in the political system.

We know that education and income are correlated. The more education a person has, the more money he or she is likely to make. It should not be a surprise then, to see in Figure 11-3 that income differences also result in a turnout bias. The level of underrepresentation for those in the bottom third of income has increased slightly over the last thirty years, from a ratio of just under 0.9 in 1964 to just over 0.8 in 1992. The same is true for the overrepresentation of those with incomes in top third of the nation. In 1964, they were overrepresented with a ratio of 1.14; in 1992 the ratio was 1.23. In all, of the three demographic measures presented here, it is interesting to note that education provides the sharpest contrast. In 1992, the difference in representation between whites and African Americans was 0.12; for income the difference was 0.36; and for education the gap was larger still at 0.56. Education is strongly related to political activity, and as a consequence, differences in education lead to large inequalities in the level of activity for different groups. Equally important, these biases have not disappeared in recent years but have remained consistent or even increased.

1992 and Ross Perot

Tables 11-1 and 11-2 and Figures 11-1 through 11-3 all provide evidence that every election is unique in some way. We have already noted that the general decline in turnout since

Figure 11-3   Income Bias in Turnout, 1964–1992

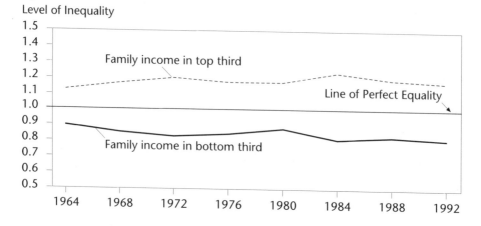

1960 was reversed in 1992, when turnout was about 5 percent higher than it had been in 1988. In this section we examine briefly a unique aspect of the 1992 election: Ross Perot. Perot's candidacy illustrates how political events and actors can dramatically affect political attitudes. Perot, a symbol of the growing disenchantment with the major parties, mobilized many voters. We may not know exactly why he had the influence he did, but we do know that the mechanisms we have cited in this chapter were central to his efforts. Perot made people more concerned about the outcome of the race; he made the race more salient to a sizable portion of the electorate; and he helped to heighten the contrasts between the parties. In short, he stimulated interest in the campaign and thereby helped increase turnout.

To examine Perot's influence on turnout, we divided the electorate into three groups. The first group is people who did not vote in 1992. We label these people nonvoters. The second group is those who voted in both the 1992 and 1988 elections; we label them voters. The third group is people who voted in 1992 but not in 1988. These people, called newcomers, were somehow convinced to vote in 1992 after sitting out the prior election.[6] Every election has newcomers, but for 1992 the percentage of newcomers was twice as large as in 1988, and is second only to the election of 1972—an election in which the United States dramatically expanded the electorate by allowing eighteen-year-old citizens to vote for the first time. So something in 1992 brought an unusual number of newcomers into the voting booths, and Perot accounts for at least part of that increase.

The best way to identify Perot's role is to look at what percentage of each candidate's vote can be accounted for by newcomers. Only 16 percent of George Bush's vote and 19 percent of Bill Clinton's vote came from people who had not voted in 1988. Perot received the highest level of support from newcomers: 20 percent of his votes came from people who had not voted in 1988.[7] In all, Bush received only 29 percent of the newcomers' votes while he earned 34 percent of the votes of those who had also voted in 1988. Although these differences are relatively small, we can make two inferences. First, the majority of newcomers cast a vote against the incumbent. Second, Perot did well among the newcomers, a fact that supports the idea that his candidacy helped mobilize the electorate.

Further evidence can be found through examining attitudes toward Perot and the other two candidates. In the 1992 survey, respondents were asked to place themselves and each of the candidates on an ideological spectrum ranging from 1 to 7. We can compare how far people placed themselves from the candidates and how far apart they placed the candidates from one another. These scores tell us whether individuals saw themselves as being ideologically closer to one of the candidates and whether they perceived ideological distinctions between the candidates. Using these scores, we find that newcomers in 1992 saw Bush and Perot as being much closer together than were Clinton and Perot. More important, new voters saw either Clinton or Perot as being closer to themselves than Bush.

Finally, we should note that Perot was not a salient candidate to most voters. Out of a possible 20 responses, the mean number of comments about Perot was 1.3, which compares with 3.1 for Bush and 2.7 for Clinton. Clearly, people knew and thought more about the major party candidates, especially the incumbent. Among newcomers, however, Perot was more salient. These voters averaged 1.5 comments on Perot, a difference of +0.2 from the rest of the voters. This difference between newcomers and the overall mean is larger than for either of the other candidates; those differences are +0.1 for Bush and 0 for Clinton. Such differences are not statistically significant, but they reinforce the pattern seen above. They indicate that Perot's candidacy contributed to increasing turnout in 1992.

Conclusions

Many factors affect political participation in the United States. Demographic characteristics are among the most important. Higher levels of age, education, income, and social involvement are associated with higher turnout. But these characteristics have not changed much over time, and so although they can help to explain turnout in any one election, they are less helpful in explaining changes in turnout.

In comparison, political attitudes changed significantly over the last three decades, and many of these attitudes are strongly related to turnout. Many of these changes are direct sources of declining participation in the United States. For example, partisan identification and external efficacy declined between 1964 and 1992, while cynicism increased. The 1992 candidacy of Ross Perot, however, tapped into some of these attitudes and provided an incentive to participate for some Americans.

So what does this portend for the future? Given the relative stability of most socioeconomic variables, further attitudinal shifts will contribute to changes in turnout. And while no one can predict which attitudes will change, we can foresee a general pattern. Turnout will continue to drop unless the parties, and more probably the candidates, are able to foster attitudes that are more supportive of political engagement. In an era of negative campaigns, that kind of change in attitudes would be difficult to achieve.

Notes

1. Party salience is the sum of the number of times a respondent mentioned something that he or she "liked" about a party and something that he or she "disliked." Scores ranged from 0 to 20.

2. Candidate salience is the sum of the number of times a respondent mentioned something he or she "liked" about a major party candidate and something he or she "disliked." Scores ranged from 0 to 20.

3. To compute the difference in predicted turnout, we used logistic regression to calculate the predicted probability of voting. This is done by setting all variables to their mean, computing the probability of voting, then raising one variable by 1 standard deviation and computing a new probability of voting. All other variables were held constant at their means. The difference between the second and first probabilities is the change in the likelihood of voting.

4. The predicted change in turnout is computed by estimating the mean likelihood of voting for the 1992 sample, adjusting the characteristics of the 1992 sample to represent their 1964 compatriots, and reestimating the mean likelihood of voting. The difference between the two means is the predicted change in turnout. The significance for the cell entries is based upon the significance level for the 1992 coefficients. See Lieske (1994) for more details on this methodology.

5. The changes in internal efficacy may be due to the effects of the Perot campaign in mobilizing those who previously thought politics was too complicated to understand.

6. We confine this analysis to voters over the age of twenty-two to avoid categorizing newly enfranchised adults as newcomers.

7. This is calculated by dividing the number of newcomers who voted for a candidate by the total number of votes cast for that candidate.

12 The Cultural Divide in American Politics: Moral Issues and Presidential Voting

Alan I. Abramowitz

According to conventional wisdom, the 1992 presidential election was about economics. The slow recovery from the 1991 recession and continued high unemployment made many Americans worry about their own and their country's economic well-being. Indeed, exit polls showed that the economy was the most salient issue on voters' minds and that Bill Clinton's victory over George Bush was based largely on dissatisfaction with the incumbent's handling of the economy (Pomper 1993).

Despite widespread public concern about the economy, however, the 1992 presidential election was not just a choice between two different economic programs. The 1992 presidential election also presented the American people with a choice between two different sets of values.[1] At their national conventions, the Democratic and Republican Parties took sharply contrasting positions on value-laden issues such as access to abortion and the rights of homosexuals (Congressional Quarterly 1993, 59A–65A, 78A–99A). The Democratic platform strongly endorsed the Supreme Court's 1973 decision legalizing abortion (*Roe v. Wade*) and called for an extension of federal civil rights laws to prohibit housing and job discrimination against AIDS victims and homosexuals. The Republican platform, in contrast, called for a virtual ban on abortion and opposed any extension of civil rights protection to homosexuals. Despite the dramatic differences between the parties' positions, however, very little is known about how this conflict over values affected the electorate.

One of the longest-standing debates in the study of American elections and voting behavior involves the influence of policy issues on decision-making strategies of voters and the outcomes of elections. Early research on voting behavior, including the sociological studies of the Columbia school (Lazarsveld, Berelson, and Gaudet 1944; Berelson, Lazarsveld, and McPhee 1954) and the social-psychological studies of the Michigan school (Campbell et al. 1960) generally downplayed the importance of policy issues. During the 1960s and 1970s, however, a number of studies indicated that policy differences in areas such as civil rights, the Great Society programs of the Johnson administration, and the Vietnam War did influence voters' decision making in presidential elections (Abramson, Aldrich, and Rohde 1983, chap. 6; Converse et al. 1969; Miller et al. 1976; Nie, Verba, and Petrocik 1979; Pomper 1972; RePass 1971). While scholarly opinion remained divided on the importance of these issues (Margolis 1977), a growing consensus emerged among voting-behavior researchers that policy issues could, under certain conditions, sway large numbers of voters.

During the 1970s and 1980s, a new set of policy issues began to divide the parties. In the aftermath of the Supreme Court's decisions prohibiting school prayer and legalizing abortion, evangelical Christian groups began to mobilize in support of candidates, primarily Republicans, who promised to overturn the Court's rulings and restore "traditional" values. At the same time, feminist and gay rights groups increasingly demanded that Democratic candidates defend abortion rights and support civil rights protection for gays and lesbians. Religious affiliation and beliefs were becoming increasingly important influences on partisanship and voting behavior (Green and Guth 1991; Kellstedt, Smidt, and Kellstedt 1991).

The first condition for policy-based voting is the existence of clear differences between the parties on policy issues. Without such differences, voters cannot choose between the parties on policy grounds. But in American presidential elections, clear policy differences are not always present. Two-party competition often leads the major parties and their candidates to adopt similar or ambiguous positions on controversial policy issues (Downs 1957, chap. 8; Page 1978). When this happens, voters find it difficult to choose between the parties on policy grounds (Key 1966). The absence of clear differences between the parties on major issues may explain why studies of voting in the presidential elections of the 1950s found little evidence of policy-based voting.

Even if the parties take clear and distinguishable positions, however, no guarantee exists that voters will perceive the differences between the parties and act on them. Voters must both perceive parties' positions and care about the issues to translate policy differences into policy voting. However, perceptual accuracy may be impeded by voters' party loyalties. Voters can avoid psychological conflict between their party loyalty and their issue positions through selective perception, the process of recognizing only the information that fits with their existing beliefs (Page and Brody 1972). Furthermore, even if voters perceive candidates' positions accurately, they may not strongly prefer one party's position over the other's.

We can infer, then, that the potential for policy voting should vary directly with the degree of polarization of opinion on an issue. If most voters take a similar position on the issue, both major parties probably will gravitate toward that position; voters will find it difficult to distinguish between the parties' positions, and voters who do perceive a difference will not strongly prefer one party's position to the other's. However, when opinion is polarized on an issue, parties can be expected to take opposing positions, and voters should be more likely to perceive a clear difference between the parties' positions and to strongly prefer one party's position to the other's.

Polarization should also increase the salience of an issue. Voters with extreme views are more likely to care about an issue than voters with moderate views. Therefore, the larger the proportion of voters with extreme positions on an issue, the larger should be the proportion of voters who care enough about the issue to use it in their voting decision.

Moral Issues in the 1992 Presidential Election

No set of issues in recent years has had a greater potential to produce policy-based voting than those involving moral values. Perhaps more than any other type of issue, moral values tend to polarize voters. Issues such as legalized abortion and gay rights involve fundamental beliefs about right and wrong. Opponents of legalized abortion and gay rights see these policies as directly contrary to religious teaching and family values. On the other side, advocates of legalized abortion and gay rights see these policies as protecting basic individual rights and freedom of choice. As a result, it is very difficult for political leaders to find a middle ground that will be acceptable to voters on both sides of these issues (Cook, Jelen, and Wilcox 1992).

Moral values would appear to fit Edward Carmines and James Stimson's (1980) definition of an easy issue. Gay rights and legalized abortion are symbolic and emotional issues that involve policy ends rather than means. As such, moral issues are easy for voters to understand. This is demonstrated by the extremely small proportion of citizens who are unable or unwilling to express an opinion on these issues—for example, less than 1 percent of respondents in the 1992 American National Election Study (ANES) had no opinion about the legality of abortion.

Since 1980, the two major parties have taken dramatically different positions with regard to value-laden issues such as sexual equality, legalized abortion, and gay rights. The Republican Party's platforms, reflecting the influence of right-to-life activists and conservative evangelicals, have opposed the Equal Rights Amendment and civil rights protection for homosexuals and have advocated a virtual ban on abortion. Meanwhile, the Democratic Party's platforms, reflecting the influence of prochoice, homosexual, and feminist activists, have advocated greater civil rights protection for homosexuals and AIDS victims, and they have strongly endorsed the Equal Rights Amendment and the Supreme Court's 1973 decision legalizing abortion. In 1992, Bill Clinton became the first major-party presidential candidate to openly campaign for gay votes. Given the clear differences between the parties' positions on moral issues, conservative voters should strongly prefer the Republican Party's position while liberal voters should strongly prefer the Democratic Party's position.

Data: The 1992 American National Election Study

The 1992 American National Election Study provides the data for this analysis. The study included two batteries of questions measuring attitudes toward abortion and gay rights.

Respondents also were asked to give their perceptions of the positions of the Democratic and Republican presidential candidates on legalized abortion. This question allows us to compare awareness of party differences on a moral issue with awareness of party differences on other types of issues.

The ANES survey did not ask respondents to rate their concern with moral issues compared with other kinds of issues. However, as in previous years, the 1992 survey did include several series of open-ended questions asking respondents what they liked and disliked about the political parties and presidential candidates, what they regarded as the most important differences between the two major parties, and what they considered the most important problems facing the country. These questions were used to measure concern about moral issues by coding answers according to whether or not any of these issues were mentioned. We assume that the more concerned a voter was about moral issues, the more likely it is that he or she would have mentioned these issues in response to one or more of these open-ended questions.

In addition to legalized abortion and gay rights, the 1992 ANES survey included questions about a wide variety of domestic and international issues including the death penalty, civil rights, social welfare policy, defense spending, and the Gulf War. Respondents also were asked to evaluate their personal financial situation and the state of the national economy. These questions allow us to compare the influence of moral values on the vote with that of economic conditions and other policy issues.

Measures

The first question that must be addressed before analyzing the effects of moral values on voters' decision making is whether moral issues formed a separate and distinct policy dimension in the minds of voters. To answer this question, I subjected all of the questions dealing with policy issues to a factor analysis, using principal components extraction and a varimax rotation. Factor analysis identifies issues that are highly correlated, meaning that voters who are conservative on one issue in a given factor will be more likely to be conservative on others as well. The results of the factor analysis are shown in Table 12-1.

The results of the factor analysis provide clear evidence that moral issues formed a separate and distinct issue dimension. The questions dealing with abortion and gay rights loaded on a separate factor from questions dealing with all other issues. In addition to this moral values dimension, three other issue dimensions emerged from the factor analysis. These involved attitudes toward racial issues, attitudes toward social welfare issues, and attitudes toward military and national security issues.

Based on the results of the factor analysis, I combined the seven questions dealing with abortion and gay rights into a single moral values scale. Scores on this scale ranged from

Table 12-1 Results of Factor Analysis of Policy Issues in 1992

Issues	Social Issues	Racial Issues	Social Welfare Issues	Military/ Security Issues
Gay rights laws	.528	.237	.379	−.318
Gays in military	.628	.210	.311	−.225
Gay adoption	.658	.216	.198	−.088
Legalized abortion	.744	−.080	.013	.107
Parental consent for abortion	.658	.108	−.111	.268
Spousal notification for abortion	.718	.017	−.163	.185
Abortion funding	.566	.111	.181	.147
Job preference for blacks	−.016	.707	−.001	.349
College preference for blacks	.000	.759	.062	.277
Civil rights progress	.213	.577	−.098	.041
School integration	.067	.605	.175	−.200
Help for blacks	.126	.514	.334	.268
Whether blacks are treated fairly	.133	.654	.122	−.094
Government-guaranteed jobs	−.040	.243	.665	.237
Government-provided services	−.118	−.168	−.664	.022
Government-backed health care	.074	.016	.710	.207
Defense spending	−.307	−.090	−.178	−.454
Gulf War	−.104	−.141	−.277	−.552

Source: 1992 American National Election Study.

Notes: Analysis includes only respondents who reported voting in presidential election. Coefficients shown are factor loadings based on principal components extraction with varimax rotation. Coefficients of .5 (−.5) or larger are underlined.

−14 (most conservative) to +14 (most liberal), with a mean of −0.9 and a standard deviation of 7.6.

I used the questions included in the factor analysis to create scales measuring attitudes toward three other sets of issues: civil rights, social welfare, and national security. The civil rights scale ranged from −10 (most conservative) to +10 (most liberal), with a mean of −2.4 and a standard deviation of 4.8; the social welfare scale ranged from −9 (most conservative) to +9 (most liberal), with a mean of 0.2 and a standard deviation of 3.7; and the national security scale ranged from −4 (most promilitary) to +4 (most antimilitary), with a mean of 0.1 and a standard deviation of 1.7.

Attitudes toward national economic conditions were measured by two questions asking about how conditions had changed in the past year and in the past four years. These two questions were combined into a scale with scores ranging from –4 (most negative) to +4 (most positive). This scale had a mean of –2.3, with a standard deviation of 1.6, indicating that evaluations of economic conditions were overwhelmingly negative.

Personal economic well-being was measured by a scale consisting of eight questions. In addition to the traditional item asking respondents whether they were personally doing better, about the same, or worse than a year earlier, I included seven items dealing with voters' personal economic experiences. These questions asked respondents whether they had been able to make necessary purchases, save money, obtain medical care, and make mortgage or rental payments, and whether they had used savings, borrowed money, or looked for an additional job in order to meet current expenses. Combining these seven questions with the traditional personal finances question should produce a more reliable measure of personal economic well-being than the personal finances question alone. The scale of personal economic well-being ranged from –5 (most negative) to +5 (most positive) with a mean of 0.7 and a standard deviation of 2.2. Thus, on average, voters evaluated their own financial situation much more positively than the national economic situation.

Polarization of Opinion

I have argued that the potential for policy-based voting on an issue should be related to the degree of opinion polarization on that issue. To compare the degree of opinion polarization on different policy issues, we can examine the distribution of scores on each of the policy scales. Figure 12-1 presents histograms for each of the policy scales, including the two subscales—abortion and gay rights—that make up the moral issues scale. The figures show the percentage of respondents who fall at each position on the scale, with the most liberal respondents on the left and the most conservative ones on the right.

The data summarized in Figure 12-1 indicate that opinions on legalized abortion and gay rights were much more polarized than opinions on social welfare, national security, or even civil rights. Opinions about social welfare, national security, and civil rights issues all followed a unimodal distribution, with opinions clustered around the middle of the scale and relatively few respondents holding extreme opinions. On all of these issues, only 4 to 6 percent of respondents were found at the extreme positions. In contrast, opinions about abortion and gay rights followed a multimodal distribution, with substantial numbers of respondents holding extreme opinions. On the abortion subscale, 13 percent of the respondents were located at the liberal or conservative ends of the scale; on the gay rights subscale, 25 percent of the respondents were located at the liberal or conservative ends of the scale.

To measure opinion polarization, I converted the raw scores on the various policy scales into percentage scores, with 0 representing the most conservative score and 100 the most liberal score. We can then compare the standard deviations of the scales: the larger the stan-

Figure 12-1   Distributions of Opinion on Policy Scales

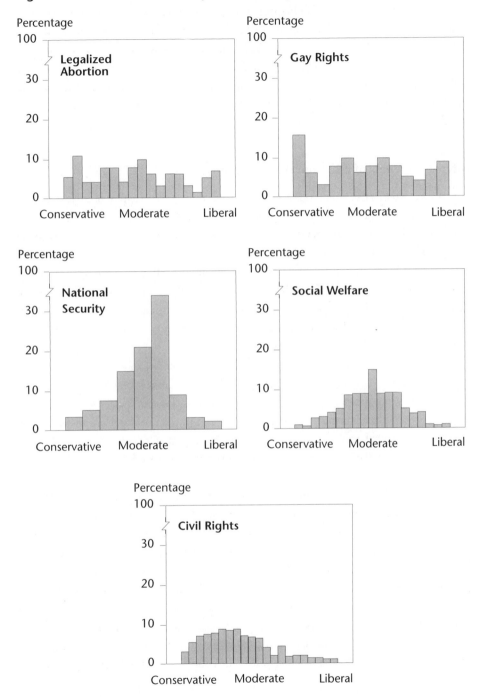

dard deviation, the greater the degree of polarization. The results show, once again, that opinions on abortion and gay rights were much more polarized than opinions on other issues. The standard deviations of the social welfare, national security, and civil rights scales were 20.5, 20.9, and 23.7, respectively. In contrast, the standard deviation of the abortion scale was 30.3 and the standard deviation of the gay rights scale was 32.6. The high degree of opinion polarization on these issues, along with the clear difference between the parties' positions, should have created a strong potential for policy-based voting on moral issues.

Voters' Awareness of and Concern About the Issues

I have argued that two conditions for policy-based voting are perception of party differences and concern about an issue. Table 12-2 presents data bearing on these two conditions. In this table, perception of party differences and concern with moral issues are compared with perception of party differences and concern about three other sets of issues: racial issues, social welfare issues, and national security issues. Perception of party differences is measured by the percentage of voters who placed the presidential candidates on opposite sides of an issue. Concern is measured by the percentage of voters who mentioned an issue at least once in response to the open-ended questions dealing with party and candidate likes and dislikes, party differences, and national problems.

The data in Table 12-2 indicate that voters were much more likely to view the parties as being on opposite sides of moral issues than to perceive differences on other types of issues. (Unfortunately, no questions were asked about party positions on racial issues.) Fifty-nine percent of voters placed the parties on opposite sides on the issue of legalized abortion, compared with 32 percent on social welfare issues and 26 percent on defense spending. Not only was the electorate polarized on moral issues, but voters also viewed the parties as polarized on these issues.

The data in Table 12-2 also underscore the salience of moral issues in the electorate. Thirty percent of voters mentioned abortion or gay rights at least once in response to the open-ended questions, while only about 10 percent of voters mentioned either social welfare or national security issues and only 5 percent of voters mentioned racial issues. Thus, moral issues appear to be more salient in 1992 than any other set of policy issues.

I have argued that the salience of moral issues in 1992 reflected the polarization of public opinion on these issues. If this was the case, then we should find the highest levels of concern among voters with the most extreme views. To test this hypothesis, Table 12-3 displays the relationships between concern and extremism, measured by the consistency of opinion in either a liberal or a conservative direction. Thus the "very high" category

Table 12-2 Perceptions of Party Differences and Issue Salience, 1992 Presidential Election (in Percentages)

Issue Area	Perceive Parties on Opposite Sides	Issue Salient
Moral issues	59[a]	30
Racial issues	NA	5
Social welfare issues	32[b]	11
Defense/military issues	26[c]	9

Source: 1992 American National Election Study.

Notes: Percentages based on respondents who reported voting in presidential election. Number of cases is approximately 1,700. NA = question not available.

[a] Based on question on legal status of abortion.
[b] Average of questions on government responsibility for jobs and living standards and tradeoff between government services and taxes.
[c] Based on question on defense spending.

includes those with either consistently liberal or consistently conservative positions on moral issues.

The data in Table 12-3 strongly support the extremism hypothesis. Voters at the liberal and conservative poles of the moral issues scale were more than three times as likely to express concern about moral issues than voters with moderate positions. Extremism definitely led to heightened concern with moral issues. What remains to be determined is how perceptions of party differences and concern affected policy voting.

Moral Values and Candidate Choice

I have hypothesized that awareness of party differences is a necessary condition for policy-based voting and that salience should magnify the influence of policy attitudes on the vote. To test these hypotheses, Table 12-4 displays the relationships between attitudes toward moral issues and presidential candidate choice among three groups of voters: those who perceived no difference between the parties' positions on moral issues, those who perceived a difference but for whom these issues were not salient, and those who perceived a difference and for whom these issues were salient.

The data in Table 12-4 provide strong support for both hypotheses concerning the conditions for policy-based voting. Among voters who did not perceive a difference between the

Table 12-3 Salience of Moral Issues by Extremism, 1992 Presidential Election

Extremism Score	Percentage Concerned	Nnumber of Cases
Very low (0–2)	18	(341)
Low (3–5)	22	(323)
Moderate (6–8)	25	(318)
High (9–11)	36	(247)
Very high (12–14)	62	(246)
Tau c	.30*	

Source: 1992 American National Election Study.

Note: Based on respondents who reported voting in presidential election.

* Statistically significant at the .01 level.

parties' positions on moral issues, no relationship existed between policy attitudes and the presidential vote (tau c = –.00). In contrast, among voters who perceived a difference between the parties' positions, a strong relationship existed between attitudes toward moral issues and the presidential vote. The data in Table 12-4 also provide strong evidence for the salience hypothesis: among voters who perceived a difference between the parties' positions, the relationship between policy attitudes and candidate preference was much stronger among those for whom moral issues were salient (tau c = .79) than among those for whom these issues were not salient (tau c = .48).

To compare the effect of moral issues on presidential candidate preference with the effects of economic conditions and other types of issues, I conducted two probit analyses.[2] One analysis included all Bush and Clinton voters. The second analysis included only Bush and Clinton voters who perceived a difference between the parties' positions on moral issues and for whom these issues were salient. This group constituted almost one-fourth of the entire electorate. The results of these two probit analyses are presented in Table 12-5.

Among all Clinton and Bush voters, moral issues had a stronger influence on candidate choice than any other set of issues, including national economic conditions and personal economic well-being. In fact, the only variable that had a stronger influence on candidate choice was party identification. Furthermore, among the subset of aware and concerned voters, the effect of these issues was about twice as strong as among the electorate as a whole. For these voters, moral issues were much more important than any other set of issues, including the economy. In fact, among these voters the influence of moral issues on the vote was virtually identical to the influence of party identification.

Table 12-4 Issue Awareness, Issue Salience, and the Effect of Moral Issues on the Presidential Vote, 1992

Position on Moral Issues	Percentage of Major Party Vote for Clinton Among Voters		
	Unaware of Differences (n = 353)	Aware but Not Concerned (n = 486)	Aware and Concerned (n = 339)
Very conservative	63	19	4
Somewhat conservative	49	49	22
Slightly conservative	45	67	36
Moderate	55	71	33
Slightly liberal	51	84	61
Somewhat liberal	56	90	76
Very liberal	75	98	95
Tau c	−.00	.48*	.79*

Source: 1992 American National Election Study.

* Statistically significant at the .01 level.

The Sources of Moral Values

The data presented here demonstrate that the American people and the two major political parties were deeply divided over moral issues in 1992. What explains this sharp division in American public opinion? Differences over issues such as gay rights and legalized abortion appear to reflect a cultural division in contemporary American society—a division between a religious culture and a secular culture. Adherents of the religious culture believe that public policy should be based on traditional Judeo-Christian teachings found in the Bible and other religious texts; adherents of the secular culture believe that public policy should be based on humanistic values informed by scientific knowledge.

If attitudes toward moral issues reflect a person's cultural orientation, we should find a strong relationship between religious affiliation and beliefs and attitudes toward such issues as gay rights and legalized abortion. Based on the traditional teachings of their churches, practicing Protestants and Roman Catholics should be more inclined to oppose gay rights and legalized abortion than the religiously unaffiliated and Jews. Furthermore, regardless of affiliation, religiosity should be associated with opposition to legalized abortion and gay rights.

In addition to religious affiliation and beliefs, education should also have a strong influence on a person's cultural orientation. In the United States, education, and especially higher education, is generally associated with the promotion of secular values such as personal

Table 12-5 The Influence of Moral Issues on the Vote, 1992 Presidential Election

Independent Variables	All Voters (n = 891)			Aware and Concerned (n = 253)		
	Coefficient	Ratio	Change in Probability	Coefficient	Ratio	Change in Probability
Party identification	.470	12.55*	.35	.487	4.95*	.37
Ideology	.388	3.91*	.14	.330	1.42	.11
Social welfare	.034	1.48	.05	.019	0.33	.02
Civil rights	.024	1.34	.04	.028	0.70	.05
Military issues	.005	0.12	.00	.024	0.20	.02
Personal economic condition	−.032	−0.99	−.03	−.098	−1.20	−.09
National economic condition	−.149	−3.38*	−.10	−.069	−0.63	−.05
Moral issues	.055	5.10*	.16	.115	4.40*	.33
Age	−.003	−0.66	−.02	−.006	−0.58	−.04
Gender (female)	−.314	−2.33*	−.06	.084	0.26	.03
Race (black)	.577	2.00*	.05	−.716	−0.97	−.07
Education	−.104	−1.33	−.04	−.318	−1.56	−.12
Family income	−.014	−1.11	−.03	−.002	−0.07	−.00
Constant	.828			1.287		

Source: 1992 American National Election Study.

Notes: Dependent variable is presidential vote, coded as "1" for Clinton and "0" for Bush. Change in probability is estimated effect of increase of one standard deviation on each independent variable on probability of voting for Clinton for voter with initial probability of .50.

* Statistically significant at the .01 level.

freedom and tolerance of alternative lifestyles. Therefore, the more schooling a person has completed, the more likely he or she should be to support gay rights and legalized abortion.

Members of groups that have been the victims of discrimination should also be less likely than members of socially dominant groups to support traditional values that have, in the past, been used to justify such discrimination. Thus, women and African Americans should be more likely to support gay rights and legalized abortion than white men.

Table 12-6 shows the relationships between attitudes toward moral issues and personal characteristics, including religious affiliation, church attendance, education, race, and gender. To compare attitudes toward moral issues among members of different groups, I have converted scores on the moral issues scale into percentages, with 100 representing the most liberal position on all issues and 0 representing the most conservative position on all issues.

All of the relationships in this table are in the expected direction. Protestants and Catholics

Table 12-6 Group Differences in Liberalism on Moral Issues

Characteristic	Percentage Liberal
Religion	
Protestant (n = 886)	42
Roman Catholic (n = 366)	46
Jewish (n = 31)	78
None (n = 180)	64
Church Attendance	
Never (n = 462)	59
Rarely (n = 215)	55
Occasionally (n = 202)	48
Regularly (n = 178)	42
Weekly (n = 430)	31
Education	
Some high school (n = 176)	35
Graduated high school (n = 460)	41
Some college (n = 381)	48
Graduated college (n = 433)	55
Race	
White (n = 1,286)	46
Black (n = 175)	50
Gender	
Male (n = 709)	42
Female (n = 780)	51

Source: 1992 American National Election Study.

Note: Based on respondents who reported voting in the 1992 presidential election.

were much more conservative than Jews and those with no religious affiliation. Likewise, persons who attended church regularly were much more conservative than those who seldom or never attended. Blacks were only slightly more liberal than whites, but there was a somewhat larger gap between men and women.

To test our hypotheses about the sources of moral values, it is necessary to estimate the effect of each of our independent variables while controlling for all of the others. For example, the gap between blacks and whites may be larger than it appears in Table 12-6 because blacks tend to be more religious than whites. Thus the effect of religion may be masking the effect of race. I therefore conducted a multiple regression analysis with the moral issues scale as the dependent variable. The independent variables were religious affiliation,

Table 12-7 Explaining Attitudes Toward Moral Issues

Independent Variables	b	t-ratio	Beta
Church attendance	−1.82	−14.98*	−.385
Roman Catholic	1.07	2.50*	.060
Jewish	6.50	5.36*	.123
No religion	2.62	4.27*	.110
West	−0.83	−1.57	−.044
Midwest	−1.31	−2.68*	−.078
South	−1.59	−3.10*	−.091
Education	1.85	9.53*	.243
Family income	0.03	0.92	.024
Gender (female)	3.21	9.15*	.209
Race (black)	3.09	5.44*	.130
Age	−.00	−0.35	−.008
Constant	−2.73		
R^2	.33		

Source: 1992 American National Election Study.

Notes: Dependent variable is cultural issues scale ranging from −14 (most conservative) to +14 (most liberal). Coefficients shown are unstandardized regression coefficients (b), ratios of regression coefficients to standard errors (t-ratio), and standardized regression coefficients (Beta).

* Statistically significant at the .01 level (one-tail test).

church attendance, education, race, and gender. Region, age, and family income were included in the analysis as control variables. The results of the regression analysis are presented in Table 12-7.

The data in Table 12-7 strongly support our hypotheses concerning the importance of religious affiliation and beliefs in shaping attitudes toward moral issues. Religiosity, as measured by church attendance, had by far the strongest influence of any of the variables included in the analysis on support for gay rights and legalized abortion. The more regularly a person attended church services, the more conservative he or she tended to be on moral issues. Furthermore, Jews held by far the most liberal attitudes on moral issues of any religious group. Catholics and the religiously unaffiliated were only slightly more liberal than Protestants. (Because the Protestant category has been excluded from the analysis, the coefficients for all of the other religious groupings represent a comparison with Protestants.)

As expected, a strong positive relationship existed between education and liberal attitudes toward moral issues. In fact, after religiosity, education had the strongest influence on these attitudes of any of the variables in the analysis. The data show that after controlling for all of the other variables in the analysis, college-educated respondents were much more likely to support gay rights and legalized abortion than respondents with only a high school education.

Finally, both gender and race were strongly related to attitudes toward moral issues. As expected, women tended to hold more liberal attitudes on these issues than men and African Americans tended to hold more liberal attitudes than whites.

After controlling for the other variables in the regression analysis, neither age nor family income had any discernible impact on attitudes toward moral issues. However, some regional differences did persist: southerners and midwesterners held somewhat more conservative attitudes than residents of the Northeast (the excluded category in the analysis). These differences were fairly modest, however. Thus, while the balance of power between the religious and secular cultures may differ slightly from one region to another, with the religious culture strongest in the South and the secular culture strongest in the Northeast, the conflict between the two cultures extends to all regions of the country.

Conclusions

Although voters' dissatisfaction with economic conditions was the major reason George Bush lost the 1992 presidential election, the economy was not the only issue on the minds of voters as they cast their ballots. Data from the 1992 American National Election Study indicate that Americans were deeply divided over moral issues such as legalized abortion and gay rights, and that these issues strongly influenced their choice of a presidential candidate. In fact, moral issues had a stronger influence on voters' decision making than any other type of issue, including the economy. The politicization of moral issues may be one of the most important and enduring political developments of the 1990s.

The relatively strong influence of moral issues on voters' decision making reflected two facts: more voters perceived a difference between the parties' positions on moral issues than on other types of issues, and more voters were concerned about these issues than about other types of issues. Approximately two-thirds of voters perceived a difference between the parties' positions on moral issues, and nearly one-third of voters mentioned moral issues in response to the open-ended questions included in the survey. Among the subset of aware and concerned voters, a group that comprised more than one-fifth of the electorate, the influence of moral issues on candidate choice was far greater than that of any other type of issue and almost equal to that of party identification. While these citizens were not pure single-issue voters, they did weigh moral issues very heavily in their voting decision.

The impact of moral issues on the 1992 presidential election reflected the polarization of public opinion on these issues. One large bloc of voters viewed gay rights and legalized abortion as violations of fundamental religious principles; another large bloc viewed these policies as protecting basic personal freedoms. The high degree of polarization of the electorate and intense pressure from activists on opposite sides of these issues resulted in a sharp divergence between the two major parties' positions and a clear choice for voters. Thus, voters with liberal or conservative views on moral issues had reason to strongly prefer one party's position to the other's.

Our findings indicate that polarization of public opinion on an issue is an important condition for policy voting. Polarization increases the pressure on the parties to take divergent positions. Furthermore, once parties diverge, polarization increases the intensity of voters' preferences. Given the continuing sharp division within the American electorate over issues such as gay rights and legalized abortion and the opportunities for activists on both sides of these issues to influence the presidential nominating process, it is likely that moral issues will remain a potent influence on voters' decision making in future presidential elections.

Notes

1. The term *values* here refers to issues that involve fundamental religious or moral principles. Thus, these issues tend to be viewed in terms of right and wrong.
2. Probit is used because the dependent variable is dichotomous.

Part 5   Political Institutions and Public Opinion

The linkage between public opinion and governmental actions lies at the heart of democratic theory. Most Americans believe that governmental institutions, such as Congress, should represent public opinion in their policy enactments. Based on their views of government's proper roles, the public also judges officeholders. The chapters in this part of the book explore both public evaluations of the government and the representation of public opinion in public policy.

The public's evaluations of president fluctuates widely. Many researchers match these swings in presidential evaluations with the negative effects of war and a poor economy, temporary upswings in response to short international crises, and a general decline in presidential popularity over the course of a four-year term. Lyn Ragsdale's chapter provides further structuring to our understanding of presidential popularity by positing that components of these evaluations can be ascribed to personal characteristics of presidents, historical trends, and institutional behaviors.

The American public, since the early 1960s, has become very cynical toward government. Only 3 percent of Americans in 1992 felt they could trust the federal government to do "what is right" almost always, with only another one-quarter feeling they could trust the government most of the time. Similarly, three-quarters felt that the government is run for the benefit of a few big interests rather than for all Americans, and nearly half of U.S. citizens believed that quite a few of the people holding public office are crooked (Luttbeg and Gant 1995, 137–138).

In light of events since 1960 (Vietnam, Watergate, falling living standards for many Americans), such cynicism is understandable. The government does not stand alone in this crisis of confidence. The public has less faith today than in the recent past in a wide variety of institutions, including big business, schools, doctors, and organized religion (Lipset and Schneider 1983, 48–49).

Within this realm of cynicism, Congress often falls toward the bottom of people's confidence rankings. As John Hibbing and Elizabeth Theiss-Morse report in their chapter, only about one in six Americans has a great deal of confidence in the U.S. Congress. Hibbing and Theiss-Morse posit a new explanation for this negative attitude toward Congress: that Americans view Congress as too powerful and as using its power to obstruct change.

Thomas Marshall's chapter searches for matches between public opinion and public policy in a most unusual institutional setting—that of the Supreme Court. After all, the Constitution insulates the third branch from public pressure, setting up a process of selection through presidential appointment and congressional confirmation rather than direct election; furthermore, justices are granted lifetime terms of office. Yet Marshall demonstrates that the rate of consistency between public opinion and Supreme Court decisions is quite high; his Supreme Court figures are as high as Alan Monroe's (1994) figures for policies in general. Marshall presents five explanations for this high level of congruency.

13 Disconnected Politics: Public Opinion and Presidents

Lyn Ragsdale

P eople used to say of me that I . . . divined what the people were going to think. I did not 'divine.' I simply made up my mind what they ought to think, and then did my best to get them to think it." Theodore Roosevelt, speaking at the turn of the twentieth century, made clear that his strategy was to create rather than to follow public opinion (1926, vol. 20, 414). Near the end of the century, Ronald Reagan modified speeches according to what internal White House polls and focus groups showed public opinion to support. George Bush received daily poll reports on American attitudes toward Iraq months before the start of the Gulf War. These polls helped administration officials to establish the ultimate direction of American involvement in the war and to frame their justification for the war. In the aftermath of a Republican sweep of the House and Senate in the 1994 elections, Bill Clinton's specially prepared White House polls showed that the public felt the president should be more faithful to his centrist campaign promises. In the ensuing days, Clinton made announcements backing a middle-class tax cut, denouncing the size of the federal government, and calling for a line-item veto. Unlike Roosevelt, three presidents at the end of the century followed, rather than created, public opinion.

The nature of presidents' relations with the public has changed technologically, philosophically, and politically in the twentieth century. Technological changes have affected how presidents present themselves to the public, how the public responds, and how the public's responses are measured. Presidents no longer have the luxury afforded Theodore Roosevelt to divine public opinion. Instead, monthly (sometimes even weekly) public opinion polls, taken by various polling organizations and inside the White House, monitor public opinion. These polls began in 1938 when the Gallup Organization first asked a random sample of Americans the question, "Do you approve or disapprove of the way [the incumbent] is handling his job as president?" Since that initial poll—in which 60 percent of Americans approved of Franklin D. Roosevelt's job performance—presidential popularity, or presidential approval, has become a part of the body politic. The question was asked about Harry S. Truman during his first term (1945–1948) just fifteen times. But the advent of computer-assisted telephone polling has made these surveys far more numerous. Polls measured George Bush's approval 110 times during his four years in office. The polls do not merely inquire about a president's overall job performance; they capture public opinion on specific presidential decisions and White House problems. It is not uncommon to see poll results on whether the Senate should confirm a controversial presidential nominee, whether the president should fire a wayward aide, or whether the president has taken an appropriate stance on a factious issue, such as the pardon of Richard Nixon, the American hostage crisis in Iran, or allowing homosexuals to serve in the military.

Other technological changes grant the public greater access to more information about the president from more varied sources than ever before. Theodore Roosevelt counted on newspaper and wire service reports as the primary outlets for presidential news. Today, presidential news may appear through live coverage, network and local television and radio news broadcasts, news talk shows, entertainment talk shows, news magazines, newspapers, radio call-in shows, and on-line computer services.

These technological changes have worked in tandem with and accentuated philosophical changes. Philosophically, Theodore Roosevelt and his successor, Woodrow Wilson, made the presidency a public office and the president a public representative in new ways. The prevailing notion in the nineteenth century was that presidents might be seen, but they were rarely heard on policy issues before the nation. Presidents typically did not advance their own policy views or take positions on matters before Congress. Roosevelt changed that by insisting that the president could offer policy reforms as the "steward of the people" who was "bound actively and affirmatively to do all he could for the people. . . . My belief was that it was not only his right but his duty to do anything that the needs of the nation demanded unless such action was forbidden by the Constitution or by the laws" (Roosevelt 1913, 389). In Roosevelt's view, the public provided the president with a mandate for policy activism.

Roosevelt also saw the president as a particular kind of representative. Two views have long been associated with the idea of representation: that a representative may act as a *delegate* on behalf of the expressed desires of the public or as a *trustee* in the best interests of the public (as the representative construes those interests). Roosevelt, as the only nationally elected official, believed that presidents should act as trustees to do what was best for the country, even if their actions were controversial.

Today's philosophy is different. Presidential stewardship and the accompanying policy activism are bolder and broader than Roosevelt could have imagined. Furthermore, today's presidents must take into account the omnipresence of public opinion polls, which present an immediate and continuous plebiscite on their performance. The frequency and visibility of public opinion surveys put pressure on presidents to conform with the known preferences of the public as documented in the polls. Consequently, presidents are more likely to behave as delegates who react to public opinion than as trustees who may shape it. This is not to say that presidents do not attempt to act as trustees, but that they will have greater difficulty doing so.

These technological and philosophical changes have fundamentally changed the politics of the presidency. Politically, the omnipresence of the president as national representative and the ongoing popular plebiscite change the way presidents do their public business. Both place considerable pressure on the chief executives to take their case directly to the American people all of the time. To be sure, Theodore Roosevelt's voice captured the public's attention "nosily, clamorously; while he is in the neighborhood the public can no more look the other way than the small boy can turn his head away from a circus parade followed by a steam calliope" (quoted in Cornwell 1965, 15). But it was a voice that was heard only sporadically and only in direct appeals at public rallies. The president's voice was not heard live across the nation or in daily news broadcasts, subject to an immediate critique by officials of the other party, momentary media analysis, and overnight public evaluation. Contemporary presidents are seen and heard daily on all major and minor issues facing the nation. Their messages may actually have less impact on public opinion than those of their predecessors did, because the communication takes on the quality of background noise.

In addition, with so many polls available, a president's job performance is overevaluated. The poll results become "political facts" about the president that people in Washington cite, regularly update, and, most important, use to construct political strategies. Consequently, the opening for presidential success may not extend beyond the next poll. It is increasingly difficult for presidents to get ahead of Americans' opinions on various issues. Instead, presidents often choose courses of action that are, in the vernacular of the Reagan administration's pollsters, "resonators"—positions and issues that people generally like or do not find controversial (Brace and Hinckley 1992, 3). The more presidents do or say counter to these resonators, the less likely they will be to be able to follow public opinion satisfactorily. Activist presidents have difficulty faring well amidst these political changes.

This chapter addresses the changing relationship between presidents and the public by highlighting three dimensions to public opinion toward presidents: personal, historical, and institutional. The personal dimension defines the individual differences that occur among presidents in their relations with the public. The historical dimension marks different periods in the relationship between presidents and the public; within these periods, presidents share similar problems and resources in dealing with the public. The institutional dimension identifies regularly occurring patterns of behavior which all presidents follow: every president engages in certain policy activities and public activities that are expected of the occupant of the White House. The chapter concludes with an assessment of how the three dimensions together affect the way the public approves of presidents' performance in office. The interweaving of the three dimensions makes presidents less important to the public at the same time as the public becomes more important to, but less manageable by, presidents.

Personal Differences Among Presidents

People in and out of the Clinton administration commented on the low approval ratings of President Clinton during his first year. Clinton's approval peaked in his second month in office, February 1993, at 59 percent and dropped to its lowest point, 38 percent, just four months later. Most of the explanations for these low marks centered on Clinton himself—as a novice in Washington; someone ill at ease in foreign affairs; an advocate of an aggressive, but not well thought out, domestic agenda; and a figure plagued by charges of sexual harassment and financial misdealings.

Of the three dimensions of public opinion toward presidents, the personal dimension is the most vivid and easiest to grasp. It points to unique decisions and mistakes that presidents make in office and the unique circumstances that confront them. These individual differences also lead sometimes to exceptional ebbs and flows of popularity. Bill Clinton was not alone in facing large swings in presidential approval ratings. Gerald Ford's popularity plummeted 21 points when he pardoned Richard Nixon. Jimmy Carter enjoyed a 14-point increase in approval after the Iranian seizure of American hostages. George Bush's approval ratings shot up 25 percentage points in just twenty days in January 1991 as the nation sat transfixed by the nightly television war in the Persian Gulf. He gained 6 more points by the end of February to reach an 89 percent approval rating, the highest approval ever recorded for any president. During the next year, Bush's popularity was in free fall; it dropped 51 percentage points from February 1991 to February 1992.

Table 13-1 provides a more systematic look at the approval ratings of individual presidents from Franklin Roosevelt to Clinton. The table shows a wide variation in popularity among the eleven presidents. Presidents Truman and Nixon (in their second terms) shared the lowest average popularity for a term, at 36 percent approval and 35 percent approval, respectively. President Roosevelt achieved the highest average popularity rating during his third term: 74 percent approval. The standard deviation column in the table also reveals the volatility of several presidents' popularity. In particular, Truman, Johnson, Nixon (in his second term), Carter, and Bush had wide swings in approval ratings during their terms, as shown in the "difference" column in the table, which subtracts the lowest approval rating from the highest approval rating. Presidents Truman and Bush experienced the largest shifts in their approval—a 55 percentage point difference for Truman in his first term and the 51 percentage point gap noted for Bush.

The personal dimension seems to provide analysts with reassurance that what they see is what they get. A drop or rise in approval can be matched with a specific event, decision, or activity during a president's term. Seemingly, these events, conditions, and decisions are unique to a given president. People assume that Vietnam could have happened only on Johnson's watch. No one but Nixon would have let Watergate get out of hand. Other presidents

Table 13-1 The Personal Dimension: Approval of Individual Presidents, Franklin Roosevelt to Bill Clinton

President	Average	Standard Deviation	High	Low	Difference	Number of Polls
Roosevelt						
2d term (1938–1940)	59%	3.2	65%	54%	11%	19
3d term (1941–1943)	74	3.9	84	66	18	24
Total (1938–1943)	67	8.3	84	54	30	43
Truman						
1st term (1945–1948)	52	16.9	87	32	55	15
2d term (1949–1952)	36	11.3	69	23	46	29
Total (1945–1952)	42	16.0	87	23	64	44
Eisenhower						
1st term (1953–1956)	69	5.4	79	57	22	52
2d term (1957–1960)	60	5.8	73	49	24	55
Total (1953–1960)	65	7.2	79	49	30	107
Kennedy (1961–1963)	71	6.9	83	58	25	40
Johnson (1964–1968)	56	13.4	80	36	44	81
Nixon						
1st term (1969–1972)	57	5.3	65	48	17	60
2d term (1973–1974)	35	12.4	67	23	44	34
Total (1969–1974)	49	13.2	67	23	44	94
Ford (1974–1976)	47	7.0	71	37	34	35
Carter (1977–1980)	47	12.0	75	28	47	88
Reagan						
1st term (1981–1984)	50	7.6	68	35	33	76
2d term (1985–1988)	56	6.9	65	40	25	46
Total (1981–1988)	52	8.0	68	35	33	122
Bush (1989–1992)	61	14.8	83	32	51	110
Clinton (1993–1994 only)	48	5.5	59	38	21	56

Sources: Roosevelt to Ford calculated from *Gallup Opinion Index,* October–November 1980, 13–59. Polls on Roosevelt began in 1938; no polls were conducted in 1944. Carter to Clinton calculated from successive volumes of *Gallup Poll Monthly.*

would not have handled the Iranian hostage crisis the way Carter did. Thus, the personal dimension allows presidency watchers to focus on differences among presidents as individuals: Johnson is not Nixon who is not Carter. And these differences are confirmed in their approval ratings.

Yet, although the personal dimension is the simplest aspect of presidential popularity to understand, it is surely the most misleading. The personal dimension reveals that there are variations in presidents' approval ratings. Those variations, however, may not be wholly attributable to the uniqueness of individual chief executives. Bill Clinton's early-term popularity problems may have been only partly his own doing. Forgotten in the simplicity of the personal dimension are systematic comparisons across presidents. Without such comparisons, students of public opinion do not really know how much of the variations across presidents are actually the result of personal differences. With such comparisons, the importance of personal differences is not denied but is placed in a more appropriate context.

Historical Trends

One type of comparison that can be made is to examine differences across time periods. The historical dimension denotes whether technological, philosophical, and political shifts over time have altered the way people view presidents. If such historical trends exist, then presidents of one time period will have approval ratings that look distinctly unlike those of another era regardless of who the presidents are, what they do, or what they encounter during their terms. For instance, people often commented on the personal popularity of Ronald Reagan. Early in his first term, the press dubbed Reagan the "Teflon president." Problems encountered by his administration never seemed to stick to him, and his honeymoon never completely ended. Many likened Reagan's personal popularity to that of Dwight Eisenhower, a spectacularly successful general of World War II turned highly popular president of the 1950s. Others suggested that Reagan had revitalized public impressions of the presidency after the disappointments of Jimmy Carter.

Despite these characterizations, each of which stresses the unique personal nature of Reagan's approval, a comparison of Eisenhower's and Reagan's popularity from Table 13-1 reveals marked differences. And a comparison of Reagan's, Carter's, and Clinton's approval ratings shows stunning similarities. Eisenhower's average popularity for his first term was 69 percent; his highest popularity point was 79 percent approval and his lowest popularity point was only 57 percent approval. In contrast, Reagan's average popularity for his first term was just 50 percent; his highest approval was 68 percent and his lowest rating was 35 percent. Reagan's average ratings were higher in his second term, but they still did not match those of Eisenhower in either term. Eisenhower's popularity was more like that of his immediate successor, Kennedy, whose popularity rating averaged 71 percent.

Reagan's approval was more like the ratings of two Democratic presidents—his predecessor, Carter, whose average popularity was 47 percent, and Clinton, whose midterm popularity averaged 48 percent.[1] Indeed, the levels of public approval that Carter and Reagan received during their first two years in office were nearly identical, and they were quite similar during their third years (see Ragsdale 1993, 148). Only in the fourth year of their terms did their approval ratings drastically diverge. Both Carter and Reagan saw their honeymoons fade toward the end of their first year in office; both faced growing disillusionment over the next two years, as economic problems worsened—Carter's primarily inflation, Reagan's primarily unemployment. Although Reagan may have projected a more comfortable image than Carter, he was no more a Teflon president than his predecessor had been. In addition, his midterm average approval rating was 50 percent, only slightly better than Clinton's 48 percent approval. This pattern suggests that there are similarities in public opinion from one president to another relevant to the period of presidential politics in which they served. The supposed personal difficulties of Clinton and the supposed personal fortunes of Reagan can be placed in clearer perspective by considering political similarities within time periods of the presidency.

Historical eras are examined more closely in Table 13-2, which provides a breakdown of approval and disapproval during two periods of the presidency—from Franklin Roosevelt to Lyndon Johnson (1938–1968) and from Richard Nixon to Bill Clinton (1969–1994). Presidents from Roosevelt to Johnson received notably higher approval ratings during their terms than presidents since Nixon have. President Johnson's average popularity, which significantly eroded with worsening problems in Vietnam, still was higher than that of any of the presidents since Nixon, except Bush. Johnson's annual approval ratings for the years 1964 through 1966 were above 50 percent. It was only in 1967 and 1968 that Johnson's approval ratings dipped below that mark. In this vein, Johnson's popularity fits better with the earlier pattern than with the later one.

The differences between the two periods in average approval and in annual approval for each year of the term are striking. Average approval during the early period is 61 percent, while average approval during the later period is 52 percent. The large gap between the periods holds for both the first term and the second term. The table also reveals how the average approval ratings per year were lower in every year of the later period except the eighth. Presidential honeymoons are decidedly less happy affairs in the later period, when presidents received an average of only 56 percent approval for their first year in office; 72 percent approval was the average for presidents in the earlier period. The gap is no less pronounced in the second term. The later presidents start their second terms with an average 50 percent approval rating, whereas the earlier presidents had received a 67 percent approval rating.

The long-term downward shift in popularity may point to certain systematic changes in the environment within which presidents perform and within which the public evaluates their performance. Three such changes are discussed here: changes in media coverage of presidents,

Table 13-2 The Historical Dimension: Average Approval for Year in Term, Comparing Roosevelt Through Johnson (1938–1968) with Nixon Through Clinton (1969–1994)

	1938–1968 Approval	1969–1994 Approval	Difference
Average	61%	52%	−9%
Average first term	63	53	−10
Average second term	57	48	−9
First Term			
First year	72	56	−16
Second year	61	52	−9
Third year	58	54	−4
Fourth year	53	46	−7
Second term			
Fifth year	67	50	−17
Sixth year	58	44	−14
Seventh year	54	48	−6
Eighth year	52	53	1

Sources: Calculated from all available Gallup polls from 1938 to 1994. For 1938 to 1976, poll results found in *Gallup Opinion Index*, October–November 1980, 13–59. For Carter to Clinton, poll results found in successive volumes of *Gallup Poll Monthly*.

changes in presidents' luck in facing unfolding political events, and changes in economic conditions in the country.

Bad Press

One fundamental historical change involves press coverage of presidents. Figure 13-1 charts negative coverage of presidents from Truman (in his second term) to Clinton, as displayed in the *New York Times*.[2] It is immediately clear from the figure that negative press coverage soared, as one would expect, during Watergate, soon returned to levels relatively like those from before the scandal, and then since 1985 has slowly increased. During the earlier period (1949–1968) 14 percent of stories (twenty-six stories per quarter) in the *New York Times* were negative. The bad press more than doubled, to 30 percent of presidential news stories, in the period since 1969, amounting to seventy-seven negative stories per quarter. Even excluding the Watergate years 1973 and 1974, negative stories amounted to 28 percent of total coverage in the later period. The negative coverage during the 1990s is especially striking. Fully

Figure 13-1 The Rise of Bad Press for Presidents, 1949–1994

Mean number of negative stories

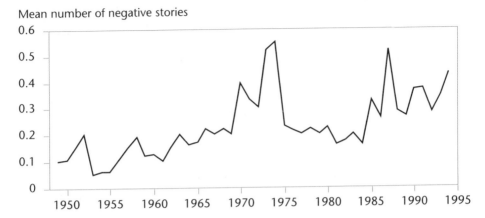

Note: Negative stories are coded and counted from the *New York Times*.

36 percent of coverage was negative during the first half of the decade. Even during 1991, as the Persian Gulf War unfolded, negative news climbed, accounting for 37 percent of the coverage. Bad news continued for Bill Clinton: 35 percent of news coverage was negative in 1993 and 43 percent was negative in 1994.[3]

To understand this rise in bad press, one must first consider the more general increase in media coverage of presidents. As illuminated in Figure 13-2, the beginnings of this overall increase in presidential news coverage occurred in 1963 and can be traced in part to the Kennedy assassination. Journalists were distressed about their inability to provide immediate coverage of the assassination, in part because of the growing size of the White House press corps. There were so many press vans in the Dallas motorcade and they were so far behind the presidential limousine that no reporter or camera operator witnessed the assassination or even knew it had taken place. The press vans merely followed the chase to Parkland Memorial Hospital, where the president was taken. The last van pulled up to the hospital well after all members of the presidential and vice presidential entourages were inside. From this event, the "body watch" in presidential news evolved.

The body watch dictates that members of the press cover presidents' every public move just in case, in Ronald Reagan's words, "the awful, awful" happens—the president is shot, becomes ill, has an accident, or dies. A Washington bureau chief for *Newsweek* elaborated: "The worst thing in the world that could happen to you [as a journalist] is for the President of the United States to choke on a piece of meat, and for you not to be there" (Grossman and Kumar 1981, 43). The body watch expanded further in the 1960s as technological advances in satellites created more opportunities for live coverage. The body watch also intensified as

Figure 13-2 Media Coverage of Presidents, 1949–1994

Total number of stories

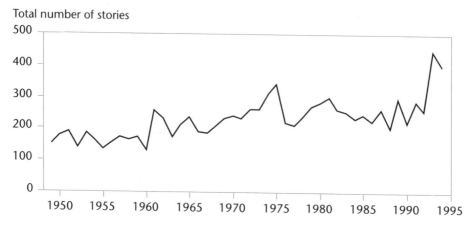

nightly network news shows enlarged their formats from fifteen minutes to thirty minutes in the early 1960s and had more time for presidential news.

The consequence of the body watch is total coverage of presidents, from their most trivial and mundane public actions to their sometimes dramatic official announcements. Total coverage means that many more personal and official mistakes are captured and critiqued than would have been with less comprehensive coverage. As one example, Lyndon Johnson enjoyed playing with his two beagles, pulling them up by their long floppy ears. One day photographers recorded Johnson's play session on the White House lawn. The next day newspapers across the country ran the picture of the president smiling broadly and holding one of the dogs up by its ears. Dog owners were enraged. The White House swiftly announced that Johnson would abandon the practice. In earlier times the event would not have been recorded and no controversy would have occurred.

In recent years the body watch has focused attention on the personal foibles and past liaisons of presidents and presidential candidates. For example, during the 1988 presidential campaign, rumor had it that Sen. Gary Hart, a contender for the Democratic nomination, was having an affair. Hart denied the rumors and cavalierly challenged reporters to follow him. They did. Reporters watched as he left the woman's home early one morning. Since then, what might be called the "Gary Hart rule" has been invoked on all candidates and chief executives. Reporters question all details—whether recent or from the distant past—of the politicians' personal lives. This replaces a starkly different "Franklin Roosevelt rule" previously followed by reporters: never disclose details of presidents' or presidential candidates' personal lives. This earlier practice began as an informal agreement among reporters and camera operators that they would never mention or photograph Franklin Roosevelt in his wheel-chair. The practice was later extended to not covering Roosevelt's problematic marriage. Under the Gary Hart rule invoked during the 1992 presidential campaign, it was not surprising to see NBC News correspondent Stone Phillips ask George Bush about an affair the president was rumored to have had with a state department official. Bush's brusque retort—"You don't ask questions like that in the White House"—did little to dampen the controversy. Nor, given the new scope of the body watch, did it seem shocking to see Bill and Hillary Clinton discuss their marriage on the news show *60 Minutes*.

Coupled with the body watch has been a notable rise in skepticism, if not outright cynicism, among the White House press corps about presidents' actions and, in particular, about presidential accounts of those actions. Reporters witnessed the so-called credibility gap of the Johnson administration during the Vietnam War. The gap was identified when the troop levels and casualty figures announced by the administration were lower than figures found independently by reporters. Reporters helped to expose the outright lies of President Nixon during the Watergate cover-up and the web of deception and illegality in the Iran-contra affair in the Reagan administration. The melodrama of these episodes was deepened by the lack of candor from presidents in several other less divisive actions, including the U-2 incident in 1960, the Bay of Pigs invasion in 1961, and troops sent to the Dominican Republic in 1965. Consequently, as the columnist Max Frankel observed, White House reporters increasingly treat "virtually every official utterance as a carefully contrived rendering that needs to be examined for the missing word or phrase, the sly use of statistics, the slippery syntax or semantics" (1971, 16).

The now total coverage of presidents partially reflects technological advances in broadcasting which make it feasible for reporters to cover every move a president makes. But the body watch has prompted a not so subtle shift in the philosophical tenets of the office as well. Theodore Roosevelt's public representative faces assessments of moral and ethical conduct that were not undertaken before. Moreover, distinctions among official public activities, personal activities done in public, and personal activities have collapsed. There is an ever widening domain of what is considered an acceptable, if not highly sought after, topic for a presidential news story. Evolutions of this kind are not easily stopped or even slowed. An uneasy shift in presidential politics has accompanied this philosophical change. The body watch draws up new definitions of success and failure for presidents, which include how adept they are at handling past or present personal problems, how they face political battles which may erupt from any and all activities covered in the watch, and how well they handle the media.

Bad Luck and a Bad Economy

Beyond the bad press presidents received in the later period, they also encountered more bad luck and worse economic times than their predecessors. Table 13-3 provides a summa-

Table 13-3 Political and Economic Differences Between 1949–1968 and 1969–1994
(Quarterly Averages)

	1949–1968	1969–1994	Difference
Media coverage (number of stories)	180	255	75
Negative coverage (percent of stories)	14.30	30.10	15.80
Positive coverage (percent of stories)	48.30	36.00	−12.30
Negative events (number)	0.13	0.63	0.50
Unemployment (percent)	6.85	6.57	−0.28
Consumer price index (total change)	1.91	31.52	29.61

Sources: Data on media coverage are from Michael Grossman and Martha Kumar, *Portraying the President* (Baltimore: Johns Hopkins University Press, 1981), as updated by the author. Data on negative events as described in the text were coded and calculated by the author. Data on unemployment and consumer prices are taken from successive volumes of the U.S. Department of Commerce, *Survey of Current Business.*

ry comparison for the two periods on a number of political and economic measures. Presidents in the later period encountered five times more negative events than presidents in the earlier period had.[4] These events are relatively long-lived and prominent; they are national or international in scope; they specifically involve some form of presidential action; and they have a directly adverse consequence for the president. Some of these events presidents bring on themselves, but others are out of their control. They include negative international events (the communist victory in Vietnam in September 1974), massive political protests and riots (the Los Angeles riots in 1991), the failure of major legislation or a key nomination actively sought by a president before Congress (the demise of health care reform in 1994, the defeat of Robert Bork's nomination to the Supreme Court in 1987), and highly unpopular executive actions, staff misdealings, or personal problems (such as Ford's pardon of Nixon in 1974). While presidents encountered only ten such negative events in the early period, they were plagued by forty-six negative events in the later period. The economy was also much more problem-filled in the later period. Unemployment rates during the two periods are quite similar (an average of 6.9 percent for the early period as compared with 6.6 percent for the later period). But consumer price increases were fifteen times greater in the later period than in the earlier era.

Thus, later presidents coped with a much more rough-and-tumble political and economic environment than their earlier counterparts. The historical increase in negative events included terrorist campaigns, civil wars in newly organized countries, and presidents' own political scandals in the Watergate and the Iran-contra affairs. Economic woes of the later period also were more complicated and difficult to handle—problems of stagflation (a combination of slow growth and high inflation) and oil-price shocks in the 1970s, the rising budget deficit in the 1980s, and severe budget cuts in the 1980s and 1990s to cope with the deficit. Press coverage devoted attention to these big problems and bad economic times, thereby amplifying the negative environment within which presidents worked and within which the public evaluated their work.

Institutional Behavior

This chapter has examined the ways presidents are affected by factors outside the institution. But one can also look at the presidency itself in different eras. An institution has a life of its own, independent of the people who participate in it. The institution establishes a set of regular patterns of behavior that individuals within it follow, whatever they do at other times in their life. Institutional behavior thus involves the extent to which different individuals faced with similar circumstances respond in much the same way. This is not to say that institutional behavior remains static—it may change with the times. But presidents abandon established patterns of behavior at their peril. If they do so, they violate expectations people have of someone who holds the chief executive's job. The institution of the presidency thus guides the behavior of presidents. This means that presidents with very different backgrounds, political skills, and policy agendas nonetheless behave in certain similar ways. Two types of institutional behavior exist for presidents: policy activism and public appearances.

Policy Activism

Theodore Roosevelt originated presidential policy activism with his shift in the philosophical tenets of the office. According to the principle of activism, presidents, as Roosevelt's stewards of the people, make independent policy actions and are fully involved in the legislative policy debate in Congress. Contemporary presidents, regardless of individual differences, are all but required to engage in policy activity; it comes with the job. For example, many people typecast Bill Clinton as a "policy wonk," someone who immersed himself in the details of policy and offered many, perhaps too many, policy items for the national agenda. Yet Clinton's personal interests had seemingly less to do with his policy activity than institutional requirements at hand. His first-year policy activism was no greater than Truman's, nearly fifty years before—both made 159 policy requests to Congress.

In the contemporary period, Roosevelt's legacy has taken three key forms. First, presidents since Truman have submitted annual legislative programs to Congress, in an effort to influence, if not define, the congressional agenda. Second, presidents take positions on numerous matters before Congress, beyond their own legislative proposals. Finally, presidents since Franklin Roosevelt have used executive orders as a device to fashion substantive policy decisions bypassing the legislative process. Executive orders are documents signed by presidents which carry the same weight in law as a statute but do not require passage by

Table 13-4 Presidents' Institutional Behavior Differences Between 1949–1968 and 1969–1994 (Quarterly Average Number)

	1949–1968	1969–1994	Difference
Total policy activity	60	51	−9
Legislative requests	22	15	−7
Policy positions (taken on roll calls)	20	22	2
Executive orders	18	14	−4
Total public appearances	41	61	20
Major addresses	1	1	0
News conferences	7	4	−3
Minor policy speeches	2	3	1
Ceremonial appearances	31	53	22

Source: Data from Lyn Ragsdale, *Vital Statistics on the American Presidency* (Washington, D.C.: Congressional Quarterly, 1996).

Congress. Presidents have signed executive orders to accomplish such things as the desegregation of the military, implementation of affirmative action guidelines, and enacting restrictions on abortion counseling. Policy activism, then, is a key form of institutional behavior in the presidency. Combining the three types of activities, presidents have made about fifty-five policy actions per quarter during the period from 1949 to 1994. As shown in Table 13-4, there has been a slight drop in policy activism between the two historical periods discussed here. Presidents in the early period took an average of sixty policy actions per quarter, while presidents in the later period took fifty-one quarterly policy actions. Much of the drop can be attributed to Ronald Reagan, who made a limited number of legislative requests to Congress in his terms.[5]

Public Appearances

Theodore Roosevelt also enlarged the public face of the presidency. Roosevelt's philosophical view of the president as key public representative instructed chief executives to take their case directly to the public. In Roosevelt's words, "I achieved results only by appealing over the heads of the Senate and House leaders to the people, who were the masters of both of us" (1926, vol. 20, 342). This philosophical perspective coupled with technological advances in broadcasting and air travel invite current presidents to go to the public often.

In considering presidents' public appearances, it is important to distinguish among four types of appearances: major national addresses, news conferences, minor policy speeches, and ceremonial appearances. The appearances target different audiences and contain varying degrees of policy content. Major national addresses are prime-time speeches before the nation which include State of the Union messages, other speeches to joint sessions of Congress, and special addresses from the White House. The major addresses typically contain substantive policy remarks, but, more than any other forum, they also depict the president as the nation's symbolic leader. News conferences contain policy content and attract national audiences but the give-and-take between reporters and the president offers a far different format from that of major addresses. Minor policy speeches are made before a specific audience, often at a university commencement or business or labor convention. In the speech, the president may outline a significant policy proposal, but the forum is less visible than a major national address or news conference. Ceremonial appearances involve presidents' greeting specific groups at the White House or being welcomed to various communities in rallies and motorcades across the country. As shown in Table 13-4, major addresses and minor policy speeches have remained relatively constant over the total forty-five-year period. There has been a small drop in the number of news conferences but a distinct rise in the number of ceremonial appearances. Although ceremonial appearances were certainly an important form of institutional behavior in the earlier period, they have become decidedly more a part of presidents' activities in the later period. Combining the appearances, presidents in the later period made sixty-one public appearances per quarter, while presidents in the earlier period made only forty-one appearances; the increase is almost completely accounted for by the rise in ceremonial appearances.

With these appearances, presidents have adopted a fundamental political strategy. They engage in a perpetual campaign of public appearances which continues long after the election is over. Driving this perpetual campaign is the assumption that maximum public exposure leads to maximum popular benefit. Campaigners typically assume that they should make as many appearances in as many forums as they have time, energy, and money to make. The rationale is that appearances can only help the campaign. Presidents have applied this assumption to their appearances in office, especially the ceremonial ones, believing that public exposure can only help in their efforts to maintain or build a favorable public image and gain public support for particular policy decisions. The assumption holds a kind of self-generating quality which pushes presidents to make ever more public appearances, thus helping to account for their increase from the earlier period to the later period. This cycle makes public appearances as a form of institutional behavior all the more entrenched.

Institutional Behavior and the Public

The problem for presidents is that neither policy activism nor public appearances pay off much in their popularity ratings. Table 13-5 examines the average popularity obtained by presidents when they engaged in low and high levels of policy activism and public appearances during the two periods of presidential politics (1949–1968 and 1969–1994). In both eras, more active presidents have lower approval ratings. In the early period, more active pres-

Table 13-5 Effects of Policy Activism and Public Appearances on Popularity, 1949–1968 and 1969–1994

	1949–1968		1969–1994	
	%	(n)	%	(n)
Low policy activism	61	(36)	54	(53)
High policy activism	54	(34)	49	(52)
Low public appearances	59	(49)	52	(54)
High public appearances	57	(31)	51	(51)

Notes: The low and high categories are broken at the mean. The numbers of cases are in parentheses. Policy activism combines legislative requests, policy positions on roll calls, and executive orders. Public appearances combine major addresses, news conferences, minor policy speeches, and ceremonial appearances.

idents average 54 percent approval, while less active presidents earn 61 percent approval. In the later period, more active presidents receive 49 percent approval; again less active presidents have higher approval, with 54 percent. Above average numbers of public appearances likewise do not guarantee higher approval ratings. In fact, there is not much difference in either period in approval ratings between presidents who make above average numbers of appearances and those who make below average numbers of appearances. Perhaps the perpetual campaign does not help a president govern.

Putting the Pieces Together

It is now important to consider the relative contribution of the three components of presidential approval to the overall direction of presidential approval. Table 13-6 presents results of a model estimating the effects of personal, historical, and institutional factors on presidential popularity for the two eras of presidential politics—1949–1968 and 1969–1994 and the entire time period (1949–1994). The dependent variable is average presidential approval during a given three-month period. As measures of individual presidents, variables denote whether a particular president is serving in office or not.[6] The variables are designed to capture differences among presidents' popularity ratings. As indicators of historical circumstances, bad press, negative events, unemployment, and consumer prices are incorporated in the model.[7] Measures of institutional behavior include the number of major addresses, news conferences, minor speeches, ceremonial appearances, and total policy requests made by a president in a quarter.[8] Also included in the model is a measure of past popularity—the popularity rating attained by the president during the previous quarter. This measure accommodates an inertial effect that has long been noted in presidents' approval ratings (Kernell

Table 13-6 Personal, Historical, and Institutional Effects on Presidential Popularity, 1949-1994

Variable	1949–1968			1969–1994			1949–1994		
	b	t-ratio	Impact	b	t-ratio	Impact	b	t-ratio	Impact
Individual Presidents									
Truman	-11.23	-4.15*	-2.36	—	—	—	-6.05	-1.93***	-.54
Eisenhower, I	-.78	-.31	-.13	—	—	—	5.07	1.81***	.35
Kennedy	8.46	3.23*	1.35	—	—	—	3.26	1.15	.20
Johnson	6.99	2.15**	2.03	—	—	—	-.06	-.02	-.01
Nixon	—	—	—	-7.77	-2.63*	-1.70	-1.41	-.48	-.68
Ford	—	—	—	3.70	1.06	.37	.78	.23	.05
Carter	—	—	—	-1.75	-.55	.26	-1.65	-.56	-.15
Reagan, I	—	—	—	3.81	1.11	.58	-2.66	-.83	-.24
Reagan, II	—	—	—	—	—	—	-.23	-.07	-.02
Bush	—	—	—	5.45	1.66***	.66	4.20	1.30	.29
Clinton	—	—	—	-2.64	-.63	-.21	-2.37	-.62	-.11
Historical Circumstances									
Negative media	-47.59	-5.26*	-17.64	-14.55	-1.66***	-4.36	-14.93	-1.87***	-3.58
Negative events	-.86	-.47	-.12	-1.03	-1.26	-.65	-.55	-.72	-.24
Consumer price change	-.09	-3.38*	-.17	-.07	-2.45*	-2.21	-.06	-2.54*	.98
Unemployment	.05	1.05	.36	-3.52	-4.24*	-23.13	-.03	-.50	-.21
Institutional Behavior									
Policy activity	-.11	-2.59*	-6.59	-.14	-2.79*	-7.14	-.12	-3.24*	-6.54
Major addresses	.78	1.22	.97	1.97	2.98*	2.54	1.60	3.01*	1.99
News conferences	.11	.48	.80	-.34	-1.10	-1.24	-.20	-.87	-1.02
Minor speeches	.11	.32	.22	-.07	-.28	.24	-.24	-1.11	-.69
Ceremonial appearances	-.02	-.47	.66	.02	.50	1.05	.03	.81	1.34

(Table continues)

Table 13-6 (*Continued*)

Variable	1949–1968			1969–1994			1949–1994		
	b	*t-ratio*	*Impact*	*b*	*t-ratio*	*Impact*	*b*	*t-ratio*	*Impact*
Prior popularity	.47	7.38*	27.22	.63	8.61*	32.60	.64	12.04*	34.69
Constant	52.11	7.65		54.46	6.30		28.82	6.40	
Number of cases		(80)			(105)			(185)	
Explained variance (R²)		.92			.70			.77	

Notes: b = unstandardized regression coefficient. Impact = unstandardized regression coefficient times mean of variable. Critical t-ratio values: * p = .01, t = 2.36; ** p = .05, t = 1.98; *** p = .10, t = 1.66.

1978; Ragsdale 1984). Specifically, past approval is typically the best predictor of current approval.

The table offers three types of information from the model estimated using ordinary least squares regression. The first column for each time period lists the unstandardized regression coefficient (b). The coefficient is interpreted as follows: a 1 unit change in the independent variable prompts a change in the dependent variable equivalent to the size of the coefficient. For example, during the period 1949–1994, the unstandardized coefficient for negative press is −14.93. This means that if all news stories printed in the *New York Times* in a given quarter were negative, popularity would decline by 15 percentage points.

The second column of each group lists the t-ratio of the coefficient (calculated as the coefficient divided by its standard error). This is a measure of the statistical significance of the variable and indicates whether or not the effect of the independent variable observed could have simply happened by chance. For instance, the negative media variable for the period 1949–1994 has a t-ratio of −1.87, which means it is statistically significant at the $p = .10$ level— which means in turn that there is a 10 percent probability that a result like this one could be due to chance. Generally, the higher the t-ratio, the more confidence we have in the relationship. With coefficients that are not statistically significant, we have no confidence that the independent variable truly affects presidential popularity.

The third column of each group records the "impact" of each variable. This impact is calculated by multiplying the coefficient found in the first column (b) by the mean of the variable.[9] This provides a more precise calculation for the effect of the independent variable on the dependent variable. For instance, on average, negative stories account for 23 percent of news stories, not 100 percent. Thus, the impact of the negative news variable is more accurately calculated by taking this mean percent of negative stories into account. The impact shows roughly a 3.6 percent drop in approval ($-14.93 \times .23 = -3.58$).

The findings reveal that individual presidents have a much greater influence in the first period than in the second. In the early period, the variables for Truman, Kennedy, and Johnson are statistically significant. The Johnson variable is of particular interest because its positive coefficient underscores Johnson's higher approval ratings and justifies his placement in the early period. In the later period, only the variables for Nixon and Bush are significant. Not surprisingly, the Nixon effect is negative; the Bush effect is positive. None of the variables for the other presidents has a statistically significant effect on popularity. This means that presidents are much less able to make their own personal mark in the later period.

Among the historical circumstances confronting presidents, the findings show surprisingly that the impact of bad press on popularity is four times greater in the earlier period than in the later period. In the early period, the impact of the negative press variable reveals that in a quarter with average negative press, presidents experience a nearly 18 percentage point drop in approval. This drop suggests that because there were fewer negative stories in the earlier period, each story was worth more in adversely affecting presidential approval. The impact is only 4 percentage points in the later period. In part this smaller effect is a result of the influence of the Nixon variable on popularity, since much of the negative press during the later period was associated with Watergate.

Consumer prices, but not unemployment, significantly affect presidents' popularity in the early period. By contrast, both consumer prices and unemployment significantly affect presidents' approval ratings in the later period. The impact of consumer prices is ten times greater in the later period than in the earlier one. An average change in consumer prices in the early period prompts popularity to drop by only .17 percentage point. An average change in consumer prices in the later period drops approval by over 2 percentage points. Among the variables in the later period, unemployment has a greater effect on the decline of presidential popularity than any other variable, except prior approval. This effect results from the very high unemployment figures in the Ford and especially Reagan years. Negative events do not affect presidential approval in either period.

Considering institutional behavior, presidents' public appearances—major addresses, news conferences, minor policy speeches, or ceremonial appearances—do not influence their popularity ratings in the earlier period. In the later period, presidents' major national addresses boost their approval by 2.5 percentage points per quarter. They receive no such help from news conferences, minor policy speeches, or ceremonial appearances. Of equal import, they experience a decline in approval from their policy initiatives. Their policy actions cost them 6.6 percentage points in the early period and over 7 percentage points in the later period. Presidents in the later period are especially disadvantaged by this factor because their approval ratings are lower overall and the policy activism, which is actually less extensive than in the earlier period, drops the public's evaluations of their performance still further.

Overall, the findings show how the office of the presidency has changed between the two time periods. Presidents have much less personal flexibility in the later period to affect their own approval ratings. Instead, they are confronted by serious economic conditions that erode their popularity. Although the impact of bad press is actually greater in the earlier period, the greater amounts of bad press in the later period cannot make presidents feel more sanguine about the media environment within which they work. Moreover, in the recent period, presidents see their institutional behavior working at cross purposes. While they gain approval from their speeches, they lose far more than they gain from their policy actions.

Conclusion: Presidential Disconnections

Theodore Roosevelt died in 1919, before radio broadcasts had begun. In 1924, Calvin Coolidge made the first nationally broadcast address to the nation from the back platform of a railroad car. Two decades later, public opinion polls began to capture popular reactions to these addresses and presidents' other actions. And only ten years after that, presidents began to appear on live television; meanwhile, poll results, as ingredients to make or break a presidential decision, were increasingly commonplace. Roosevelt would have been pleased that since the 1930s presidents have ardently expanded the philosophical tenets of policy activism and public representation which he espoused. He would be dismayed that those tenets coupled with around-the-clock media coverage and continual public opinion polls have made the philosophical requirements no longer politically feasible.

Presidents face a bitter irony. The current philosophy of the presidency requires that they be policy stewards and public representatives. Presidents have adopted political strategies to fit these philosophical requirements. They have taken numerous policy actions and have spent a considerable time in office making public appearances in Washington and around the country. But these activities confront the ever present public opinion polls within which presidents are punished for policy activism and get no credit for their public appearances, except major addresses (and only in the recent period). Although Americans may say that they prefer activist presidents who get the job done, evidence belies such statements. The more active presidents are, the more unpopular they are. Media coverage has made the president a public figure with little, if any, private space. This coverage has so enlarged the requirements of presidents' public representation that people may become distrustful of presidents about whom they know so much. Presidents make ever more varied national appearances, but their messages are buried in their own avalanche.

With the ability to measure minute shifts in public opinion on literally everything that occurs during a presidency, presidents have lost much, although not all, of their ability to shape and focus public opinion, as either policy activists or public representatives. Thus, the combination of public representation, policy activism, media coverage, and public opinion polls fundamentally recalibrates the metric by which presidents' success in office is measured. Success is equated with popularity, failure with disapproval.

To accommodate this new equation, presidents must offer grand simplifications in their policy actions and public appearances. They must offer bold, clear-cut solutions to complex problems which can be portrayed in media coverage as major administration victories. Two Carter administration officials asked "whether any president can be perceived as successful today unless his governing victories are overwhelming" or are depicted as overwhelming (Heineman and Hessler 1980, 108). Reagan's early budget- and tax-cutting victories and Bush's Persian Gulf War victory stand as elegant examples of the inelegant new requirements of the office. Too, presidents are judged harshly when their defeats appear overwhelming, as Clinton's health care reform defeat did. Far more ordinary achievements such as trade agreements, budget deals, and executive reorganizations do not provide items for the clear-cut ledger of success and failure. Similarly, presidents' public appearances must be dramatic rather than routine and less frequent rather than more frequent.

Thus, the rationales behind policy activism and the perpetual campaign are in need of reexamination. Although successive presidents have offered numerous policy proposals and maintained a breakneck pace of appearances, the evidence here suggests they would be better off making policy suggestions and public appearances less often and more strategically. Presidents run the risk of overexposure from both forms of institutional behavior and a devaluation of the political import of the presidency in the process.

While one might believe that technological, philosophical, and political changes have brought presidents and the public closer together, in some ways the changes have actually forced them further apart. The very polls and media used to establish the connection between presidents' performances in office and the public's evaluations of them are responsible for the disconnection between president and public. The disconnection occurs because the public is not persuaded by most presidential public appearances and dislikes policy activism. They continue to hold presidents responsible for economic conditions that are becoming increasingly international, complex, and out of presidents' hands. Presidents attempt to make economic and other decisions with public opinion in mind, but the public is much less persuaded by the merits of the actions. Presidents do not get credit for acting as delegates, even when the web of public opinion prevents them from acting as trustees. This disconnection between presidents and the public is one that Theodore Roosevelt would neither have envisioned nor praised.

Notes

1. Reagan's midterm popularity (1981–1982) averaged 50 percent.

2. Newspaper coverage data have not yet been gathered for Roosevelt or Truman in his first term. So the remainder of the discussion is based on quarterly data from Truman (1949) to Clinton (1994). The news data come from a content analysis of the *New York Times* in which all stories on the presidency are coded as having positive, negative, or neutral tone. The original content analysis from 1953 to 1978 was conducted by Michael Grossman and Martha Kumar (1981, 253–272). Their time series has been extended and updated by the author. Ideally, data on television coverage would also be useful in ascertaining the nature of good and bad press, since the presidency has become such a television-oriented office during the period since Truman. Television news data for this time period, however, are not fully available. The Grossman and Kumar study does include an analysis of CBS News coverage of the presidency; it shows great similarity between CBS News and the *New York Times,* which is recognized as a national newspaper with extensive, often leading, coverage of the presidency.

3. Others also have observed this increase in negative coverage in television news (see Lichter and Noyes 1991; Smoller 1986).

4. Identification of these negative events for the period 1949 to 1994 was based on matching of material presented in weekly issues of *Facts on File* and monthly breakdowns of the *World Almanac.* An event had to be consistently mentioned for at least four consecutive weeks in the *File.* In addition, the event had to be discussed in the almanac's monthly chronology of major world occurrences. Both sources also had to note specifically the presence of presidential involvement in the event: Did the president

take some action? The two sources were evaluated to establish the negative impact of an event on a president's administration.

5. The policy measure discussed is an additive index of the following three measures: (1) the annual number of legislative requests presidents make to Congress in their State of the Union messages, as first determined by Light (1991, 42) and extended and updated by the author; (2) the quarterly number of policy positions presidents take on legislation being voted on before Congress, as calculated in successive volumes of the *Congressional Quarterly Almanac;* and (3) the quarterly number of executive orders signed by a president. These data are all found in Ragsdale (1996).

6. These are a series of dummy variables, coded 1 for when a president is in office, 0 for when any other president is in office. In the full time period and the early period, Eisenhower's second term is the excluded category. In the later time period, Reagan's second term is the excluded category.

7. Bad press is the percentage of stories in the *New York Times* which carry a negative tone toward a president. The variable for negative events is coded for the number of negative events that occur in a given quarter. Unemployment is the quarterly unemployment rate as taken from the U.S. Department of Commerce, *Survey of Current Business.* Inflation is measured as the quarterly change in consumer prices, as calculated from data also taken from the U.S. Department of Commerce, *Survey of Current Business.*

8. Major addresses, news conferences, minor speeches, and ceremonial appearances are coded and calculated by the author and found in Ragsdale (1996). The total number of policy requests adds together the number of requests the president makes to the Congress in his State of the Union message, the number of policy positions he takes on roll call votes before Congress, and the number of executive orders signed, also found in Ragsdale (1996). Preliminary tests indicated that the additive index outperformed the three measures taken separately.

9. For a discussion of the impact measure, see Achen (1982) and Finkel (1993).

14 Public Opinion and Congressional Power

John R. Hibbing and Elizabeth Theiss-Morse

Americans are angry and upset with their government. Extreme antigovernment feelings were behind the Oklahoma City bombing in April 1995. After the gut-wrenching aftermath of the bombing, several commentators and politicians, including President Clinton, began an important discussion about people's disgust with government by raising two questions. The first was related directly to the Oklahoma City bombing: "How could some people hate their government so much that they would be willing to kill innocent people?" The second was potentially even more troubling because of its broader ramifications: "Why are feelings of disgust toward the U.S. government apparently so strong and so widespread?"

The second question suggests that we cannot simply point to a small lunatic fringe and say "There's the problem." So many people are disgusted with politics in the United States that this negative public mood is surely a defining feature of public opinion in the 1990s. Although feelings of disgust do not lead most people to go to the extremes of the Oklahoma City bombers, negative public opinion does have ramifications for the workings of the American political system. According to historian David Kennedy in a 1995 *Los Angeles Times* article, "Democracy, which Abraham Lincoln defined as government of, by and for the people, cannot easily survive in an atmosphere of cynical and contemptuous regard for government itself." It is imperative that we gain a better understanding of public opinion toward the American government, and especially toward the parts of the system that most upset the public.

In this light, we offer thoughts and evidence on public attitudes toward government, specifically toward the U.S. Congress. Although Americans are disgusted with government in general, Congress is the institution at the focal point of much of the public's dissatisfaction with politics. David Broder and Richard Morin (1994), for example, ask why the public hates Congress. Alan Ehrenhalt (1992) refers to Congress as the embattled institution. Congress faces a wave of public criticism that is unprecedented in recent memory (Uslaner 1992, 1). But why? Why are Americans especially angry with Congress?

Research on the power of the presidency would lead us to expect people to be most upset with the president. According to Doris Graber, "The president is the single most important figure in American politics" and "a president with good leadership abilities can make Congress do his . . . bidding" (1982, 1). Morris Fiorina states, "On the national level most analysts have viewed the presidency as stronger than the Congress at least since the time of FDR" (1992, 79).

If people's perceptions of an institution's power are related to how disgusted they are with that institution when things go wrong, then in light of conventional wisdom people should be angry with the president, not Congress. To take one example, scholars examining economic conditions and vote choice argue that citizens hold the president responsible for the state of the economy and reward or punish his party accordingly (Peffley 1985). When the economy is bad, they blame the president. But if the president has the power and is held responsible for much that goes on in the political system, then why are people particularly upset with Congress? Perhaps people are just confused. Or perhaps their disgust with Congress makes sense given their perceptions of the national institutions. We argue that, contrary to the implication of political science research, people in actuality perceive Congress to be very powerful, even more powerful than the president, but they believe Congress uses its power in primarily an obstructionist rather than a proactive way.

Our claims and conclusions are based on two data sets collected in 1992. One data set was derived from a random national sample of 1,433 American adults. During the summer of 1992, respondents were asked more than a hundred questions about their attitudes toward Congress and other political institutions. Interviews lasted approximately thirty minutes and were conducted over the telephone. The second data set was produced by a series of eight focus group sessions conducted across the country, also during the summer of 1992. In focus groups a small number of people (usually eight to twelve) meet and talk together for about two hours in a setting that is much less structured than telephone surveys. Although focus groups lack the systematic qualities of traditional surveys, they do permit participants to express themselves with greater flexibility and in a more nuanced and interactive fashion than is possible in surveys, particularly on topics that are not constantly on their minds, such as attitudes toward political institutions.

This combination of data from a new survey instrument and from focus group discussions on perceptions of Congress should make possible a much more thorough accounting of public attitudes toward Congress than has been undertaken in previous research. We begin our analysis by presenting information on public approval of the three institutions of government during the past few decades. To try to understand these patterns, especially Congress's consistently poor image, we investigate perceptions of institutional power, comparing the perceived power of Congress, the presidency, and the Supreme Court. We then assess people's beliefs about the specific powers of Congress. (What powers does Congress have? Upon what are these powers based?) Finally, we examine the connection between perceptions of congressional power and attitudes toward Congress.

Comparing Public Support for Congress, the Presidency, and the Supreme Court

We have argued that Congress is the focus of many people's anger. We need to determine whether this is so and, if it is, whether people's distaste for Congress is a recent phenomenon. Fortunately for our study, over the past thirty years or so the Harris organization has consistently posed questions on public support for the three branches of government. Specifically, people have been asked to report the amount of confidence they have in the leaders of Congress, the presidency, and the Supreme Court. Figure 14-1 shows how confidence has shifted over time (see Hibbing and Theiss-Morse 1995).

Despite incredible political changes and momentous events for individual political institutions, the public has been remarkably consistent in its confidence. To be more precise, during the last three decades, the public has always placed more confidence in the Supreme Court than in Congress. The mean percentage with a "great deal" of confidence in the Supreme Court is 29, and the range is from 22 to 40. The mean percentage with a "great deal" of confidence in Congress is just 15, and the range is from 8 to 28.

What about the executive branch? As with the Supreme Court, but to a slightly lesser degree, the public places more confidence in the executive branch than in the Congress (the mean percentage with a "great deal" of confidence in the executive branch is 21, and the figure ranges from 9 to 42). As might be expected, however, confidence in the executive branch is by far the most volatile of the measures, fluctuating both within and across presidencies. Given the hierarchical structure of the presidency, confidence in the person occupying the pinnacle of that institution will obviously go a long way toward determining confidence in the entire executive branch. As a result, although confidence in the executive branch is usually higher than confidence in the Congress and lower than confidence in the Supreme Court, it actually rose above confidence in the Court on two occasions (1977 and 1984) and fell below confidence in Congress on three occasions (1979, 1986, and 1995). Still, the general pattern is clearly for the public to be least confident in Congress and most confident in the Court, with confidence in the executive swinging somewhere in between.

Another noteworthy aspect of these patterns is the virtual absence of a significant upward or downward overall trend since the mid-1970s. The increase in confidence appearing around 1984 was apparently generated by confidence in Ronald Reagan, a strong economy, and the feel-good nature of that time. Setting aside the 1984 blip, the decades covered in the figure produced no major changes in confidence levels. Indeed, dissatisfaction with Congress in the early 1990s was actually fairly similar to dissatisfaction with Congress in the late 1970s.

What we find very surprising, though, are the 1995 figures. The 1994 midterm elections led to a historic shift in the partisan makeup of Congress, and in January 1995, for the first

Figure 14-1 Confidence in Congress, the Presidency, and the Supreme Court, 1971–1995

Percent having great deal of confidence

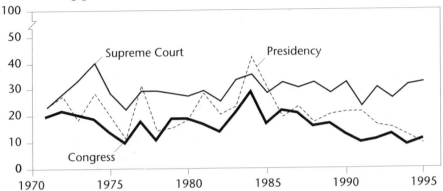

Source: Harris poll data.

Note: No data for Congress 1973, Presidency 1975.

time in forty years, the Republicans assumed control of both houses of Congress. The Republican leadership's "Contract with America" and the expectations raised by the promises of policy advances in the first hundred days of the 104th Congress led many people to assume that confidence in Congress would increase appreciably. After all, a newly elected president often experiences a honeymoon period—that is, high approval ratings early in the first term. Why should a new Congress not experience the same increase in approval? Yet the Harris data for 1995 show that Congress was not given much of a honeymoon period, if any. Confidence in Congress increased only 2 points between March 1994 and March 1995. Although it is true that confidence in the presidency decreased in the same period, even falling below Congress by 1 percentage point, the new Congress elicited basically the same low confidence ratings as the old Congress.

The unavoidable conclusion is that Congress is the least-liked political institution. At times, less than 10 percent of the population admits to having a great deal of confidence in Congress. Even these numbers, in many ways, do not capture public attitudes. Many people in the 1990s have moved beyond an absence of confidence in Congress to a more vitriolic and emotional dislike. Negative feelings lead many citizens to advocate basic changes in the nature of Congress, such as term limitations. Our focus group participants made comments such as this: "[Members of Congress] tell you one thing and then do something else. And I think the American people, the public, is just—everybody is fed up with it. They're a bunch of crooks. They don't care."

Figure 14-2 Perceptions of Institutional Power

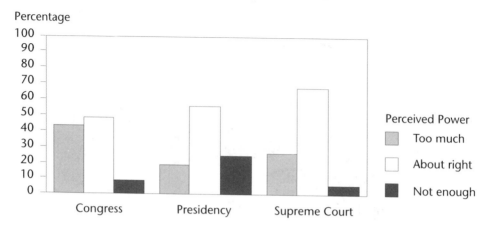

So the public is more negative about Congress than it is about the other institutions. And this situation is not new but rather has been with us, more or less, for approximately three decades. If anything, people's attitudes toward Congress have become more strongly negative. Certainly the press has paid more attention to public dissatisfaction with Congress, and citizens have been professing their displeasure with louder voice and more raw emotion. All this leads us back to the question we posed in the introduction to this chapter. Why has the public turned against Congress if, as some political scientists and others tell us, the president is all-powerful and therefore responsible for the current condition of the nation (see Lowi 1985)?

Which Institution Has Power?

Political scientists and commentators alike often assume that the presidency is the most powerful branch of government. But does the public share their assumption? To understand public wrath toward government, and specifically toward Congress, it is essential that we examine the assumption regarding presidential power. One possible explanation for Congress's low standing, of course, is that people are disgusted with Congress because they perceive it to be weak and powerless. Citizens in this scenario would prefer a much stronger Congress to counteract the overwhelming power of the presidency, and when they do not see Congress acting powerfully, they respond with disgust. Another possibility—and the one we think most likely—is that people dislike Congress because they perceive it to be extremely powerful. Congress, they might argue, is so powerful that it is unconscionable for members not to use this power for the betterment of the citizenry and the nation as a whole. People then become disgusted because Congress is not doing what it ought to be doing.

Do people think Congress is powerful or powerless? We asked our survey respondents if they thought each of the three individual political institutions had too much power, about the right amount of power, or too little power. Figure 14-2 provides strong support for our contention that people think Congress is too powerful. Only 19 percent of respondents thought the presidency had too much power; more than twice as many respondents, 43 percent, thought Congress had too much power. And it is not the case that the rest of the respondents were satisfied with the power of the presidency and Congress. Only 9 percent thought Congress should have more power, while 25 percent thought the presidency should have more power.

Discussions among focus group participants corroborate the survey results. Participants believed that the presidency was quite weak relative to Congress, and they made clear their sense that Congress rules the roost in Washington. When asked which branch is most powerful, a Houston resident said: "The Congress. They're the ones that the president and everybody else has to go to to get them to approve things." A Minnesotan said: "I think the presidency is kind of a figurehead position limited in power by the Congress. And no matter how much you like an individual, he can probably put a little bit of pressure on, but it's owned and regulated and operated by our Congress." Another focus group participant said: "I think the whole thing basically goes into the Congress rather than the president. All he's got is the veto power. He doesn't, I don't feel, have any power as far as the law is concerned. Neither does the Supreme Court. All they do is interpret it. I think the problem is basically in the Congress."

Several focus group participants even compared the presidency to the monarchy in England, arguing that both were simply figureheads. One participant said: "I thought the president had become almost more of a monarchy. I mean, the president is just more of a figurehead and we pay him for his service, and that no real decision making of any lasting consequence is made by the president."

According to the survey respondents and focus group participants, the presidency is significantly weaker than Congress. One focus group respondent suggested that the United States no longer has a system of checks and balances because the Supreme Court and presidency are too weak to have any control over Congress. But just what powers does Congress have? What makes the people think Congress is so powerful that the president is only a figurehead? We examine these questions next.

Public Perceptions of Congressional Powers

According to Lawrence Dodd, "The power of Congress rests on the ability of its elected members to legislate; to respond effectively to policy needs, interests and demands; in short, to act" (1981, 411). Citizens, however, do not view Congress's power in the same terms. In fact, according to the public, Congress's power rests in procedures that actually inhibit action. That is, Congress's power rests on its ability to be obstructionist. The strongest evidence for this point is found in the focus group discussions.

Most often, focus group discussions of power pitted Congress against the president, and Congress nearly always won, but not by being active. According to several participants, the president desperately tries to get things done, but Congress often gets in the way. Members of Congress bicker among themselves, they allow interest groups to jump into the process, they conduct study after study on an issue, they are tremendously inefficient, and ultimately they accomplish nothing. And this is exactly where Congress's power lies, according to the focus group discussions: members of Congress could contribute to taking care of the nation's problems in a simple, straightforward way, but instead they choose to make the task much more difficult than it needs to be and thereby keep things from getting done.

Survey results provide supportive, albeit less direct, evidence. If we are correct that people believe Congress is too powerful because its flawed procedures and structures prevent things from getting done, then we should find that the more people dislike the workings of Congress, the more they will think Congress is too powerful.

We considered two aspects of perceived structures and procedures: professionalization and representation. Professionalization refers to how structured and formalized an institution is. Congress has become more complex and devoted to standardized operating procedures, has larger staffs, has more defined boundaries setting it apart from other parts of the government and from citizens, has members who stay longer in office, has a more elaborate infrastructure, and has well-defined norms and rules (see Polsby 1968). Representation refers to perceptions of Congress's ability to represent diverse interests and the interests of ordinary people, but it also includes concerns about the role interest groups play in the political process. (Refer to this chapter's appendix for a listing of questions.)

Figure 14-3 shows that whether people like or dislike congressional processes and structures is related to their assessment of Congress's power. Among those who like professionalization and feel Congress does a good job at representation, about the same percentage of people think Congress has too little power as think it has too much power. The big difference is among those who dislike professionalization and view Congress as failing on representation. Only about 8 percent of people who dislike congressional processes and structures think Congress has too little power, whereas over 45 percent of this group think it has too much.

So people hold Congress to be a very powerful branch, especially in relation to the presidency, and the basis of Congress's perceived power lies in its obstructionist processes and structures. The professionalization of Congress—with its bewildering array of committees and subcommittees, its armada of entrenched staffers, its complicated insider rules and elaborate infrastructure, and its ponderous, multistage legislative process—contributes to this perception. And the representational procedures evident in Congress, with its reliance on pro-

Figure 14-3 Democratic Processes and Power

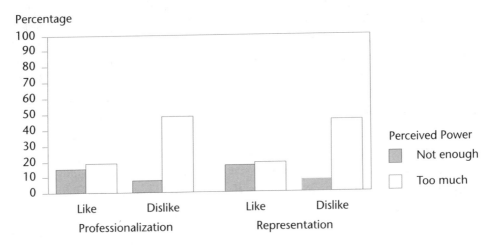

Percentage

Perceived Power
- Not enough
- Too much

Professionalization: Like, Dislike
Representation: Like, Dislike

fessional lobbyists rather than regular citizens, contribute in the same way to perceptions of the power of Congress.

A professionalized Congress is one that is set apart in many ways from the world around it. Its boundaries are less permeable, its tasks are accomplished in-house, it has large staffs, and it allows for and promotes specialization. The professionalized Congress is therefore potentially able to shut out input from external sources, whether from the president or the public. Citizens' perception of this process, then, intensifies their view that Congress's power is to obstruct the enactment of good laws. Congress can choose to pay attention and react to the president or it can ignore him. Congress can choose to work with the people to find solutions to the nation's problems or it can choose to ignore them. Professionalization leads, in the public's mind, to isolation and to a Congress unwilling to work with its constituents to solve the nation's problems.

The nature of modern representation also adds to Congress's perceived obstructionism. People believe that a truly representative Congress would reflect the interests of ordinary individuals. Now, theoretically, this type of representation could be achieved through interest groups. Pluralist theorists state that interest groups are important to a democracy because they aggregate interests in such a way as to allow for fair competition among interests (Truman 1951). In a pluralist democracy, interest groups are supposed to provide a healthy, even vital, linkage between the diverse interests of people and the government. But rather than seeing interest groups as a useful link, people view interest groups as insidious. The fact that congressional processes promote interest group influence obviously says something about Congress. By turning to interest groups rather than ordinary people, Congress has lost touch with what people want to see done in America. When the president tries to address problems of importance to the public, Congress becomes obstructionist in part because it protects the favored positions of established special interests, which have also become the favored positions of members of Congress themselves. Congress is obstructionist because it operates with a skewed vision of what needs to be accomplished in the nation.

So the nature of Congress and congressional processes promotes inaction. By not being proactive, Congress is able to stall the whole political system. People believe that the president generally wants to do what is necessary to take care of the nation's problems. They also assume widespread agreement among citizens concerning what needs to be done. But the public believes solutions to national problems are rarely enacted because Congress does not use its power to solve problems. Instead, they believe the power of Congress often contributes to the problems.

Consequences of People's Perceptions of Congressional Power

In this section, we describe three consequences of popular perceptions of congressional power. First, we argue that perceptions of congressional power are related to overall approval of Congress. People are less likely to approve of Congress if they are focused on Congress's power to obstruct. Second, people's feelings toward Congress are likely to be affected by perceptions of its power. Finally, Congress is likely to be held more responsible for problems facing the nation than the other institutions because of its perceived power.

Approval of Congress

If people believe that Congress uses its power to impede progress rather than to address major problems facing the nation, then they are not likely to approve of the job Congress is doing. Survey data show this to be true. The more people think Congress has too much power, the less likely they are to approve of the job members of Congress are doing ($r = -.36$; $p < .01$). But perhaps this relationship exists merely because a certain group of people, say Republicans, is more negative toward Congress (remember, the survey was done before the Republican takeover of Congress) and more inclined to believe Congress possesses a great deal of power.

To test for this relationship, we must take other possible influences on congressional disapproval into account. Table 14-1 shows the results of a regression analysis with approval of members of Congress as the dependent variable and perceptions of congressional power, education, and party identification as independent variables.[1] Even after controlling for the effects of education and party identification, perceptions of congressional power are strongly and negatively related to approval of members of Congress. Whether a Republican or a

Table 14-1 Explaining Approval of Members of Congress

Variable	Unstandardized Regression Coefficient	Standard Error	t-ratio
Education	−.04	.02	−1.87
Party identification	−.08	.02	−4.45*
Perceived power	−.22	.02	−12.32*
Adjusted R^2	.14		
F (df = 3, 1,295)	72.7		

Notes: All variables range from 0 to 1.

* Statistically significant at the .01 level.

Democrat, whether highly educated or not, someone who thinks Congress has too much power is much more likely to disapprove of the job its members are doing.

Emotional Reactions to Congress

Aside from approval or disapproval, which can be a simple, straightforward assessment of the job government is doing, we often hear in the popular press that Americans have strong negative feelings toward government. It comes as no surprise that people feel negatively toward Congress as well. What exactly is the nature of this negative mood, though? Is it hatred? If our argument is correct, and people are upset at Congress's power to obstruct, then we would expect people to feel frustrated by Congress. Why, they might ask, don't members do something to help out? Why do they make government grind to a halt? Frustration, in turn, is likely to lead people to feel angry toward and disgusted by the membership of Congress. On the other hand, since Congress's obstruction takes place in full view of everyone, people are less likely to feel afraid of than angry at members of Congress. Congress is not doing its job surreptitiously or sneakily, so there is little reason to be afraid or uneasy.

We asked the survey respondents a series of questions concerning their emotional reactions to members of Congress: "Now we would like to know something about the feelings you have about members of Congress. Have members of Congress ever made you feel angry? . . . Afraid? . . . Disgusted? . . . Uneasy?" Respondents answered yes or no to these questions. Using the answers only of people who think Congress has too much power, we can determine what feelings these people have toward the members of a Congress they believe to be too powerful.

Figure 14-4 provides fairly strong evidence that Congress's obstructionist powers lead people to feel angry at and disgusted by members of Congress. Eighty-seven percent of respon-

Figure 14-4   Congressional Power and Emotions

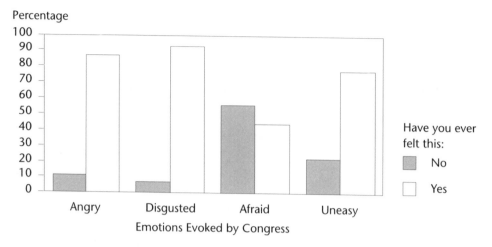

Note: Respondents include only those who say Congress is "too powerful."

dents who think Congress is too powerful said they had felt anger toward members of Congress, and fully 93 percent said they had felt disgusted. Feelings of fear and uneasiness, as expected, are less common among these respondents. Though 78 percent still said they had felt uneasy, only 44 percent had felt afraid. So perceptions that Congress has too much power are related to feelings of anger and disgust, presumably due to the frustration people feel about Congress's obstructionism.

Congressional Responsibility

A final consequence of citizens' perceptions of congressional power relates to ascribing responsibility for the problems facing the nation. Citizens are naturally more likely to blame a powerful institution for not doing anything to take care of the problems than they are to blame a weak and impotent institution. Therefore, one of the worst possible situations for an institution would be to be perceived to have more power than it really does and thus to be held culpable for problems it did not bring about. The perception that Congress is powerful may place it precisely in this situation.

By employing our survey data, we can test for the extent to which Congress is held responsible for national problems. We asked respondents: "What part of the government is most responsible for the massive budget deficits currently facing the U.S. government? Would you say it is Congress or the Presidency?" The easiest, and probably most accurate, response is "Both," which was given by 27 percent of the respondents. What we found surprising is that 52 percent pointed the finger of blame solely at Congress whereas less

Figure 14-5 Power and Responsibility for Deficit

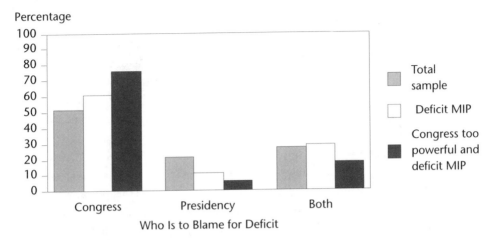

Percentage

Who Is to Blame for Deficit

Note: "Deficit MIP" refers to respondents who said the deficit was the most important problem facing the nation. "Congress too powerful and deficit MIP" refers to respondents who believe Congress is too powerful and that the deficit is the most important problem facing the nation.

than half that many—only 21 percent—blamed the presidency alone (see Figure 14-5).

These percentages reflect the opinions of the entire survey sample. What about people who are especially concerned about the deficit? We asked respondents what they felt to be the most important problem facing the nation. Not surprisingly, given the mood of the nation in 1992, 51 percent pointed directly to some type of economic concerns, and 17 percent specifically mentioned the budget deficit. This "most important problem" screen allows us to determine whether people who are particularly worried about the deficit are more likely to put the responsibility for the problem on Congress's shoulders. Figure 14-5 shows this to be true: 61 percent of individuals who are very concerned about the budget deficit blame Congress for the deficit, whereas only 11 percent of these respondents blame the presidency and 29 percent blame both branches.

Finally, if people perceive Congress to be very powerful, they are likely to believe it ought to be able to do something about the nation's problems, especially problems that really matter to them. If they perceive Congress as not doing anything, then they are likely to view Congress as truly to blame. To test this argument, we focused on people who think the budget deficit is the most important problem facing the nation *and* who think Congress is too powerful. Figure 14-5 shows that 76 percent of these people point the finger of blame at Congress and only 6 percent at the presidency. Those who blame both Congress and the presidency dropped to 18 percent.

Our survey data allow us to examine ascribed responsibility further, but in a less direct way. Although we do not have measures of who is blamed in each issue area, we did ask a series of questions on how good a job Congress, the presidency, and the Supreme Court were doing dealing with what respondents considered the most important problem facing the nation. Respondents were asked if each of the three institutions was doing a good job, a fair job, or a poor job handling whatever they thought was the most important problem, from the economy to moral issues to foreign policy. Whatever the problem, results show that 75 percent of respondents thought Congress was doing a poor job, 62 percent said the presidency was doing a poor job, and 46 percent said the Supreme Court was doing a poor job.

The public believes Congress is a powerful institution. Moreover, as is made clear by responses to questions on the budget deficit, many people believe that Congress is not using its power to take care of pressing national problems. The fact that people who believe the deficit is the most important problem are especially likely to point the finger of blame at Congress paints an even bleaker picture for Congress. The budget deficit is likely the result of the combined efforts of Congress and the presidency. Yet people who believe the deficit is a serious problem and who think Congress is too powerful are over twelve times more likely to blame Congress than the president for the deficit. Our results further show that in general, people think Congress is doing a poor job taking care of a wide variety of the nation's problems.

Conclusion

Contrary to what we would expect, given the prevailing wisdom in political science, the American public perceives Congress to be very powerful, maybe too powerful. Is the image of an all-powerful Congress a recent phenomenon? We do not have data to address this point directly. It may be that during the time of Franklin D. Roosevelt and perhaps even during the era of the so-called imperial presidency (see Schlesinger 1973), the public believed that the presidency was the most powerful institution. But we would caution against being too quick to arrive at such a conclusion. People may have been convinced for quite some time that Congress is the most powerful governmental branch. Nearly a quarter of a century ago, Roger Davidson and Glenn Parker (1972) and Jack Dennis (1973), using different data, arrived separately at the conclusion that "Congress emerges as the institution perceived to have [the] greatest impact upon people's lives" (Dennis 1973, 12). The data these scholars present for the early 1970s are as convincing as ours are for the early 1990s.

We suspect that the feature of public opinion that has changed over the years is not the perception that Congress is powerful but rather the extent to which people view congressional power positively or negatively. Writing in the early 1970s, Donald Devine noted that people prefer congressional power overwhelmingly to presidential power (1972, 158–163).

At about the same time, Dennis reached a similar conclusion, demonstrating that "Congress appears to have an edge over other institutions in the level of support for its power" (1973, 15). These descriptions of public support for congressional power seem strangely out of place in the mid-1990s. As our survey data indicated, only 9 percent of voting-age Americans want Congress strengthened, whereas nearly half want it weakened. More poignantly, comments in the focus groups leave no doubt that the public is quite disgusted with the power of Congress.

Why would people be so much less approving of a powerful Congress now than they were twenty-five years ago? We have argued in this chapter that perceptions of Congress's power are in part based on structures and processes employed in Congress. To work within a modern democratic political system, Congress must be able to address a wide range of issues with as much expertise as possible and to represent diverse and often contending interests. But it is in part Congress's move toward greater professionalization and interest group representation that gets it in the most trouble with citizens. These modern democratic processes are significantly related to perceptions that Congress's power is obstructionist. People have the impression that members of Congress squabble, delay, are inefficient, get swept up in the Washington scene, and keep things from happening. In this view, the president may want to accomplish something and citizens know what needs to be done; but Congress can prevent things from getting done. Congress's power rests not in action but in inaction. This is an immense power, and the modern Congress's structure and processes nourish this power.

To be sure, Congress has had significant power for most of the Republic's history, and this power is more often than not a power to stop things from being done. As designed, the legislature's detachment from the executive branch, the two separate houses, the multiple decision points and associated need to build successive coalitions, and the distinct geographical constituencies all conspire against action. An important part of the reason that the public has become less tolerant of the deliberate pace and apparent obstructionism of Congress is the extent to which congressional processes and structures are visible. Even casually attentive citizens are now aware of partisan disputes, attempts at interbranch compromise, dilatory tactics, the plethora of committees and subcommittees, caustic debate, platoons of staffers, office perquisites, junkets with lobbyists, and money-raising cocktail parties with fat cats.

The inherent openness of a collegial institution such as Congress combined with the increased exposure made possible by modern technology, media, and societal tendencies has made Congress particularly vulnerable. The public is now more likely to know something about the increasing institutionalization of Congress, from banks to pensions. The public is now more likely to be aware of the interaction of lobbyists and members of Congress. And the public is now more likely to acquire a better sense of the power of Congress, beyond its constitutional mandates. Needless to say, the public does not like what it sees. Most people dislike virtually every facet of the professionalization of Congress, from lengthy service to six-figure salaries. Most people deplore the influence of special interests and are reluctant to accept that special interests may be representing a valid view of some portion of the citizenry.

As if all this were not bad enough for those concerned about public approval of Congress, the perceived clout of the institution, as detailed in this chapter, moves popular support into an even lower category. Most people refuse to believe that a legislative body should be slow to act, reluctant to adopt new ideas, and anxious to debate and compromise for the sake of uniting diverse public opinion. Most people want Congress to have the power to check the president, but they do not want to see this power in action. Both institutions should work together to solve problems. The public wishes not to see partisan conflict on the nightly news when problems require action. In adopting such a position, we believe the public is being patently unrealistic. But our task is not to pass judgment; it is to explain why the public is so negative toward Congress. We believe the perceptions of congressional power, when combined with the other factors described, contribute to such an explanation.

These perceptions of congressional power have serious consequences for public opinion toward Congress in the 1990s. As we have shown, people who believe Congress has too much power are much more disapproving of the job performance of members of Congress than are those who are more satisfied with Congress's level of power. People who see Congress as powerful also feel much more disgust and anger toward Congress. This disgust with Congress clearly came through in the 1994 midterm elections, when citizens voted out the party in power.

Public opinion concerning congressional power may be even more damaging to Congress than the disapproval or anger attracting so much editorial comment. Because people believe Congress is very powerful, they place the full blame on Congress for problems facing the nation, such as the budget deficit, even when the problems are likely not all Congress's fault. Congress in the 1990s is often seen as failing when it is not. Not dealing with an important national problem might not spell trouble for the public approval of an institution if that institution were not viewed as being in a position to do something about the problem. The Supreme Court enjoys this latter situation in a variety of policy areas, but Congress does not. People see Congress as powerful and capable of solving myriad problems. Thus, the perception that Congress is failing to deal with major problems is especially damaging because the institution is believed to have the power to make a difference.

To understand public opinion toward political institutions in the 1990s, it is essential that we appreciate public perceptions of the potential and clout of those institutions. Contrary to what is often assumed, people believe Congress is more powerful than the presidency and the Court, and this belief affects other opinions and feelings about Congress and about the entire political system. Public opinion toward Congress is so negative partly because Congress is doing its job in representing diverse interests, in wrestling openly with complicated issues, and in using its power to check other institutions.

Appendix

Two data sets were used in this study: a national telephone survey and focus groups (for more information, see Hibbing and Theiss-Morse 1995). The telephone survey data were collected by the Bureau of Sociological Research at the University of Nebraska. The bureau hired and trained interviewers for this project. The bureau purchased a list of telephone numbers from a national random sample and then randomly generated the last digit of the telephone number. When interviewers called a household, they asked to speak to the person in the household who was at least eighteen years old and who had the most recent birthday (Salmon and Nichols 1983). The telephone interviews were conducted from July to October 1992 and had a 57 percent response rate, comparable to most recent telephone surveys of this kind. A total of 1,433 people completed the survey.

The dependent variable in Table 14-1 is a standard four-point approval question on members of Congress. The approval question asked respondents if they, in general, strongly approved, approved, disapproved, or strongly disapproved of the way the members of Congress are handling their jobs.

The party identification question is the standard seven-point American National Election Studies (ANES) question (strong Democrat, weak Democrat, independent leaning toward Democrats, independent, independent leaning toward Republicans, weak Republican, strong Republican). The education question, the standard ANES question, asked respondents to indicate the highest level of schooling they had completed.

The "most important problem" question asked respondents in an open-ended format, "What do you think is the single most important problem facing this country?" They were then asked, "How good a job is the U.S. Congress doing in dealing with this problem, a good job, a fair job, or a poor job?" followed by questions referring to the presidency and to the Supreme Court.

To ascertain respondents' assessment of institutional power, we asked, "The institutions of government in Washington, no matter who is in office, need a certain amount of power for the good of the country and the individual person. Please tell me if the institution has too much power, not enough power, or about the right amount of power. The U.S. Supreme Court? . . . What about the Presidency? . . . What about the U.S. Congress?"

The professionalization and representation variables were created by summing responses to several five-point Likert questions that ranged from strongly disagree to strongly agree. We reversed coding where necessary so that pro-professionalization and pro-representation responses were assigned higher numbers. Professionalization: Congress addresses difficult issues in a reasonably efficient way; there are too many staffers or assistants in Congress (reversed); just a few members of Congress have all the power (reversed); members of Congress focus too much on events in Washington (reversed). Representation: Congress does a good job representing the diverse interests of Americans, whether black or white, rich or poor; Congress is too far removed from ordinary people (reversed); Congress is too heavily influenced by interest groups when making decisions (reversed).

The independent variables used in the regression analysis were standardized to range from 0 to 1, making comparisons across variables easier. See King (1986) and Luskin (1991) for a discussion of how to interpret scales using this method of standardizing variables.

The focus groups were conducted in two communities in each of four parts of the country: Nebraska, the Minneapolis-St. Paul area, Houston, and upstate New York. The eight locations varied in terms of socioeconomic status, population size of the community, and minority makeup of the community. The focus groups included from six to twelve people and lasted about two hours. Participants were promised and received $20 for their involvement.

The focus group moderator worked from a list of prepared questions. An assistant tape recorded the sessions and kept track of participants' comments with pen and paper. The tape recordings were later transcribed. The transcripts were systematically analyzed for the connections respondents made among various political objects and then for the topics of comments. Using this method, we were able to examine both the evaluations made about certain institutions or members and the linkages among various attitudes.

Note

1. We use respondents' approval of the members of Congress here because when people are asked about "Congress" they tend to respond in terms of the members of Congress (see Hibbing and Theiss-Morse, 1995). Since people think about Congress as its members, we think it appropriate to use the membership approval measure.

15 Public Opinion and the Supreme Court: The Insulated Court?

Thomas Marshall

At first glance, the U.S. Supreme Court may appear to be far removed from American public opinion. Unlike members of Congress, the nine justices are appointed for life terms, at least with "good behavior." In the twentieth century, not a single justice has faced an impeachment hearing. Nor do hostile congressional committees summon the justices to appear before televised hearings—a fate that even the Federal Reserve Board's governors sometimes face. The last five justices to retire averaged twenty-six years on the Court before retiring at advanced ages. During the last half century, not a single justice has used the Court as a springboard to launch a bid for elective office.

Justices' careers before coming to the Supreme Court also seem increasingly removed from public opinion. In decades past, many Supreme Court justices arrived at the Court with personal experience in running for elective office. Among current Supreme Court justices, however, only Sandra Day O'Connor has ever faced voters in an election. Today, a Supreme Court nominee's resume typically shows experience as an attorney, an appointed official, or a judge.

Compared with Congress or the White House, the Supreme Court makes little effort to sway public opinion. Many opinions are announced in a rush during the term's last few weeks. The Court's staff does not try to put a public relations "spin" on the Court's rulings, and even the best-known decisions are couched in obscure legal jargon that few Americans could easily follow. Unlike many lower courts, the Supreme Court does not allow televised coverage when oral arguments are held or when decisions are announced. The Court also exempts itself from Open Meetings Act requirements, and makes its decisions in closed conference, behind closed doors, far away from C-SPAN's watchful eye.

Several of the justices have written dismissively of public opinion. In *Furman v. Georgia* (1972), a landmark death penalty case, for example, Justice Thurgood Marshall wrote that "while a public opinion poll obviously is of some assistance in indicating public acceptance or rejection of a specific penalty, its utility cannot be very great." Justice Lewis Powell commented in the same case that "public opinion polls [have] little probative relevance." In *Stanford v. Kentucky* (1989) Justice Antonin Scalia called public opinion polls "uncertain foundations" upon which to base a Supreme Court decision.

Not surprisingly, Americans seldom focus on the Supreme Court. On average, only a quarter of the Court's full written opinions receive any television newscast coverage (Katsh 1983; Slotnick, Segal, and Campoli 1994; Slotnick 1991). Only one-half to two-thirds of Americans correctly understand even the most famous Supreme Court rulings, such as its flag-burning or abortion rulings (Marshall 1991). Shortly after Ruth Bader Ginsburg was nominated to the Supreme Court, only 45 percent of Americans said they knew who she was or what she did.[1] One survey even reported that only 9 percent of Americans could name Chief Justice William Rehnquist, although 54 percent of Americans could name Judge Joseph Wapner, from a popular television series.[2]

Reassessing the Court and Public Opinion

Upon closer examination, however, the U.S. Supreme Court is not so far removed from American public opinion. Perhaps surprisingly, a review of nationwide public opinion polls suggests that most Supreme Court decisions are consistent with the opinions of a majority of Americans.

Since the mid-1930s pollsters often have surveyed public opinion on high-profile Supreme Court cases. In an earlier study of Court decisions from the mid-1930s until the Rehnquist Court's first term in fall 1986, some 146 Supreme Court decisions could be directly matched, in substance, with a poll item from a major nationwide poll, such as the Gallup, Harris, or CBS News/*New York Times* polls (Marshall 1989). This chapter compares (or matches) another twenty-six Supreme Court decisions with poll questions from nationwide polls during the Rehnquist Court's first term (1986/87) through the 1992/93 term.[3] Where an issue raised in a Supreme Court decision could be compared, in substance, with a carefully worded poll item from a major nationwide poll, the Supreme Court's decision can be classified as either "consistent" or "inconsistent" with American public opinion, or in a few cases, as "unclear."

As an example, consider the Supreme Court's ruling in *Michigan Department of State Police v. Stitz* (1990). In that dispute, a 6–3 Court majority upheld a Michigan policy of randomly stopping motorists to check for drunk drivers. That ruling was consistent with a 74–25 percent majority in a 1990 Harris poll favoring "the use of random police checks at toll booths to check drivers for signs of alcohol and drug intoxication."[4] The *Stitz* decision is classified as consistent with public opinion.

Now consider another example: the very controversial Supreme Court decision in *Planned Parenthood of Southeastern Pennsylvania v. Casey* (1992). One part of the *Casey* decision invalidated a Pennsylvania law requiring a woman to notify her husband before obtaining an abortion. The Court's decision to invalidate that section of the Pennsylvania law was inconsistent with a 73–25 percent majority in a January 1992 Gallup poll which supported "a law requir-

Table 15-1 Supreme Court Consistency with Public Opinion, by Court Period, 1935–1993

	Hughes Court (1934/35– 1940/41)	Stone Court (1941/42– 1945/46)	Vinson Court (1946/47– 1952/53)	Warren Court (1953/54– 1968/69)	Burger Court (1969/70– 1985/86)	Rehnquist Court (1986/87– 1993)
Consistent	65%	54%	68%	52%	53%	54%
Unclear	12	—	—	14	15	—
Inconsistent	24	46	32	33	33	46
Number of cases	(17)	(13)	(19)	(21)	(76)	(26)

Notes: For all 172 poll-to-decision matches, 96 (or 56 percent) were consistent, 16 (or 9 percent) were unclear, and 60 (or 35 percent) were inconsistent. The sums of percentages in each column (for each Court) add to 100 except where the rounding of entries changes the total slightly. Results insignificant at the .05 level.

ing that the husband of a married woman be notified if she decides to have an abortion."[5] This part of the *Casey* decision is therefore classified as "inconsistent" with public opinion.

In a few instances, public opinion was very closely divided (within the .05 level of sampling error) on a Supreme Court decision, and the decision is classified as unclear. None of the 26 Rehnquist Court poll-to-decision matches considered in this chapter is classified as unclear, although 11 percent of the earlier 146 decisions were.

To be sure, these poll-to-decision matches do not represent a purely random sample of the Supreme Court's docket. Civil liberties, civil rights, and death penalty cases more often spark public controversy and poll questions than do economic cases, and it is only on controversial matters that pollsters assess public opinion. This sample of poll-to-decision matches is a diverse but nonrandom sampling of the Court's high-profile agenda.

Overall, in these twenty-six decision-to-poll matches, the Rehnquist Court's decisions were consistent with nationwide poll majorities fourteen times (54 percent of the matches) and were inconsistent with poll majorities twelve times (46 percent of the matches). The 54 percent consistent figure for the Rehnquist Court compares with the Supreme Court's earlier 1935–1986 average of 56 percent consistent, 33 percent inconsistent, and 11 percent unclear decisions (Marshall 1989, 78–79; see also Barnum 1985). Table 15-1 compares the Rehnquist Court with earlier Courts since the mid-1930s.

A more direct comparison of the Rehnquist Court and earlier Court periods would set aside poll-to-decision matches where American public opinion was itself evenly divided. In this comparison the Rehnquist Court appears to be somewhat less consistent with American public opinion than earlier Courts were. Where the polls were clear, earlier Courts agreed with the polls in 63 percent of their decisions; the figure for the Rehnquist Court is 54 percent.

In several instances, a Supreme Court decision was consistent with a large and one-sided poll majority. According to available polls, the Rehnquist Court's most popular ruling was *Skinner v. Railway Labor Executives' Association* (1989), upholding mandatory drug testing for public safety workers. Matching the *Skinner* decision, an 88–12 percent public opinion majority favored mandatory drug testing for public safety workers, according to a 1986 CBS News/*New York Times* poll.[6] The Rehnquist Court's two other most popular decisions came in upholding the requirement that a woman give her written "informed consent" for an abortion, in *Planned Parenthood of Southeastern Pennsylvania v. Casey* (1992); and in upholding the parental notification requirement for a minor to have an abortion, in *Ohio v. Akron Center for Reproductive Health* (1990). In each of these decisions, at least six times as many Americans agreed with the Court's decisions as disagreed.

The Rehnquist Court's decisions have not always enjoyed so much public consensus, however. In several instances, the Court's decisions have been decidedly unpopular. The Rehnquist Court's least popular decision was its denial of an application for stay in the "Baby Jessica" custody case, *DeBoer v. Schmidt* (1993). In that case, Justice Stevens, for the Court, refused to overturn a state court decision returning a two-year-old child to her Iowa biological parents over the objections of the child's Michigan custodial parents, who had raised the child since infancy. According to a Gallup poll item, only 8 percent of Americans favored returning Baby Jessica to her biological parents, while 78 percent of Americans favored leaving Baby Jessica with the couple who had raised her.[7]

The two other least popular Rehnquist Court decisions were *Cruzan v. Director, Missouri Department of Health* (1990), allowing a state agency to keep alive—over the objections of the parents—a car crash victim who had lapsed into a persistent vegetative coma; and *Sable Communications v. Federal Communications Commission* (1989), upholding the right to operate sexually explicit commercial telephone talk lines for adults. In each of these decisions, at least three times as many Americans disagreed with the Court's decision as approved it. To put these unpopular rulings into perspective, the *DeBoer, Cruzan*, and *Sable* decisions were about as unpopular as the 1989 and 1991 congressional pay raises.[8]

Is the Court more consistent with American public opinion on some issues than on others? Prior to the Rehnquist Court, the Court's rulings were most often consistent with American public opinion when the issues involved transportation and commerce (80 percent consistent with public opinion), business regulation and taxes (77 percent consistent), or racial issues (75 percent consistent). Court rulings were least often consistent with public opinion in religion cases (only 50 percent consistent with public opinion); criminal rights, courts, and police cases (48 percent); and federalism cases (46 percent) (Marshall 1989, 89).

The twenty-six decisions examined here are only a small sample of the Rehnquist Court's rulings, but some comparisons are possible. The Rehnquist Court appears to reflect the polls most closely in its abortion and women's rights rulings—where two-thirds (eight of twelve) of the decisions match the polls. In First Amendment cases, involving free speech, religion, and obscenity claims, the Rehnquist Court was consistent with the polls in only one-third (two of six) of its rulings. For the remaining eight decisions, the Court was consistent with the polls exactly half the time in four criminal penalty cases and four miscellaneous cases.

Because justices typically record their individual votes when deciding a case, it is possible to compute how often each justice's votes are consistent with nationwide public opinion. The evidence suggests that some justices are much more consistent with the polls than others are.

Consider, for example, the Court's opinion in *Rust v. Sullivan* (1991), where a 5–4 majority upheld a federal regulation forbidding workers at publicly funded health clinics to counsel pregnant women on the availability of abortion. That decision was inconsistent with a 71–23 percent CBS News/*New York Times* poll majority. Justices Rehnquist, Souter, White, Scalia, and Kennedy made up the Court's majority, and were therefore inconsistent with public opinion. Justices Blackmun, Marshall, Stevens, and O'Connor dissented, and were therefore consistent with public opinion.

When each justice's vote is scored as consistent or inconsistent with public opinion, striking differences appear. Of justices who recorded at least ten votes on these twenty-six decisions, Justices Rehnquist and White were the most often consistent with majority public opinion, with each scoring 72 percent consistent. Justice Brennan was the least consistent with public opinion, reflecting poll majorities in only 29 percent of his votes.

Because several justices cast only a few votes during this period, it may be more meaningful to divide the justices by their liberal-versus-conservative voting patterns. Five justices (Stevens, Blackmun, Marshall, Brennan, and Powell) voted conservative in fewer than one-third of these cases and can be considered the liberal bloc. The remaining seven justices (Thomas, Rehnquist, Scalia, Kennedy, Souter, White, and O'Connor) voted conservative in over two-thirds of these cases and can be considered the conservative bloc.[9]

Overall, the conservative bloc's votes were more often consistent with the polls. Together, the conservative bloc cast 132 votes, of which 67 percent were consistent with poll majorities or pluralities. By comparison, the liberal bloc together cast ninety votes, of which only 43 percent were consistent with poll majorities or pluralities.

The Rehnquist Court shows several other patterns in how often justices are consistent with public opinion. Republican justices were slightly more consistent with public opinion than were Democrat justices (60 percent consistent versus 51 percent consistent). Republican justices appointed since 1980 were the most consistent with public opinion (63 percent consistent). Minority (Catholic, Jewish, African American, or women) justices were slightly less consistent with nationwide public opinion majorities than were white male Protestant justices (57 percent consistent, versus 60 percent consistent).

Interestingly, the Rehnquist Court's decisions represented the attitudes of several large demographic groups equally well. For example, these twenty-six Rehnquist Court decisions were consistent with majorities of men about as often as with majorities of women, and they were consistent with majorities of the college-educated as often as with majorities of high school-educated Americans. These results are similar to those reported for the Supreme Court going back to the early 1950s (Marshall 1992).

Has the Rehnquist Court represented American public opinion in the liberal-versus-conservative content of its decisions? Of the twenty-six Rehnquist Court rulings examined here, twenty-four had a clear liberal-versus-conservative content.[10] Of these twenty-four rulings, the Supreme Court handed down conservative decisions in 75 percent of the cases. By comparison, public opinion majorities also supported the conservative position in 75 percent of the cases. Overall, American public opinion and Supreme Court rulings during the Rehnquist Court have fit well; both were quite conservative on these high-profile cases.

Although both American public opinion and the Rehnquist Court took conservative positions on three-quarters of these disputes, they did not necessarily take a conservative position on the same specific cases. For example, public opinion took a liberal position on five disputes for which the Rehnquist Court handed down a conservative ruling. On another five disputes, public opinion was conservative but the Rehnquist Court issued a liberal ruling. On the remaining fourteen disputes, public opinion and the Rehnquist Court adopted the same ideological stance.

How does the Supreme Court's record in representing American public opinion compare with that of elected officeholders? Overall, the Supreme Court appears to be roughly as consistent with the polls as directly elected officeholders are. One study by Alan Monroe (1994) examined a much larger number of poll-to-policy comparisons during the period 1980–1991. Monroe reported that 55 percent of public policies were consistent with nationwide polls during the 1980–1991 period, reflecting a slight decline in poll-to-policy agreement compared to the 63 percent level for the 1960–1979 time period. By comparison, some 56 percent of Supreme Court decisions were consistent with nationwide public opinion polls during the same 1980–1991 period.[11]

Linkages Between Public Opinion and the Court

How can we explain why an unelected, life-tenured Court is as often consistent with public opinion as federal officeholders who must face the voters are? Five explanations help us to understand the linkages, or ties, between American public opinion and Supreme Court decision making.

A first explanation is that the Supreme Court often upholds the decisions of federal policy makers, such as the president, Congress, or the federal agencies. The Supreme Court typically does so whether or not the federal action was consistent with public opinion. However, federal laws and policies under review at the Court usually do reflect American public opinion. By upholding federal laws and policies, the Supreme Court, in turn, itself reflects public opinion.

This pattern may explain why the Supreme Court so often agrees with American public opinion in federal-level disputes. Since the mid-1930s, the Supreme Court has considered a challenged federal law or policy in seventy-three cases where a nationwide poll item was available for comparison. Three-quarters (72 percent) of these federal laws or policies were themselves consistent with public opinion. When the disputed law or policy was consistent with the polls, the Supreme Court upheld it 79 percent of the time.

The Court also upheld most federal laws and policies that were inconsistent with public opinion—doing so 60 percent of the time. However, because challenged federal laws and policies much more often than not reflect nationwide polls—and because the Court typically deferred to federal laws and policies—the Supreme Court was consistent with nationwide polls 74 percent of the time in federal-level disputes. Judicial restraint, then, helps to explain why the Supreme Court is so often consistent with American public opinion, at least when federal laws and policies are involved.

When state or local laws and policies are involved, however, this picture changes considerably. Since the mid-1930s, state or local laws and policies reviewed by the Supreme Court were consistent with nationwide polls only 58 percent of the time. When a state or local law or policy was consistent with nationwide polls, the Supreme Court upheld it 60 percent of the time. In these instances, the Supreme Court also reflected nationwide opinion. When a state or local law or policy disagreed with nationwide polls, however, the Supreme Court upheld it only 50 percent of the time. For state or local cases, judicial deference is not as strong an explanation as for federal cases.

As judicial scholars (Brisbin and Kilween 1994; Savage 1992; Smith and Hensley 1993) have observed, the conservative Rehnquist Court is more likely to defer to elected officials' decisions than earlier Courts were. Of the twenty instances here in which a state or local law or policy reached the Supreme Court, for example, the Rehnquist Court upheld the challenged law or policy 75 percent of the time.[12] This commitment to judicial restraint on behalf of state or local laws and policies, however, may reduce the frequency with which the Court reflects nationwide public opinion. Several disputed state or local laws are not consistent with nationwide public opinion—for example, Texas's use of the death penalty for mentally retarded convicted murderers.[13]

In short, judicial restraint may, in part, explain why the Supreme Court is so often consistent with American public opinion, at least when federal laws and policies are involved.

Most federal laws and policies reflect American public opinion, and in most cases, the Supreme Court upholds the challenged law or policy—thereby also making a ruling consistent with the polls.

A second linkage concerns the type of dispute involved. The Supreme Court most often represents American public opinion in high-profile cases, or where public opinion is very one-sided. In these instances, the justices may find it much easier to determine prevailing public opinion. For example, from the mid-1930s to the mid-1980s, Supreme Court decisions were consistent with nationwide polls 76 percent of the time when the issue involved was a top national concern. When the issue involved was not as important to the American public, the Supreme Court was consistent with public opinion only 59 percent of the time (Marshall 1989, 82–83).

The Rehnquist Court was much more often consistent with public opinion when public sentiment on an issue was extremely one-sided. For example, when two-thirds (or more) of Americans took the same position, the Supreme Court was consistent with public opinion 58 percent of the time.[14] Where public opinion was more closely divided, the Supreme Court was consistent with the poll majority only 40 percent of the time.

A third linkage is that some justices may believe their proper role is to reflect majority public opinion in their decision making. To be sure, no justice has ever openly argued that the Court should simply defer to public opinion. Several justices have even argued that indirectly expressed public opinion—such as a legislature's laws or a jury's decisions, not public opinion polls—are the best indicators of public attitudes.[15] Even so, several justices have conceded that they are influenced by major public opinion shifts. As Chief Justice William Rehnquist wrote:

I was recently asked . . . whether the justices were able to isolate themselves from the tides of public opinion. My answer was that we are not able to do so, and it would probably be unwise to try. We read newspapers and magazines, we watch news on television, we talk to our friends about current events. No judge worthy of his salt would ever cast his vote in a particular case simply because he thought the majority of the public wanted him to vote that way, but that is quite a different thing from saying that no judge is ever influenced by the great tides of public opinion that run in a country such as ours. Judges are influenced by them. . . . (1987, 98)

A fourth, and more indirect, linkage is that the Supreme Court's unpopular decisions are much more likely to be overturned, either by Congress, by a presidential action, or by a subsequent Supreme Court decision. From the mid-1930s to the mid-1980s, for example, only 10 percent of Supreme Court decisions were overturned if the Court's decision was consistent with the polls. However, over one-third (37 percent) of Court decisions were overturned if the decision was not consistent with public opinion (Marshall 1989, 177). A well-known example of an unpopular Supreme Court ruling later overturned is *Oregon v. Mitchell*

(1970), a decision (in part) restricting Congress's ability to grant voting rights for eighteen-to-twenty-year-olds to federal elections only. This ruling was later overturned by the Twenty-Sixth Amendment in 1971.[16]

A fifth linkage between public opinion and Supreme Court decision making also operates indirectly, through the nomination and confirmation process. Supreme Court nominees are more easily and more often confirmed by the Senate if they are perceived as moderates. Extremely conservative or extremely liberal nominees are more likely to provoke a confirmation fight and are less likely to win Senate confirmation (Cameron, Cover, and Segal 1990; Overby et al. 1992). In some instances, a president may even seek to avert a full-scale Senate confirmation battle by choosing a nominee who is either little known or perceived as politically moderate (Davis 1994; Van Winkle 1994).

Since 1980, for example, nine Supreme Court nominees faced Senate confirmation. At the time of their nominations, five nominees (O'Connor, Souter, Kennedy, Ginsburg, and Breyer) were generally described as moderates or moderate conservatives; on average, only four senators voted against their confirmation. The remaining four nominees (Scalia, Bork, Thomas, and Chief Justice Rehnquist) were widely described as clearly conservative; on average, thirty-five senators voted against confirmation. All of the more moderate nominees were easily confirmed, while one conservative nominee (Bork) was rejected by the Senate, and another (Thomas) was confirmed by only a four-vote margin.

That ideologically moderate nominees are more easily confirmed by the Senate also increases the chances that the Supreme Court will reflect public opinion. Since the mid-1930s, moderate justices have agreed with American public opinion in 63 percent of their votes. By comparison, more conservative or more liberal justices less often agreed with nationwide polls (58 percent or 54 percent, respectively) (Marshall 1989, 120). Moderate justices are also more sensitive to swings in public opinion than their conservative or liberal brethren (Sheehan and Mischler 1993; Wood and Flemming 1993).

Each of the five linkages discussed above helps to explain why an unelected, life-tenured Supreme Court represents American public opinion about as often as elected officials do. Interestingly, another often discussed linkage can be rejected. This linkage is the "manipulation model," which argues that because the Supreme Court is highly respected, its rulings influence (or manipulate) public opinion on specific issues. In other words, public opinion follows the Court.

The evidence does not support the manipulation model. Where identically worded poll questions are available both before and after a Court ruling, public opinion support for the Court's decisions as often declines as increases. Historically, the average public opinion poll (percentage) shift from before to after a Supreme Court ruling is almost 0 (Marshall 1989, 146–155; see also Baas and Thomas 1984; Page, Shapiro, and Dempsey 1987; Rosenberg 1991).[17]

Consider, for example, the Supreme Court's 1986 decision in *American Booksellers Association v. Hudnut* (1986). In *Hudnut,* the Court affirmed a lower court ruling striking down an Indianapolis ordinance which, in part, had banned the depiction of graphic sexual violence toward women. Before the Supreme Court's ruling, 73 percent of Americans favored a total ban on magazines showing sexual violence. After the Court's ruling, 76 percent of Americans favored the ban.[18] In this instance, not only did an overwhelming majority of Americans take a position different from the Supreme Court's, but the percentage of Americans in disagreement with the Court's ruling also slightly increased.

Why do Supreme Court decisions have so little impact on American public opinion? One explanation is that many Americans do not understand even the Court's highest-profile decisions. For example, only about one-half to two-thirds of Americans correctly understood the Supreme Court's flag-burning, school prayer, or abortion decisions (Marshall 1989, 327).

Another reason may be that the Supreme Court is simply not sufficiently popular to influence attitudes. In 1994, for example, 42 percent of Americans said they had a "great deal" or "quite a lot" of confidence in the Supreme Court.[19] However, even more Americans reported having only "some" confidence (38 percent) or "very little" (16 percent) or "none" (1 percent), or having no opinion (3 percent). True, the Supreme Court's approval ratings are above average for American political institutions. Even so, fewer than half of Americans usually give clearly positive ratings to the Court. This middling level of popularity is probably insufficient to sway nationwide public opinion on specific Court rulings.

Conclusion

Two hundred years ago, Alexander Hamilton wrote that the Supreme Court would be "an excellent barrier" against "the effects of occasional ill humors" of majority public opinion. To Hamilton and some of the founding generation of Americans, the Supreme Court seemed well positioned to resist public opinion and to protect the rights of minorities (Hamilton 1961, 79).

At first glance, the modern Supreme Court may indeed seem to be far removed from American public opinion. Yet a closer look suggests that the modern Supreme Court's decisions have been consistent with American public opinion about as often as the actions of other American policy makers.

Supreme Court decision making is linked to American public opinion in several ways. First, the Court often exercises judicial restraint to uphold federal laws and policies. Since federal laws and policies are themselves typically consistent with American public opinion, the Court's custom of judicial deference at the federal level leads the Court to reflect public opinion. Second, the Court is more often consistent with public opinion on high-profile issues, or where public opinion is very one-sided. Third, justices may be influenced by the "great tides" of public sentiment. Fourth, over time, unpopular Supreme Court rulings are more often overturned by Congress, the president, or the Court itself. Finally, ideologically moderate nominees more often win seats on the Court, and moderate justices are more often consistent with public opinion than either liberal or conservative justices.

Contrary to Hamilton's expectations, the Supreme Court is not insulated from American public opinion.[20] American public opinion has at least a modest independent impact on Supreme Court decision making (Marshall and Ignagni 1994; Mishler and Sheehan 1993), and public opinion also influences the Court through the five linkages just described. If the founding generation of Americans expected the Supreme Court to be a barricade against majority public opinion, they considerably underestimated the influence of public opinion in American politics.

Notes

1. Gallup poll, June 18–21, 1993.
2. "Wapner v. Rehnquist: No Contest," *Washington Post,* June 23, 1989, sec. A.
3. The twenty-six decision-to-poll matches, and the issue involved, from the Rehnquist Court include: *South Dakota v. Dole* (1987), drinking-age-based federal funding restrictions; *Hazelwood School District v. Kuhlmeier* (1988), censorship of student newspapers; *Johnson v. Transportation Agency of Santa Clara County* (1987), affirmative action in hiring and promotion; *Board of Directors of Rotary International v. Rotary Club of Duarte* (1987), clubs' right to restrict memberships by sex; *Edwards v. Aguillard* (1987), creation science; *Wilkins v. Missouri* (1989) and *Stanford v. Kentucky* (1989), execution of teenage criminals; *Skinner v. Railway Labor Executives' Association* (1989), mandatory drug testing; *Texas v. Gregory Lee Johnson* (1989), flag burning; *Penry v. Lynaugh* (1989), execution of mentally retarded criminals; *Webster v. Reproductive Health Services* (1989), public hospital restrictions and fetal viability tests; *Planned Parenthood of Southeastern Pennsylvania v. Casey* (1992), husband notification, informed consent, twenty-four-hour waiting periods, and one-parent consent for abortion; *Rust v. Sullivan* (1991), abortion counseling gag rule; *Sale v. Haitian Centers Council* (1993), Haitian refugees; *Bray v. Alexandria Women's Health Clinic* (1993), Operation Rescue anti-abortion tactics; *Hodgson v. Minnesota* (1990), two-parent notification for abortion; *Ohio v. Akron Center for Reproductive Health* (1990), one-parent notification for abortion; *Sable Communications v. Federal Communications Commission* (1989), commercial telephone sex to adults; *Barnes v. Glen Theater* (1991), nude dancing performances; *Michigan State Police v. Stitz* (1990), highway sobriety checkpoints; *Board of Education v. Mergens* (1990), religious group meetings in high schools; *Cruzan v. Director, Missouri Department of Health* (1990), withdrawal of life-sustaining treatment; *DeBoer v. Schmidt* (1993), parental custody of adopted children.
4. Harris poll, January 11 to February 11, 1990, and November 6 to December 13, 1989.
5. Gallup poll, January 16–19, 1992.
6. CBS News/*New York Times* poll, August 18–21, 1986.
7. *Gallup Poll Monthly,* August 1993, 33.
8. According to a July 25–28, 1991 Gallup poll, 77 percent of Americans disapproved of the congressional pay increase, 18 percent approved, and 5 percent reported no opinion.
9. Justices Ginsburg and Breyer did not participate in any of the twenty-six decisions analyzed here.

10. *DeBoer v. Schmidt* (1993) and *Cruzan v. Director, Missouri Department of Health* (1990) are not included here, since neither involved a traditional liberal-versus-conservative conflict.

11. The 56 percent consistent figure reported here for Supreme Court decisions is based on excluding a few instances in which available polls were inconsistent or evenly divided. Excluding these instances makes the Supreme Court computation comparable to the Monroe figures, which exclude instances of closely divided or inconsistent poll results. If all instances of decision-to-poll matches were counted for the 1980–1991 period, the Supreme Court figures would be 52 percent consistent, 40 percent inconsistent, and 7 percent unclear.

12. The Rehnquist Court upheld state or local laws or policies nine of twelve times (75 percent) when that law or policy was consistent with nationwide polls. It also upheld state or local laws or policies equally often (75 percent, or six of eight times) when the law or policy was inconsistent with nationwide polls.

13. The Court upheld applying the death penalty to a mentally retarded murderer in *Penry v. Lynaugh* (1989), although a 71–21 percent majority opposed doing so, according to a 1988 Harris poll. Sentencing a mentally retarded murderer to the death penalty was also opposed by 73 percent of Texans.

14. A typical example of a one-sided public opinion distribution is the Court's upholding of a twenty-four-hour waiting period for abortions in part of *Planned Parenthood of Southeastern Pennsylvania v. Casey* (1992). According to a December 12–15, 1991, Gallup poll, a 73–23 percent majority agreed with "a law requiring women seeking abortions to wait 24 hours before having the procedure done."

15. See, for example, Justice O'Connor's arguments in *Penry v. Lynaugh* (1989), at 288–289; or Chief Justice Burger's arguments in *Furman v. Georgia* (1972), at 441–442.

16. By a 5–4 vote, the Court ruled that Congress could not lower the voting age to eighteen in state elections without a constitutional amendment. By comparison, a 60–35 percent public opinion majority favored "lowering the voting age to 18 for local and state elections," according to a March 1971 Gallup poll.

17. The Supreme Court's actions may, however, affect the Court's own approval ratings (Caldeira 1986; Gibson and Caldeira 1992) or polarize public opinion (Canon 1992; Franklin and Kosaki 1989). For evidence that the Court's rulings and justices' resignations affected public opinion during the 1930s, see Caldeira (1987).

18. Gallup poll, March 1985 and July 1986.

19. Gallup poll, March 25–27, 1994.

20. For historical reviews of the Supreme Court's ties to public opinion, see Dahl (1957) and Casper (1976). For research which unscrambles the impact of legal influences versus public opinion or other extralegal influences on Supreme Court decision making, see Epstein and Kobylka (1992) and George and Epstein (1992).

Appendix
A Primer on Statistics and Public Opinion

The contributors to this book use survey data to test their hypotheses, and they rely on statistical techniques to determine whether these data support their ideas. All scientific disciplines develop standards of adequate evidence to support claims, and political science is no different. The statistics used in this book are all widely accepted in the discipline, but they may be unfamiliar to many readers. This appendix presents a short primer in statistics to help readers obtain a deeper understanding of the analyses presented in the chapters.

Statistics can be used to describe the attitudes of members of a sample or of various groups within the sample. For example, we might want to know how many Americans believe that President Clinton is doing a good job, or how men and women differ in their assessments of his presidency. Statistics can also help us untangle the multiple sources of attitudes. For example, statistics can tell us whether race, sex, income, or partisanship is more important in explaining evaluations of Clinton's job performance.

Survey Sampling and Statistical Significance

The chapters in this book all report data from national surveys. Because it is impossible to interview every American in a survey, researchers must draw samples of citizens. There are many different ways to draw samples, but nearly all social scientists use some variation on random sampling. A truly random sample is one in which every element of the population has an equal chance of selection.

Using random samples allows social scientists to estimate how closely the sample represents the general public. Consider support for Patrick Buchanan, who ran for the presidency in Republican primaries in 1996. Assume that if we could ask all Americans whether they think that Buchanan would make a good president, 25 percent would say yes. We cannot actually interview the entire population, but we can draw a sample of 1,500 or 2,000.

The Central Limit Theorem tells us that if we were to draw an infinite number of samples and calculate the average rating of Buchanan in each sample, the average of those sample means would form a normal distribution (a symmetrical bell curve, as in Figure A-1) around 25 percent. Some samples would by chance have higher means because we would

Figure A-1   Normal Distribution and Percent of Cases Between Selected Points Under the Curve

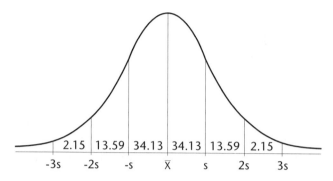

| 2.15 | 13.59 | 34.13 | 34.13 | 13.59 | 2.15 |

-3s   -2s   -s $\overline{X}$ s   2s   3s

Note: $\overline{X}$ = population mean; s = standard deviation.

have selected a greater proportion of Buchanan supporters, and some would have lower means because we would have selected a greater proportion of his opponents. But if we draw samples that are sufficiently large, most will have close to 25 percent Buchanan supporters. For any given sample size, we can estimate just how close we are to the true population average.

Of course, there is always the random chance of drawing a truly unusual sample. We could select a sample that would be mostly composed of Buchanan voters, for example, or a sample of very liberal Democrats who detest Buchanan. The odds of drawing such a sample would be very low. In general, we report the confidence interval with 95 percent certainty, meaning that for a given sample size, 95 percent of all samples drawn at random will have a sample mean that is within a certain distance from the true population mean (and 5 percent will not). A common confidence interval is ±3 percent. Thus if we drew a sample that had 23 percent Buchanan supporters, we could estimate that the true population figure would be between 20 percent and 26 percent.

If we are trying to determine if a relationship can be generalized to the larger public, we consider two factors—the magnitude of the relationship and the size of the sample. Imagine, for example, that we are interested in gender differences in responses to Patrick Buchanan. If we surveyed a random sample of 20 people and found that nearly all of the women disliked Buchanan and most men liked him, we would not be confident that this pattern could generalize to the larger public. If we surveyed 2,000 individuals at random, however, we would be more confident that these differences were real. There are precise formulas for determining just how likely we would be to find any given relationship by chance, given the size of the sample.

By convention social scientists say that if they are 95 percent certain that a relationship can be generalized to the larger population, that relationship is statistically significant. Most of the tables in this book have notes indicating that a single asterisk means statistical significance at the .01 level and two asterisks mean statistical significance at the .05 level. If a relationship is significant at the .05 level, it means that there is about a 5 percent chance that the relationship is not valid in the general public.

Average Responses and Distributions:
Means, Medians, and Standard Deviations

If we want to know what Americans believe on a given issue, we can examine polling data, which are reported in percentages. For example, for many years Gallup and other pollsters have asked Americans whether they approve of the job the president is doing (see Chapter 13). Newspapers and television newscasts report the approval percentage and tell us whether that number is higher or lower than previous ratings.

Some poll questions are far more complex. Consider, for example, a question asking respondents to place themselves on a seven-point scale, where 1 indicates that they believe that the government should provide many fewer services and cut spending a lot, and 7 indicates that they believe the government should provide many more services and increase spending a lot.

Perhaps we would like to summarize the responses of all those who answered the survey. We can report an average position by calculating the mean response. In the 1992 American National Election Study, the government services question was asked; the frequencies for each response category are shown in Figure A-2. The mean response is simply obtained by adding together all the responses given (1s, 2s, 3s, and so on) and dividing by the number of people who answered the question. The mean response to this item is 4.12.

Means are appropriate with interval-level measures—when each unit of measurement is the same. But means are skewed when a few cases are far from the mean. Consider a question about the role of women, where a response of 1 indicates a strong view that women should be given an equal role in society, and a response of 7 indicates a strong view that a woman's place is in the home. The distribution of responses to this question in the 1992 ANES is shown in Figure A-3. Here the mean is 2.23, even though most of the cases are in the 1 category. The small number of cases at 6 and 7 have a strong influence on the mean.

Sometimes, a median, rather than a mean, response is reported for the average American's position. The median is the score for the middle-ranked person on the question. For instance, assume we ask five friends how much money they have in their wallets and we get the following responses: $3, $5, $10, $20, $500. The median, or middle, response is $10; the mean, or average, is $107.60. Medians are a more appropriate way to evaluate items that are badly skewed, like income, and to describe ordinal data, where the values represent an

Figure A-2 Distribution of Responses on Government Services Question

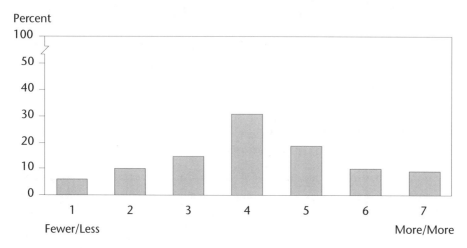

Source: 1992 American National Election Study.

Note: Respondents were asked to place themselves on a seven-point scale according to how they felt about government services and spending.

ordering but the intervals between the categories are not of the same size. In the case of the government services question, the median is 4, while the median of the women's role question is 1. Ted Jelen in Chapter 4 compares the mean positions of various religious groups on attitudes toward sexual morality, feminism, and school prayer. Barbara Norrander in Chapter 7 compares the median responses of Republicans and Democrats on ideology and policy issues.

We can describe the distribution of issue positions by depicting the shape or using a statistic that measures the variation around the average response. When we describe the shape of a distribution, we often count the number of peaks. For example in Figure A-2, there is one peak in the middle of the distribution, and we refer to this as a unimodal distribution. In addition, the distribution is almost perfectly symmetrical, with more of the responses toward the center of the scale and few responses on the ends. Such a distribution is called a normal distribution or a bell-shaped distribution, as in Figure A-1. In contrast, Figure A-4 shows a bimodal distribution on a hypothetical attitude, with large numbers of conservatives opposing an even larger number of liberals and few responses between.

If we wish to use a statistic to describe the distribution of cases, we most often use the standard deviation. The standard deviation is calculated by taking each case and subtracting the mean; this value is then squared (multiplied by itself). We make this calculation for each case then add up the squared values. This sum is then divided by the total number of

Figure A-3 Distribution of Responses on Role of Women Question

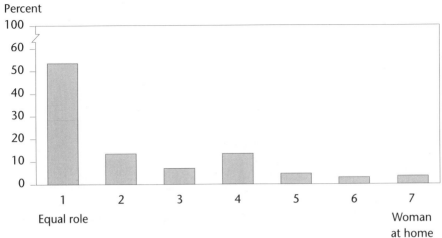

Percent

Source: 1992 American National Election Study.

Note: Respondents were asked to place themselves on a seven-point scale according to their opinion about women's roles in society.

cases and the square root is taken. (The squaring process is used to eliminate negative values, since we do not care whether cases fall above or below the mean, but how far they are from the mean.) The standard deviation for the guaranteed services question is 1.58, and for the women's role scale it is 1.68. If the distribution of cases falls into a normal curve, we know that two-thirds of the cases fall between one standard deviation below and one standard deviation above the mean; 95 percent of the cases fall within two standard deviations of the mean.

Standard deviations are used to compare attitudes and respondents' qualities that are measured on different scales. For instance, we cannot directly compare the impact of age (measured in years) with the effects of ideology (measured on a 1–7 scale) on abortion attitudes. However, if we convert both items to standardized scales, measuring each as the distance from the mean for each question, then we can compare age to ideology. This is approximately what happens when we report standardized regression coefficients or calculate changes in probabilities in probit, which are discussed in the following sections.

Measuring the Relationship Between Two Opinions

A variety of statistics can be used when we want to compare survey respondents' answers on one question to those on another question. These statistics are usually called correla-

Figure A-4 Distribution of Responses on Hypothetical Attitude Question

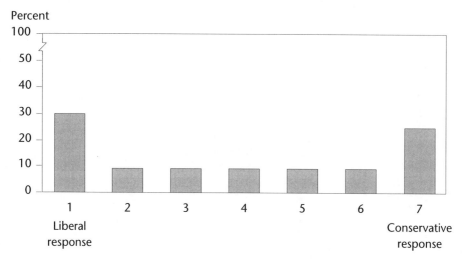

Source: 1992 American National Election Study.

tions, and all of them tell us how closely aligned answers are between the two questions. If answers were to line up perfectly—such that, for example, all Democrats were liberals, all independents were moderates, and all Republicans were conservatives—then correlation statistics would take on the value of 1.0. If all answers were to line up perfectly, but in reverse order—say our result was that all Democrats were conservatives and all Republicans were liberals—then the correlation statistics would have a value of –1.0. The positive sign for a coefficient merely means that high scores on one variable are associated with high scores on the other; negative signs mean that a high score on the first is associated with a low score on the second.

In survey research, the patterns are never perfect. In fact, because of the wide variety of opinions and traits of Americans, most correlations in studies of public opinion fall in the range from 0, no pattern, to .3, a fairly strong pattern. Which statistic is used to report the opinions depends on the way the opinions are measured (interval, ordinal, or nominal levels of measurement) and the type of patterns the research is seeking. Correlations are appropriate when both variables are at least measured at the ordinal level—that is, where the numbers assigned to the response categories represent some kind of ordering. Ted Jelen in Chapter 4 uses Pearson's r to measure the strength of the relationship, while Alan Abramowitz in Chapter 12 uses tau c. All of the correlation statistics can generally be interpreted in the same manner. The closer the statistic is to 1.0 or –1.0, the stronger the relationship is; the closer the statistic is to 0, the weaker the relationship is.

Explaining Opinions Through Other Opinions and Personal Traits: Regression and Probit

We often believe that a variety of attitudes and personal traits explains a person's opinions on a complex issue. Thus Elizabeth Cook in Chapter 8 hypothesizes that abortion opinions are shaped by demographic factors such as education, religion, and other attitudes. She is seeking to explain a single attitude, the attitude toward abortion, which in this case becomes the dependent variable because she believes that abortion attitudes will depend upon education and religion.

The traits and other opinions that are used to explain abortion attitudes are called the independent variables. Although we can correlate each of these variables with abortion attitudes, we cannot simply add up their effects because some of the explanatory power of one variable may be shared by another. For example, frequency of church attendance correlates with abortion attitudes in the General Social Survey at .34, and general ideology correlates with abortion attitudes at .17. Yet church attendance and ideology are also correlated with each other, at .15. In other words, some of the reason that attendance is so highly correlated with abortion attitudes is because those who attend church regularly are more likely than others to call themselves conservatives, and some of the reason that ideology is so highly correlated with abortion attitudes is that conservatives go to church more often than liberals. We need a way to sort out the impact of these two independent variables. In regression and probit analyses we attempt to explain a dependent variable by using a variety of independent variables.

A number of statistics are reported from a regression analysis. The explanatory power of all the independent variables together on the dependent variable is given by R^2 (R-squared). The R^2 can be interpreted as the amount of variation explained in the dependent variable. For example, in Chapter 10 William Jacoby describes the explanatory power of various sets of independent variables by referencing the R^2. In Table 10-1, for example, about a quarter of the variation in evaluations of personal economic conditions is explained by demographic variables and economic behavior.

The impact of each independent variable is explained by two statistics. The first is the unstandardized regression coefficient, sometimes referred to as b. This tells how much change occurs in the dependent variable for a single unit change in the independent variable when all the other independent variables are held constant. In Table 8-7, for example, the unstandardized coefficient for race is .37, and for education it is .06. Because race is measured as a simple dichotomy (black/white), the coefficient here represents the entire impact of race, and blacks were on average 0.37 points more liberal on this 6-point abortion scale. But education is measured in years, which means that for each year of education, respondents were on average .06 points more liberal on abortion.

The impact of different independent variables, however, cannot be directly compared if the variables are not measured on the same scale. To facilitate comparison, the regression coefficients are standardized (using the standard deviations of both the independent and dependent variables). These standardized regression coefficients can then be used to judge the relative impact of each of the independent variables. Notice in Table 8-7 that although the unstandardized coefficient for race is larger than that for education, the standardized coefficient (or beta) is higher for education. This is because once the entire range of educational attainment is considered (from 0 to 26 years), education has a greater impact on abortion attitudes than race. Standardized regression coefficients have the virtue of allowing us to compare the importance of different variables within a given model. If we seek to compare across different models, however, we must use the unstandardized coefficients.

Probit is similar to regression in that several independent variables are used to explain positions on one dependent variable. Probit is appropriate when the dependent variable is measured at the ordinal level, and it is most often used when the dependent variable has only two categories. Probit estimates the probability that a person will fall in one category versus the other of the dependent variable. The overall fit of the model is given by the percentage of cases classified correctly or by a pseudo-R^2. The equivalent of the unstandardized regression coefficient in probit is maximum likelihood estimates (MLEs). As with unstandardized regression coefficients, MLEs cannot be directly compared if the independent variables are measured on different scales. To compare the impact of a variety of independent variables, changes in the probabilities of falling into one category of the dependent variable are calculated. All the independent variables except one are held constant, usually at their mean values, while the remaining independent variable is changed by some value (often by one standard deviation). The change in probability of falling in the selected category of the dependent variable is then measured. For example, in Chapter 3, Steven Tuch and Lee Sigelman estimate the probabilities that whites and blacks in different social classes will take particular positions on affirmative action (see Table 3-4).

Scaling: Factor Analysis and Cronbach's Alpha

Often a political science concept is too complex to be measured with a single survey question. In these cases, survey researchers ask many questions, and analysts seek ways to combine them into a single measure of a concept. Before combining questions, however, scholars must first determine whether all of the items measure the same attitude. The answer may depend on who is being surveyed. Consider the underlying concept of feminism. We might attempt to measure support for feminism by asking for respondents' evaluations of organizations such as the National Organization for Women (NOW); their attitudes toward general equality and rights for women; and for their opinions about specific policies such as equal pay for equal work, access to child care for working mothers, parental leave to care for a baby or for a sick child, prosecuting sexual harassment, legal abortion, and lesbian rights.

If we were conducting a survey of activists in feminist and antifeminist organizations, then all of these items would almost surely measure the central idea of feminism. But if we were conducting a survey of Catholic and fundamentalist working women, then the items on lesbian rights and abortion might tap into a different, religious, dimension of attitudes. We could see this by looking at the correlations. Among Catholic women employed outside the home, there might be a far lower correlation between attitudes on equal pay for equal work and parental leave on the one hand, and abortion and lesbian rights on the other, than we would find among feminist activists. If so, then we would need to create separate scales to measure these different attitudes among Catholic working women.

Factor analysis is a statistic based on correlations. It is used by researchers who want to find sets of variables that are highly correlated with one another, and therefore measure the same underlying dimension. In Chapter 10, William Jacoby used factor analysis to determine which items measured the same economic attitudes. Once he had selected these items, he verified that they formed a reliable scale using a statistic called Cronbach's alpha.[1] In Chapter 12, Alan Abramowitz used factor analysis to identify items that he included in a scale measuring attitudes on social issues; his results are in Table 12-1.

Statistics and Replication

Many people are critical of statistics because there may be different ways to examine the same question, and it is possible that they will yield different answers. The old adage that there are "lies, damn lies, and statistics" conveys the thought that statistics can produce misleading portraits of reality, wrapped in scientific credibility. Although it is certainly possible to create misleading results using statistics, social science guards against this problem in a number of ways. Most important is the possibility of replication.

Most of the chapters in this book use data from large national surveys such as the American National Election Studies and the General Social Surveys, which are available to most social scientists. If, say, Roger Smith reports a result that is surprising, that contradicts other published results, or that is inconsistent with established theories, then it is likely that another scholar—call her Jane Jones—will use the same data to examine the same problem. If Professor Jones concludes that the previous study reached an erroneous result by using the wrong statistic or by considering the problem in the wrong way, then she will try to publish a rebuttal article in a scientific journal. If the blind reviewers of her critique (that is, they do not know whose article they are reading) accept the validity of her analysis, then the paper will probably be published. In this way, social science guards against the misuse of statistics.

Statistics are powerful tools that enable social scientists to test their hypotheses, refine their theories, and describe the world. They are used not only by scholars, but by professional pollsters, consultants, and others who study public opinion.

Note

1. This means, of course, that there is a 5 percent chance that the survey will produce a mean that is further from the mark. Campaigns that track public opinion toward a candidate on a nightly basis are familiar with this result—often a single poll will give radically different results than those done the day before and the day after. We can often identify these nonrepresentative samples by simply looking at the frequencies of various demographic variables—sex, race, age, education—or of basic political attitudes such as partisanship and general ideology. If we have a sample with 45 percent blacks, or where nearly everyone has a college education, we can be certain that the sample is an outlier (that is, that it would fall in the extreme ends of a distribution of all possible samples).

References

Abramowitz, Alan I. 1994. "Issue Evolution Reconsidered: Racial Attitudes and Partisanship in the U.S. Electorate." *American Journal of Political Science* 38: 1–24.

___. 1995. "It's Abortion, Stupid." *Journal of Politics* 57: 176–186.

Abramson, Jeffrey, F. Christopher Arterton, and Gary R. Orren. 1988. *The Electronic Commonwealth: The Impact of New Media Technologies on Democratic Policies.* New York: Basic Books.

Abramson, Paul. 1976. "Generational Change and the Decline of Party Identification in America: 1952–1974." *American Political Science Review* 70: 469–478.

___. 1979. "Developing Party Identification: A Further Examination of Life-Cycle, Generational, and Periodic Effects." *American Journal of Political Science* 23: 78–96.

Abramson, Paul R., and John H. Aldrich. 1982. "The Decline of Electoral Participation in America." *American Political Science Review* 76: 502–521.

Abramson, Paul R., John H. Aldrich, and David W. Rohde. 1983. *Change and Continuity in the 1980 Elections,* rev. ed. Washington, D.C.: CQ Press.

Achen, Christopher. 1982. *Interpreting and Using Regression.* Beverly Hills, Calif.: Sage Publications.

Aldrich, John H. 1991. "Rational Choice and Turnout." *American Journal of Political Science* 37: 246–278.

Aldrich, John H., Richard G. Niemi, George Rabinowitz, and David W. Rohde. 1982. "The Measurement of Public Opinion About Public Policy: A Report on Some New Issue Question Formats." *American Journal of Political Science* 26: 391–414.

Allport, Gordon W. 1935. "Attitudes." In *A Handbook of Social Psychology,* ed. C. Murchison. Worcester, Mass.: Clark University Press.

Allsop, Dee, and Herbert Weisberg. 1988. "Measuring Change in Party Identification in an Election Campaign." *American Journal of Political Science* 32: 996–1017.

Almond, Gabriel. 1950. *American People and Foreign Policy.* New York: Harcourt Brace.

Arterton, F. Christopher. 1987. *Teledemocracy: Can Technology Protect Democracy?* Newbury Park, Calif.: Sage Publications.

Aufderheide, Patricia. 1992. "Cable Television and the Public Interest." *Journal of Communication* 42 (Winter): 52–65.

Baas, Larry, and Dan Thomas. 1984. "The Supreme Court and Policy Legitimation." *American Politics Quarterly* 12: 335–360.

Barber, Benjamin. 1984. *Strong Democracy: Participatory Politics for a New Age.* Berkeley: University of California Press.

Bardes, Barbara A., and Robert W. Oldendick. 1978. "Beyond Internationalism: The Case for Multiple Dimensions in the Structure of Foreign Policy Attitudes." *Social Science Quarterly* 59: 496–508.

Barnum, David. 1985. "The Supreme Court and Public Opinion: Judicial Decision Making in the Post-New Deal Period." *Journal of Politics* 47: 652–666.

Bartels, Larry M. 1993. "Messages Received: The Political Impact of Media Exposure." *American Political Science Review* 87: 267–285.

Barton, Allen H., and R. Wayne Parsons. 1977. "Measuring Belief System Structure." *Public Opinion Quarterly* 41: 159–180.

Beck, Paul, and Frank J. Sorauf. 1992. *Party Politics in America,* 7th ed. New York: Harper Collins.

Behr, Roy L., and Shanto Iyengar. 1985. "Television News, Real-World Cues, and Changes in the Public Agenda." *Public Opinion Quarterly* 49: 38–57.

Bennett, Stephen E. 1991. "Left Behind: Declining Turnout Among Noncollege Young Whites, 1964–1978." *Social Science Quarterly* 72: 314–333.

Bennett, Stephen E., and Linda L. M. Bennett. 1992. "From Traditional to Modern Conceptions of Gender Equality in Politics: Gradual Change and Lingering Doubts." *Western Political Quarterly* 45: 93–111.

Bennett, Stephen E., and David Resnick. 1990. "The Implications of Nonvoting for Democracy in the United States." *American Journal of Political Science* 34: 771–804.

Bennett, W. Lance, and David L. Paletz. 1994. *Taken by Storm: The Media, Public Opinion, and U.S. Foreign Policy in the Gulf War.* Chicago: University of Chicago Press.

Berelson, Bernard R., Paul F. Lazarsfeld, and William N. McPhee. 1954. *Voting.* Chicago: University of Chicago Press.

Berger, Ronald J., W. Lawrence Neuman, and Patricia Searles. 1991. "The Social and Political Context of Rape Law Reform: An Aggregate Analysis." *Social Science Quarterly* 72: 221–238.

Berke, Richard L. 1995. "The 'Contract' Gets New Ally on the Right." *New York Times,* January 18, D19.

Bobo, Lawrence D., and James R. Kluegel. 1993. "Opposition to Race-Targeting: Self-Interest, Stratification Ideology, or Racial Attitudes?" *American Sociological Review* 58: 443–464.

Bonk, Kathy. 1988. "The Selling of the Gender Gap: The Role of Organized Feminism." In *The Politics of the Gender Gap,* ed. Carol M. Mueller. Newbury Park, Calif.: Sage Publications.

Boston, Thomas D. 1988. *Race, Class, and Conservatism.* Boston: Unwin Hyman.

Brace, Paul, and Barbara Hinckley. 1992. *Follow the Leader.* Chicago: University of Chicago Press.

Brisbin, Richard, Jr., and John Kilween. 1994. "U.S. Supreme Court Review of State High Court Decisions." *Judicature* 78: 33–40.

Broder, David, and Richard Morin. 1994. "Why Americans Hate Congress." *Washington Post National Weekly Edition,* July 11–17, 6–7.

Brody, Richard A., and Benjamin I. Page. 1972. "The Assessment of Policy Voting." *American Political Science Review* 66: 450–458.

Brody, Richard A., and Lawrence Rothenberg. 1988. "The Instability of Partisanship: An Analysis of the 1980 Election." *British Journal of Political Science* 18: 445–466.

Brody, Richard A., and Paul M. Sniderman. 1977. "From Life Space to Polling Place." *British Journal of Political Science* 7: 337–360.

Brown, Clifford, Jr., Lynda Powell, and Clyde Wilcox. 1995. *Serious Money: Fundraising and Contributing in Presidential Nomination Campaigns.* New York: Cambridge University Press.

Buell, Emmett, and Lee Sigelman. 1985. "An Army That Meets Every Sunday? Popular Support for the Moral Majority." *Social Science Quarterly* 66: 426–434.

___. 1987. "A Second Look at 'Popular Support for the Moral Majority: A Second Look.'" *Social Science Quarterly* 68: 167–169.

Burstein, Paul. 1985. *Discrimination, Jobs, and Politics.* Chicago: University of Chicago Press.

Caldeira, Gregory. 1986. "Neither the Purse nor the Sword: Dynamics of Public Confidence in the Supreme Court." *American Political Science Review* 80: 1209–1226.

___. 1987. "Public Opinion and the U.S. Supreme Court: FDR's Court-Packing Plan." *American Political Science Review* 81: 1139–1155.

Cameron, Charles, Albert Cover, and Jeffrey Segal. 1990. "Senate Voting on Supreme Court Nominees: A Neoinstitutional Model." *American Political Science Review* 84: 525–534.

Campbell, Angus, Philip E. Converse, Warren E. Miller, and Donald E. Stokes. 1960. *The American Voter.* New York: Wiley.

Canon, Bradley. 1992. "The Supreme Court as a Cheerleader in Politico-Moral Disputes." *Journal of Politics* 54: 637–653.

Carmines, Edward G., and Michael Berkman. 1994. "Ethos, Ideology, and Partisanship: Exploring the Paradox of Conservative Democrats." *Political Behavior* 16: 203–218.

Carmines, Edward G., and Harold W. Stanley. 1990. "Ideological Realignment in the Contemporary South: Where Have All the Conservatives Gone?" In *The Disappearing South?*

Studies in Regional Change and Continuity, ed. Robert P. Steed, Lawrence W. Moreland, and Tod A. Baker. Tuscaloosa: University of Alabama Press.

Carmines, Edward G., and James A. Stimson. 1980. "The Two Faces of Issue Voting." *American Political Science Review* 74: 78–91.

———. 1989. *Issue Evolution: Race and the Transformation of American Politics.* Princeton: Princeton University Press.

Carroll, Susan J. 1988. "Women's Autonomy and the Gender Gap: 1980 and 1982." In *The Politics of the Gender Gap,* ed. Carol M. Mueller. Newbury Park, Calif.: Sage Publications.

Caspary, William R. 1970. "The 'Mood Theory': A Study of Public Opinion and Foreign Policy." *American Political Science Review* 64: 536–547.

Casper, Jonathan. 1976. "The Supreme Court and National Policy Making." *American Political Science Review* 70: 50–63.

Center for Media and Public Affairs. 1995. "1994: The Year in Review." *Media Monitor,* January-February.

Chappell, Henry, and William R. Keech. 1990. "Citizen Information, Rationality, and the Politics of Macroeconomic Policy." In *Information and Democratic Processes,* ed. John A. Ferejohn and James H. Kuklinski. Urbana: University of Illinois Press.

Charity, Arthur. 1995. *Doing Public Journalism.* New York: Guilford Press.

Chittick, William, and Keith Billingsley. 1989. "The Structure of Elite Foreign Policy Beliefs." *Western Political Quarterly* 33: 201–224.

Claggett, William. 1981. "Partisan Acquisition Versus Partisan Intensity: Life Cycle, Generation, and Period Effects, 1952–1976." *American Journal of Political Science* 25: 193–214.

Compaine, Benjamin M. 1988. *Issues in New Information Technology.* Norwood, N.J.: Ablex.

Congressional Quarterly. 1993. *Congressional Quarterly Almanac.* Washington, D.C.: Congressional Quarterly, Inc.

Conover, Pamela Johnston. 1988. "Feminists and the Gender Gap." *Journal of Politics* 50: 985–1010.

———. 1991. "Where Is the Scheme? Critiques." *American Political Science Review* 85: 1364–1369.

Conover, Pamela Johnston, Ivor Crewe, and Donald Searling. 1991. "The Nature of Citizenship in the United States and Great Britain: Empirical Comments on Theoretical Themes." *Journal of Politics* 53: 800–832.

Conover, Pamela Johnston, and Stanley Feldman. 1981. "The Origins and Meaning of Liberal/Conservative Self-Identification." *American Journal of Political Science* 25: 617–645.

———. 1986. "Emotional Reactions to the Economy: I'm Mad as Hell and I'm Not Going to Take It Anymore." *American Journal of Political Science* 30: 50–78.

Conover, Pamela Johnston, Stanley Feldman, and Kathleen Knight. 1986. "Judging Inflation and Unemployment: The Origins of Retrospective Evaluations." *Journal of Politics* 48: 565–588.

Conover, Pamela Johnston, and Virginia Sapiro. 1993. "Gender, Feminist Consciousness and War." *American Journal of Political Science* 37: 1079–1099.

Converse, Philip E. 1964. "The Nature of Belief Systems in Mass Publics." In *Ideology and Discontent,* ed. D. Apter. New York: Free Press.

___. 1975. "Public Opinion and Voting Behavior." In *The Handbook of Political Science,* ed. Fred I. Greenstein. Reading, Mass.: Addison-Wesley.

___. 1976. *The Dynamics of Party Support: Cohort Analyzing Party Identification.* Beverly Hills, Calif.: Sage Publications.

___. 1979. "Rejoinder to Abramson." *American Journal of Political Science* 23: 97–100.

___. 1990. "Popular Representation and the Distribution of Information." In *Information and Democratic Processes,* ed. John A. Ferejohn and James H. Kuklinski. Urbana: University of Illinois Press.

Converse, Philip E., Warren E. Miller, Jerrold R. Rusk, and Arthur C. Wolfe. 1969. "Continuity and Change in American Politics: Parties and Issues in the 1968 Election." *American Political Science Review* 63: 1083–1105.

Conway, M. Margaret. 1981. "Political Participation in Midterm Congressional Elections." *American Politics Quarterly* 9: 221–244.

Cook, Elizabeth Adell, Frederick Hartwig, and Clyde Wilcox. 1993. "The Abortion Issue Down Ticket: The Virginia Lieutenant Governor's Race of 1989." *Women and Politics* 12: 5–18.

Cook, Elizabeth Adell, Ted G. Jelen, and Clyde Wilcox. 1992. *Between Two Absolutes: Public Opinion and the Politics of Abortion.* Boulder, Colo.: Westview Press.

___. 1993. "Generational Differences and Abortion Attitudes." *American Politics Quarterly* 21: 31–53.

___. 1994. "Issue Voting in Gubernatorial Elections: Abortion and Post-*Webster* Politics." *Journal of Politics* 56: 187–199.

___. 1995. "Issue Voting in U.S. Senate Elections: The Abortion Issue in 1990." *Congress and the Presidency* 21: 99–112.

Cook, Elizabeth Adell, and Clyde Wilcox. 1991. "Feminism and the Gender Gap: A Second Look." *Journal of Politics* 53: 1111–1122.

Corbett, Michael. 1991. *American Public Opinion: Trends, Processes, and Patterns.* New York: Longman.

Cornwell, Elmer. 1965. *Presidential Leadership of Public Opinion.* Bloomington: Indiana University Press.

Costain, Anne M., and Steven Majstorovic. 1994. "Congress, Social Movements and Public Opinion: Multiple Origins of Women's Rights Legislation." *Political Research Quarterly* 47: 111–135.

Craig, Stephen C. 1993. *The Malevolent Leaders.* Boulder, Colo.: Westview Press.

Dahl, Robert. 1957. "Decision-making in a Democracy: The Supreme Court as a National Policy-Maker." *Journal of Public Law* 6: 279–295.

———. 1989. *Democracy and Its Critics.* New Haven: Yale University Press.

Dalton, Russell J. 1988. *Citizen Politics in Western Democracies.* Chatham, N.J.: Chatham House.

Davidson, Roger H. 1969. *The Role of the Congressman.* New York: Western.

Davidson, Roger H., and Glenn R. Parker. 1972. "Positive Support for Political Institutions: The Case of Congress." *Western Political Quarterly* 25: 600–612.

Davis, James A., and Tom W. Smith. 1991. *General Social Surveys, 1972–1991.* Chicago: National Opinion Research Center.

Davis, Richard. 1994. "The Ginsburg Nomination: The Role of the Press, Interest Groups, and the Public in the Selection of a Supreme Court Nominee." Presented at the Annual Meeting of the American Political Science Association, New York.

Dearing, James W. 1989. "Setting the Polling Agenda for the Issue of AIDS." *Public Opinion Quarterly* 53: 309–329.

Deitch, Cynthia. 1988. "Sex Differences in Support for Government Spending." In *The Politics of the Gender Gap,* ed. Carol M. Mueller. Newbury Park, Calif.: Sage Publications.

Dennis, Jack. 1973. "Public Support for American National Political Institutions." Presented at the Conference on Public Support for the Political System, Madison, Wis.

Devine, Donald J. 1972. *The Political Culture of the United States.* Boston: Little, Brown.

Dillingham, Gerald. 1981. "The Emerging Black Middle Class: Class Consciousness or Race Consciousness?" *Ethnic and Racial Studies* 4: 432–447.

Dixon, Richard D., Dianne E. Levy, and Roger C. Lowery. 1988. "Asking the 'Born-Again' Question." *Review of Religious Research* 30: 33–39.

Dodd, Lawrence. 1981. "Congress, the Constitution, and the Crisis of Legitimation." In *Congress Reconsidered,* 2d ed., ed. Lawrence Dodd and Bruce Oppenheimer. Washington, D.C.: CQ Press.

Dodson, Debra L., and Lauren Burnbauer with Katherine Kleeman. 1990. *1989: The Abortion Issue in New Jersey and Virginia.* New Brunswick, N.J.: Eagleton Institute of Politics.

Downs, Anthony. 1957. *An Economic Theory of Democracy.* New York: Harper and Row.

Durr, Robert H. 1993. "What Moves Policy Sentiment?" *American Political Science Review* 87: 158–170.

Duverger, Maurice. 1955. *The Political Role of Women.* Paris: UNESCO.

Ehrenhalt, Alan. 1992. "An Embattled Institution." *Governing,* January, 28–33.

Entman, Robert M. 1989. *Democracy Without Citizens: Media and the Decay of American Politics.* New York: Oxford University Press.

Epstein, Lee, and Joseph Kobylka. 1992. *The Supreme Court and Legal Change: Abortion and the Death Penalty.* Chapel Hill: University of North Carolina Press.

Erikson, Robert S., and David W. Romero. 1990. "Candidate Equilibrium and the Behavioral Model of the Vote." *American Political Science Review* 84: 1103–1126.

Erikson, Robert S., and Kent L. Tedin. 1995. *American Public Opinion: Its Origin, Content and Impact,* 5th ed. Boston: Allyn and Bacon.

Erskine, Hazel. 1971. "The Polls: Women's Role." *Public Opinion Quarterly* 35: 275–290.

Faludi, Susan. 1991. *Backlash: The Undeclared War Against American Women.* New York: Crown.

Falwell, Jerry. 1980. *Listen, America!* Garden City, N.Y.: Doubleday.

Feagin, Joe R. 1991. "The Continuing Significance of Race: Antiblack Discrimination in Public Places." *American Sociological Review* 56: 101–116.

Feldman, Stanley. 1982. "Economic Self-Interest and Political Behavior." *American Journal of Political Science* 26: 446–466.

____. 1988. "Structure and Consistency in Public Opinion: The Role of Core Beliefs and Values." *American Journal of Political Science* 32: 415–440.

Festinger, Leon. 1957. *A Theory of Cognitive Dissonance.* Evanston, Ill.: Row, Peterson.

Finkel, Steven. 1993. "Reexamining the 'Minimal Effects' Model in Recent Presidential Campaigns." *Journal of Politics* 55: 1–21.

Fiorina, Morris. 1981. *Retrospective Voting in American National Elections.* New Haven: Yale University Press.

____. 1992. *Divided Government.* New York: Macmillan.

Firestone, Charles M. 1993. *Towards a Reformulation of the Communications Act: A Report of the 1993 Aspen Communications Counsel's Forum.* Washington, D.C.: Aspen Institute.

Fishbein, Martin, and Icek Ajzen. 1975. *Belief, Attitude, Intention, and Behavior.* Reading, Mass.: Addison-Wesley.

Fiske, Susan T., and Shelley E. Taylor. 1984. *Social Cognition.* New York: Random House.

Fite, David, Marc Genest, and Clyde Wilcox. 1990. "Gender Differences in Foreign Policy Attitudes." *American Politics Quarterly* 18: 492–513.

Frankel, Max. 1971. "The Press and the President." Letter to *Commentary,* July 16, 16.

Franklin, Charles, and John E. Jackson. 1983. "The Dynamics of Party Identification." *American Political Science Review* 77: 957–973.

Franklin, Charles, and Liane Kosaki. 1989. "Republican Schoolmaster: The U.S. Supreme Court, Public Opinion, and Abortion." *American Political Science Review* 83: 751–777.

Frankovic, Kathleen A. 1982. "Sex and Politics: New Alignments, Old Issues." *PS: Political Science and Politics* 15: 439–448.

Free, Lloyd A., and Hadley Cantril. 1967. *The Political Beliefs of Americans: A Study of Public Opinion.* New Brunswick, N.J.: Rutgers University Press.

___. 1968. *The Political Beliefs of Americans.* New York: Simon and Schuster.

Gallup Report. 1983. "Reagan Popularity Drops Below 40 Percent Approval Mark for First Time Since Taking Office." March, 13–28.

Gant, Michael M., and Norman R. Luttbeg. 1991. *American Electoral Behavior.* Itasca, Ill.: F. E. Peacock.

Garry, Patrick M. 1994. *Scrambling for Protection: The New Media and the First Amendment.* Pittsburgh: University of Pittsburgh Press.

George, Tracey, and Lee Epstein. 1992. "On the Nature of Supreme Court Decision Making." *American Political Science Review* 86: 323–337.

Gibson, James, and Gregory Caldeira. 1992. "Blacks and the United States Supreme Court: Models of Diffuse Support." *Journal of Politics* 54: 1120–1145.

Gilbert, Christopher P., Timothy R. Johnston, and David A. Peterson. 1994. "The Religious Roots of Third-Party Voting: A Comparison of Perot, Anderson, and Wallace Voters." Presented at the Annual Meeting of the American Political Science Association, New York.

Gilliam, Franklin D. 1986. "Black America: Divided by Class?" *Public Opinion* 8: 53–57.

Gilliam, Franklin D., and Kenneth Whitby. 1989. "Race, Class, and Attitudes Toward Social Welfare Spending: An Ethclass Interpretation." *Social Science Quarterly* 70: 89–100.

Gilligan, Carol. 1982. *In a Different Voice: The Changing Political Attitudes of American Women.* Cambridge: Harvard University Press.

Golding, Peter. 1990. "Political Communication and Citizenship: The Media and Democracy in an Egalitarian Social Order." In *Political Communication: The New Imperatives,* ed. M. Ferguson. London: Sage Publications.

Graber, Doris. 1982. "Introduction: Perspectives on Presidential Linkage." In *The President and the Public,* ed. Doris Graber. Philadelphia: ISHI.

___. 1984. *Processing the News: How People Tame the Information Tide.* White Plains, N.Y.: Longman.

___. 1991. "From 'Cold War' to 'Tepid Peace': The Soviet Image in Transition." Presented at the Annual Meeting of the American Association for Public Opinion Research, Phoenix, Arizona.

___. 1993. *Mass Media and American Politics, 4th ed.* Washington, D.C.: CQ Press.

Granberg, Donald. 1982a. "A Comparison of Members of Pro- and Anti-Abortion Organizations in Missouri." *Social Biology* 28: 239–252.

___. 1982b. "Family Size Preferences and Sexual Permissiveness as Factors Differentiating Abortion Activists." *Social Psychology Quarterly* 45: 15–23.

Green, John C., and James L. Guth. 1991. "The Bible and the Ballot Box: The Shape of Things to Come." In *The Bible and the Ballot Box: Religion and Politics in the 1988 Election,* ed. James L. Guth and John C. Green. Boulder, Colo.: Westview Press.

Grossman, Lawrence K. 1994. "Reflections on Life Along the Electronic Superhighway." *Media Studies Journal* 8: 27–40.

Grossman, Michael, and Martha Kumar. 1981. *Portraying the President.* Baltimore: Johns Hopkins University Press.

Guth, James L., and John C. Green. 1993. "Salience: The Core Concept?" In *Rediscovering the Religious Factor in American Politics,* ed. David C. Leege and Lyman A. Kellstedt. Armonk, N.Y.: M. E. Sharpe.

Hadden, Jeffrey K. 1969. *The Gathering Storm in the Churches.* Garden City, N.Y.: Doubleday.

Hamill, Ruth C., Milton Lodge, and Frederick Blake. 1985. "The Breadth, Depth and Utility of Class, Partisan, and Ideological Schemata." *American Journal of Political Science* 29: 850–870.

Hamilton, Alexander. 1961. "Federalist 78: The Judges as Guardians of the Constitution." *The Federalist Papers,* ed. Benjamin Wright. Cambridge: Belknap.

Hamilton, Richard F., and James D. Wright. 1986. *The State of the Masses.* Hawthorne, N.Y.: Aldine.

Hammond, Phillip E., Mark A. Shibley, and Peter M. Solow. 1994. "Religion and Family Values in Presidential Voting." *Sociology of Religion* 55: 277–290.

Harris, Frederick. 1994. "Something Within: Religion as a Mobilizer of African-American Political Activism." *Journal of Politics* 56: 42–68.

Hart, Stephen. 1992. *What Does the Lord Require? How American Christians Think About Economic Justice.* New York: Oxford University Press.

Hartsock, Nancy. 1983. *Money, Sex and Power: Toward a Feminist Historical Materialism.* New York: Longman.

Hastie, Reid. 1986. "A Primer of Information Processing Theory for the Political Scientist." In *Political Cognition,* ed R. Lau and D. Sears. Hillsdale, N.J.: Erlbaum.

Hastings, Philip K. 1960. "Hows and Howevers of the Woman Voter." *New York Times Magazine,* June 12, 14, 80–81.

Hedlund, Ronald D., and H. Paul Friesema. 1972. "Representatives' Perceptions of Constituency Opinion." *Journal of Politics* 34: 730–752.

Heineman, Ben, and Curtis Hessler. 1980. *Memorandum for the President: A Strategic Approach to Domestic Affairs in the 1980s.* New York: Random House.

Herbst, Susan. 1995. "On Electronic Public Space: Talk Shows in Theoretical Perspective." *Political Communication* 12: 263–274.

Hess, Robert, and Judith Torney. 1967. *The Development of Political Attitudes in Children*. Garden City, N.Y.: Doubleday.

Hibbing, John R., and Elizabeth Theiss-Morse. 1995. *Congress as Public Enemy: Public Attitudes Toward American Political Institutions*. New York: Cambridge University Press.

Hibbs, Douglas A., Jr. 1987. *The American Political Economy: Macroeconomics and Electoral Politics*. Cambridge: Harvard University Press.

Hill, David B., and Norman R. Luttbeg. 1983. *Trends in American Electoral Behavior*. Itasca, Ill.: F. E. Peacock.

Hinckley, Ronald H. 1988. "Public Attitudes Toward Key Foreign Policy Events." *Journal of Conflict Resolution* 32: 295–318.

———. 1994. "The Domestication of Foreign Policy Attitudes: Has the End of the Cold War Had an Impact?" Presented at the Annual Meeting of the American Association for Public Opinion Research, Danvers, Mass.

Hinich, Melvin J., and Michael C. Munger. 1994. *Ideology and the Theory of Political Choice*. Ann Arbor: University of Michigan Press.

Hochschild, Jennifer L. 1981. *What's Fair? American Beliefs About Distributive Justice*. Cambridge: Harvard University Press.

Hodgson, Godfrey. 1980. *All Things to All Men: The False Promise of the American Presidency*. New York: Simon and Schuster.

Hollander, Richard. 1985. *Video Democracy: The Vote-from-Home Revolution*. Mt. Airy, Md.: Lomond.

Holmes, John E. 1985. *The Mood/Interest Theory of American Foreign Policy*. Lexington, Ky.: Lexington Press.

Holsti, Ole R. 1992. "Public Opinion and Foreign Policy: Challenges to the Almond-Lippmann Consensus." *International Studies Quarterly* 36: 439–466.

Holsti, Ole R., and James N. Rosenau. 1979. "Americans' Foreign Policy Agenda: The Post-Vietnam Beliefs of American Leaders." In *Challenges to America: United States Foreign Policy in the 1980s*, ed. Charles Kegley and P. J. McGowan. Beverly Hills, Calif.: Sage Publications.

———. 1984. *American Leadership in World Affairs and the Breakdown of Consensus*. Boston: Allen and Unwin.

———. 1986. "Consensus Lost, Consensus Regained? Foreign Policy Beliefs of American Leaders, 1976–1980." *International Studies Quarterly*, December, 375–410.

Huckfeldt, Robert. 1979. "Political Participation and the Neighborhood Social Context." *American Journal of Political Science* 23: 579–592.

Huckfeldt, Robert, and Carol Weitzel Kohfeld. 1989. *Race and the Decline of Class in American Politics*. Urbana: University of Illinois Press.

Hughes, Janice. 1994. "The Changing Multimedia Landscape." *Media Studies Journal* 8: 53–58.

Hunter, James Davison. 1991. *Culture Wars: The Struggle to Define America.* New York: Basic Books.

Hurwitz, Jon, and Mark Peffley. 1990. "Public Images of the Soviet Union: The Impact on Foreign Policy Attitudes." *Journal of Politics* 52: 3–28.

Iannaccone, Laurence R. 1993. "Heirs to the Protestant Ethic? The Economics of American Fundamentalists." In *Fundamentalisms and the State: Remaking Polities, Economies, and Militance,* ed. Martin E. Marty and R. Scott Appleby. Chicago: University of Chicago Press.

Jackman, Mary R., and Robert W. Jackman. 1983. *Class Awareness in the United States.* Berkeley: University of California Press.

Jackson, John E. 1975. "Issues, Party Choices and Presidential Voting." *American Journal of Political Science* 19: 161–186.

Jacoby, William G. 1986. "Levels of Conceptualization and Reliance on the Liberal-Conservative Continuum." *Journal of Politics* 48: 423–432.

___. 1988. "The Impact of Party Identification on Issue Attitudes." *American Journal of Political Science* 32: 643–661.

___. 1991. "Ideological Identification and Issue Attitudes." *American Journal of Political Science* 35: 178–205.

Janda, Kenneth, Jeffrey M. Berry, and Jerry Goldman. 1995. *The Challenge of Democracy: Government in America,* 4th ed. Boston: Houghton Mifflin.

Jaynes, Gerald, and Robin M. Williams, eds. 1989. *A Common Destiny: Blacks and American Society.* Washington, D.C.: National Academy Press.

Jelen, Ted G. 1988. "The Effects of Gender Role Stereotypes on Political Attitudes." *Social Science Journal* 25: 353–365.

___. 1990. "Religious Belief and Attitude Constraint." *Journal for the Scientific Study of Religion* 29: 118–125.

___. 1991. *The Political Mobilization of Religious Beliefs.* New York: Praeger.

___. 1993. *The Political World of the Clergy.* Westport, Conn.: Praeger.

___. 1994. "Religion and Foreign Policy Attitudes: Exploring the Effects of Denomination and Doctrine." *American Politics Quarterly* 22: 381–400.

___. 1996. "Catholicism, Conscience, and Censorship." In *Judeo-Christian Traditions and the Mass Media: Religious Audiences and Adaptations,* ed. Daniel A. Stout and Judith M. Buddenbaum. Newbury Park, Calif.: Sage Publications.

Jelen, Ted G., Corwin E. Smidt, and Clyde Wilcox. 1990. "Biblical Literalism and Inerrancy: A Methodological Investigation." *Sociological Analysis* 51: 307–313.

____. 1993. "The Political Effects of the Born-Again Phenomenon." In *Rediscovering the Religious Factor in American Politics,* ed. David C. Leege and Lyman A. Kellstedt. Armonk, N.Y.: M. E. Sharpe.

Jelen, Ted G., and Clyde Wilcox. 1990. "Denominational Preference and the Dimensions of Political Tolerance." *Sociological Analysis* 51: 69–80.

____. 1995. *Public Attitudes on Church and State.* Armonk, N.Y.: M. E. Sharpe.

Jennings, M. Kent, and Richard G. Niemi. 1974. *The Political Character of Adolescence.* Princeton: Princeton University Press.

____. 1981. *Generations and Politics.* Princeton: Princeton University Press.

Jentleson, Bruce W. 1992. "The Pretty Prudent Public: Post Post-Vietnam American Opinion on the Use of Military Force." *International Studies Quarterly* 36: 49–74.

Katona, George. 1975. *Psychological Economics.* New York: Elsevier.

Katsh, Ethan. 1983. "The Supreme Court Beat: How Television Covers the U.S. Supreme Court." *Judicature* 67: 6–12.

Keith, Bruce E., David B. Magleby, Candice J. Nelson, Elizabeth Orr, Mark C. Westlye, and Raymond E. Wolfinger. 1992. *The Myth of the Independent Voter.* Berkeley: University of California Press.

Kellstedt, Lyman A. 1989. "The Meaning and Measurement of Evangelicalism: Problems and Prospects." In *Religion and Political Behavior in the United States,* ed. Ted G. Jelen. New York: Praeger.

Kellstedt, Lyman A., and John C. Green. 1993. "Knowing God's Many People: Denominational Preference and Political Behavior." In *Rediscovering the Religious Factor in American Politics,* ed. David C. Leege and Lyman A. Kellstedt. Armonk, N.Y.: M. E. Sharpe.

Kellstedt, Lyman A., John C. Green, James L. Guth, and Corwin E. Smidt. 1994a. "It's the Culture, Stupid: 1992 and Our Political Future." *First Things* 42: 28–33.

____. 1994b. "Religious Voting Blocs in the 1992 Election: The Year of the Evangelical?" *Sociology of Religion* 55: 307–326.

Kellstedt, Lyman A., and Mark Noll. 1990. "Religion, Voting for President, and Party Identification, 1948–1984." In *Religion and American Politics,* ed. Mark A. Noll. New York: Oxford University Press.

Kellstedt, Lyman A., and Corwin E. Smidt. 1993. "Doctrinal Beliefs and Political Behavior: Views of the Bible." In *Rediscovering the Religious Factor in American Politics,* ed. David C. Leege and Lyman A. Kellstedt. Armonk, N.Y.: M. E. Sharpe.

Kellstedt, Lyman A., Corwin E. Smidt, and Paul M. Kellstedt. 1991. "Religious Tradition, Denomination, and Commitment: White Protestants and the 1988 Election." In *The Bible and the Ballot Box: Religion and Politics in the 1988 Election,* ed. James L. Guth and John C. Green. Boulder, Colo.: Westview Press.

Kennedy, David. 1995. "Savage Words, Deadly Deeds: The Allure of Malignant Ideas." *Los Angeles Times,* April 30, M1.

Kenski, Henry C. 1988. "The Gender Factor in a Changing Electorate." In *The Politics of the Gender Gap,* ed. Carol M. Mueller. Newbury Park, Calif.: Sage Publications.

Kenski, Henry C., and William Lockwood. 1989. "The Catholic Vote from 1980 to 1986: Continuity or Change?" In *Religion and Political Behavior in the United States,* ed. Ted G. Jelen. New York: Praeger.

Kerber, Linda K. 1980. *Women of the Republic: Intellect and Ideology in Revolutionary America.* Chapel Hill: University of North Carolina Press.

Kernell, Samuel. 1978. "Explaining Presidential Popularity." *American Political Science Review* 72: 506–522.

Key, V. O., Jr. 1966. *The Responsible Electorate.* Cambridge: Harvard University Press.

Kiewiet, D. Roderick. 1983. *Macroeconomics and Micropolitics: The Electoral Effects of Economic Issues.* Chicago: University of Chicago Press.

Kinder, Donald R. 1986. "The Continuing American Dilemma: White Resistance to Racial Change 40 Years After Myrdal." *Journal of Social Issues* 42: 151–171.

Kinder, Donald R., and D. Roderick Kiewiet. 1979. "Economic Discontent and Political Behavior: The Role of Personal Grievances and Collective Economic Judgments in Congressional Voting." *American Journal of Political Science* 23: 495–527.

Kinder, Donald R., and D. Roderick Kiewiet. 1981. "Sociotropic Politics: The American Case." *British Journal of Political Science* 11: 129–131.

King, Gary. 1986. "How Not to Lie with Statistics." *American Journal of Political Science* 39: 666–687.

Klein, Ethel. 1984. *Gender Politics: From Consciousness to Mass Politics.* Cambridge: Harvard University Press.

Klingberg, Frank. 1983. *Cyclical Trends in American Foreign Policy Moods: The Unfolding of America's World Role.* New York: University Press of America.

Kluegel, James R. 1990. "Trends in Whites' Explanations of the Black-White Gap in Socioeconomic Status, 1977–1989." *American Sociological Review* 55: 512–525.

Kluegel, James R., and E. Smith. 1986. *Beliefs About Inequality.* New York: Aldine de Gruyter.

Knight, Kathleen. 1985. "Ideology in the 1980 Election: Ideological Sophistication Does Matter." *Journal of Politics* 47: 828–853.

Knight, Kathleen, and Carolyn Lewis. 1992. "Ideology and the American Electorate." In *Perspectives on American and Texas Politics,* ed. Kent L. Tedin, Donald S. Lutz, and Edward P. Fuchs. Dubuque, Iowa: Kendall/Hunt.

Kramer, Gerald H. 1971. "Short-Term Fluctuations in U.S. Voting Behavior: 1896–1964." *American Political Science Review* 65: 131–143.

Kritzer, Herbert. 1996. "The Data Puzzle: The Nature of Interpretation in Quantitative Research." *American Journal of Political Science* 40: 1–32.

Kuklinski, James, Robert Luskin, and John Bolland. 1991. "Where Is the Schema? Going Beyond the S-Word in Political Psychology." *American Political Science Review* 85: 1341–1356.

Ladd, Everett Carl. 1995. "1994 Vote: Against the Backdrop of Continuing Realignment." In *America at the Polls, 1994,* ed. Everett Carl Ladd. Storrs, Conn.: Roper Center.

Lane, Robert. 1959. *Political Life: Why People Get Involved in Politics.* Glencoe, Ill.: Free Press.

Lau, Richard. 1986. "Political Schemata, Candidate Evaluation and Voting Behavior." In *Political Cognitions,* ed. Richard Lau and David O. Sears. Hillsdale, N.J.: Lawrence Erlbaum.

Lau, Richard R., and David O. Sears. 1981. "Cognitive Links Between Economic Grievances and Political Responses." *Political Behavior* 3: 279–302.

Laver, Murray. 1989. *Information Technology: Agent of Change.* New York: Cambridge University Press.

Lazarsfeld, Paul, Bernard Berelson, and Hazel Gaudet. 1944. *The People's Choice.* New York: Columbia University Press.

Leege, David, and Lyman Kellstedt, eds. 1993. *Rediscovering the Impact of Religion on Political Behavior.* Armonk, N.Y.: M. E. Sharpe.

Leighley, Jan. 1990. "Social Interaction and Contextual Influences on Political Participation." *American Politics Quarterly* 18: 459–475.

Lenart, Silvo. 1994. *Shaping Political Attitudes: The Impact of Interpersonal Communication and Mass Media.* Thousand Oaks, Calif.: Sage Publications.

Levering, Ralph B. 1978. *The Public and American Foreign Policy, 1918–1978.* New York: William Morrow.

Levitan, Teresa E., and Warren E. Miller. 1979. "Ideological Interpretations of Presidential Elections." *American Political Science Review* 73: 751–771.

Lewis, Peter H. 1994a. "Censors Become a Force on Cyberspace Frontier." *New York Times,* June 29, A1.

____. 1994b. "You Can't Roller-Skate on Electronic Highway." *New York Times,* June 28, C6.

Lewis-Beck, Michael S. 1988. *Economics and Elections: The Major Western Democracies.* Ann Arbor: University of Michigan Press.

Lichter, Robert, and Richard E. Noyes. 1991. "In the Media Spotlight: Bush at Midpoint." *The American Enterprise* 2: 50.

Lieske, Joel. 1994. "How Culture Affects the Probability of Voting: A New Answer for the Turnout Riddle." Presented at the Annual Meeting of the American Political Science Association, New York.

Light, Paul. 1991. *The President's Agenda,* rev. ed. Baltimore: Johns Hopkins University Press.

Lippmann, Walter. 1922. *Public Opinion.* New York: Harcourt, Brace.

___. 1956. *The Public Philosophy.* New York: Mentor.

Lipset, Seymour Martin. 1960. *Political Man.* Garden City, N.Y.: Doubleday.

Lipset, Seymour Martin, and William Schneider. 1978. "The *Bakke* Case: How Would It Be Decided at the Bar of Public Opinion?" *Public Opinion,* March/April, 38–44.

___. 1983. *The Confidence Gap.* New York: Free Press.

Lopatto, Paul. 1985. *Religion and the Presidential Election.* New York: Praeger.

Lowi, Theodore. 1985. *The Personal Presidency.* Ithaca, N.Y.: Cornell University Press.

Luker, Kristin. 1984. *Abortion and the Politics of Motherhood.* Berkeley: University of California Press.

Luskin, Robert C. 1987. "Measuring Political Sophistication." *American Journal of Political Science* 31: 856–899.

___. 1991. "Abusus non tollit usum: Standardized Coefficients, Correlations, and R^2s." *American Journal of Political Science* 35: 1032–1046.

Luskin, Robert C., John P. McIver, and Edward G. Carmines. 1989. "Issues and the Transmission of Partisanship." *American Journal of Political Science* 33: 440–458.

Luttbeg, Norman R., and Michael M. Gant. 1985. "The Failure of Liberal/Conservative Ideology as a Cognitive Structure." *Public Opinion Quarterly* 49: 80–93.

___. 1995. *American Electoral Behavior 1952–1992.* Itasca, Ill.: F. E. Peacock.

Lyon, David. 1988. *The Information Society: Issues and Illusions.* Cambridge: Polity Press.

Maddox, William S., and Stuart A. Lilie. 1984. *Beyond Liberal and Conservative: Reassessing the Political Spectrum.* Washington, D.C.: Cato Institute.

Margolis, Michael. 1977. "From Confusion to Confusion: Issues and the American Voter." *American Political Science Review* 71: 31–43.

Marshall, Thomas. 1989. *Public Opinion and the Supreme Court.* Westchester, Mass.: Unwin Hyman.

___. 1991. "Public Opinion and the Rehnquist Court." *Judicature* 75: 322–329.

___. 1992. "The Supreme Court and the Grass Roots: Whom Does the Court Represent Best?" *Judicature* 76: 22–28.

Marshall, Thomas, and Joseph Ignagni. 1994. "Supreme Court and Public Support for Rights Claims." *Judicature* 78: 146–151.

Martin, Elizabeth. 1983. "Surveys as Social Indicators: Problems in Monitoring Trends." In *Handbook of Survey Research,* ed. Peter Rossi, James Wright, and Andy Anderson. New York: Academic Press.

Maxwell, Carol J. C. 1994. "Meaning and Motivation in Pro-Life Direct Action." Unpublished Ph.D. dissertation, Washington University, St. Louis.

Mayer, William G. 1992. *The Changing American Mind: How and Why American Public Opinion Changed Between 1960 and 1988.* Ann Arbor: University of Michigan Press.

McClosky, Herbert, and John Zaller. 1984. *The American Ethos: Public Attitudes Toward Capitalism and Democracy.* Cambridge: Harvard University Press.

McCrone, Donald J., and James H. Kuklinski. 1979. "The Delegate Theory of Representation." *American Journal of Political Science* 23: 278–300.

McDermott, Monica. 1994. "Race/Class Interactions in the Formation of Political Ideology." *Sociological Quarterly* 35: 347–366.

McLean, Iain. 1989. *Democracy and New Technology.* Cambridge: Polity Press.

McNamara, Patrick H. 1992. *Conscience First, Tradition Second: A Study of Young Catholics.* Albany: State University of New York Press.

Meier, Kenneth J., and Cathy M. Johnson. 1990. "The Politics of Demon Rum: Regulating Alcohol and Its Deleterious Consequences." *American Politics Quarterly* 18: 404–429.

Meyers, Edward. 1997. *Public Opinion and the Future of the Nation's Capital.* Washington, D.C.: Georgetown University Press.

Mickiewicz, Ellen. 1991. "Images of America." In *Beyond the Cold War: Soviet and American Media Images,* ed. Everette E. Dennis, George Gerbner, and Yassen N. Zassoursky. Newbury Park, Calif.: Sage Publications.

Miller, Arthur. 1988. "Gender and the Vote: 1984." In *The Politics of the Gender Gap,* ed. Carol M. Mueller. Newbury Park, Calif.: Sage Publications.

Miller, Arthur H., Warren E. Miller, Alden S. Raine, and Thad H. Brown. 1976. "A Majority Party in Disarray: Policy Polarization in the 1972 Election." *American Political Science Review* 70: 753–778.

Miller, Warren E. 1980. "Disinterest, Disaffection, and Participation in Presidential Elections." *Political Behavior* 2(1): 7–32.

———. 1991. "Party Identification, Realignment, and Party Voting: Back to Basics." *American Political Science Review* 85: 557–568.

———. 1992. "The Puzzle Transformed: Explaining Declining Turnout." *Political Behavior* 14: 1–43.

Miller, Warren E., Donald R. Kinder, Steven J. Rosenstone, and the National Election Studies. 1993. *American National Election Study, 1992: Pre- and Post-Election Survey [Enhanced with 1990 and 1991 Data].* [Computer file.] ICPSR ed., conducted by University of Michigan, Center for Political Studies. Ann Arbor: University of Michigan, Center for Political Studies, and Inter-university Consortium for Political and Social Research [producers]. Ann Arbor: Inter-university Consortium for Political and Social Research [distributor].

Miller, Warren E., and J. M. Shanks. 1982. "Policy Directions and Presidential Leadership." *British Journal of Political Science* 12: 299–356.

Miller, Warren E., and Donald E. Stokes. 1963. "Constituency Influence in Congress." *American Political Science Review* 57: 45–57.

Mills, C. Wright. 1959. *The Sociological Imagination.* New York: Oxford University Press.

Mischler, William, and Reginald Sheehan. 1993. "The Supreme Court as a Countermajoritarian Institution? The Impact of Public Opinion on Supreme Court Decisions." *American Political Science Review* 87: 87–101.

Moen, Matthew C. 1992. *The Transformation of the Christian Right.* Tuscaloosa: University of Alabama Press.

___. 1994. "From Revolution to Evolution: The Changing Nature of the Christian Right." *Sociology of Religion* 55: 345–357.

Monroe, Alan. 1994. "Public Opinion and Policy Outcomes, 1960–1991." Presented at the Annual Meeting of the American Political Science Association, New York.

Morgenthau, Hans. 1978. *Politics Among Nations,* 5th ed. New York: Knopf.

Mueller, Carol M. 1988. "The Empowerment of Women: Polling and the Women's Voting Bloc." In *The Politics of the Gender Gap,* ed. Carol M. Mueller. Newbury Park, Calif.: Sage Publications.

Mueller, John. 1970. "Presidential Popularity from Truman to Johnson." *American Political Science Review* 64: 18–34.

___. 1973. *Wars, Presidents, and Public Opinion.* New York: Wiley.

___. 1994. *Policy and Opinion in the Gulf War.* Chicago: University of Chicago Press.

Muncy, Robyn. 1991. *Creating a Female Dominion in American Reform 1890–1935.* New York: Oxford University Press.

Myrdal, Gunnar. 1944. *An American Dilemma: The Negro Problem and Modern Democracy.* New York: Random House.

Nadeau, Richard, and Harold W. Stanley. 1993. "Class Polarization in Partisanship among Native Southern Whites, 1952–90." *American Journal of Political Science* 37: 900–919.

Negroponte, Nicholas P. 1995. *Being Digital.* New York: Alfred A. Knopf.

Nesmith, Bruce. 1994. *The New Republican Coalition: The Reagan Campaign and White Evangelicals.* New York: Peter Lang.

Neuman, W. Russell. 1991. *The Future of the Mass Audience.* New York: Cambridge University Press.

Nice, David C. 1992. "The States and the Death Penalty." *Western Political Quarterly* 45: 1037–1048.

Nie, Norman H., Sidney Verba, and John R. Petrocik. 1979. *The Changing American Voter.* Cambridge: Harvard University Press.

Niemi, Richard G., and M. Kent Jennings. 1991. "Issues and Inheritance in the Formation of Party Identification." *American Journal of Political Science* 35: 970–988.

Niemi, Richard G., John Mueller, and Tom W. Smith. 1989. *Trends in Public Opinion: A Compendium of Survey Data.* New York: Greenwood Press.

Norrander, Barbara, and Clyde Wilcox. 1993. "Rallying Around the Flag and Partisan Change: The Case of the Persian Gulf War." *Political Research Quarterly* 46: 759–770.

____. 1994. "State Differences in Abortion Attitudes and Policy." Presented at the Annual Meeting of the Midwest Political Science Association, Chicago.

Norris, Pippa. 1988. "The Gender Gap: A Cross-National Trend?" In *The Politics of the Gender Gap,* ed. Carol M. Mueller. Newbury Park, Calif.: Sage Publications.

____. 1994. "Gender-Related Influences on Voting Behavior and Public Opinion." Presented at the conference on Women and American Politics: Agenda Setting for the 21st Century, Center for the American Woman and Politics, Eagleton Institute, Rutgers University, New Brunswick, N.J.

Office of Technology Assessment, U.S. Congress. 1988. *Science, Technology, and the First Amendment.* OTA-CIT-369. Washington, D.C.: Government Printing Office.

Okin, Susan Muller. 1979. *Women in Western Political Thought.* Princeton, N.J.: Princeton University Press.

____. 1991. *Justice, Gender and the Family.* New York: Basic Books.

Overby, L. Marvin, Beth M. Henschen, Julie Strauss, and Michael H. Walsh. 1992. "Courting Constituents? An Analysis of the Senate Confirmation Vote on Justice Clarence Thomas." *American Political Science Review* 86: 997–1003.

Page, Benjamin I. 1978. *Choices and Echoes in Presidential Elections: Rational Man and Electoral Democracy.* Chicago: University of Chicago Press.

Page, Benjamin I., and Richard A. Brody. 1972. "Policy Voting and the Electoral Process: The Vietnam War Issue." *American Political Science Review* 55: 979–995.

Page, Benjamin I., and Robert Y. Shapiro. 1983. "Effects of Public Opinion on Policy." *American Political Science Review* 77: 175–190.

____. 1992. *The Rational Public: Fifty Years of Trends in Americans' Policy Preferences.* Chicago: University of Chicago Press.

Page, Benjamin, Robert Shapiro, and Glenn Dempsey. 1987. "What Moves Public Opinion?" *American Political Science Review* 81: 23–44.

Page, Benjamin I., Robert Y. Shapiro, Paul W. Gronke, and Robert M. Rosenberg. 1984. "Constituency, Party, and Representation in Congress." *Public Opinion Quarterly* 48: 741–756.

Paget, Karen M. 1993. "The Gender Gap Mystique." *The American Prospect* 15 (Fall): 93–101.

Palfrey, Thomas R., and Keith T. Poole. 1987. "The Relationship Between Information, Ideology, and Voting Behavior." *American Journal of Political Science* 31: 511–530.

Parent, Wayne, and Paul Stekler. 1985. "The Political Implications of Economic Stratification in the Black Community." *Western Political Quarterly* 38: 521–538.

Peffley, Mark. 1985. "The Voter as Juror: Attributing Responsibility for Economic Conditions." In *Economic Conditions and Electoral Outcomes,* ed. Heinz Eulau and Michael Lewis-Beck. New York: Agathon Press.

Peffley, Mark, and Jon Hurwitz. 1992. "International Events and Foreign Policy Beliefs: Public Response to Changing Soviet-U.S. Relations." *American Journal of Political Science* 36: 431–461.

Peretz, Paul. 1983. *The Political Economy of Inflation in the United States.* Chicago: University of Chicago Press.

Peterson, Steve. 1992. "Church Participation and Political Participation: The Spillover Effect." *American Politics Quarterly* 20: 123–139.

Pierce, Patrick. 1993. "Political Sophistication and the Use of Candidate Evaluation." *Political Psychology* 14: 21–35.

Piston, Walter. 1978. *Harmony,* 4th ed. New York: W. W. Norton.

Polsby, Nelson. 1968. "The Institutionalization of the U.S. House of Representatives." *American Political Science Review* 62: 144–168.

Pomper, Gerald M. 1972. "From Confusion to Clarity: Issues and American Voters, 1956–1968." *American Political Science Review* 66: 415–428.

___. 1993. "The Presidential Election." In *The Election of 1992,* ed. Gerald M. Pomper, F. Christopher Arterton, Ross K. Baker, Walter Dean Burnham, Kathleen A. Frankovic, Marjorie Randon Hershey, and Wilson Carey McWilliams. Chatham, N.J.: Chatham House.

Pomper, Gerald M., with Susan S. Lederman. 1980. *Elections in America: Control and Influence in Democratic Politics,* 2d ed. New York: Longman.

Popkin, Samuel L. 1991. *The Reasoning Voter: Communication and Persuasion in Presidential Campaigns.* Chicago: University of Chicago Press.

Powell, Lynda W. 1982. "Issue Representation in Congress." *Journal of Politics* 44: 658–678.

___. 1989. "Analyzing Misinformation: Perceptions of Congressional Candidates' Ideologies." *American Journal of Political Science* 33: 272–293.

Ragsdale, Lyn. 1984. "The Politics of Presidential Speechmaking." *American Political Science Review* 78: 971–984.

___. 1993. *Presidential Politics.* Boston: Houghton Mifflin.

___. 1996. *Vital Statistics on the American Presidency: Washington to Clinton.* Washington, D.C.: Congressional Quarterly.

Reed, Ralph. 1994. *Politically Incorrect: The Emerging Faith Factor in American Politics.* Dallas: Word.

Rehnquist, William. 1987. *The Supreme Court.* New York: William Morrow.

RePass, David E. 1971. "Issue Salience and Party Choice." *American Political Science Review* 65: 289–400.

Rheingold, Howard. 1993. *The Virtual Community: Homesteading on the Electronic Frontier.* Reading, Mass.: Addison-Wesley.

Richman, Al. 1994. "The American Public's 'Rules of Military Engagement' in the Post Cold War Era." Presented at the Annual Meeting of the American Political Science Association, New York.

Ridout, Christine F. 1993. "News Coverage and Talk Shows in the 1992 Presidential Campaign." *PS: Political Science and Politics* 26: 712–716.

Roosevelt, Theodore. 1913. *Theodore Roosevelt: An Autobiography.* New York: Macmillan.

___. 1926. *The Works of Theodore Roosevelt.* New York: Scribner.

Rosenberg, Gerald. 1991. *The Hollow Hope: Can Courts Bring About Social Change?* Chicago: University of Chicago Press.

Rosenstone, Steven J., and John Mark Hansen. 1993. *Mobilization, Participation, and Democracy in America.* New York: Macmillan.

Rozell, Mark, and Clyde Wilcox. 1995. *God at the Grassroots.* Lanham, Md.: Rowman and Littlefield.

___. 1996. *Second Coming: The Christian Right in Virginia Politics.* Baltimore: Johns Hopkins University Press.

Rucinski, Dianne. 1991. "The Centrality of Reciprocity to Communication and Democracy." *Critical Studies in Mass Communication* 8: 184–194.

Ruddick, Sara. 1980. "Maternal Thinking." *Feminist Studies* 6: 342–347.

Salmon, Charles, and John Spicer Nichols. 1983. "The Next-Birthday Method of Respondent Selection." *Public Opinion Quarterly* 47: 270–276.

Sapiro, Virginia, and Pamela Johnston Conover. 1993. "Gender in the 1992 Electorate." Presented at the Annual Meeting of the American Political Science Association, Washington, D.C.

Savage, David. 1992. *Turning Right: The Makings of the Rehnquist Supreme Court.* New York: Wiley.

Schlesinger, Arthur M., Jr. 1973. *The Imperial Presidency.* Boston: Houghton Mifflin.

Schlozman, Kay L., Nancy Burns, and Sidney Verba. 1994. "Gender and the Pathways to Participation: The Role of Resources." *Journal of Politics* 56: 963–990.

Schlozman, Kay L., and Sidney Verba. 1979. *Injury to Insult: Unemployment, Class and Political Response.* Cambridge: Harvard University Press.

Schudson, Michael. 1995. *The Power of News.* Cambridge: Harvard University Press.

Schuman, Howard, Charlotte Steeh, and Lawrence D. Bobo. 1985. *Racial Attitudes in America: Trends and Interpretations.* Cambridge: Harvard University Press.

Scott, Joan. 1986. "Gender: A Useful Category of Historical Analysis." *American Historical Review* 91: 1053–1075.

Sears, David O., and Jack Citrin. 1985. *Tax Revolt: Something for Nothing in California*, enlarged ed. Cambridge: Harvard University Press.

Sears, David O., and Carolyn L. Funk. 1990. "Self-Interest in Americans' Political Opinions." In *Beyond Self-Interest*, ed. Jane J. Mansbridge. Chicago: University of Chicago Press.

Segal, Howard P. 1994. *Future Imperfect: The Mixed Blessings of Technology in America*. Amherst: University of Massachusetts Press.

Segers, Mary C. 1995. "The Catholic Church as a Political Actor." In *Perspectives on the Politics of Abortion*, ed. Ted G. Jelen. Westport, Conn.: Praeger.

Seltzer, Richard, and Robert C. Smith. 1985. "Race and Ideology: A Research Note Measuring Liberalism and Conservatism in Black America." *Phylon* 46: 98–105.

Shapiro, Robert, and Harpreet Mahajan. 1986. "Gender Differences in Policy Preferences: A Summary of Trends from the 1960s to the 1980s." *Public Opinion Quarterly* 50: 42–61.

Shapiro, Robert Y., and Benjamin I. Page. 1988. "Foreign Policy and the Rational Public." *Journal of Conflict Resolution* 32: 211–247.

Sheehan, Reginald, and William Mischler. 1993. "Explaining the Influence of Public Opinion on Supreme Court Decision-making." Presented at the Annual Meeting of the Southern Political Science Association, Atlanta.

Sigelman, Lee. 1991. "Jews and the 1988 Election: More of the Same?" In *The Bible and the Ballot Box: Religion and Politics in the 1988 Election*, ed. James L. Guth and John C. Green. Boulder, Colo.: Westview Press.

Sigelman, Lee, and Susan Welch. 1991. *Black Americans' Views of Racial Inequality: The Dream Deferred*. New York: Cambridge University Press.

Sigelman, Lee, Clyde Wilcox, and Emmett Buell. 1987. "An Unchanging Minority: Popular Support for the Moral Majority, 1980 and 1984." *Social Science Quarterly* 68: 876–884.

Simon, Rita J., and Jean M. Landis. 1989. "The Polls—A Report: Women's and Men's Attitudes About a Woman's Place and Role." *Public Opinion Quarterly* 53: 265–276.

Skocpol, Theda. 1992. *Protecting Soldiers and Mothers: The Political Origins of Social Policy in the United States*. Cambridge: Harvard University Press.

Slotnick, Elliot. 1991. "Media Coverage of Supreme Court Decision-making: Problems and Prospects." *Judicature* 75: 128–142.

Slotnick, Elliot, Jennifer Segal, and Lisa Campoli. 1994. "Television News and the Supreme Court." Presented at the Annual Meeting of the American Political Science Association, New York.

Smidt, Corwin E. 1988. "Evangelicals Within Contemporary American Politics: Differentiating Between Fundamentalist and Non-Fundamentalist Evangelicals." *Western Political Quarterly* 41: 601–620.

____. 1989. "Identifying Evangelical Respondents: An Analysis of 'Born-Again' and Bible Questions Used Across Different Surveys." In *Religion and Political Behavior in the United States,* ed. Ted G. Jelen. New York: Praeger.

Smith, A. Wade. 1987. "Problems and Progress in the Measurement of Black Public Opinion." *American Behavioral Scientist* 30: 441–455.

Smith, Christopher, and Thomas Hensley. 1993. "Assessing the Conservatism of the Rehnquist Court." *Judicature* 77: 83–89.

Smith, Robert C., and Richard Seltzer. 1992. *Race, Class, and Culture: A Study in Afro-American Mass Opinion.* Albany: State University of New York Press.

Smith, Tom W. 1978. "In Search of House Effects: A Comparison of Responses to Various Questions by Different Survey Organizations." *Public Opinion Quarterly* 42: 443–463.

____. 1984. "The Polls: Gender and Attitudes Toward Violence." *Public Opinion Quarterly* 48: 384–396.

____. 1990a. "Classifying Protestant Denominations." *Review of Religious Research* 31: 225–245.

____. 1990b. "Liberal and Conservative Trends in the United States." *Public Opinion Quarterly* 54: 609–626.

Smoller, Fred. 1986. "The Six O'Clock President: Patterns of Network News Coverage of the Presidents." *Presidential Studies Quarterly* 16: 40–42.

Sniderman, Paul M. 1993. "The New Look in Public Opinion Research." In *Political Science: The State of the Discipline II,* ed. Ada W. Finifter. Washington, D.C.: American Political Science Association.

Sniderman, Paul M., and Richard A. Brody. 1977. "Coping: The Ethic of Self-Reliance." *American Journal of Political Science* 21: 501–521.

Sniderman, Paul M., Richard A. Brody, and Philip E. Tetlock. 1991. *Reasoning and Choice: Explorations in Political Psychology.* New York: Cambridge University Press.

Sniderman, Paul M., and Philip Tetlock. 1986. "Symbolic Racism: Problems of Motive Attribution in Political Analysis." *Journal of Social Issues* 42: 129–150.

Sowell, Thomas. 1981. *Markets and Minorities.* New York: Basic Books.

____. 1984. *Civil Rights: Rhetoric or Reality?* New York: Morrow.

Squire, Peverill, Raymond E. Wolfinger, and David Glass. 1987. "Residential Mobility and Turnout." *American Political Science Review* 81: 45–65.

Stimson, James A. 1984. "Pursuing Belief Structure: A Research Narrative." In *The Research Process in Political Science,* ed. W. Phillips Shively. Itasca, Ill.: F. E. Peacock.

____. 1991. *Public Opinion in America: Moods, Cycles, and Swings.* Boulder, Colo.: Westview Press.

Sullivan, John L., James E. Pierson, and George E. Marcus. 1978. "Ideological Constraint in the Mass Public: A Methodological Critique and Some New Findings." *American Journal of Political Science* 22: 233–249.

Sundquist, James L. 1973. *Dynamics of the Party System.* Washington, D.C.: Brookings Institution.

Tamney, Joseph B., Ronald Burton, and Stephen D. Johnson. 1989. "Fundamentalism and Economic Restructuring." In *Religion and Political Behavior in the United States,* ed. Ted G. Jelen. New York: Praeger.

Tate, Katherine. 1993. *From Protest to Politics: The New Black Voters in American Elections.* New York: Russell Sage.

Teixeira, Ruy A. 1992. *The Disappearing American Voter.* Washington, D.C.: Brookings Institution.

Television and Cable Fact Book. 1992. Washington, D.C.: Warren.

Tetlock, Philip E. 1986. "A Value Pluralism Model of Ideological Reasoning." *Journal of Personality and Social Psychology* 50: 819–827.

Times Mirror Center for the People and the Press. 1993. *The Vocal Minority in American Politics.* Los Angeles: Times Mirror.

___. 1994. *Technology in the American Household.* Los Angeles: Times Mirror.

Tolleson-Rinehart, Sue, and Jeannie Stanley. 1994. *Claytie and the Lady: Ann Richards, Gender, and Politics in Texas.* Austin: University of Texas Press.

Truman, David. 1951. *The Governmental Process.* New York: Alfred Knopf.

Tuch, Steven A., Lee Sigelman, and Jack Martin. 1994. "Fifty Years After Myrdal: Blacks' Racial Policy Attitudes in the 1990s." *Challenge* 5: 44–57.

Uhlaner, Carole. 1989. "Rational Turnout: The Neglected Role of Groups." *American Journal of Political Science* 33: 390–422.

U.S. Bureau of the Census. 1992. *Statistical Abstract of the United States,* 112th ed. Washington, D.C.: U.S. Government Printing Office.

Uslaner, Eric. 1992. "Can Reform Change Congress? The New Institutionalism and Social Engineering." Presented at the Annual Meeting of the American Political Science Association, Chicago.

Van Winkle, Stephen. 1994. "Supreme Court Nominations and Public Opinion: Implications for Judicial Policy Making." Presented at the Annual Meeting of the American Political Science Association, New York.

Verba, Sidney, and Norman H. Nie. 1972. *Participation in America.* New York: Harper and Row.

Verba, Sidney, Kay L. Schlozman, and Henry Brady. 1995. *Voice and Equality: Civic Voluntarism in American Politics.* Cambridge: Harvard University Press.

Verba, Sidney, Kay L. Schlozman, Henry Brady, and Norman Nie. 1993a. "Citizen Activity: Who Participates? What Do They Say?" *American Political Science Review* 87: 303–318.

___. 1993b. "Race, Ethnicity, and Political Resources: Participation in the United States." *British Journal of Political Science* 23: 453–497.

Wald, Kenneth D. 1992. "Religious Elites and Public Opinion: The Impact of the Bishops' Peace Pastoral." *Review of Politics* 54: 112–143.

Wald, Kenneth D., Lyman A. Kellstedt, and David C. Leege. 1993. "Church Involvement and Political Behavior." In *Rediscovering the Religious Factor in American Politics,* ed. David C. Leege and Lyman A. Kellstedt. Armonk, N.Y.: M. E. Sharpe.

Warf, Barney. 1995. "Telecommunications and the Changing Geographies of Knowledge Transmission in the Late 20th Century." *Urban Studies* 32: 361–378.

Wattenburg, Martin P. 1990. *The Decline of American Political Parties: 1952–1988.* Cambridge: Harvard University Press.

___. 1991. *The Rise of Candidate-Centered Politics: Presidential Elections of the 1980s.* Cambridge: Harvard University Press.

Weilhouwer, Peter, and Brad Lockerbie. 1994. "Party Contacting and Political Participation, 1952–1990." *American Journal of Political Science* 38: 211–229.

Weissberg, Robert. 1976. *Public Opinion and Popular Government.* Englewood Cliffs, N.J.: Prentice Hall.

Welch, Michael R., David C. Leege, Kenneth D. Wald, and Lyman A. Kellstedt. 1993. "Are the Sheep Hearing the Shepherds? Cue Perceptions, Congregational Responses, and Political Communications Processes." In *Rediscovering the Religious Factor in American Politics,* ed. David C. Leege and Lyman A. Kellstedt. Armonk, N.Y.: M. E. Sharpe.

Welch, Susan, and Michael W. Combs. 1985. "Intra-Racial Differences in Attitudes of Blacks: Class Cleavages or Consensus?" *Phylon* 46: 91–97.

Welch, Susan, and Lorn S. Foster. 1987. "Class and Conservatism in the Black Community." *American Politics Quarterly* 4: 445–470.

Welch, Susan, and Lee Sigelman. 1989. "A Black Gender Gap?" *Social Science Quarterly* 79: 120–133.

Williams, Frederick, and John V. Pavlik, eds. 1994. *The People's Right to Know: Media, Democracy and the Information Highway.* Hillsdale, N.J.: Lawrence Erlbaum.

Wilcox, Clyde. 1986. "Fundamentalists and Politics: An Analysis of the Effects of Differing Operational Definitions." *Journal of Politics* 48: 1041–1051.

___. 1987. "Popular Support for the Moral Majority in 1980: A Second Look." *Social Science Quarterly* 68: 157–167.

___. 1988. "Political Action Committees and Abortion: A Longitudinal Analysis." *Women and Politics* 9: 1–20.

___. 1989. "The New Christian Right and the Mobilization of the Evangelicals." In *Religion and Political Behavior in the United States,* ed. Ted G. Jelen. New York: Praeger.

___. 1990. "Race, Gender Role Attitudes and Support for Feminism." *Western Political Quarterly* 43: 113–121.

___. 1991. "Religion and Electoral Politics Among Black Americans in 1988." In *The Bible and the Ballot Box: Religion and Politics in the 1988 Election,* ed. James L. Guth and John C. Green. Boulder, Colo.: Westview Press.

___. 1995. "The Sources and Consequences of Public Attitudes on Abortion." In *The Politics of Abortion,* ed. Ted G. Jelen. New York: Praeger.

Wilcox, Clyde, and Ted G. Jelen. 1990. "Evangelicals and Political Tolerance." *American Politics Quarterly* 18: 25–46.

___. 1991. "The Effects of Employment and Religion on Women's Feminist Attitudes." *International Journal for the Psychology of Religion* 1: 161–171.

Wilcox, Clyde, and Leonard Williams. 1990. "Taking Stock of Schema Theory." *Social Science Journal* 27: 373–395.

Williams, Walter C. 1982. *The State Against Blacks.* New York: New Press.

Wilson, William J. 1980. *The Declining Significance of Race.* Chicago: University of Chicago Press.

___. 1987. *The Truly Disadvantaged.* Chicago: University of Chicago Press.

Wittkopf, Eugene R. 1990. *Faces of Internationalism: Public Opinion and American Foreign Policy.* Durham, N.C.: Duke University Press.

Wlezien, Christopher. 1995. "The Public as Thermostat: Dynamics of Preferences for Spending." *American Journal of Political Science* 39: 981-1000.

Wolfinger, Raymond E., and Steven J. Rosenstone. 1980. *Who Votes?* New Haven: Yale University Press.

Wood, Dan, and Roy Flemming. 1993. "Supreme Court Liberalism and American Political Moods." Presented at the Annual Meeting of the Southern Political Science Association, Atlanta.

Wright, Gerald C., Jr., Robert S. Erikson, and John P. McIver. 1987. "Public Opinion and Policy Liberalism in the American States." *American Journal of Political Science* 31: 980–1001.

Wriston, Walter B. 1992. *The Twilight of Sovereignty: How the Information Revolution Is Transforming Our World.* New York: Scribner's.

Yeric, Jerry L., and John R. Todd. *Public Opinion: The Visible Politics,* 2d ed. Itasca, Ill.: F. E. Peacock.

Zaller, John R. 1992. *The Nature and Origins of Mass Opinion.* New York: Cambridge University Press.

Zaller, John, and Stanley Feldman. 1992. "A Simple Theory of the Survey Response: Answering Questions and Reviewing Preferences." *American Journal of Political Science* 36: 579–616.

Index

Cook, Elizabeth, 7, 31, 129, 131–149, 163, 287
Coolidge, Calvin, 248
Correlation coefficient, 12–13
Correlation statistics, 285–286
Correlations
    feminism and voting, 30
    parent/child attitudes, 17
Cost of living, 172–178
Credibility gap, 239
Criminal law, 273
Criminal rights, 272
Cronbach's alpha, 289
Cruzan v. Director, Missouri Department of Health, 272
C-SPAN, 76, 84, 85
Culture, 20, 221–225
Culture wars, 55–68
Custody cases, 272

Data
    reliability of, 11
    statistical manipulation of, 12–14
Davidson, Roger, 264
Death penalty. *See* Capital punishment
DeBoer v. Schmidt, 272
Defense spending, 26, 114–119, 218
Democracy, 167, 252
Democratic Party
    abortion issue, 131
    age of members, 62–66
    candidate evaluations, 28
    citizen's perception of ideology, 104–107
    conservative wing, 20
    demographic characteristics of, 119–123
    denomination of members, 58
    economic policies, 183
    factions, 120–123
    gender support for, 28–30, 31, 34, 35
    ideology vote, 107–109
    influence on economic beliefs, 173–178
    issues opinions, 113–119
    midterm elections, 55
    party loyalty, 37
    party/ideology relationship, 95–98
    religious affiliation/attitudes relationship, 61–66
    sophistication of voters, 100–101

and the South, 112
    Supreme Court decisions, 273–274
    understanding, 95–98
    values, 211–212
Demographic characteristics, 5–6
    abortion attitudes, 136–139, 287
    as voter turnout predictor, 204–207
    influence on economic beliefs, 174–181, 182–186
    issues consistency, 123–125
    partisanship relationship, 201–202
    party factions, 121, 122
    party relationship, 112–123
    political beliefs and, 19–20
    political participation and, 209
    probability of voting and, 201–202, 205
    Supreme court decisions, 274
    See also specific demographic characteristic, i.e., Income; Race; Sex
Dennis, Jack, 264–265
Dependent variables, 5, 12–13, 30
Descriptive statistics, 12
Desert Storm. *See* Operation Desert Storm
Devine, Donald, 264
Direct democracy, 85–86
Discrimination, 222
Disposable income, 182–186
Dole, Robert, 189
Domestic issues, 153
Dominican Republic, 239
Downs, Anthony, 92, 110n.1
Downs model, 92–95, 108–109
Drug testing, 272
Drunk driving, 270
Duverger, Maurice, 23
Dynamics of the Party System, 19

East
    issue consistency, 123–125
    party factions, 121, 122
Economic issues, 123–125, 271
    attitudes toward, 181–186
    domestic economy, 2
    effectiveness of policy, 178–181
    influence on beliefs, 173–178
    media coverage, 239–241, 248
    overview, 170–172
    perceptions of, 172–178

Militarism, 30, 31, 160–162
Military issues, 161, 214–218
    Haiti, 168
    support for, 164–165
Mills, C. Wright, 14–15
Minorities, 121, 122, 123–125
Mobility, 202, 204–205
Mode, 12
Modems, 75, 81, 82
Moderates, 94, 103, 110n.5
    demographic characteristics, 119–123
    party vote relationship, 95–98
    trends in identification, 99–102
Monroe, Alan, 228, 274
Mood cycles, 103
Mood theory, 152–153, 154–155
Moral issues, 7, 17, 20, 57, 63–64, 159
    political nature and, 20
    and presidential election (1992), 213–216
    salience of, 218, 220
    See also Values
Moral Majority, 68n.7
Morgenthau, Hans, 151
Morin, Richard, 252
MTV, 77
Mueller, John, 22, 153, 157–158, 165, 167

National Opinion Research Center, 39, 154, 156
National Organization for Women, 32, 288–289
National Public Radio, 84, 85
National security issues, 214–218
Nesmith, Bruce, 64
Neuman, W. Russell, 80, 86–87
New York Times, 9, 20, 35, 70–71, 236–237, 250n.2, 251n.7
New York Times Magazine, 20
News broadcasts, 84–85
News conferences, 243, 248
News magazines, 69, 78, 230
News stories
    distribution of, 70, 71
    framing of, 70, 76–78
    sources of, 82–85
    Soviet news, 70–71
Newspapers, 69, 70, 78, 84–85, 230, 230, 250n.2

as public issues forum, 81–82
as source of information, 6
use of, 83
Newsweek, 237
Nicaraguan contras, 165
Niemi, Richard, 17, 22
Nixon, Richard M., 230
    approval rating, 233–234, 235–236, 245–248
    media coverage, 248
    Watergate, 232, 236, 239, 248
Nonconformists, 59–66
Nonideological voters, 91–92
Normal-shaped distribution, 282, 284
Norrander, Barbara, 90, 111–130, 284

Obscenity, 273
Obstructionism, 258, 259, 261–262
O'Connor, Sandra Day, 269, 273
Ohio v. Akron Center for Reproductive Health, 272
Oklahoma City bombing, 252
Oldendick, Robert, 160
On-line computer services, 74, 230
Open Meetings Act, 269
Operation Desert Storm, 150
Oregon v. Mitchell, 276–277

Pack journalism, 72–73
Page, Benjamin, 69, 152–155
Paget, Karen, 32
Panama invasion, 165
Parker, Glenn, 264
Parsons, R. Wayne, 123
Partisanship
    convergence with ideology, 100–102
    ideology and, 89–90
    issue consistency and, 123–125
    religion and, 58
    values loyal to, 212
Party identification, 90, 101, 104–107, 195–197, 200, 209
    as voter turnout predictor, 204–205
    conservative positions and, 64
    economic beliefs and, 173–178, 179, 182–186
    issues and, 113–119
    issues consistency, 123–125